D0816501

The Royal Palaces of Tudor England

The Royal Palaces of Tudor England

ARCHITECTURE AND COURT LIFE 1460–1547

SIMON THURLEY

Published for
THE PAUL MELLON CENTRE
FOR STUDIES IN BRITISH ART
by
YALE UNIVERSITY PRESS
NEW HAVEN & LONDON 1993

For C.H.C., R.T. and T.M.T., and in memory of M.E.H.

Frontispiece: Anon., *The Family of Henry VIII* (detail), *c.*1545
(The Royal Collection, Windsor Castle, © 1993 Her Majesty the Queen).

Copyright © 1993 by Yale University

All rights reserved. This book may not be reproduced, in whole or in part,
in any form (beyond that copying permitted by Sections 107 and 108
of the U.S. Copyright Law and except by reviewers for the public press),
without written permission from the publishers.

Designed by Gillian Malpass
Set in Linotron Bembo by Best-set Typesetter Ltd, Hong Kong
Printed in Singapore by C.S. Graphics PTE Ltd

Library of Congress Cataloging-in-Publication Data

Thurley, Simon, 1962–
    The royal palaces of Tudor England : architecture and court life,
1460–1547 / Simon Thurley.
        p.   cm.
    Includes bibliographical references and index.
    ISBN 0-300-05420-3
    1. Henry VIII, King of England, 1491–1547 — Homes and haunts.
2. England — Social life and customs — Medieval period, 1066–1485.
3. England — Social life and customs — 16th century.   4. Great
Britain — Kings and rulers — Dwellings.   5. Great Britain — History —
Tudors, 1485–1603.   6. Palaces — England — History — 16th century.
7. Great Britain — Court and courtiers.   8. Tudor, House of.
9. Architecture, Domestic — England.   I. Title.
DA332.T49   1993
942.06′2′092 — dc20   93-4183
                                                                               CIP

A catalogue record for this book is available from The British Library

Contents

Preface

THIS BOOK IS THE PRODUCT of work undertaken for a PhD thesis between 1986 and 1989 and my employment first by the Crown Buildings Group of English Heritage (1988–90) and subsequently for The Historic Royal Palaces Agency. In the first period I came to know the documentary sources for Tudor royal houses intimately, in the second I grew to know the buildings themselves. All work on royal buildings must take as its basis *The History of the King's Works*, published by HMSO between 1963 and 1982, and a debt to its authors is here acknowledged. However, the present work takes the subject much further, drawing on evidence either not appropriate or not available to *The King's Works*. It also takes an entirely different approach, using the copious documentation to illustrate the life of the Court, rather than the growth of a government department. Yet *The Royal Palaces of Tudor England* is not a history of the Tudor Court.

It is fundamentally a social history of royal building in the early sixteenth century and as such, I hope, fills the gap left by *The King's Works*.

I must acknowledge here the grants I received from the British Academy between 1986 and 1989 and the very large number of people who have helped me in various ways. These include Tom Campbell, James Carley, John Cloake, Howard Colvin, Alan Cook, Daphne Ford, Derek Gadd, Phillipa Glanville, Michael Green, Susanne Groom, Christoph Grunenberg, Peter Gwynn, John Harvey, Alisdair Hawkyard, the late Gerald Heath, David Honour, Maurice Howard, Edward Impey, Phillip Lindley, Gillian Malpass, Clare Murphy, John Newman, Geoffrey Parnell, Neil Samman, J.T. Smith, David Starkey, John Thorneycroft, Josephine Turquet, Michael Turner, Juliet West and Kate Woodruff.

1. Hampton Court, Surrey. Detail of fig. 97.

Glossary

Bayne Bath.

Camera Chamber or room

Court Defined by Sir Geoffrey Elton as 'all those who at any given time were within "his grace's house"'. The Court was thus a group of courtiers who had an architectural locus, the king's house. Both the houses and the courtiers varied in numbers and composition, but the focus of the organism, the king, remained the same in all circumstances. (G. R. Elton, 'Tudor Government: The Points of Contact. III: The Court', *Transactions of the Royal Historical Society*, 5 ser. 26 (1976) p. 217.)

Domus House or household.

Domus regis King's house or household.

Donjon A tower lodging containing the private rooms of the owner; cf. D. J. Cathcart King, *The Castle in England and Wales* (London, 1988), pp. 188–96.

Garderobe Latrine.

Giests Lists delineating the movements of the Court on progress.

Hall place An area, lobby or space before the door of a room.

Halpace A word with several meanings: a great halpace is often a staircase; a halpace can be a hearth.

Halfpace A landing on a staircase with straight flights of stairs.

Haut place Literally a high place. Either a staircase with a deep well or a raised platform, often with a seat.

Palace In England, the principal seat of the sovereign, i.e. the Palace of Westminster.

Platt A plan.

Tennis-play A tennis-court.

Vice A spiral stair.

A note on capitalisation

The names of rooms are not given capital letters, thus: guard chamber, privy chamber, wardrobe, privy kitchen. Departments of the royal household are, so Privy Chamber, Wardrobe, Privy Kitchen. The word household itself has two meanings. Capitalised it represents the 'below stairs' functions of the Court under the Lord Steward. In the lower case it means the domus of the king, all those making up his Court. All titles of officers are given capital letters: Cofferer, Gentleman of the Privy Chamber, Captain of the Guard.

A note on plans

The most commonly referred to plans of the major buildings are grouped together at the back of the book in an appendix. These are referred to in the text as 'plan 00'. All illustrations within the text, whether plans or not, are referred to as 'fig. 00'. The conventions used in all the plans are as follows: solid black lines and areas represent extant walls or features, or features seen in excavation; broken lines represent conjectural walls or features; unbroken lines represent walls or features seen in historic plans and views.

facing page: Hampton Court, Surrey. Detail of fig. 172

Chapter 1

ROYAL HOUSES IN THE MIDDLE AGES

When Henry VIII died at Whitehall in the early hours of 28 January 1547 he possessed over sixty houses. This remarkable sequence of magnificent buildings was largely of the King's own making. Henry VIII was an energetic — and unflagging — builder of houses, alone of his passions his enthusiasm for the construction of houses never diminished. The outcome of this was that in 1547 the English Crown owned more houses than it ever had previously, or would again (fig. 4). After 1547 the history of royal houses in England is one largely of declining numbers and of unrealised projects for new buildings. There was to be no English counterpart to Versailles or Schönbrunn. Instead, by a quirk of fortune, by 1700 the principal palace of the kings of Britain was one of Henry VIII's lesser subsidiary houses, St James's Palace.

The houses of the kings and queens of England up to the eighteenth century were far more than residences, they were centres of power, the hub of the country's interests, hopes and aims, all of which focused on an individual — the monarch. The monarch's daily existence was shrouded in mystery, tradition, ceremony and etiquette, indeed a whole liturgy for life. This liturgy, like that of the Church, demanded a certain architectural framework to make it function properly, and from the earliest times royal houses were built to accommodate the liturgy of monarchy.

Under the Angevin kings the royal household was a peripatetic organisation, almost constantly on the move. The king's *domus*, or household, numbered only about one hundred and he was able to move with ease and speed between his houses. The itineraries taken by the Court were not haphazard and the Court usually stayed in specific places for the great feasts of the year. After the Conquest, the largest royal establishments were at Westminster and Winchester and these two sites tended to provide the ceremonial centres of the kingdom, yet neither house assumed the position of the principal or normal residence of the king. The king's household grew steadily in size from the early twelfth century to the early fourteenth. From about 100 to 150 in 1100, it grew to 500 or more by about 1300. The increase in size, together with a greater desire for comfort, meant that the household moved less frequently and certainly less quickly than before.[1]

Coupled with the increasing size of the household in the fourteenth century was a reduction in its administrative function. At first the king's *domus* had embodied all the administrative offices of the kingdom, but from the late eleventh century it began to shed routine administrative work. First the Treasury and Exchequer and later the Chancery moved out of the king's household and were set up at Westminster.[2] Thus from the mid-fourteenth century, although the king ruled from his household, wherever it might be staying, the administrative heart of England was at Westminster. The choice of Westminster, rather than Winchester, ensured that Westminster became the 'official' residence of the king. As such it became his *palatium*, his palace, the seat of power. Westminster, throughout the period dealt with in this book, was the only residence that was ever referred to as a palace. This is supported by the fact that Westminster quickly became the most extensive and frequently

3. The White Tower, the Tower of London. The earliest royal residence to survive in anything like its original form.

4. Graph showing the number of occupied royal houses from the reign of Henry VIII to the Commonwealth.

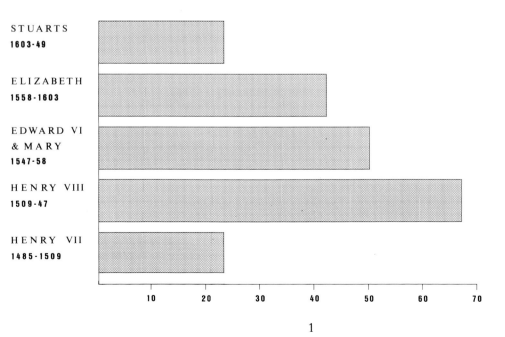

STUARTS
1603-49

ELIZABETH
1558-1603

EDWARD VI
& MARY
1547-58

HENRY VIII
1509-47

HENRY VII
1485-1509

10   20   30   40   50   60   70

5. Maps showing the increasing concentration of residences in and around London between the reigns of Henry II and Henry VIII. Top left: royal residences 1154–1216; top right: royal residences 1216–72; bottom right: royal residences 1327–77; bottom left: royal residences 1509–47.

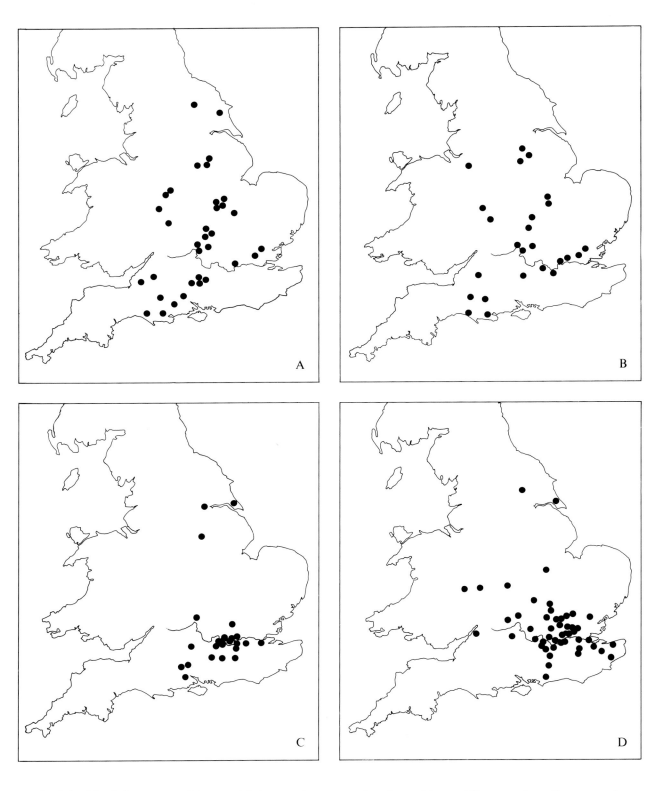

used of the king's houses until its partial destruction by fire and subsequent abandonment as a residence in the early part of Henry VIII's reign.[3]

The reigns of Henry III and Edward III mark important watersheds in the evolution of the royal palace. Henry III spent heavily — at least £28,000[4] — on the houses at Windsor, Westminster, Clarendon, Woodstock, Havering and Guildford, finding small, often timber-framed, buildings and transforming them into large, stone ones. To do this

2

he created the embryonic Office of Works. As a result two significant changes took place. First there was a reduction in the number of royal houses and a narrowing of the King's itinerary, as not all the King's residences could be embellished to the standard of Clarendon, for instance. Second, there was a permanent administrative staff to repair and maintain the existing stock of houses.

These two changes were further consolidated under Edward III who built as lavishly as his great-grandfather. He undertook considerable works at Windsor, Sheen, Havering, the Tower of London and Leeds. In addition he acquired or built half a dozen hunting lodges.[5] This great outburst of building, like that undertaken by Henry III, had the effect of reducing the number of royal houses and concentrating the majority of them in one area. Most of Edward III's houses were located in the Thames valley (fig. 5).

Thus, from the early Middle Ages to the beginning of the fifteenth century there were two overall trends: a decrease in the number of royal houses with a corresponding increase in their size and convenience, and an increase in the size of the royal household with a corresponding decrease in its mobility. Neither of these trends seems to have affected the form of the buildings themselves and the plans of royal houses during the fifteenth century were very much the same as they had been in the twelfth. The long-term success of the original principles behind the design of early-medieval English royal houses is remarkable, and on account of their eventual abandonment and replacement in the late fifteenth century they are briefly summarised here.

Royal domestic accommodation to 1272

The evidence relating to the houses and Courts of the Anglo-Saxon kings is scanty and confusing. Even after the Norman Conquest, knowledge of the household and castles of William the Conqueror is slight; little is known about his household, that is to say those subjects who were with the King at any one time, and only the White Tower, in the Tower of London (fig. 3), completed after his death, reveals anything about his accommodation. However, a document drawn up in 1136 for King Stephen called *constitutio domus regis* (the constitution of the king's household) lists all the principal servants of the King's *domus* and can be taken to represent the sort of household that William the Conqueror developed.

The *domus*, which seems to have had a permanent establishment of about one hundred, was divided into five departments headed by the Chancellor,

Steward, Master-butler, Master-chamberlain and Constable. The most important person, as far as the organisation of the King's domestic life was concerned, was the Master-chamberlain. He was in charge of the King's chamber, his *camera*, the room in which the King lived. Such a room survives in the White Tower, mutilated, but a precious survivor of Norman royal life.

The White Tower had three storeys and a basement which was entered separately. A timber external stair led to the now much-altered entrance on the first floor. Although three storeys high, the building actually only comprised two floors, the second floor being two storeys high (fig. 6). The plan of each floor was very simple as it was divided into three compartments: a large one filling the whole of the western half and on the east two smaller ones, one apsidal.

The King's floor (fig. 7) had only one access point, the great north-eastern spiral stair which probably led into a passageway with access to a galleried hall, the centre of life for the majority of the King's household, the place where they ate and slept. Next door, divided off from the hall was the King's *camera* which had three doors. One allowed the King to arrive and depart via the north-east stair, another provided private access to the chapel and the third access to the hall. The door to the hall was probably directly adjacent to the King's seat or

6. Cut-away section of the White Tower, the Tower of London *c*.1100. On the second floor on the right is the king's chapel; next to it on the left is the king's double-height chamber; and running the whole width of the building is his hall.

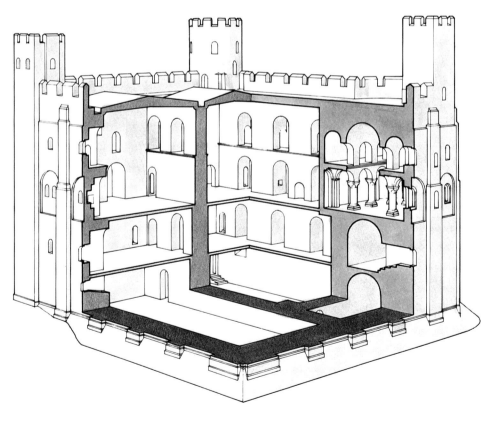

3

7. The White Tower, the Tower of London. Second-floor plan *c.*1100. A: the king's hall; B: the king's chamber; C: the king's chapel.

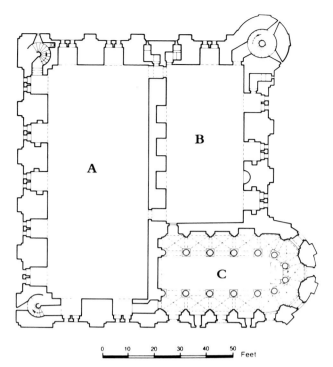

8. The Tower of London. Block plan showing distribution of royal lodgings in *c.*1250. A: the White Tower; B: the great hall; C: the queen's chamber; D: the queen's hall; E: the king's chamber; F: the king's hall; G: the watergate.

canopy. This room was the great royal bedsit; here he slept in a heavily hung bed, bathed in a wooden tub, worked at his table, amused himself and sometimes also ate. The Master-chamberlain, the man in charge of this room, and a close circle of

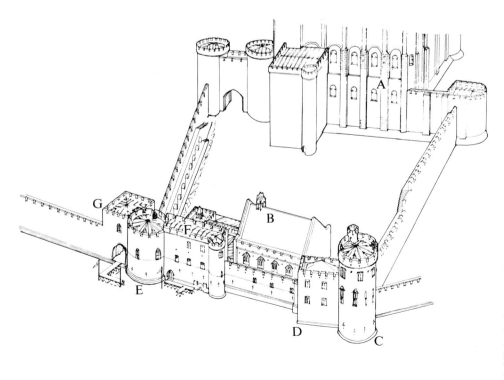

friends and counsellors would attend the King and at night sleep around his bed.

The kings of England were not to live in one room for long: evidence from Nottingham Castle in the reign of Henry II (1154–89) shows how more extensive accommodation was built alongside the donjon for both himself and his Queen (fig. 22). The King's lodgings were immediately adjacent to the donjon and probably formed an extension of it. They comprised three rooms; the King's chamber, a hall and a great chamber. The latter must have been the principal room where he ate and slept, for it had a garderobe and a wardrobe attached. The Queen's lodgings were less extensive, they comprised only two rooms with a privy and garderobe.[6]

Henry II's works at Nottingham no longer survive but the new residential accommodation built by his grandson, Henry III, at the Tower of London does in part. To the south of the White Tower there had been, since the 1220s, an inner ward containing some sort of royal accommodation; during the reign of Henry III the inner ward was reconstructed in a grand style with permanent accommodation for the King and Queen (fig. 8). Accommodation centred on an aisled great hall measuring 65 by 58 feet, serviced by a kitchen on the west. The hall was built up against the curtain wall of the fortress and a passage led from it to two halls, one on the east for the Queen and a western one for the King. Neither hall survives in its entirety, but the footings of the King's hall have been excavated and show that Henry could enter his lodgings via a riverside postern and stair directly from the royal barge. Both the King's and the Queen's halls were attached to great chambers in massive mural towers. Only the King's great chamber, today called the Wakefield Tower (fig. 9), survives. It conveys more vividly than any other surviving structure the way that the early medieval kings lived.

Vaulted with what was originally a timber vault, with windows looking out over the Thames, the interior of the Wakefield Tower is a magnificent piece of architecture. The king was provided with a large chapel, screened from the chamber proper, there was a large hooded fireplace and a recess, probably for his bed, and somewhere on the north side was a garderobe, now lost. In this room, on the occasions when he visited the Tower, Henry III passed the day and night.[7]

The most extensive residential accommodation built by Henry III was at Westminster (plan 12). None of this now survives, but the work of nineteenth-century antiquaries allows comparison with the King's lodgings at the Tower.[8] The heart of the palace was the Norman great hall, the largest great hall in Europe whose very size made it impractical for everyday use and had spawned a lesser hall built to its south in the twelfth century, as was the King's great chamber, built at right-angles to it. Henry III left the lesser hall as it was but completely rebuilt the great chamber, subsequently known as the painted chamber, and two rooms to its south which seem to have been the Queen's chamber and chapel (plan 12).

Much is known of Henry III's painted chamber (fig. 10) and it can be closely compared to his great chamber at the Tower. The essential elements were the same, a bed, a fireplace and a chapel, all in magnificent painted surroundings. At Westminster a refinement was that the chapel was close to the head of the bed and an open quatrefoil allowed the King to hear mass. The painted chamber was clearly designed to be the premier chamber in the land — indeed the *palatium* — the king's principal residence.

By the time of Henry III, the dual role of the Palace of Westminster as both administrative headquarters and domestic accommodation had begun to spawn a descriptive vocabulary. The offices of Exchequer and Chancery and the great hall became the great palace, those rooms beyond the lesser hall were the privy palace. It is important to note that 'privy', in this context, did not mean exclusive or private as it came to by the late fifteenth century. At Westminster in the thirteenth century it meant 'distinct from those areas in which the administration is accommodated'.

Royal domestic accommodation from 1272 to 1399

Henry III's son, Edward I, is chiefly remembered for his extraordinary achievement in military architecture, but Edward never overlooked his personal comfort. He modified and improved his father's buildings particularly at the Tower and at Westminster and his building works at the Tower survive largely intact. By building an outer curtain wall beyond the pre-existing inner defences Edward I transformed the Tower of London into the great concentric fortress that it is today. In doing this he rendered useless his father's magnificent accommodation in the Wakefield Tower which was left high and dry, sandwiched between the two walls (figs 11, 14). To remedy this the King built himself new riverside accommodation in what has become known as St Thomas's Tower.

St Thomas's Tower, which contained a new hall and great chamber, was linked to the earlier buildings by a walk, providing the King with four chambers in addition to the great hall (fig. 11). Edward's hall was much larger than Henry III's, lit by two great windows looking out on to the river and heated by an enormous projecting hooded

fireplace placed between them. In the corner turret was a small chapel. Beyond was the great chamber, with two windows and a fireplace like the outer room. The corner turret contained a strong-room near which was a garderobe.[9]

Documentary evidence as to the precise use of these rooms is entirely lacking, but a comparison

9. The Wakefield Tower, the Tower of London. The Wakefield Tower was built by Henry III as his great chamber; it is the only complete surviving, if altered, early medieval, royal residential building.

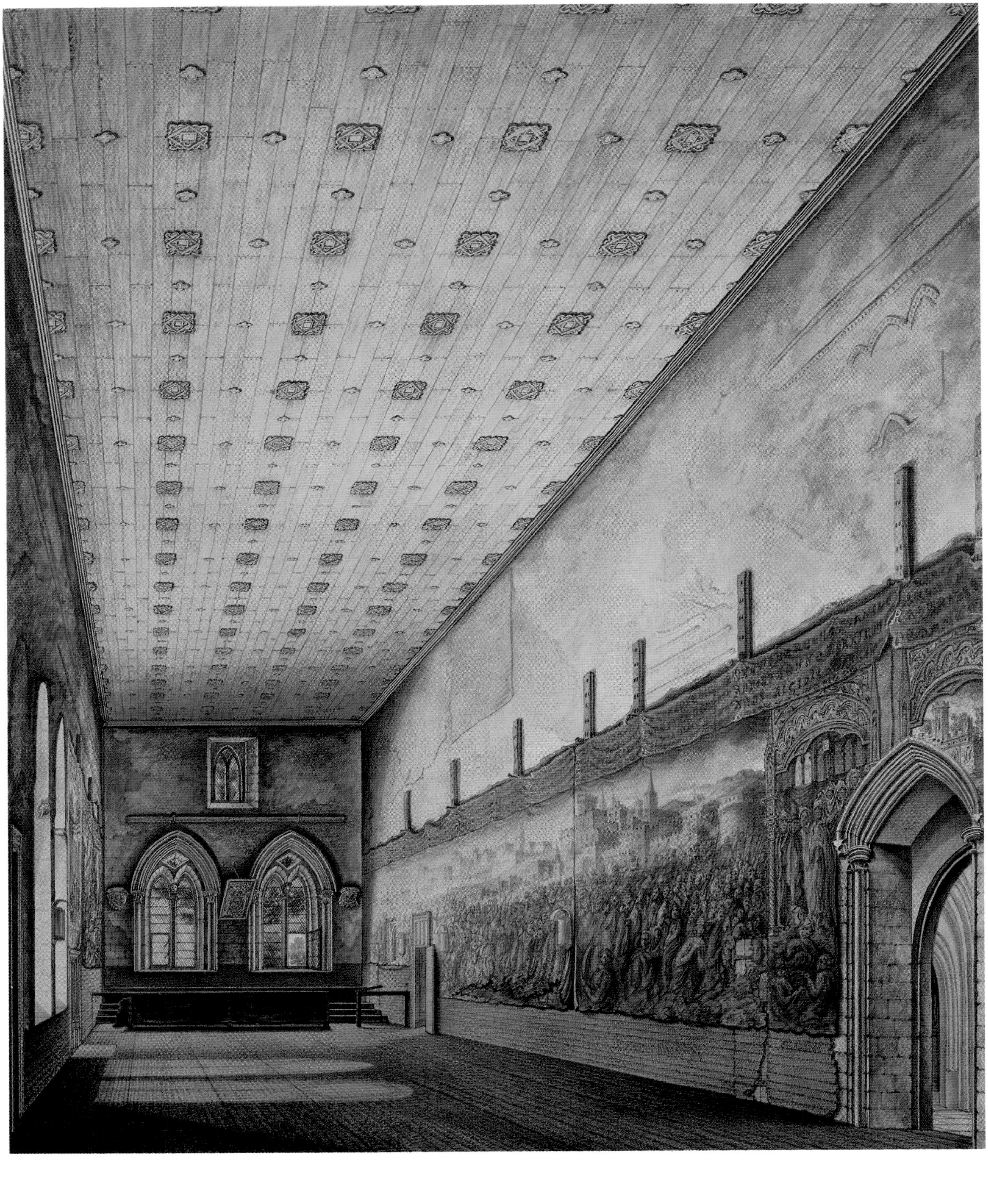

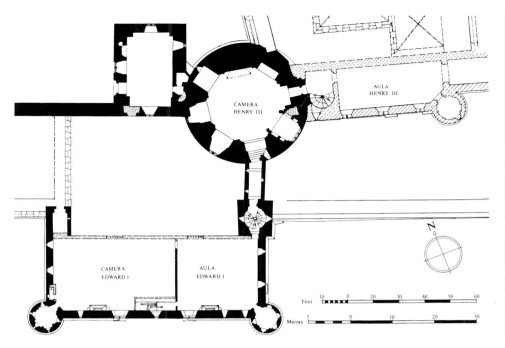

11. Edward I's lodgings, the Tower of London. Plan showing the probable arrangement of the lodgings in 1300.

12 (above right). Conway Castle, Caernarvonshire. Aerial view showing the king's lodging with its four towers in the inner ward.

13 (right). Conway Castle, Caernarvonshire. Plan showing location of Edward I's lodgings in the inner ward.

10 (facing page). The Painted Chamber, Westminster Palace. View of the interior, before the discovery of its painted murals by William Capon, 1799. The king's bed enclosure would have been on the left-hand side beyond the fireplace.

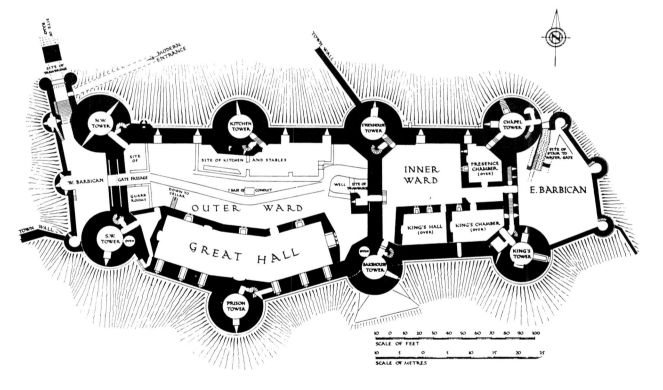

with Conway Castle (Gwynedd) would suggest that the Wakefield Tower was used as a presence chamber for the receipt of visitors and the transaction of formal state business. Conway (figs 12–13), like the Tower, had an outer ward for the King's household and companions and an inner ward for the King's own use. Unroofed, the King's lodgings survive and comprise a hall and great chamber, an inner and an outer room; but also a separated presence chamber with an attached chapel. The great chamber lies against a tower in which there was an oratory, strong room and gardrobe, the essential adjuncts to a medieval king's bedroom.

Edward I was also responsible for extending his father's accommodation at Westminster (plan 12). Unfortunately, as with so many alterations to the palace, it is hard to gain a clear idea of their topography. The accounts refer to a new chamber for the Queen, and many of his alterations seem to have been intended to improve his wife's lodgings.[10] But what of more private accommodation? At Westminster, Henry III had two chambers, one in a garden and the other probably sited beneath the painted chamber on the river front. Both were richly painted and both had fireplaces, so they may have been reserved for his more private moments. Castles, owing to their compact and secure nature, tended not to provide space for private accommodation; it was at the manors like Westminster, and particularly Woodstock, where special provision was made. At Woodstock Henry II and Henry III built a detached complex called Everswell or Rosamund's some two hundred yards from the main house. This was a self-contained retreat for the king and queen with its own kitchen, chapel and residential accommodation set in gardens with a spring feeding pools in the middle. At Windsor Castle a similar retreat was provided, called Windsor Manor, which was much extended by Edward I, once again to provide more convenient accommodation than the castle.[11]

The next major developments in the domestic accommodation of the English monarchy came under Edward III, a builder almost as prolific as Henry III. Little now survives of the magnificent works at Sheen, Havering, the Tower and Leeds, nor of his half-dozen or so hunting lodges. Of his lodgings at Windsor Castle, however, considerably more survives in terms both of fabric and of documentation.[12]

The royal lodgings at Windsor in 1350, immediately before King Edward embarked on his reconstruction, were essentially those of Henry III's time. They were grouped around two courtyards and provided space for not only the King and Queen but also for the royal children. It seems as if the King's lodging was principally a hall and great chamber, but attached to the great chamber were two mural towers which presumably provided further accommodation. Edward III almost completely reconstructed the royal lodgings, building a new hall, converting the old one into a great chamber for himself, reconstructing the second courtyard and building a third as a new kitchen court.

At the end of the account roll for 1363–5 is a list of furniture required for the King's new rooms and this gives a good idea of their extent.[13] Next to the hall was the King's great chamber and a room called the painted chamber; these rooms formed one unit of accommodation. A second group of rooms was situated around the second court to the west. The accounts describe five rooms, none of which is identified in terms of function. Yet the fifth room, a chamber called 'La Rose', may provide the key to their identification. La Rose (today John's Tower) was drastically altered by Jeffrey Wyatville from 1824, but its original configuration is still clear.[14] It was originally built to contain three elements, an upper chamber with a fireplace, a garderobe and a stair leading directly down to the upper ward. From the account rolls we know that the interior of the upper chamber was vaulted and painted by twenty-one men. Thus within La Rose were all the elements needed for the King's innermost sanctum. The room next to it, what the furnishing account calls the fourth room, would therefore seem to have been his great chamber, or bedchamber. This is perhaps borne out by the fact that it was the only room to contain 'screens', and that it had more furniture than the other four rooms. The third chamber had tables and trestles suggesting that it was perhaps the King's hall furnished for eating. The other two chambers were small rooms in the gate tower.

At Windsor under Edward III a division similar to that which existed at Westminster appears to have been formed. There were the formal, 'state' rooms — the great hall, the King's great chamber and the painted chamber; then there were the rooms in which the King spent the majority of his time, culminating in a lavish closet. It is important to remember that this division did not mean that either set of lodgings was more extensive than those occupied by Henry III, for the core of both kings' accommodation was an outer and an inner chamber with a closet (or closets) beyond. What had become more formalised by the reign of Edward III was the fact that the King had a public and a less public function and these two were made architecturally distinct. Richard II created a similar but even more private retreat at Sheen where he built a house with several chambers and a kitchen on a nearby island in the Thames called 'La Nayght'.[15]

* * *

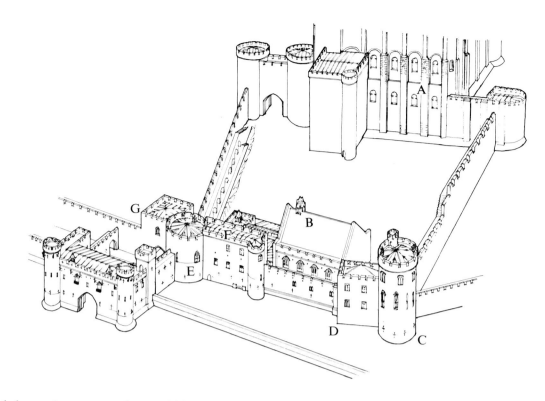

14. The royal lodgings at the Tower of London, *c.*1300. After Edward I built St Thomas's Tower as a new watergate, the royal lodgings were moved into the building from Henry III's mural tower and chamber. Compare figure 8.

Royal domestic accommodation 1399–1461

With the advent of the House of Lancaster a gradual but marked change in the layout of English royal houses is discernible, a change well illustrated by the history of the building works at the royal house at Sheen. There had been a royal residence at Sheen since the early fourteenth century, which Richard II had ordered to be demolished after the death of his first wife there in 1394. Sheen was chosen by Henry V at his accession in 1413 as the site for a trio of religious foundations and a splendid dynastic residence for himself and his heirs. Work began within a year on constructing temporary accommodation (called 'Byfleet') and also on a great donjon, but not much progress had been made when Henry died eight years later. It was left to his successor, the infant Henry VI, to complete the house.[16]

The resumption of work at Sheen in 1429 coincided with the coronation of the boy-king and the end of the Duke of Gloucester's protectorate. This return to work after a seven-year break was a recognition by the King's council that Henry VI would need accommodation suitable to his status as King of France as well as of England. Between 1429 and 1435, £2,575 was spent on finishing the main building, and subsequently, in preparation for the King's marriage to Margaret of Anjou in 1445, it was further extended. The plan of the Lancastrian house was very similar to those of the Tudor period (plan 11);[17] there was a great moated stone donjon

linked to an outer court beyond the moat. In form Sheen must have been very similar to Raglan Castle (Gwent) (figs 33 and 34), which was under construction at almost exactly the same time. The builder of Raglan, Sir William ap Thomas, had served under Henry V at Agincourt and both King and subject seem to have been influenced by the castles they had seen whilst on campaign in France.[18]

At Sheen there was an unprecedented innovation. Unlike previous royal houses there was a physical barrier between the accommodation of the monarch and that of the Court. A moat divided the lodgings of the King and Queen from the remainder of the house. This division was symptomatic of a trend which was to come to dominate the minds of the monarchs of England: the quest for privacy. What Sheen provided was a potential for privacy within the main building and, more important, a bid for the legitimacy of privacy for a monarch. Kings of England began to place more and more barriers, both physical and organisational, between themselves and their courtiers.

The full implications of the innovation introduced at Sheen seem not to have been understood initially; at least, the basic principle of its design was not applied elsewhere by Henry V. At Kenilworth Castle the King followed the example of his predecessors in building himself a remote pleasure-ground. The Pleasance was a moated retreat with a hall and several other chambers set in gardens on the

9

other side of the great pool before the castle.[19] Like Rosamund's, and La Nayght, The Pleasance was separate from the house proper.

Other than his works at Sheen, Henry VI is not known for his secular building works and, on Edward IV's succession, there were only nine royal houses: the Palace of Westminster, Baynard's Castle, Eltham, Greenwich, Sheen, Woodstock, Langley, Minster Lovell and Tickenhill. In addition there were the residential castles: Windsor, the Tower, Fotheringhay, Nottingham, Leeds, Kenilworth and Warwick. Edward IV, unlike his predecessor, was a great patron of the secular arts, and it was in his reign that the changes in the structure of the Court and the very nature of the monarchy began to show in the form of the King's houses.

Chapter 2

THE YORKISTS, BURGUNDY AND MAGNIFICENCE

SIR JOHN FORTESCUE in his political treatise *The Governance of England*, written about 1470, set out what he believed to be the principles of kingship:

> Item, it shall nede that the kyng haue such tresour, as he mey make new bildynges whan he woll, ffor his pleasure and magnificence; and as he mey bie hym riche clothes, riche furres . . . riche stones . . . and other juels and ornamentes conuenyent to his estate roiall. And often tymes he woll bie riche hangynges and other apparell ffor his howses . . . ffor yff a king did not so, nor myght do, he lyved then not like his estate, but rather in miserie, and in more subgeccion than doth a priuate person.[1]

For Fortescue it was essential that a king should be rich enough to buy beautiful and expensive objects both for his own pleasure and to appear magnificent. Expenditure, extravagance and magnificence went hand in hand. Being magnificent was the art of being visibly richer and more powerful than others. It was not enough that a king should rule, he must be seen to be ruling by being surrounded by richness which fitted his elevated state. The concept of magnificence is crucial to the understanding of the buildings and Court culture of the age.

Guillaume Fillastre, Chancellor of the Burgundian Order of the Golden Fleece, in his book *La Toison d'or* (c.1470), stated that the chief virtue of a prince was magnificence.[2] In doing so he followed Aristotle's concept of the term in the *Nicomachean Ethics*, where the Greek philosopher had said that 'The magnificent man is a sort of connoisseur; he has an eye for fitness, and can spend large sums with good taste'. These sums were spent 'not upon himself but upon public objects'.[3] The magnificent prince is more interested in 'how he can achieve the finest and most appropriate result rather than how much it will cost and how it can be done most cheaply'.[4] Money was never to be stinted, nor the cost counted by a prince, whether in a programme of buildings, in displays of faith and piety or in promoting entertainments or festivals.[5] Thus, for

Fillastre magnificence was the princely art of lavish provision which was both a reflection and a physical expression of the prince's personal standing and authority.

Fillastre's definition of magnificence allowed a prince to spend without due thought or taste. Not everyone followed Fillastre's definition in its totality. In his play *Magnificence* (fig. 15), written in the early 1520s John Skelton considers the problem of finding a compromise between ostentation and meanness. He takes as his central theme the proverb 'measure is treasure'.[6] The central figure, Magnificence, falls because he drives his chief minister,

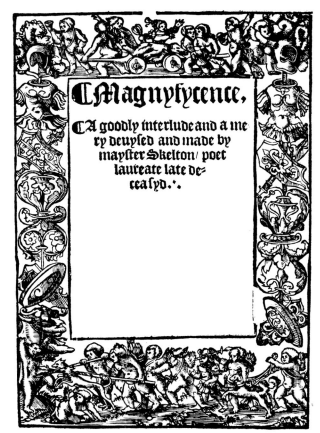

15. The title-page of *Magnificence* by John Skelton, published c.1532.

Measure, from office and gives another, Liberty, full reign. Magnificence, at the start of the play says:

> For doubtless I perceive my Magnificence
> Without measure lightly may fade,
> Of too much liberty under the offence,
> Wherefore, Measure, take Lyberte with
>   you hence,
> And rule hym after the rule of your scole.[7]

So for Skelton, magnificence signified the physical expression of power by properly measured liberality in all things.

Magnificence was a concept well understood by the late medieval kings of England. The courts of Richard II, Henry V and Edward IV matched and rivalled any of their European counterparts and in 1466 a visitor to the Court of Edward IV observed, without irony, that the English king had 'the most splendid Court that could be found in all Christendom'.[8] Only Henry VI conspicuously failed to observe the concept, earning nearly universal contempt and disparagement for his almost total neglect of suitable royal magnificence, the splendour of his Chapel Royal being a single exception which was not rated enough to redeem his general omission. Even Henry VI's personal appearance and choice of clothes disappointed and shocked his subjects, and in 1471 his entry into London was described as being 'more lyker a play than the shewing of a prynce to wynne mennys hertys', and that 'evyr he was shewid in a long blew goune of velvet as thowth he hadd noo moo to chaunge with'.[9] As Sir John Fortescue noted, one of Henry VI's worst flaws was his 'grete pouertie', his reluctance to keep a 'worshipfull and grete housolde' with the attendant social consequences.[10] Neither Edward IV nor Henry VII were to repeat Henry VI's mistake: they both understood that the illusion of wealth, power and status was as important as the real thing. In his will Henry VII directed that his newly finished chapel at Westminster should be painted with 'our arms, badges, cognisants, and other convenient painting', not because 'such a work requireth' such embellishment, but, more importantly, because such lavish decoration 'to a king's work appertaineth'. In other words Henry VII commanded the embellishment because the chapel should signify its royal ownership by its magnificence.[11]

A proper understanding of what exactly magnificence meant is the key to appreciating the art and architecture of the Tudor Court. The Tudors did not share the modern obsession for the aesthetic achievement of Italy, or even the Netherlands, France or anywhere else, but concentrated on the creation of a magnificent effect. This effect was achieved by four principal considerations most, or all, of which were necessary for success. The first was expense, that is the cost of the item; the second cunning, the skill with which it was wrought; the third novelty, its originality; and fourth was placement — its juxtaposition with other objects.

Contemporary accounts of Court festivals and reports of visits abroad by Englishmen reveal how these four yardsticks were used to judge *objets d'art*. The two fullest accounts of the festivals and feasts of the Tudor Court are those of Edward Hall in his *Chronicle* (1548) and of George Cavendish in his contemporary *Life of Wolsey*. Both applied the concept of magnificence to judge what they saw. In a famous passage, Cavendish described in great detail the splendour with which Wolsey entertained the French ambassadors at Hampton Court in 1527, paying special attention to the expense of the preparations and how much gold and silver had been displayed. He continued . . .

> the kyng was privye of all this worthy feast, who entendyd ferre to exed the same . . . But to discrybe the disshes, the subtyllties, the many straynge devysis and order in the same I do bothe lake wytt in my grosse old hed and cunnyng in my bowelles to declare the wonderfull and curious Imagynacions in the same Inventyd and devysed . . . yet dyd thys bankett ferre exed the same as fynne gold dothe siluer in waytt and valewe.[12]

The value of the items displayed, their curiosity, their size and diversity, are the features most remarked upon. Almost any page of Hall's *Chronicle* will reveal the same attitude. The design of the arras at the jousts of 1510–11 was 'curiously made and plesaunt to beholde, it was solempne and ryche, for every post or piller therof, was covered with fryse golde'.[13] The palace at the Field of Cloth of Gold (fig. 66) 'lumyned the eyes of the beholders' by the 'great connynge and sumpteous woorke' and 'no livyng creature might but joye' at the gilt cornice 'with fine Golde'.[14] The canopy over the high altar there was 'of merveilous greatnes' and the altar in the Queen's closet 'lacked neither Pearles nor Stones of riches'.[15]

Conversely, on great occasions where there was no lavish show of magnificence, the courtiers of Henry VIII were wont to complain. Bishop Clerk reported of a masque held at the Court of Francis I, 'there was done no notable . . . nor no great excess in charges; we can assure you . . . our opinion that the king spent not in this feast . . . one hundred crowns above his ordinary, for as for . . . masquering habits, they were but coarse'.[16] During Wolsey's mission to France in 1527 observers were struck by the magnificence and solemnity displayed by the English, as compared with the alleged simplicity, frugality and absence of all ceremony on the part of the French.[17] This supposed lack of magnificence was a source of contempt. The Court of Henry VIII was not the first to set such store by the creation of lavish physical settings. The idea of magnificence as practised by the early Tudor monarchy was a continuation of the spectacular precedent set by Edward IV who had been profoundly influenced by the most fashionable Court in Europe, the Court of the dukes of Burgundy.

From the fourteenth century the Court of France under the Valois family had been surrounded by a group of ducal sub-Courts, of which Anjou, Burgundy, Berry, Bourbon, Brittany and Foix were the most important. The natural role of the French Court as the leader of fashion which the ducal Courts could follow was seriously undermined in the early fifteenth century by a combination of civil war and invasion from England. As a result the individual ducal Courts were able to develop distinctive courtly cultures of their own. By the 1430s the Court of Burgundy, through its wealth and the determination of its dukes, had outshone not only the other ducal Courts but also the royal Courts of France and England.[18]

The primacy of the Burgundian Court was reflected in elaborate Court ceremonial and festivals as well as in artistic patronage. Court etiquette reached a peak of complex subtlety under Charles the Bold, and to record and regulate the points of issue raised by such elaboration Duke Charles's Master of Ceremonies, Olivier de la Marche, wrote *L'estat de la maison du duc Charles de Bourgogne* (1474).[19] Even the Duchess, Isabel of Burgundy, had frequently to consult a work on etiquette to ensure that the correct forms were being observed.[20] This ceremony reached frequent peaks during Court festivals, marriages, treaties and receptions. The earliest of this extraordinary sequence, Philip the Bold's wedding at Ghent in 1369, had been magnificent enough,[21] but during the 1460s, at occasions such as Charles the Bold's wedding, the spectacle reached extraordinary proportions (see p. 16).

The function of these lavish and elaborate ceremonies was to enhance the Duke's prestige and to display his wealth and power. In short, it was the creation of *magnificence*. This was produced by an army of artists and craftsmen working on tapestries, jewellery, manuscripts, clothes and buildings:[22] in the words of Otto Cartellieri 'the sovereign's hand might touch nothing common, and even the homeliest articles were made and beautified by famous craftsmen and artists'.[23]

For the Burgundians the courtly culture of magnificence was underpinned by the idea of chivalry and the perpetuation of the chivalric values

of the thirteenth century.[24] One of the clearest expressions of this was the creation, by Philip the Good, of the Order of the Golden Fleece. This was established in 1430 'from the great love which we bear to the noble order of chivalry, whose honour and prosperity are our only concern, to the end that the true catholic faith . . . may be defended and preserved . . . and for the furtherance of virtue and good manners'.[25] The dukes of Burgundy filled their libraries with chivalric romances and their tournaments promoted the values and aims of chivalry.[26] Chivalry was the essence of medieval courtly life and Burgundian magnificence in the late Middle Ages flourished in its golden age.

Burgundian magnificence was given a highly particular expression in the residences of the dukes of Burgundy. The fourteenth-century dukes of Burgundy had had residences in Brussels, Dijon, Ghent, Hesdin in Artois, Valenciennes in Hainault and at the Hôtel d'Artois in Paris. All but one of these residences were in an urban setting where the ducal house was the most magnificent of the town houses of the nobility. The one exception was the Palace of Hesdin, set, as it was, in the country. Nothing survives of it now but much is known about it from building accounts which describe in great detail, among other things, the gallery of practical jokes set up in the 1450s.[27] Valenciennes was another large palace, now entirely vanished, but about which a little is known from manuscripts. Of Philip the Good's palace at Lille, the Palais Richour, fragments survive; the original building was abandoned as too small in 1461 and a contract was awarded for a new palace which was completed by 1473.

At Champmol, near Dijon, Philip the Bold (d. 1404) built a Charterhouse not far from the ducal palace.[28] Of the Charterhouse, demolished at the French Revolution, only the main porch remains. Similarly, the palace with its Sainte-Chapelle, the headquarters of the Order of the Golden Fleece, is also almost entirely lost, only a hall, two kitchens and two towers survive. Philip the Good (d. 1467) was responsible for several important additions between 1452 and 1463, including the Tour de la Terrasse and the Salle des Gardes.[29]

Until the time of Philip the Good, the dukes of Burgundy were based mainly in Paris, and it was only after 1420 that they took up residence mainly in the Netherlands. When in Paris they occupied the Hôtel d'Artois, which was mostly demolished in 1543,[30] leaving one small fragment, the Tower of John the Fearless, built between 1408 and 1411.[31] This donjon was the Duke's private tower containing his bedroom, and beneath it a bathroom. Philip the Good was the first duke to reside mainly outside Paris. In addition to his work at Champmol

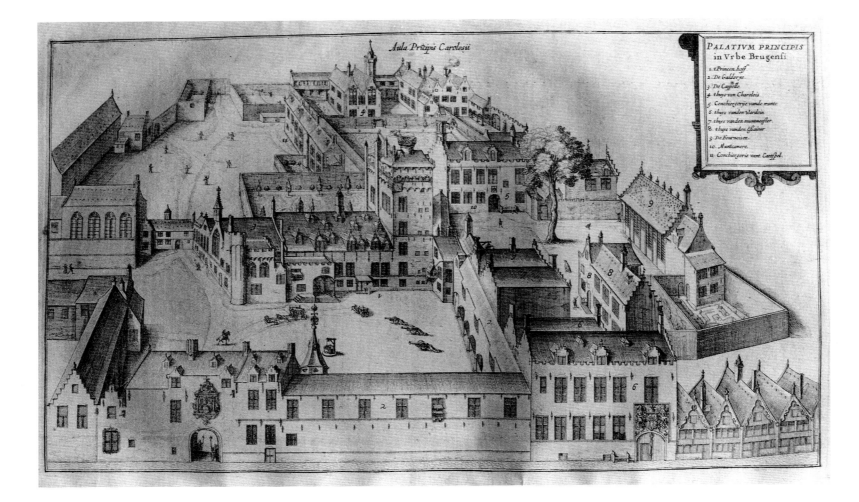

Aula Prīcipis Carolesii

PALATIVM PRINCIPIS
in Vrbe Brugensi.

1. 't Princen hof
2. De Gallerye
3. De Cappelle
4. thuys van Charolois
5. Conciergerye vande munte
6. thuys vanden Wardein
7. thuys vanden muntmeester
8. thuys vanden Essaieur
9. De Fournoisen
10. Muntcamere
11. Conciergerie vant Cartsel

16. Princenhof, Bruges.
Engraving from A.
Sanderus, *Flandria Illustrata*,
1644 edn.

he undertook substantial building operations at most
of the palaces which were to be occupied by the
fifteenth-century dukes: Bruges, Brussels and
Ghent.[32]

Princenhof (fig. 16), the ducal residence at Bruges,
was the biggest of the houses of the fifteenth-
century dukes of Burgundy, and is known today
from Anthonis Sanderus's engraving in *Flandria
Illustrata* (1641). It was improved with temporary
structures by Philip the Good in 1429, and then
substantially rebuilt and enlarged in the years after
his marriage in 1446.[33] In plan the palace was a
succession of courtyards. The outermost, approached
by a gatehouse, was surrounded by galleries on
loggias and contained, on its far side, the main
range. This comprised a hall, chapel and massive
donjon containing the ducal lodgings. Off the
donjon, towards the front court, the lodgings of the
Duchess faced her garden, the Duke's garden lay
behind the main range. Beyond and to the side of
the Duke's lodging was a residence for his son and
heir. The courtyards, which surrounded the main
buildings, provided lodgings for the courtiers and

recreation for the Court. The large back court could
be used for tilting, and beyond it lay tennis-courts.
The details of the internal layout are lost, but it is
known to have had extensive bathrooms on the
ground floor specially constructed for the marriage
of Philip the Good.[34]

The ducal palace at Ghent was also engraved by
Sanderus, who depicted a moated complex surrounded by gardens (fig. 17). The great court, like
that of Princenhof, was arcaded and led towards the
hall and chapel. The duke's lodgings were ranged
along one side of the court and culminated in a
donjon. The huge forecourt of the palace was used
as a tiltyard and the small group of buildings projecting into the moat contained a menagerie. Brussels
was the spot most favoured by the Burgundian
Court throughout the fifteenth century. However,
during the 1440s Bruges enjoyed a brief period of
equal popularity. The Palace of Coudenberg at
Brussels was destroyed by fire in the eighteenth
century but its appearance is known through several
drawings and views on the set of tapestries known
as the *Triumphs of Maximilian*.[35] Philip the Good

14

virtually rebuilt the palace in the 1430s and 1440s and Charles the Bold further extended it between 1468 and 1469.[36]

Most of the Burgundian palaces were built of brick. During the construction of the new hôtel at Lille in 1461, Philip the Good specified stone as the material to be used. Evidently he regarded brick as a low-grade — and decidedly humble — material. However, the practical difficulties in obtaining stone and the arguments of the builders concerning the prevailing weather conditions seem to have persuaded him to accept a brick building, as all the surviving fragments are of brick. At Coudenberg the *grande salle* was of brick, although faced in stone. Charles the Bold certainly built in brick — the new great staircase at Coudenberg being an example. All the other main palaces were made of this material, often rubbed or moulded and sometimes enriched with terracotta. The fact that the palaces of the most fashionable Court in Europe were brick-built had important consequences. Brick, which had previously been regarded as a cheap, even if convenient, building material, underwent an aesthetic revaluation and, as a result, was rated a more than acceptable material for a building, whatever its purpose.[37]

Even from this rudimentary summary there emerge clearly the main features of the fifteenth-century Burgundian palace: these features comprised a structure with numerous courtyards combining gardens and lodgings in very close proximity. The duke, duchess and heir apparent each had separate lodgings grouped around gardens and courts. Recreation was provided nearby in tennis-courts, tiltyards and gardens. A major feature was the gallery which ran round courtyards and linked outlying parts of the buildings. The main lodgings were usually on several storeys approached by a *grande vis*, and the ducal lodgings were always situated in a donjon. Stylistically the important features were the crenellated rooflines with small dormer windows ending in crow-stepped gables. Turrets were mainly octagonal and, in the views of Sanderus, crowned with lead types; rooflines were also ornamented with metal vanes and flags and ornate leadwork. The galleries were almost always on the first floor and supported by a loggia (figs 16–19).[38]

England and Burgundy

The links between England and Burgundy during the heyday of the Burgundian Court were many; mercantile, political, dynastic. The Netherlands, the prize possession of the dukes of Burgundy, was the business heart of northern Europe, and not sur-

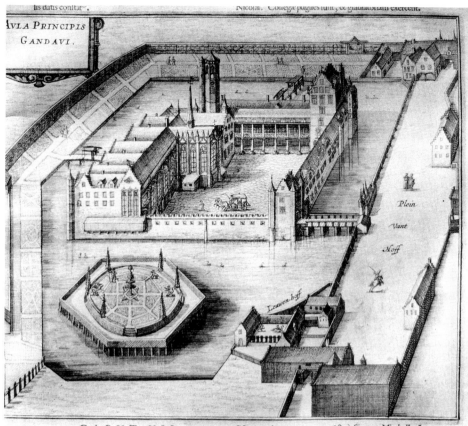

17. The ducal palace, Ghent. Engraving from A. Sanderus, *Flandria Illustrata*, 1644 edn.

prisingly England looked to the Netherlands as the main outlet for its chief product, cloth. Good relations with the Netherlands and with their Burgundian overlords were essential principles of English foreign policy and axiomatic to the survival of the English economy. The disastrous (to England) conclusion of the Hundred Years' War had been a lesson not to neglect these good relations, and 1461 offered an opportunity to put this unfortunate omission right.[39]

In both France and England there were new kings. Edward IV ascended the throne of England anxious for allies and to establish the Yorkist dynasty. Simultaneously Louis XI of France began aggressively to reassert the dominance of the French Crown. Both the Duke of Brittany, Francis II, and the Duke of Burgundy, Philip the Good, began to look for allies against the expansionist France, and Edward IV was only too happy to consolidate his position with foreign alliances.[40]

The process of reforging the traditional links between England and the Netherlands began at the very start of Edward's reign. In 1465, for the coronation of his Queen, Elizabeth Woodville, her uncle, Jacques de Luxembourg, arrived in London with a train of Burgundian knights.[41] Two years

18. The house of Louis of Gruuthuse, Bruges. Engraving from A. Sanderus, *Flandria Illustrata*, 1644 edn. Edward IV stayed here in October 1470.

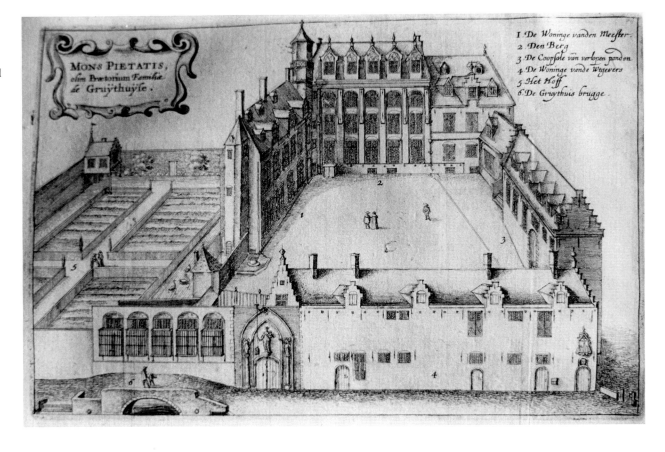

later Anthony, the Bastard of Burgundy, whose chivalrous reputation in Europe was second to none, tilted against the Queen's brother, Lord Scales.[42] These exchanges of courtly courtesies were but a prelude to the Anglo-Burgundian rapprochement when, in 1468, Edward's sister, Margaret of York, married Charles the Bold, 'accompanied by the most splendid and extravagant festivities ever contrived in the entire annals of Burgundy'.[43]

The marriage ceremonies of 1468 had a lasting effect upon those members of the English Court who witnessed them and upon the development of English courtly taste. One of those who accompanied Margaret to the Netherlands was John Paston. Paston reported to his mother:

> . . . my Lady Margaret was maryd on Sonday last past . . . sche was browt the same day to Bruggys to hyr dener, and ther sche was receyvyd as worchepfully as all the world cowd devyse, as with presessyon with ladys and lordys best beseyn of eny pepyll that euer I sye or herd of, many pagentys wer pleyed . . . the best that euer I sye.

The wedding was held in Bruges at the ducal palace of Princenhof (fig. 16), which was extended by the addition of a banqueting hall, measuring 140 by 70 feet, for the occasion. The bride made her triumphal entry into the town past nine tableaux, or pageants, to the palace, where the wedding feast was prepared. At the wedding feast itself there was a huge working model of Charles's castle at Gorinchem, out of which came musical bears, wolves and asses. The jousting in the market place which followed the feast went on for a week.[44] Paston described the jousting and the gold and silver worn by the competitors, remarking that, 'I herd neuyr of so gret plenté as her is'. Next he wrote of the Duke's Court, 'as of lordys, ladys, and gentylwomen, knytys, sqwyirs and gentylmen, I herd neuer of non lyek to it, saue Kyng Artourys cort. And by my trowthe, I have no wyt nor rememberans to wryte to yow halfe the worchep that is her.'[45]

During the winter of 1470–71 Edward IV himself was to experience the Burgundian Court when he was forced into exile at the readoption, or restoration, of Henry VI. The exiled monarch was billeted on Louis, Lord of Gruuthuse, Governor of Holland, at The Hague where he had a substantial town house with a noted library.[46] Gruuthuse's house was a courtyard house built of brick, with the *salle* and donjon constructed in the 1420s and most of the rest built by him in the 1460s. During January and February 1471 Edward stayed at Gruuthuse's house in Bruges which substantially survives today

16

(figs 18, 19).[47] Although it is impossible to assess the degree of influence of these buildings upon King Edward, Gruuthuse was to play a significant part in the construction of the King's oratory in the chancel of St George's Chapel at Windsor (fig. 20). Gruuthuse visited Windsor in 1472, not long after commissioning an almost identical oratory in the church of Notre-Dame in Bruges (fig. 21).[48]

By 1474 Edward was clearly attempting to outdo his brother-in-law in magnificence. In that year William, Lord Hastings, his Lord Chamberlain,

asked Olivier de la Marche for a signed copy of the Burgundian household ordinances, so that he could discover the degree of estate kept by the Duke on campaign. Later, foreign observers commented that the English preparations for war were as fine, if not finer, than those of the Burgundians. Hastings was an important link between the two Courts. From 1471 to 1483 he held the politically important lieutenancy of Calais and it was through Calais, England's foothold in Europe, that many Burgundian artefacts and *objects d'art* reached England.[49]

Previous English kings had bought Netherlandish tapestries to adorn their houses, but none of his predecessors had acquired as many as Edward IV. In 1478 the King bought whole sets of arras from the celebrated collection of Guillaume Hugonet, Chancellor to Charles the Bold.[50] Edward also collected Netherlandish manuscripts and commissioned manuscripts for his own collection from Flemish masters.[51] It seems as if his Court festivals were equally heavily influenced by Burgundian fashions, although lack of evidence makes it difficult to be certain.[52]

The Burgundian influence on the English Court is seen nowhere more vividly than in Edward IV's household ordinances of 1471–2, usually known as

19. The house of Louis of Gruuthuse, Bruges, today. This tall brick-built, heavily gabled courtyard house epitomises many of the strands of urban palace design found in the Netherlands in the late fifteenth century.

20. St George's Chapel, Windsor Castle. Stone and wooden oriels of the king's closet on the north side of the presbytery. The stone oriel to the left was built by Edward IV, the timber one (originally painted to resemble stone) by Henry VIII. The latter is an important surviving example of decorative timberwork from the early part of Henry VIII's reign.

21. Notre-Dame, Bruges, oratory. Commissioned by Louis of Bruges as his private oratory, the church was linked by a gallery to his house. It was probably this that inspired the oratory at Windsor.

the Black Book. In the Black Book English Court ceremonial clearly mirrors the elaborate etiquette of the Court of Burgundy.[53] For the first time the English Court had a written code of etiquette expressly designed to create magnificence. The two departments of the Court, the Lord Steward's department and Lord Chamberlain's department, were named the *domus regis magnificencie* and the *domus providencie*. It was the job of the *domus providencie*, the below-stairs part of the Court to facilitate the magnificence of the upstairs or public part of the Court — the *domus regis magnificencie*; the creation of magnificence being the stated aim of the household.[54]

Edward IV: Buildings and builders

Edward IV's architectural achievement was another expression of his pursuit of magnificence. In his lifetime the King enjoyed the reputation of being a great builder,[55] and his building works were celebrated in the poet John Skelton's elegy on his death, where the spirit of the departed King recalls:

> I made the Tower strong, I wist not why
> I knew not to whom I purchased Tattershall;
> I amended Dover on the mountain high,
> And London I provoked to fortify the wall;
> I made Nottingham a place full royall,
> Windsor, Eltham, and many other mo;
> Yet, at last, I went from them all.[56]

Five centuries have not dealt kindly with these works; some of Edward IV's ecclesiastical work, that at Windsor, survives, but the almost total disappearance of his enormous domestic construction, with the twin exceptions of ranges at Eltham and Hertford, and the lack of specificity in the extant accounts mean that the precise measure of his achievement is not easily determinable. Yet Edward's role in the development of royal buildings has been underestimated and it is now clear that many features which are often regarded as Tudor innovations were of Edwardian origin.

Outside the Thames valley Edward IV concentrated on three major domestic building projects: Fotheringhay, Nottingham and Dover. At Fotheringhay and Nottingham he erected substantial new domestic quarters for himself and his wife. Fotheringhay was Edward's favourite residence outside the Thames valley, and he spent considerable sums on what John Leland was to describe as 'very fair lodggyns in the castel'. These lodgings were probably being set up around 1463–6 when the accounts mention the 'chambers, gallery latrines, turrets and kitchen newly begun', and building was still under way in 1478 when masons were being hired in Cambridge. Later references indicate that the new chambers and gallery were approached by a staircase in the inner bailey.[57]

Edward IV's extravagant metamorphosis of the medieval fortress at Nottingham began as his work on Fotheringhay drew to a close. The work here, costing over £3,000 and completed by his brother Richard III, was described by Leland:

> the most bewtifullest part and gallant building for lodgyng is on the northe side, wher Edward the 4. began a right sumptuus pece of stone work, of the which he clerely finichid one excellent goodly toure of 3. hightes yn building, and brought up other part likewise from the foundation with stone and mervelus fair cumpacid windoes to layyng of the first soyle for chambers, . . .
>
> Then King Richard his brother as I hard ther forcid up apon that worke another peace of one lofte of tymber, making rounde wyndoes also of tymbre to the proportion of the aforesaid wyndoes of stone a good fundation for newe tymbre windowes.[58]

A plan by Robert Smythson, drawn in about 1617, shows these works in detail at ground-floor level (fig. 22). In terms of overall layout what Edward had built for himself was a privy lodging within the castle proper. The lodging range was built up against the outer wall of the castle, it had seven full-height bay windows which, judging by the fireplaces, lit three substantial rooms. These were approached by a stair from the court. The three chambers, from their size, appear to have been the state rooms of the castle. The donjon presumably contained the King's private lodgings. The three rooms may be identified as an outer chamber or hall, a withdrawing chamber and a presence chamber. The privy lodgings in the tower would be next to the presence chamber and, therefore, by inference, the easternmost turret contained the main stair leading up to the royal lodgings. The privy lodging had in its basement a privy kitchen linked to the main floors by a vice-stair.[59]

Of the two main floors, the Queen seems to have occupied the ground-floor rooms and the King those on the first floor approached by a vice-stair in the north-east corner of the courtyard.[60] If, indeed, this was the case, the model adopted was very similar to the organisation of similar lodgings in France and Burgundy, where the king, or duke, lodged above the queen and they both shared a privy lodging in the donjon. This was the case at Princenhof (fig. 16). This was very different from the traditional English plan where the king's and queen's lodgings had until then been on the same level as, for instance, at Clarendon and Westminster (see plan 12) in the thirteenth century.[61]

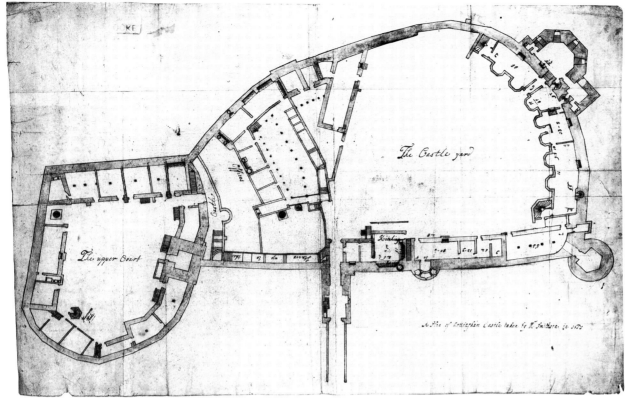

22. Nottingham Castle,
Nottinghamshire. Plan by
Robert Smythson, 1617.

Higher up the Thames at Windsor Castle the King restricted himself to modernisation. A century earlier his great-grandfather Edward III had created a splendid set of royal lodgings, but by the 1460s these had become outmoded. In 1477–8, as part of the programme of alterations, work was done in the King's great chamber and a bay window added to the Queen's great chamber.[62] An account from the same year exists for 'making of a new gallery and of a roof above a chamber situated near le jewell house'. Works were also undertaken in the garden where 'de les railez' were installed.[63] These modernisations were an attempt to introduce fashionable elements to the palace, a gallery, a garden laid out with low rails and a bay window.

A similar pattern of improvement and embellishment can also be discerned at Dover, where, according to the Elizabethan antiquarian, William Darell, the King 'laid out £10,000 in beautifying and fortifying it'. In addition to rebuilding Fiennes Tower he 'erected a stately tower, furnished with handsome apartments, and decorated it with the figures of lions and fleures-de-lys'.[64] Such a tower containing grand apartments is entirely in keeping with Edward's works elsewhere. Although Henry VI had begun to modernise the privy palace at Westminster, the real task of turning the uncomfortable medieval buildings into a set of royal

lodgings was undertaken by Edward IV. Once more, lack of evidence makes discussion of these works difficult, but Edward certainly erected new accommodation for the Queen (indeed creating a 'Queen's side' to the palace), building her a withdrawing chamber in 1464 and a great chamber in 1482. Other works seem to have included the building of a privy kitchen and a wardrobe.[65]

More is known about Eltham than of any other of Edward's works. Not only do some financial records survive, but so does his largest single building, the great hall. An early seventeenth-century plan by John Thorpe shows the palace at ground-floor level at its greatest extent (see plan 1), and excavations have revealed much about the royal lodgings.[66] After Westminster, Eltham was the largest and most favoured of the medieval royal houses. Although never an 'official' residence of the sovereign, combining state departments and domestic lodgings, it was a substantial suburban seat where important visitors could be entertained and where the whole Court could be accommodated without difficulty for a long period.[67] Eltham was what could be called a pleasure palace. It had been owned by the Crown since the death of Bishop Bek of Durham in 1311, and throughout the fourteenth century it had undergone progressive modifications and improvements. In particular Edward III had

24. Eltham, Kent. Stone bridge over the moat, now without its drawbridge and gatehouse. It probably dates from Edward IV's time.

lavished over £2,200 on the residence.[68] He seems to have built his royal lodgings on the east of the manor, although how these related to the hall excavated in 1975–9 is unclear.[69] By the reign of Richard II, Eltham was already a large and luxurious house; mention is made of a garden to the south, a bathroom, dancing chambers and extensive lodgings for the Court, and both Henry IV and Henry VI undertook further programmes of improvement.[70]

On the accession of Edward IV the exact form of the house is unclear, but it seems likely that the north and east ranges of the palace were extant (fig. 23). In addition excavation has shown that the great hall was situated in the western part of the building and to the north of it was the great chamber built over an undercroft;[71] the royal lodgings, some of which were excavated, were to the west of this. At Eltham, Edward's attention turned, not only to the privy lodgings, but also to the public aspect of the house, to the great hall and its ancillary buildings. Following the demolition of Bishop Bek's great hall and kitchens, a new hall range was built on a different alignment.[72] The old hall had been aligned north–south, the new one turned through 180 degrees to lie opposite a new stone bridge spanning the moat (fig. 24). The hall itself was built as part of a unified front facing on to a newly formed courtyard (see plan 1). Part of this range is shown in a view of 1828 by John Buckler (fig. 25) as a gabled building with a jettied upper floor and stone plinth. Its cellars survive beneath the

house which now occupies its site. The kitchens were situated at right-angles to the new hall, a significant break with tradition, the buttery and pantry occupying the usual position of the kitchens at the hall's lower end (see plan 1).[73] By realigning the hall, creating a spacious court and building a new show-front, Edward created an impressive entrance to the palace.

Beyond the great hall he constructed new royal lodgings in the shape of a 'T', the stem of which was formed by the hall (fig. 26). Northwards were the Queen's lodgings in a brick range with bay windows which ended in a gallery. Edward's lodgings were on the southern arm of the 'T'. For Queen Elizabeth Edward IV built a new range in brick, which is of great interest as it contains two features for which no earlier precedents are known, unless the almost contemporary example of an articulated facade at Nottingham was a year or two earlier. The range contained a sequence of five-sided bay windows and chimney-breasts which articulated its facade, a conceit from which evolved the free-standing bayed facades so familiar in the early Tudor royal houses. At the end of this was a gallery, the only gallery from the period about which anything is known. Contrary to expectation, this gallery was never meant to connect different parts of the building, but was designed simply for the purpose of recreation; facing west, it had a spectacular view over the Thames valley towards London.

From this brief survey it can clearly be seen how Edward IV transformed earlier antiquated houses and castles by providing himself and his family with separate privy lodgings — a house within a house for himself and his family — an innovation earlier tried successfully at Sheen by the Lancastrians. Previously neither king nor queen had enjoyed any special private provision but had lived amongst the Court merely as its greatest members. Additionally, Edward's works clearly emulated Burgundian

23. Eltham, Kent. Block plan showing the arrangement of accommodation, c.1480.

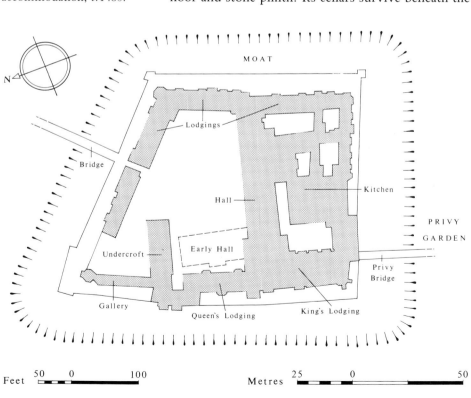

MOAT

N

Bridge

Lodgings

Hall

Kitchen

Undercroft

Early Hall

PRIVY GARDEN

Gallery

Queen's Lodging

King's Lodging

Privy Bridge

Feet   50   0   100

Metres   25   0   50

25. Drawing of the remains of Eltham by John C. Buckler for his *An Historical and Descriptive Account of the Royal Palace at Eltham*, 1828. To the right is the great hall, to the left three gables of the former service range, the space between was formerly occupied by the buttery and pantry.

architectural ideas; the gallery, the two-storey lodging, the donjon, the railed garden, all had direct Burgundian parallels. His choice of exterior design for the royal lodgings at Nottingham and Eltham furnished the next generation of English royal builders with a prototype which would be adapted and refined under the Tudors.[74]

Richard III: Duke and king

Both as royal duke and as king, Richard of York was a conspicuous builder. Not surprisingly his building works reveal interesting parallels with the works of his elder brother, Edward IV. As Duke of Gloucester, husband of a daughter of the Earl of Warwick ('the Kingmaker') and President of the Council in the North, Richard had a considerable stake in the north. He inherited his family's ancestral castle at Sandal in Yorkshire, and his marriage into the Nevilles was eventually, in 1471, to bring him two more Yorkshire castles — at Middleham and Sheriff Hutton — as well as Barnard Castle in County Durham. In the south he owned the magni-

26 and 27. Eltham, Kent, the great hall as built between *c.*1479 and *c.*1483 by Edward IV.

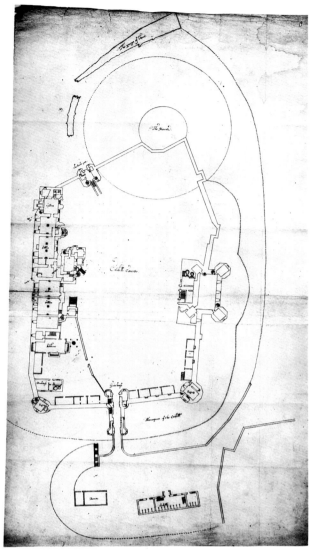

28 (above left). Middleham Castle, Yorkshire. Edward IV granted Middleham to his brother Richard, Duke of Gloucester, whose only son was born there in 1473. Richard was responsible for making several important improvements to the castle.

29 (left). Warwick Castle, Warwickshire. Aerial view showing the footings of the donjon to the left and the range containing the spy tower to the right.

30 (above right). Warwick Castle, Warwickshire. Plan by Robert Smythson, *c.*1605

ficent Sudeley Castle in Gloucestershire from 1469. At all five sites he undertook substantial improvements, and after his accession in 1583 he started a programme of rebuilding Warwick Castle as well as continuing and completing his brother's work at Nottingham and Westminster.

Of Richard III's building works those at Westminster doubtless continued — and perhaps completed — his elder brother's, as he had at Nottingham. Of his works at Barnard Castle and Middleham (fig. 28), little can be said, either through lack of evidence or because he did not take up residence there.[75] But at the other houses Richard was responsible for new tower lodgings. At Sandal this was for the convenience of his nephew John de la Pole, Earl of Lincoln, and the newly set up Council in the North.[76]

At Warwick, however, Richard began not only a tower lodging but also a range of privy lodgings. According to the antiquarian John Rous he undertook much building there,[77] and Leland indicates that one of the works was 'a mighty tower', 'began and halfe finishid'. From the remains of this tower, from excavation and from a plan by Thorpe, dating from c.1605 (fig. 30), it can be reconstructed accurately.[78] The donjon was evidently not a military installation. It contained at its lower levels a privy kitchen, and must have been intended to be similar at its (unbuilt) upper levels to Edward IV's donjon at Nottingham. Unlike the donjon at Nottingham, the accompanying lodging range was not attached to it but situated on the other side of the courtyard, built as an addition to the existing thirteenth- and fourteenth-century buildings.[79] The Spy Tower and adjacent lodgings (fig. 29) were lavishly fenestrated and highly articulated, very much in the same style as Nottingham (fig. 22). The situation of these lodgings at the upper end of the hall suggests that they provided extra accommodation for the King and Queen in the more public quarter of the castle. The private quarters seem to have been intended to be accommodated in an isolated donjon, like that at Sheen, but this donjon was never completed.

At Sudeley it seems likely that Richard was responsible for rebuilding much of the inner court-

yard, erecting a donjon, two great state rooms and a kitchen.[80] The donjon has been remodelled, but a massive state room measuring 26 feet by 49 feet survives, ruined, in something like its original form (fig. 31).[81] It is situated on the first floor with a fine parlour below. The west wall had an enormous bay window rising from the courtyard to battlement level. The east wall was almost continuous glass interrupted only by a fireplace artfully situated beneath a window; and there was a further window in the north gable-end. How this room related to the rest of the lodgings is unclear; access was certainly not via the single vice-stair in the north-east corner of the room — possibly there was once a grander processional stair elsewhere providing access.

Thus there can be no doubt that Richard shared his brother's predilection for luxurious well-lit buildings. Both brothers had a marked preference for designs consisting of a residential tower linked to spacious privy lodgings. This design for royal houses was to prove equally popular with their successor as king — and eventual brother-in-law — Henry VII.

31. Sudeley Castle, Gloucestershire. The ruins of the presence chamber on the east side of the inner court, probably constructed by Richard III when he was Duke of Gloucester.

RICHEMONT

Ant° van dei
Vmon Ca

Chapter 3

HENRY VII

IN 1485 HENRY VII, the new King of England, was twenty-eight. He had spent a hectic and hazardous life avoiding assassination or execution by successive Yorkist kings, first in confinement in Wales and later exiled in Brittany and France. Thus, Henry Tudor, unlike his son, lacked any sustained experience of English royal building. And, indeed, his perceptions, if any, must have largely been formed abroad.

Henry Tudor, Earl of Richmond, was born at Pembroke Castle on 28 January 1457, when his mother was only thirteen years old and his father had already been dead some two months. His early upbringing had been in the hands of his paternal uncle, Jasper, Earl of Pembroke, until Pembroke's support for Henry VI led to his flight abroad in 1461. Edward IV then granted the custody of the four-year-old boy to William, Lord Herbert. Herbert was an ardent Yorkist supporter and the owner of Raglan Castle (figs 33, 34) where the boy Richmond went to live, and Richmond's experience of this innovative and sumptuous building was to help to mould his own taste and expectation in houses.[1]

Following the murder of Henry VI in 1471, Richmond fled with his uncle Pembroke to Brittany, where, as a potential claimant to the English throne, following the death of Prince Henry at the Battle of Tewkesbury, he was to live for almost the next fourteen years.[2] Like Burgundy, Brittany was

one of the cluster of duchies bordering on France, technically a vassal state of the French Crown, but in reality quite independent. Although far less influential or powerful than Burgundy, Brittany nevertheless played a leading role in the power struggles between France, England and Burgundy, playing the main contestants off against each other in order to maintain Breton freedom and frustrate the expansionist ambitions of the French Crown. Architecturally Brittany was a backwater, but increasingly both the dukes and their courtiers were attempting to modernise the stock of medieval fortresses, making them more comfortable and

33 (below left) and 34. Raglan Castle, Monmouthshire. The gatehouse and donjon were under construction during the young Earl of Richmond's residence there in the early 1460s. The castle was slighted after 1646 by Parliamentary troops.

35 and 36 (following page). Château de Largöet, Elven, Morbihan. On the top floor of the donjon the future Henry VII spent two years. Figure 36 shows the layout of the castle and the extensive accommodation available in the great donjon.

32 (facing page). Richmond, Surrey. Detail of fig. 43.

37 (facing page top).
Nantes, Le Château, Loire-
Atlantique. Henry and his
uncle Jasper Tudor stayed
here for some months in
1473–4.

fashionable, although the fortress aspect could never be completely abandoned as the threat of French invasion always loomed large.[3]

On their arrival in Brittany, Richmond and Pembroke went to the Château of l'Hermine at Vannes which was the principal ducal residence. By October 1472 they had moved to Sarzeau on the

Gulf of Morbihan where they were lodged with the Admiral of Brittany, Jean de Quelenhec, at his Château of Sucinio. After staying with Quelenhec two years they briefly moved to Nantes, where in 1474 they separated. Henry was sent to the Château of Largöet, the house of the Marshal of Brittany, Jean de Rieux, where he stayed for at least two years (figs 35, 36). By 1480 Jasper and Henry were reunited and again staying at the Château of l'Hermine. There, in 1483, they were joined by a group of about four hundred English exiles from the so-called 'Buckingham rebellion'. Henry kept a small Court-in-exile at Vannes for about a year until 1484, when he eluded his Breton hosts and escaped to France.[4]

While in what amounted to virtual confinement by the Duke of Brittany, Richmond visited most of the leading ducal and seigneurial houses of Brittany; his longest stay was probably at the Château of Largöet.[5] Largöet differed little from contemporary English castles, in that there was an outer curtain wall encircling a polygonal court entered by a gatehouse. The main lodgings were built against the curtain wall on the north and south.[6] However, the most striking element of the château was the 144-foot-high donjon of six storeys, begun in the 1460s, and only nearing completion in 1475. Like the donjon at Raglan, it was isolated from the rest of the château by a moat and contained the private lodgings of the owner. On the sixth floor of this tower, the Tour d'Elven, Henry spent at least two years.

The residences of the dukes outshone Largöet but of these not much is known apart from the château at Nantes (fig. 37). At Nantes Duke Francis II had ordered a major reconstruction of the eastern and southern sides of the château in 1466. Four massive semi-circular towers were built against the curtain wall with severe machicolations relieved only by the ducal arms framed by ogee panels. But behind this defensive facade stood a luxurious four-storey grand *logis* where the duke held court. As elsewhere in western Europe, domesticity had become as important as defensibility, and within a fortified shell Francis II could live a life of luxury.[7]

Richmond's stay in France was brief, lasting barely seven months until July 1485. There was less leisure to contemplate his surroundings, but from the moment that he joined it at Langeais in October 1484 at least five months were spent travelling with the French Court. During that period the Court visited Paris, Evreux and Rouen, giving Richmond an opportunity to gain an insight into the workings of the Court and its buildings. Before setting out on his own expedition against Richard III in August 1485 Richmond probably stayed at, and certainly visited, the Louvre (fig. 38), the great thirteenth-

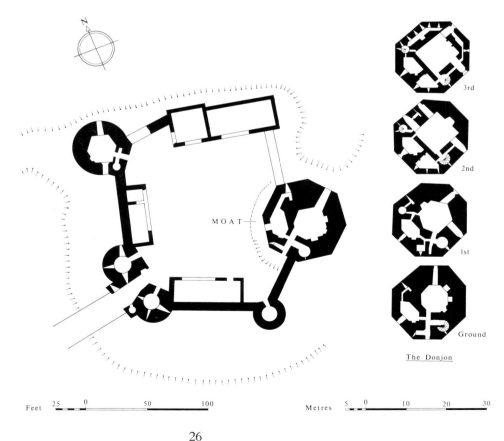

century fortress in Paris which the French King Charles V had turned into the principal royal palace of France. At the Louvre the royal lodgings were on the north side approached by a *grande vis*; this led up to the Queen's lodging on the first floor and the King's lodging above it on the second.[8]

Thus, by the time of his departure for the Bosworth expedition, Richmond had become conversant with two of the fundamental elements of French and Breton architectural practice: the donjon and the stacked lodging. Admittedly both features, the donjon with its private lodgings for the owner, and the stacked lodging with its sets of identical lodgings built on top of each other, were established fashions on both sides of the Channel. Nevertheless, Henry VII's familiarity with foreign examples from his exile abroad further sanctioned late fifteenth-century English architectual modes and resulted in their development and refinement during his reign.[9]

Henry VII's domestic building works

Political uncertainty and instability as much as almost total financial inexperience and a lack of resources meant that Henry VII was unable to contemplate much new royal building until the late 1490s.[10] Anyway, with the impressive stock of houses improved and extended by his two immediate predecessors, there was no pressing need to undertake a programme of new building. But with increasingly good fortune and more secure finances by about 1491 his thoughts turned towards building. From about 1495 Henry VII began a series of important ecclesiastical and secular projects which, although overshadowed by his son's achievements, contributed significantly to the already impressive stock of royal properties.

Unfortunately, neither the physical nor the documentary record for Henry VII's reign is as good as it is for his son's. At Richmond, his most famous residence, no more than the most fragmentary remains survive, but the evidence of early views (figs 32, 39–41, 43–4) has been corroborated by excavation. Excavation has also revealed more at Greenwich and Baynard's Castle, but not enough has emerged so far to enable full plans to be drawn. The site of Woodstock was completely levelled in the eighteenth century, so nothing remains to supplement its good run of building accounts. Despite this, a clear pattern emerges, and from the works at Richmond and Greenwich in particular, but also those at the Tower and Windsor, much can be learnt of the sort of buildings Henry VII wished to live in.

*　　*　　*

Richmond[11]

The site of what Henry VII named Richmond was that of the ancient royal manor of Sheen, which dated back to the early fourteenth century. Before 1497, when fire destroyed much of the medieval house and prompted Henry's rebuilding, there had been two successive royal houses on the site (see p. 9). The first was demolished by Richard II in 1395, the second, begun by Henry V in 1414 and completed by Henry VI was destroyed by fire in 1497. The *Great Chronicle of London* describes the fire, which at Christmas-time 1497 'began sodeynly . . . withyn the kyngis lodgyng . . . By vyolence whereof moch and grete parte of the old byldyng of that place was brent'.[12]

38. The Louvre, detail from *Les Très Riches Heures du duc de Berry*, c.1416. In general appearance the medieval fortress of the Louvre can be compared with the Lancastrian residence of Richmond (fig. 32). At the Louvre the donjon was in the inner courtyard and can be seen rising above the outer ranges of the castle.

39. Richmond, Surrey. A view from the south by an unknown seventeenth-century hand. See figure 41 for detail of facade.

Although the exact programme for the rebuilding is lost, it clearly fell into two stages. The first phase of work, which was the main one, started soon after the fire and continued to about 1501 when the *Great Chronicle* indicates that the King had 'fynysshid moch of his newe buyldyng at his manoyr of Shene and agayn ffurnysshid and repayrid that before was perysshid wyth ffyre'. This account is confirmed by the chamber accounts for 1501, which mention the glazing of the hall.[13] The second phase was started in 1502 when the house of the Friars Observant was founded to the south of the manor. This involved the planting of an orchard intersected by galleries between the friary and the house itself.[14]

The overall effect of this work can be seen in plan 11. The King kept the earlier Lancastrian donjon as the heart of his building. Made of stone, it cannot have been more than damaged by the fire of 1497 and so work on it was probably mainly a recon-struction of the interior (fig. 44). The outer two courts seem to have been totally rebuilt by the King (figs 40, 43). The whole ensemble is perhaps best described by a contemporary visitor who saw the house in late 1501 on the occasion of Prince Arthur's marriage to Catherine of Aragon:

there is a faire large and brode courte [outer court] . . . Uppon ich side of this goodly courte there are galeres with many wyndowes full lightsume and commodious; . . . Within this uttir space and large courte there is a lesser curtylage [inner court] peivyd with fyne frestone or marbill, in whoes myddill there is a conducte [fountain] . . . The pleasaunt halle is upon the right hand of this curtilage, xij or xviten greces of highte pavid with goodly tille, whoes rof is of tymber . . . In the wallys and siddys of this halle betwene the wyndowes bethe pictures of the noble kinges of this realme in their harnes and robis of goolde . . . In the lefte side of the curtilage, above over other like grees [steps], is the chapell, weell paved, glasid, and hanged with cloth of Arres . . . In the right side of the chapell is a goodly and a privy closet for the kyng . . . In the othir sid of the chapell othir by the like closettes for the Quenys Grace and the Princes, my Lady the Kynges Modir, with othir estates and gentilwomen. From the chapell and closettes extendid goodly passages and galaris — payved, glasid and poyntid, besett with bagges of gold, as rosis, portculles, and such othir — unto the Kinges chambers, the first, the secunde, the thirde enhaungyd all thre with riche and costely clothes of Arras . . . with their goodly bay windowes glasid sett owte . . . Dyvers and many moo goodly chambers there bethe for the Quenys Grace, the Prince and Princes [Arthur and Catherine of Aragon], my Lady th Kinges Mothir [Lady Margaret Beaufort], the Duke of Yorke

40. Richmond, Surrey. Two views from the north-east by A. van den Wyngaerde c.1558–62. Top, the finished studio drawing. From left to right the view shows the galleried gardens with the tennis play against the outer wall, the chapel, the central gateway to the inner court behind which lies the donjon, the great hall and the kitchens (the pointed roof of the great kitchen is faintly seen). Bottom, the site sketch. This shows in greater detail the outer court and the gable ends of the hall and chapel. In the centre can be seen the donjon.

[later Henry VIII] and Lady Margaret [Henry VII's daughter], and all the Kinges noble kynred and progeny, pleasaunt dauncyng chambers and secret closettes and most richely enhaunggid, dekkyd and beseen. Undre and beside the halle [to the north] is set and ordred the housis of office — the pantry, buttry, selary, kechon and squylery . . . ther coles and fuell in the yardes without nyghe unto the seid offices; . . . and in the leeft side of this goodly lodgyng . . . moost faire and pleasaunt gardeyns.[15]

Clearly Henry and his family lived in the donjon, as his predecessors had done, but evidence as to the internal organisation of the royal lodgings is scanty. The parliamentary surveyors of 1649 tell us that the main block was of three storeys, with twelve rooms a floor, and the description of 1501 mentions three main rooms along with other secret closets.[16] The three rooms were presumably the guard, presence and privy chambers, beyond which was the bed-chamber and 'secret closets'. The King's and Queen's lodgings occupied a block three storeys high — the lowest storey contained service rooms, the privy kitchen and wardrobe;[17] the two upper-most floors, the Queen's and King's rooms. Attached stood a great four-storeyed canted tower, in which there was a stair and a series of fine rooms.[18] This tower is clearly shown on a painting in the Fitzwilliam Museum, Cambridge (figs 39, 41), in the north-east corner of the lodgings. The stair provided the principal access to the second floor which by this token seems to have been designed for royal occupation. The 1501 account of the building states, '. . . in the leeft side of this goodly lodgyng under the Kinges wyndowes, Quenes, and othir estates, moost faire and pleasaunt gardens',[19] indicating that both the King's and Queen's lodgings faced south (see plan 11). The only way that this would have been possible, was if the King and the Queen were housed one above the other.

A close comparison can be made with the Louvre

29

as shown in an illumination from *Les Très Riches Heures du duc de Berry* (fig. 38). The Louvre too had facades articulated by a series of round and square towers. Not seen in the illumination is the *grande vis* inside the courtyard, a great vice-stair connecting the King's and Queen's lodgings which were stacked one above another. The canted tower at Richmond almost certainly performed the same purpose.[20]

Another feature of Richmond was the layout of the middle court with the hall and chapel facing each other and with the kitchens to one side of the hall (fig. 40). The plan at Raglan (fig. 42), where the great hall was centrally linked to the donjon by an outer chamber, would have been the easiest way to join the public and private sectors of the palace. At Richmond, however, there had to be a side for the Queen as well as one for the King. The plan allowed one suite to adjoin the great hall, in the traditional manner, and the other to adjoin the chapel via a *grande vis* or processional stair. A gallery linked hall and chapel to allow the King and Queen to leave the hall and arrive at their lodgings either via a bridge accross the moat or via a gallery, bridge and stair (see plan 11). The answer to who lodged on the second floor can be inferred from contemporary continental practice where the King lodged higher than the Queen.

The donjon and inner court formed only part of Henry VII's work at Richmond, for, after 1502 when the new lodgings could be occupied, the site of the old palace of Byfleet which lay to the south became free for redevelopment (fig. 43). Part of the land was used to found a friary, the remainder to plant an orchard. In 1501 this was described as

> . . . moost faire and pleasaunt gardeyns with ryall knottes aleyed and herbid — many marvelous beastes, as lyons, dragons, and such othir dyvers kynde, properly fachyoned and corved in the grownde, right well sondid and compassid in with lede — with many vynys, sedis, and straunge frute right goodly besett . . . In the lougher ende of this gardeyn beth pleasaunt galerys and housis of pleasure to disporte in.[21]

The three most notable features of the orchard were the enclosing galleries, the beasts and the recreational provisions. All these, as we have seen, were features of the Burgundian palace layout. Compare the plan of Richmond (see plan 11, and fig. 43) with that at Princenhof (fig. 16). The palace grounds at Princenhof were also intersected by galleries and gardens with tennis-courts and other recreational facilities.

The Richmond galleries were the first of their kind in England. Several influences played a part in their creation. The earlier function of a gallery,

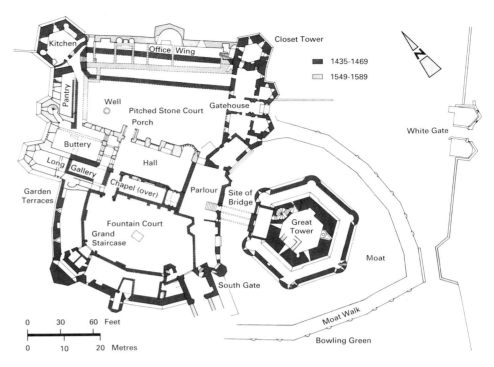

42. Raglan Castle, Monmouthshire. Plan; note the isolation of the donjon from the rest of the castle.

linking domestic accommodation with a chapel, remained important, as the Richmond galleries provided access to the friars' church.[22] Clearly modelled on the Burgundian galleries, with their open loggias at ground-floor level, the Richmond galleries departed from earlier English practice by taking a decidedly circuitous route about gardens. This design was followed in a gallery built at the Tower of London about the same time. The first-floor gallery enabled the gardens to be viewed from above which was by far the best way to view the knots and delicate layouts of the early Tudor garden. Thus the gallery some 200 feet long allowed viewing of the gardens from all angles as well as facilitating access to the friars' church and the recreational facilities in the north-east corner.

Henry VII's work at Richmond has not always been properly understood. The principal lodgings were built within the shell of the early fifteenth-century donjon of the manor of Sheen (fig. 44). This donjon displayed all the features of a French or English donjon of the period, stacked lodgings, a *grande vis* and a multi-bayed facade, moated and built in stone. Internally it was fitted out in the most up-to-date style just as were the other new additions: the great hall, chapel and outer court. The accommodation it provided for the King was almost identical to that which Edward IV and Richard III had at Nottingham; three great chambers with a series of small, private closets. This adherence to a design conceived over two decades earlier shows that Richmond was one of the last royal domestic buildings to be built on a medieval

41. Detail of fig. 39. On the right-hand corner of the donjon can be seen the great canted stair-tower; the structure to its right is the chapel. In the foreground are the galleries which ran round the gardens.

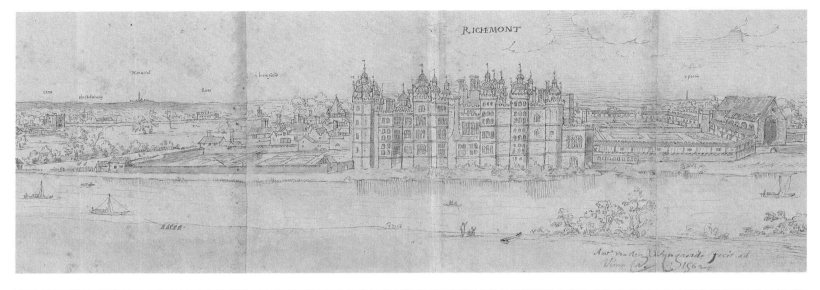

44 (above). Richmond, Surrey. A view from the south-west by an unknown seventeenth-century hand (detail). On the left is the great kitchen; just visible behind the great stone donjon is the great hall; to the right are the galleried gardens. Note the brick chimneys.

pattern. Indeed the fundamental conservatism of its design explains why within thirty years Richmond had been relegated to a third-division royal residence rarely visited by the Court.

The Tower of London and Windsor Castle

A similar conservatism of design marked Henry VII's work at the Tower and Windsor. From very early on the Tower had provided domestic as well as fortified accommodation for the kings of England. Edward II had moved the king's lodgings

eastwards from their position by the Wakefield Tower, to the Lanthorn Tower, near to which Edward III built the Cradle Tower in 1348–55 as a private watergate (fig. 8).[23] To this fourteenth-century residence Henry VII added a new gallery, a tower and a garden.

Work began on the new tower in 1501, and on the gallery in 1506.[24] These two works can be readily identified. The gallery was built on top of Henry III's curtain wall from the Lanthorn Tower across a gateway to the Salt Tower (fig. 46). Later accounts describe it as timber-framed and plastered externally.[25] Haiward and Gascoyne's 1597 bird's-eye view (fig. 45) clearly shows it with its south-

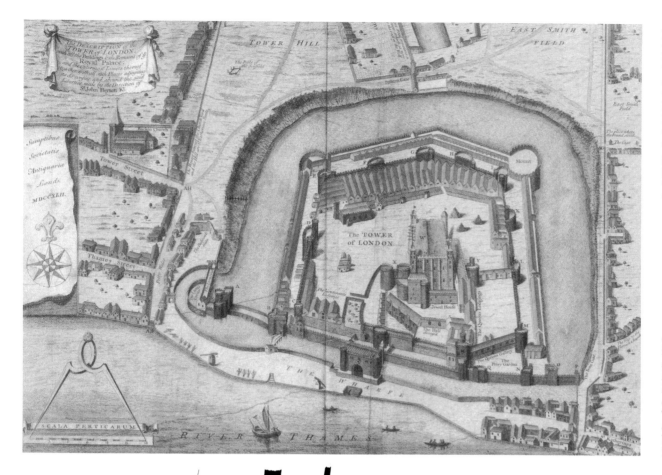

43 (facing page top). Richmond, Surrey. A view from the south-west by A. van den Wyngaerde c.1558–62 (detail). From left to right the view shows the kitchens (the great kitchen has a pointed roof), the donjon with the watergate on its right corner, the gardens surrounded by low galleries, and the ruined church of the Friars Observant.

45. The Tower of London in 1597 from G. Haiward and J. Gascoyne, *A True and Exact Draught of the Tower Liberties*. Note that the queen's gallery is the early Tudor king's gallery; the queen's lodgings are those built for Anne Boleyn in 1532.

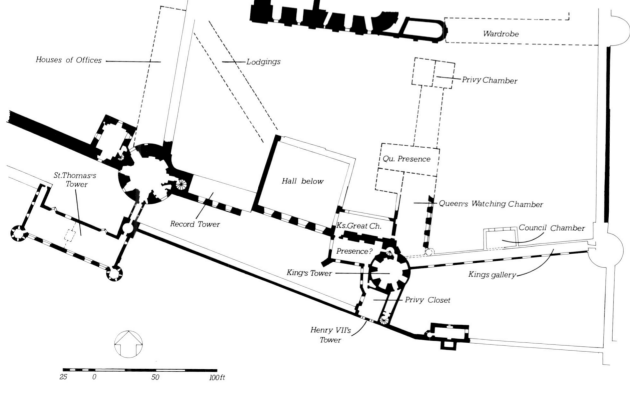

46. The Tower of London. Plan of the royal lodgings c.1540 based on documentary and archaeological evidence.

47. Windsor Castle,
Berkshire. Henry VII's new
tower; engraved in 1835.

48 (facing page top).
Greenwich from the river by
an anonymous early
seventeenth-century artist.
The blank wall on the far
right is the privy kitchen, the
donjon to its left has a
projection built by Henry
VIII as a watergate. The
royal lodgings to its left
terminate with the chapel.
Behind this can be seen the
gable of the great hall. On
the far left, in front of Henry
VIII's tiltyard towers, are
service buildings.

facing windows as well as a room formed over the medieval gateway.

The new tower can be identified from a survey of 1532 as the square building to the south and west of the Lanthorn Tower, known in the sixteenth century as the King's Tower (fig. 46). The King's Tower is described as the tower where 'the king is accustomed to lie', and a stair linked this to a garden below; the new tower built next to it contained a library overlooking the waterside and a closet. The new gallery led off the King's Tower and bisected the garden below.[26]

Henry VII's works at Windsor bear a close relation to those at the Tower. In 1485 the royal lodgings there, like those at the Tower, were essentially those of Edward III's time (fig. 14), to which the King added, again as at the Tower, a new tower and gallery. Work began at Windsor in March 1500 and accounts mention the new tower and gallery, both of which survive, albeit substantially altered (fig. 47), but early plans show the original lay-out. The function of the tower is almost certainly identical with the function of the one at the Tower of London; it bears the same relationship to the King's bedroom and presumably contained the King's private study and library.

The parallels between the works at Windsor and the Tower are striking. At both castles the lodgings built by Edward III provided satisfactory accom-

modation for the monarch's public life, but neither provided adequate private accommodation. Thus works were put under way to construct private closets, libraries and a gallery for the King's own use. However, these were only minor modifications in comparison to the major works at Richmond and Greenwich.

Greenwich[27]

If Richmond was not the innovative royal house setting a standard for future royal projects, Greenwich emphatically was. The contrast between Richmond and the house which Henry VII built at Greenwich from 1500–01 onwards could hardly be greater. For Greenwich was a courtyard house built of brick, without a moat. It had a river frontage articulated with bay windows similar in style to the range built by the Yorkist kings at Nottingham. Its site was not a new one, but of the manor of Pleasaunce begun by Humphrey, Duke of Gloucester, and extended by both Henry VI and Edward IV, nothing survived. The earlier buildings were completely demolished by Henry VII.

The chronology of Henry VII's works can be deduced from references in his chamber accounts. Work started at the house in a small way in February 1498, but that more significant building was planned is clear from the fact that by 1502 the King's mason, Robert Vertue, was busy executing work from a new 'platt' (or plan) of the Queen's design. Payments totalling more than £1,330 over the next six years include references to the garden walls, the new orchard, the gallery, the privy kitchen and the tower. The major work was complete by the end of 1504 as the payments recorded that year indicate that the house was being painted.[28]

The internal arrangement of Henry VII's house at Greenwich can be deduced only by working back from his son's reign. The riverside range contained the King's lodgings and a block lying parallel to and south of it contained the Queen's. At the west end they were joined by a gallery which also connected with the church of the Friars Observant next door. At the east end the King's and Queen's lodgings were joined by a narrow range which had the hall and chapel side by side to its east.

The King's lodgings along the waterfront were ranged between the chapel in the east and the privy kitchen in the west. East of the privy kitchen was a short length of two-storey building which ended in a five-storey tower (fig. 48, plans 3, 4). This donjon was the chief feature of the range which probably contained the King's bedroom at first-floor level. Turrets contained stairs which led up to further rooms at second and third-floor levels, doubtless

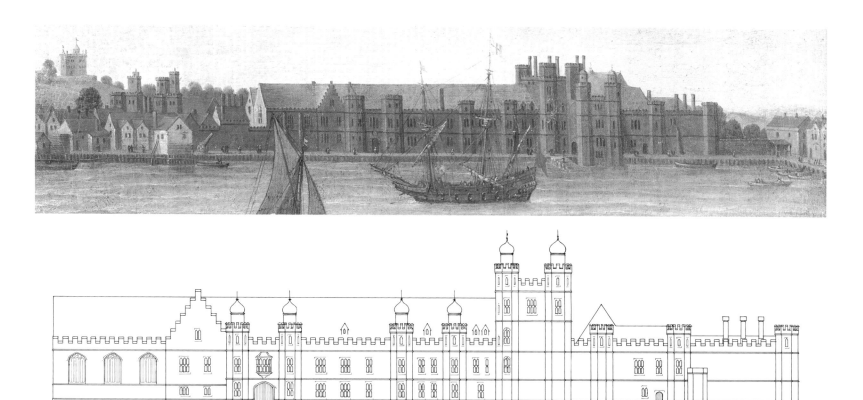

the King's most private chambers — possibly including his library and study. This arrangement bears a great affinity to the Burgundian ducal palaces discussed above. An elevation of Henry VII's river range (fig. 49) can be closely compared with Princenhof (fig. 16) and Ghent (fig. 17). It also had distinct parallels with contemporary English courtier houses. Of these, Tattershall Castle, Lincolnshire (fig. 50), had a more massive donjon than that of Greenwich, the latter having a more ambitious grouping of turrets, but the relation of the donjon to the rest of the building and its function are the same at both houses. The Bishop of Lincoln's house at Buckden, Cambridgeshire, is another at which the donjon lay behind the inner chamber. On a smaller scale, but more elaborate, is Faulkbourne Hall, Essex, and an earlier but taller donjon is found at Caister Castle, Norfolk.[29]

It was at Greenwich where the donjon, a well-established element in English and French medieval architecture, fused with the urban influence of Burgundy. A great tower, keep or donjon was a fundamental element of castle design from Norman times and it remained an important part of the plan of the English castle right through to the fifteenth century — at Raglan for example (figs 33, 42).[30] Raglan, and Richmond for that matter, were very different houses from Buckden, Tattershall and Greenwich. In the earlier houses the donjon was

separated from the rest of the castle and retained its defensive function. In the Burgundian model, developed in an urban context, the donjon was part of an urban tower-house and structurally one with the rest of the house.[31]

In terms of the development of the English royal house, the parallel with Nottingham is important. The royal lodgings at Nottingham were in almost all respects the same as those at Greenwich; there was a long, narrow, lavishly fenestrated block of public rooms, at the end of which was situated the King's donjon (fig. 22). The Nottingham donjon was, however, a separate structure from the lodging range and the lodgings were built up against the curtain wall of the castle. At Greenwich, the lodgings stood alone with the donjon assimilated into the range. Indeed, it was a courtyard house, with no vestige of fortification. Greenwich was not even moated; it had all the aspects of the urban houses of the dukes of Burgundy, notwithstanding its rural setting.

The attribution of architectural designs in the early sixteenth century is a vexed matter. Even so, Greenwich seems to have been the work of Robert Vertue, who was in charge of the building operations there from 1499 until 1504, and who in 1502 was paid for 'the new platt of Greenwich which was devised by the Queen'.[32] The reference to Queen Elizabeth's part in the design is most interesting; it testifies not only to her own fondness for Green-

49 (above). Greenwich, Kent. The elevation from the river as it would have appeared in 1509. The blank area is due to lack of information caused by the construction of Henry VIII's watergate. (Drawing David Honour)

50. Tattershall Castle, Lincolnshire. The surviving brick donjon (begun 1434–5) is very similar to that which Henry VII was later to build at Greenwich.

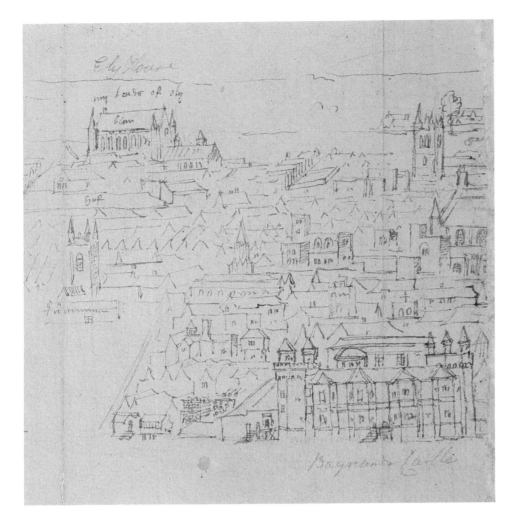

51. Baynard's Castle, London, detail from a view by A. van den Wyngaerde c.1550.

Developments in the royal household

Under the Yorkist kings and Henry VII important changes had begun to take place in the form of the royal houses. These changes were brought about by two linked developments in the royal household: an increasing desire for privacy on the part of the king and an enhanced perception of the king's status.[35] But between them these factors help to explain the development of the royal residences which have been examined so far.

The king was the centre of all power, patronage and advancement. Therefore proximity to the king was the key to success. The efficacy of royal government relied on the direct involvement of the monarch, or of the ministers upon whom he had delegated responsibility. Conscientious attendance to paperwork and discussion and approval could have absorbed all a monarch's hours, leaving no time for his courtiers. This would have created a serious dilemma, for a Court without the presence of the king was not a Court at all. The concept of privacy, as we understand it, did not exist in the Middle Ages. The king ate, drank, slept, dressed, bathed and relieved himself in public, in other words, in the company of his Court. What privacy meant, as the idea emerged and took hold, was the exclusion of those not needing to be present. What it did not mean was that the king sought to be alone. Inevitably there was a significant break among the personnel at Court between those whom the king regarded as essential attendants and those who regarded themselves as essential.[36]

Early medieval kings built themselves private retreats, often quite remote from the principal houses, where they could invite whom they wished. As the fifteenth century dawned a more determined architectural division between Court and king developed within the houses themselves — a more difficult division to manage with a populous Court. At Sheen the royal lodgings were separated from those of the courtiers, the hall and the chapel, and put in a donjon beyond a moat. This solution, in various different guises, continued throughout the fifteenth century, when kings built themselves donjons, or private towers, next to their lodgings in order to provide a more private area in which to live. The examples of Sheen, Nottingham and Greenwich — to take but a few — bear this out. Under Henry VII this architectural division, was at last given organisational expression when, in about 1495, he set up a new household department called the Privy Chamber. Staffed by a chief, the Groom of the Stool, and a small number of grooms and pages, the Privy Chamber was a way of ensuring that only those whom the King regarded as essential body-servants had access to his privy chamber and

wich, but it also suggests that the readily discernible Burgundian influences reflect her personal taste rather than the King's. Greenwich was not unique however, for what is known of Baynard's Castle in London accords very much with the King's exactly contemporaneous work at Greenwich. Baynard's Castle was as unlike a castle as Greenwich. Indeed, John Stow reports that 'Henry the seauenth about the yeare 1501. the 16. of his raigne, repayred or rather new builded this house, not imbattoled, or so strongly fortified Castle like, but farre more beautifull and commodious for the entertainment of any Prince or great Estate'.[33] Little other documentary evidence survives for Henry VII's work at Baynard's Castle, but the completed building is depicted in Wyngaerde's view of London (fig. 51) and its plan has been recovered by excavation (fig. 53).[34] As at Nottingham and Greenwich there was complex fenestration stretched between two massive octagonal towers crowned by French-looking turrets. The octagonal towers may have been either the donjon or privy towers of the house.

36

those 'secret places' — the donjons of the early Tudor royal houses.

By 1495, however, not only were there new criteria of privacy, but the very nature of the King's position had changed. In the words of one historian, 'The early Lancastrian King presided, as a first among equals, over the "joint-stock enterprise" of war with France; the Yorkists and still more the Tudors elevated themselves unapproachably above even the greatest of their Lords'.[37] The elevation of the status of the King aggravated the need to remove himself from the Court which, like the sea, surged around him. By the late fifteenth century the King could no longer live solely in public rooms as Edward III had done, but required private quarters into which he could retreat for his own purposes. This requirement was to have important architectural consequences. But Henry VII's efforts to solve his increasing need for privacy were slight beside the devices employed by his son and heir.

Chapter 4

HENRY VIII

HENRY VIII WAS CERTAINLY THE MOST prolific, talented and innovative builder to sit on the English throne. William Harrison, in his *Description of England* (c.1577), said:

> Those [palaces] that were builded before the time of Henrie the eight, reteine to these daies the shew and image of the ancient workemanship vsed in this land: but such as he erected (after his owne deuise (for he was nothing inferiour in this trade to Adrian the emperour and Justinian the lawgiuer)) doo represent another maner of paterne, which, as they are supposed to excell all the rest that he found standing in this realme, so they are and shall be a perpetuall president vnto those that doo come after, to follow in their workes and buildings of importance. Certes masonarie did neuer better flourish in England than in his time.

He was, according to Harrison, 'the onelie Phenix of his time for fine and curious masonrie'.[1]

Like many kings before him, Henry VIII was an active participant in the design of his buildings.[2] All the evidence points to his intimate involvement right down to small matters of design. In Elizabeth's reign he was regarded as 'a perfect Builder as well of fortresses as of pleasuant palaces',[3] and contemporary references bear out his design abilities. He was equally at home designing jewellery as he was with armour ('suche as no armorer before that tyme had seen') and siege engines, not to mention a new sort of tiltyard. He was deeply interested in the design of ships, guns and fortifications, and his participation in the design of coastal fortifications is well documented and certainly involved him in the drawing of platts (or plans).[4]

The inventory of his possessions taken after his death indicates that he kept plans and drawing instruments in his studies,[5] and would often request or dispatch platts during the progress of building works. When the King was at Woking in 1542 he sent one John Harwood 'for the feychyng of the kyngs platts of Mortlake at London and bryngyng them to Okyng by ye kyngs commandement'.[6] The Milanese ambassador, reporting the purchase of the lands for Whitehall Palace in 1531 stated 'his Majesty is now staying at Greenwich, and often comes to Westminster, having designed [*designato*] new lodgings there'. A year later du Bellay described how, when arriving at a royal house on progress, the King showed him around telling him what he had done, and what he was going to do.[7] While works were under way the King was a regular visitor; as new lodgings were being built at the Tower, Henry inspected the site first with the French ambassador and later with Anne Boleyn. Evidence of the King's visits and of his instructions to workmen appears in the building accounts. At Hampton Court we read of 'joyners wourking by the Kings devyese... uppon all suche prevey conceyts wiche ware devysed ther by his grace'. Another reference at Dartford in 1542 mentions 'takyng down of certyn partyssyon in the kyngs lodgyngs... at the kyngs comandemment'.[8]

This direct and persistent royal involvement meant continual changes of plan and what was probably infuriating interference for the workmen and administrators. Sometimes the King would inspect structures as they were being built, as at Greenwich in 1527, where workmen were paid 'for to hang the clothes in the kyngs syght and takyng them down again'. More often however, rooms were set up and decorated only to be altered on the King's first visit.[9] Not only did the King's constant indecision and fluctuating ideas have an important influence on royal building in this period, so did his intolerance and impatience. Once designs were settled, the King wanted to see immediate results. Often workmen laboured all night by candle-light in order to complete work in time for a royal visit.[10] Canvas tents were constructed over the works at Whitehall in 1532 to allow the workmen to work in the rain. Barrels of beer, loaves of bread and rounds of cheese were distributed to workmen bailing out waterlogged foundations at midnight.[11] Huge sums were spent on paying workmen overtime on such occasions. The resultant buildings, finished only hours before the King arrived, often had to have paint and plaster dried by charcoal braziers.[12] The great speed at which the builders had to work

52. Nonsuch, Surrey. Detail of fig. 84, showing the outer gatehouse, with the inner gatehouse on slightly higher ground behind. On the left is the gateway to the kitchen range. The whole length of the west side of the building is shown with later projections in the foreground, but the original tall chimney stacks and garderobe projections in the background.

meant that the standard of the workmanship was often very low. Sometimes payments occur to surgeons and for compensation paid for killed workmen, indicating that there were collapses during construction.[13]

Yet Henry VIII's ability, or perhaps inclination, to design or to influence the design of his many residences, did not really develop until after 1530. Before that date, the young King was dominated, architecturally, by Cardinal Wolsey. The five major works of the first part of his reign, Bridewell, Beaulieu, Greenwich, Eltham and the temporary palace at the Field of Cloth of Gold, were all managed by Wolsey. Until 1515 Henry was also engaged in completing works begun by his father at Hanworth, Woking, Wanstead, Ditton and Leeds Castle.[14]

Bridewell[15]

In 1500 there had been a cluster of ecclesiastical inns and other Church properties adjoining Fleet Street, including inns belonging to the Bishop of Salisbury

and St Davids and to the Abbot of Faversham. Another of these properties situated on the west bank of the River Fleet, had belonged to the Knights Hospitallers, who in 1507 had leased it to Henry VII's minister, Richard Empson, when it was described as a garden (fig. 53). Empson also leased the adjacent rectory house of St Bride's. On his execution in 1510 the whole property was forfeited to the Crown which almost immediately granted it to Thomas Wolsey.[16]

Wolsey, already an established figure at Court, had been employed by Henry VII on diplomatic missions and under Henry VIII had risen to Almoner, Dean of Lincoln and Prebendary of Hereford; he was soon named a councillor. Presumably the grant of St Bride's must have pleased Wolsey, as, although he did not use the rectory himself, he began to build a new house on the neighbouring land.[17] This new house became surplus to requirements in 1515, when he took a lease on Hampton Court and as Archbishop of York had the use of York Place. His interest in the lease of St Bride's was transferred to the King. After the destruction of Westminster Palace by fire three years

53. The Thames waterfront from Bridewell to Baynard's Castle in c.1540. Conjectural plan from archaeological and documentary evidence.

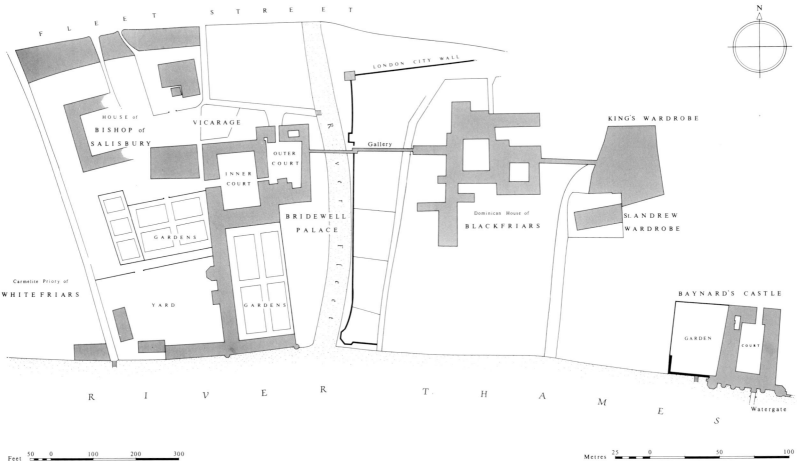

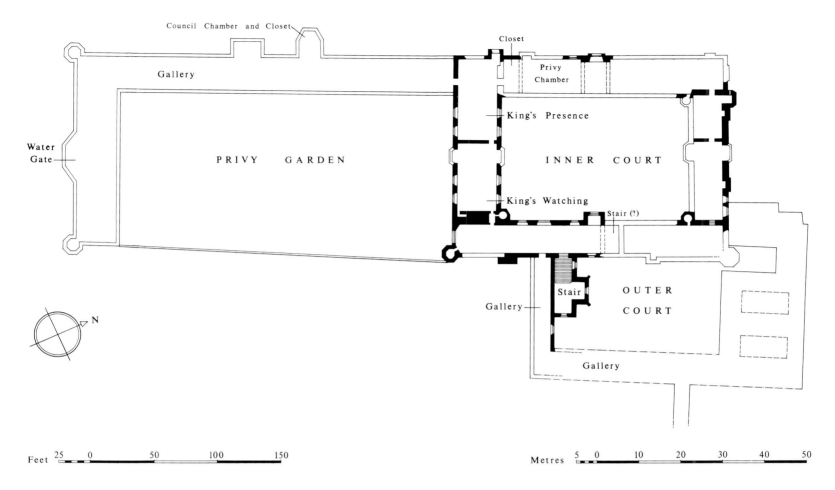

Council Chamber and Closet

Gallery

Water Gate

PRIVY GARDEN

Closet

Privy Chamber

King's Presence

INNER COURT

King's Watching

Stair (?)

N

Stair

Gallery

OUTER COURT

Gallery

Feet   25   0   50   100   150

Metres   5   0   10   20   30   40   50

earlier, Henry had lacked a house suitably near both Westminster and the capital and this requirement may help to explain why he chose Bridewell for his first new residence. The proximity of the site to the London Blackfriars may have also been a pull, as the monastery was often used for state business on account of its splendid facilities. Yet the most persuasive reason seems to have been Wolsey's building operation already under way. Wolsey's York Place accounts of 1515 show the links between his workmen there and at Bridewell.[18] It is also significant that Thomas Larke, one of Wolsey's closest friends and chief building administrators, was chosen to run the King's own building operation at Bridewell. Wolsey's involvement with Bridewell did not cease with the transfer of his lease, as he continued in his ministerial capacity to oversee Larke's work, negotiating for extra land and signing bills.[19]

Bridewell as finally completed in 1523 (figs 53–8) comprised two brick-built courtyards and a long gallery terminating in a watergate on the Thames. The royal lodgings were ranged round a three-storey inner courtyard, the King's lodgings on the south, the Queen's on the north. They were approached by a grand processional staircase (figs 58a and b) in the outer courtyard. On the north side of the outer court were a gatehouse and the kitchen block; off the east side of the inner court was a gallery about 240 feet long, running over the River Fleet and connecting Bridewell and Blackfriars (fig. 53).[20] The King's lodgings on the south comprised a guard chamber and presence chamber, both double height and situated on the second floor. Their tall windows can be seen on the 'Agas' view of 1561–8 (fig. 55). The long gallery adjoined the presence chamber and contained two rooms, one of which was a closet and the other the council chamber.[21] All these were approached by the stair, which rose up through two stories. The Queen's lodgings were also double height but were on the first floor on the other side of the courtyard; they seem to have been approached by some kind of stair between the two sets of lodgings.

Bridewell Palace is one of a group of buildings built between 1500 and 1530 in which the lodgings were arranged vertically rather than horizontally. The builders of these were all men of Henry VII's generation and not of his son's. Wolsey's Hampton Court is the most important of these. Here, between

54. Bridewell, London. Reconstructed plan based on archaeological evidence and a detailed eighteenth-century survey.

55. Bridewell, London. Detail from the woodcut *Civitas Londinium* made between 1561 and 1566 and wrongly attributed to Agas. Immediately to the right of the house is the River Fleet, the bridge between Bridewell and Blackfriars can be seen crossing it.

56 (far right). Bridewell, London. As excavated in 1978. The photograph shows the east range of the principal courtyard with the courtyard itself to the right, on the left and just discernible are the foundations of the great stair.

1515 and 1526, Wolsey built a three-storey lodging range with a processional stair and attached donjon (fig. 59). The King's lodging was situated above the Queen's and had vastly taller windows than the first-floor Queen's lodging below.[22] Another house where this arrangement existed was Thornbury Castle, Gloucestershire, where the Duchess of Buckingham was housed beneath the Duke, who

57. Bridewell, London. An engraving made for John Strype's edition of Stow's *Survey of London*, 1720. The great courtyard in the background was rebuilt after the Great Fire of 1666. In the foreground can be seen the Tudor three-storey royal lodgings approached by the great stair (left) and serviced by the kitchen courts (right).

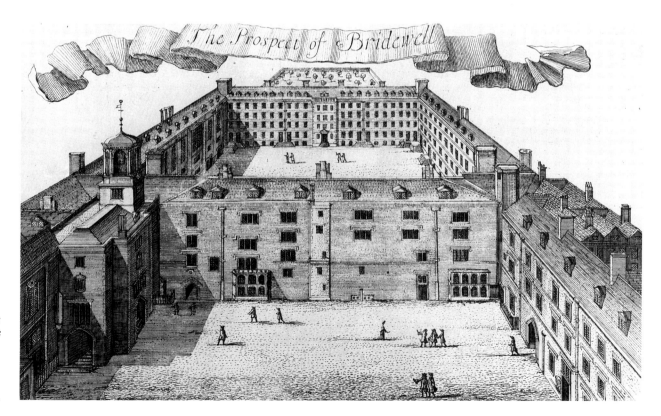

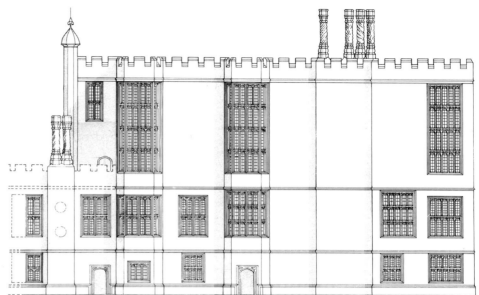

occupied first-floor rooms with hugely tall windows (fig. 60).[23] Another courtier of the same generation was the Duke of Norfolk who, at his house at Kenninghall, adopted a similar arrangement, the ducal rooms being situated on the second floor, above those of the Duchess.[24] Sir Thomas Lovell's house at Enfield also seems to have belonged to this group.[25] The immediate model in England for the arrangement followed in these buildings was Richmond, which men of Wolsey's generation regarded as the leading royal residence. Thus it comes as no surprise to discover that Henry VIII, in building his first major house was guided by Wolsey to follow current architectural practice.

Wolsey's aesthetic mentorship can be discerned more certainly in the form of the long gallery. The Bridewell gallery projected from the house for about 200 feet and ended in a watergate (figs 53–5).[26] Similar galleries, unintegrated limbs leading nowhere, but with a predominantly recreational function, were erected at all of Wolsey's houses; at

58a and b (far left top and bottom). Bridewell, London. Views by Frederick Nash (1803) of the outer court and of the great stair, showing a doorway very similar to the slightly later doorways to the great hall at Hampton Court.

59 (above). Hampton Court, Surrey. Reconstructed elevation of the west side of Thomas Wolsey's inner court. The top floor may have originally been intended for Henry VIII, but it was certainly occupied by both Catherine of Aragon and Anne Boleyn. (Drawing Daphne Ford)

60. Thornbury Castle, Gloucestershire. The south front showing the Duke and Duchess of Buckingham's stacked lodgings.

Esher,[27] The More, Hertfordshire (see plans 9, 10), York Place (see plan 15) and Hampton Court (see plan 5). The first gallery of this type that can be identified is that built by Edward IV at Eltham, which, like Wolsey's, projected from the body of the house (fig. 23, and see plan 1). The form of long gallery popularised by Wolsey was not to have a lasting influence on English royal architecture, but Bridewell did introduce two new and important features into the vocabulary of the royal builders. Bridewell, as completed for the King, did not have a conventional great hall and as such was the first of a series of hall-less royal houses built after 1530. The second innovation was the processional staircase, which gave access to the main rooms, another feature that was to dominate the King's later buildings.

Beaulieu[28]

Little now remains of Henry VIII's house at Beaulieu, Essex, yet three seventeenth-century surveys, and early views (figs 61–63) reveal something of its original form.[29] The house became Crown property in the early fifteenth century and Edward IV stayed there in 1480, but Henry VII granted it to Thomas Boteler, Earl of Ormond, who obtained a licence to crenellate in November 1491.[30] Ormond entertained Henry VIII there in 1510 and again in 1515, two months before his death, when the house passed to his daughter and her husband, Sir Thomas Boleyn. Henry VIII purchased the house from Boleyn for £1,000 and in January 1516 work on converting it had already begun.[31]

A similar pattern of works' administration as that which had occurred at Bridewell was set up at Beaulieu. Building there was entrusted to a member of Wolsey's works' organisation, William Bolton, the Prior of St Bartholomew's, Smithfield. Bolton was Wolsey's most favoured building adviser, having charge of the works at Hampton Court.[32] In 1518 Wolsey recommended him to the King for the vacant bishopric of St Asaph, giving as one of the main reasons his great skill in building. The King replied, via Richard Pace, that

> where as your Grace doith make mention in your lettres off diverse presidentes off the Kingis predecessors declarynge howe theye dydde promote unto lyke dignities the Maistres off there werks; hys Grace sayeth that itt is not lykely that they so dydde for thys qualitie oonly that they couith goodde skele in byldyngs, but for sum other great qualities (as profounde learninge) annexidde unto the same.[33]

Bolton had been Henry VII's choice to supervise the completion of his chapel at Westminster,[34] where his involvement in the design of Lady Margaret Beaufort's tomb is well documented.[35] Thus his appointment at Beaulieu brought a wealth

61. Beaulieu, Essex, as engraved for the Society of Antiquaries by George Vertue, 1786. The south, or entrance front, of the house; the central coat of arms survives (see fig. 136).

A View of the Front of the Palace of Beaulieu, commonly calld NEW HALL, in Essex, built by K. Henry VIII.

of experience to the royal works there, but it probably also ensured a degree of conservatism in the building's eventual form. Given Bolton's and Wolsey's links one would expect to find similar features at New Hall as were found at Bridewell, but these are limited to the making of a new gallery in 1517, the form of which is quite unclear.[36] Possibly Bolton's hand can be seen in the form of the chimneys on the entrance facade which echo Henry VII's Chapel, Westminster (figs 61–62). The hall and chapel lay opposite each other across a courtyard in the manner of Richmond (see plan 11) which may reflect Ormond's work as much as Bolton's. Further hints of Bolton's influence at Beaulieu may be identified in the distinctively tall first-floor windows of the gatehouse, perhaps stylistically related to those at Bridewell and the other houses from that period. There is some evidence to suggest that the royal lodgings were also stacked, as the great stair shown on the plan (fig. 63) partially survives, rising up through three storeys.

Eltham[37]

Between 1519 and 1522 an extensive scheme of modernization was carried out at Eltham by Walter Forster, the Comptroller of the King's Works. The evidence for Wolsey's participation in the ordering of these is drawn mainly from a list of 'Buyldings

62. Beaulieu, Essex, as drawn upon Cosimo III de' Medici's orders in 1669. This rather impressionistic view shows the south front of the house.

63. Beaulieu, Essex. An eighteenth-century plan of the house. A: the great hall; B: the great kitchen; C: the great stair; D: tennis play; E: north range built by the Earl of Sussex, c.1575.

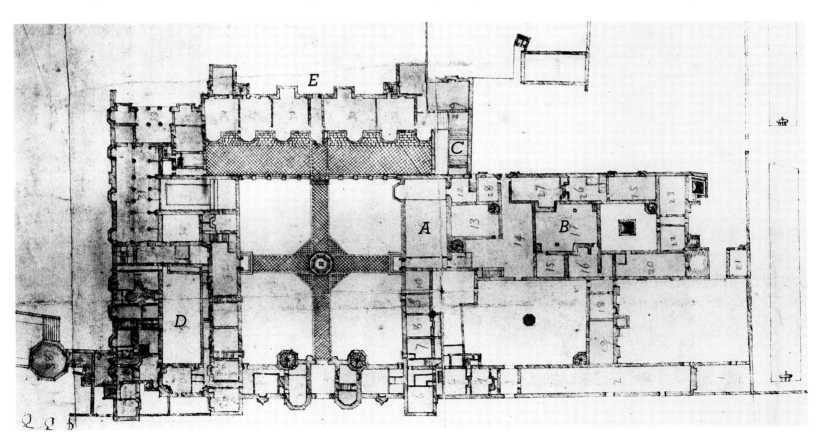

64. Eltham, Kent, seen from the west in an engraving by Peter Stent, c.1650.

65. The temporary palace at the Field of Cloth of Gold. Conjectural first-floor plan based on documentary sources.

66 (facing page). The temporary palace at the Field of Cloth of Gold, by an anonymous artist, c.1545. Although the perspective is forshortened, this view of the palace is remarkably true to the documents; the grand staircase can just be glimpsed through the archway.

and reparacions' to be undertaken at the house by Forster.[38] There are seventeen items, including a long run of alterations to be undertaken in Wolsey's lodgings, which end with a proviso enabling these works to be done 'with such other necessaries ther to bee don as he will devise',[39] thus allowing Wolsey to add more changes at will. This entry is unique in the list as the only reference to an individual person and it illustrates Wolsey's direct involvement in the works. So much so that the Venetian ambassador refered to Eltham in 1521 as 'a house belonging to the Cardinal'.[40]

The list of works provides important information on how Henry VIII altered Edward IV's house for his own use. The three principal categories of work were the remodelling of the royal lodgings, the rebuilding of the chapel and improving the layout of the gardens and outhouses. The works of Edward IV had changed the orientation of the house, as his great hall lay on an east–west axis and the royal lodgings lay to the west of it (see plan 1). The royal lodgings were therefore the buildings along the west front between the privy bridge to the south and the chapel to the north.

The rooms in the south-west corner of the house are listed in a repair account of 1533–4: 'King's bed chamber, King's raying chamber, King's breakfast chamber, King's chamber of estate, the halpace before the said chamber door, King's great chamber'.[41] In addition to these rooms, there were three closets, 'one standing above another at the south west corner of our newe lodgings'.[42] The Queen's lodgings were on the west front and were extensively altered in 1519–22 to give the Queen more and larger rooms.[43] The most important alterations were undertaken at the north end of her lodg-

ings (see plan 1). They involved enlarging the presence and withdrawing chambers at the expense of her old bedchamber and several small rooms between it and 'the king's old bedchamber'.[44] The reference to the King's old bedchamber, would indicate that the King had a bedroom on the Queen's side, probably at the north end of her lodgings.[45]

The Field of Cloth of Gold

After Bridewell and Beaulieu the largest building project undertaken in the first part of Henry VIII's reign was the temporary palace at the Field of Cloth of Gold (figs 65, 66). This was entirely managed by Wolsey. In a list of Wolsey's alleged 'prodigal and wasteful expenses' drawn up in 1529, he was accused of 'prodigal dispending of the king's treasure, as well in sumptious building made [at the Field of Cloth of Gold] only to that use, and not to endure'.[46] The construction of the temporary palace was the subject of a lengthy correspondence between Sir Nicholas Vaux and Wolsey, and one of Vaux's letters dated April 1520 clearly asks for architectural advice. Wolsey personally held the platt for the building. His close personal involvement is further borne out by his order transferring workmen from his own building projects in England to Guisnes in an attempt to finish the palace in time.[47]

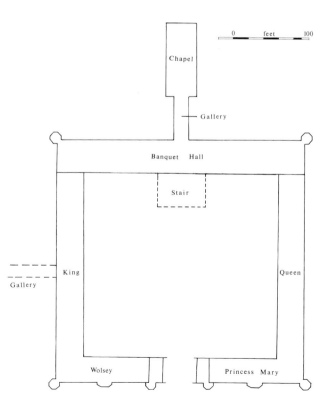

There are several lengthy contemporary accounts of the temporary palace and there have been various attempts at reconstructing its layout;[48] figure 65 is an attempt to put the evidence in plan form. The palace underwent a change of design halfway through construction. Of the several eye-witness accounts the most accurate seems to be that of the Mantuan ambassador, Soardino.[49] Soardino described a building one hundred paces long with the ranges seventeen paces wide. He went on: 'on the left side of the principal entry there are two halls and a chamber for Cardinal Wolsey . . . on the right hand two other halls and a chamber for Princess Mary',[50] which fully accords with other evidence. And 'in the middle of the long entrance hall a small building was added containing two oratories looking down on the very large church below'. This indicates that the back range of the court was used as an entrance hall, which doubled as a banqueting hall.[51] On either side of this entrance hall were the royal lodgings. 'Fronting' the gatehouse was a 'handsome covered stair in the Italian fashion'. This staircase seems to have had two flights of straight stairs and protruded into the courtyard. Beneath the main lodgings were positioned the service rooms.[52]

A few general points can be made regarding the layout of the lodgings as designed and later altered by Wolsey. The closest parallel is with Bridewell (fig. 54) where, as already mentioned, there was a quadrangular house with the King's and Queen's lodgings facing each other across a courtyard and separated by a stair. The processional stair at Guisnes was certainly a spectacular element of the composition and may be compared with that at Bridewell and the conjectured one at Beaulieu. The chapel approached by a gallery had affinities not only with the gallery at Bridewell, but with the Cardinal's own galleries (see pp. 43–4). In functional terms there were links with Bridewell too, for the King and Queen actually stayed in Guisnes Castle which was joined to the palace by a gallery, the identical expedient used at Bridewell and Blackfriars (fig. 53).

Greenwich

Building at Greenwich, unlike that at the other main buildings of the 1520s, was directed towards a fully operational completed building. The alterations to the house in the first years of Henry VIII's reign were therefore to improve the house his father had left him. The question upon whose initiative these works were undertaken is harder to answer here than elsewhere. The influence of Wolsey is difficult to detect.[53]

Henry VIII's early works at Greenwich reflect his youthful passion for recreation: tilting, hunting and revelling. To provide facilities for feats of arms and hunting, Henry built new stables; one for his stud and another for his coursers.[54] The first substantial buildings other than these were the 'two towres and a howse whiche shallbe sett over the grene before the tillt behynde the manor'.[55] These were the tiltyard towers prominent in all views of the palace (figs 67, 242–4). The towers were linked by a gallery which is described as the tiltyard gallery, in which at ground-floor level was kept tilting equipment.[56] This arrangement of towers and gallery provided the maximum space for viewing the tournaments below (see pp. 181–2) and could also be used for other sorts of entertainment. The most famous of these occasions was in 1527, when Henry entertained the French ambassadors at Greenwich. For this occasion the buildings on the west of the tiltyard were extended. Edward Hall in his *Chronicle* describes the arrangement: 'The king agaynst that night had caused a banket house to bee made on the one syde of the tylt yarde at Grenewyche wyche of an hundreth foote of length and xxx fote bredth . . . the wyndowes, were al clere stories with curious monneles [mullions] strangely wrought . . . at the one syde was a haute place for herawldes and minstrelles . . . at the nether ende were twoo broode arches . . . From thens they passed by a long galerie richely hanged into a chamber faire and large, the dores whereof was made of masonrie'.[57] This arrangement (see plan 2) is shown by Wyngaerde in some detail (fig. 67).

This complex of recreational buildings grouped on the west of the tiltyard may have been connected to the inner courtyard of the palace by a gallery, possibly the 'new gallery' for which 'Mortymer embroyderer' made 'tappets' in 1512 and for which arras was bought in 1516.[58] It seems to have joined the inner court at the Queen's great chamber. This group of works was concerned with the creation of buildings which would allow the Court to entertain itself in the winter months and evenings and provide stabling for the summer hunting.

One other addition mentioned in the chamber accounts is a library which was in the 'two lodgings there over the gallery into the Thames'.[59] This was the structure that can be seen in all the river views of the palace protruding from the face of the main building towards the Thames (fig. 48).[60]

Henry VIII: The middle years

Before 1529 Henry VIII had shown no real propensity for building. He had completed one house, almost certainly started by Wolsey, and then converted

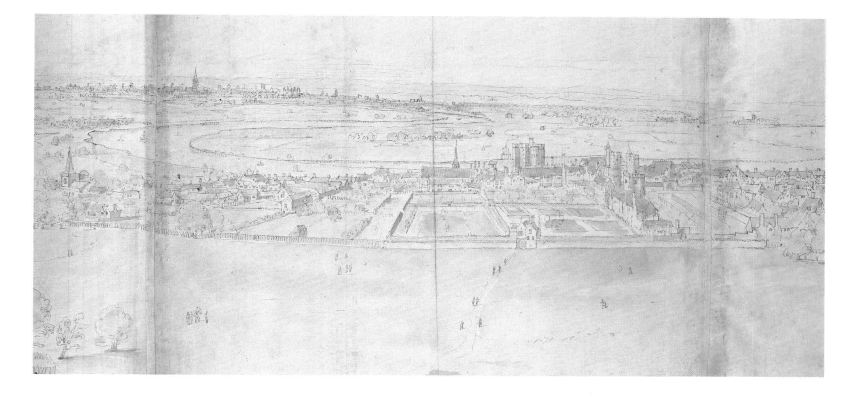

it into a dormitory for foreign ambassadors; he had bought another, Beaulieu, and extended that; he had altered one of the oldest royal properties, Eltham, and he had built the appropriately styled temporary palace for the Field of Cloth of Gold. In addition he brought to completion some of his father's lesser building works. Almost all these projects had been managed by Cardinal Wolsey, and there is no record of the King taking any great interest in them. The only house where Wolsey's hand was not apparent was at Greenwich where the young, athletic and sporting King evidently took a keen interest. Elsewhere he was content to leave it to others. In terms of what was actually built, Henry hatched no surprises; the donjon and the stacked lodging were already universal elements by 1500. Henry VIII was to save up all his surprises for after 1530 when he suddenly took up building as a passion.

1529 was a watershed in the development of the English royal house. It marks an intellectual turning point for Henry who suddenly became more interested in architecture. The reason for this change is not easy to explain; however, Anne Boleyn may have proved the catalyst; her interest in the arts seem to have stimulated the King's intellectual curiosity whereas Catherine of Aragon's had left him unresponsive. This change coincided with the downfall of Wolsey which left an architectural vacuum, with a sudden burgeoning in the number of royal properties and a diversification in their uses and with alterations in structure at Court. This remarkable combination of circumstances was to have important consequences for the form of the King's houses.

Figure 69 shows the numbers of royal domestic properties during Henry VIII's reign: for the twenty years up to 1529 the King made intermittent purchases; after 1529 there was a sudden increase in numbers followed by a steady rise until about 1536, when a second influx took place. The floodgates opened on two main counts: first, the dissolution of the monasteries necessitated the acquisition of properties which hitherto he had used as a guest during royal progresses; second, the acquisition of a large number of houses from courtiers who were either out of favour or whose properties attracted royal rapacity (fig. 68). The largest group of acquisitions consisted of properties obtained by purchase, exchange or forfeit. Early in the reign the King bought four houses, Beaulieu (1516), Ampthill (1524), Hunsdon (1525) and Petworth (1535). Four further houses fell to the Crown by forfeit: Thornbury and Penshurst from the Duke of Buckingham (1521); West Horsley from the Marquess of Exeter (1538); and Beddington from Sir Nicholas Carew (1539). But by far the commonest way of obtaining a property was by exchange. Ten houses were acquired in this manner, most of them in the late 1530s: Grafton (1526), Hackney (1535), Chelsea, Suffolk Place and Durham House (1536), Oatlands (1537),

67. Greenwich, Kent, from the south by A. van den Wyngaerde c.1558. From left to right the view shows the Friars' church, the queen's lodgings facing the privy garden, the donjon, the tiltyard towers and gallery, behind which is the great hall, and the tiltyard with the kitchens behind.

49

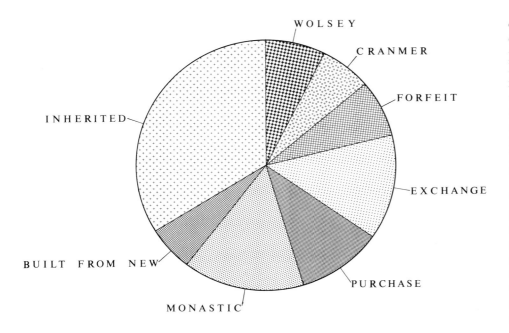

even employing many of the same workmen. However, no one was to succeed Wolsey as the King's principal architectural adviser and administrator; the King himself stepped into this breach. This new interest was fanned, if not fuelled, by Anne Boleyn, who became his enthusiastic partner in building campaigns. At Hampton Court an entirely new range of lodgings was built for Anne and she and Henry took an active role in its layout and design. The pair even spent their honeymoon there on what must have been a building site.[62]

Anne's involvement at York Place is even clearer. Two days after Wolsey pleaded guilty to the charges against him on 22 October 1529, Henry came down-river from Greenwich to view York Place accompanied only by Anne Boleyn, her mother and a gentleman of his chamber.[63] The nature of the visit seems to suggest that from the start the acquisition of the house was their joint triumph. Henry spent that Christmas at Greenwich designing the additions to the new house, and these additions

68. Pie-chart showing the sources of Henry VIII's domestic residences.

Hatfield (1538) Hull and Halnaker (1539) and Westenhanger (1540). Three other houses — Charing, Otford and Knole — were acquired from Archbishop Cranmer in 1537.[61]

At these new properties there were almost no building works, except at Beaulieu, Hull and Oatlands. The same does not hold true for the ex-monastic properties which fell into royal hands in 1538–9 (Ashridge, Canterbury, Dartford, Dunstable, Guildford, Newcastle, Reading, Rochester, St Albans, Syon and York) where the work of conversion was sometimes considerable. All these pieces of work sink into insignificance when compared to the extraordinary sequence of alterations to the King's principal houses, Greenwich, Whitehall and Hampton Court, the last two of which were gained from Cardinal Wolsey after 1530. Finally, at the end of the reign work started on new projects at Oatlands and Nonsuch, both in the recently created honour of Hampton Court.

The downfall of Wolsey in 1529 had several important implications for Henry VIII's building projects. If in the first instance the King lost his architectural mentor, he was the immediate gainer of five highly desirable properties: Hampton Court, The More, York Place, Tyttenhanger and Esher. Of these, Hampton Court and York Place were major acquisitions where building was already in progress. York Place, renamed Whitehall, was to become the King's most frequently visited residence while Hampton Court came a close third after the perennially favoured Greenwich. The works in progress at both York Place and Hampton Court were taken over in their entirety by the King, Henry

69. Graph showing the rate at which Henry VIII acquired domestic residences during his reign.

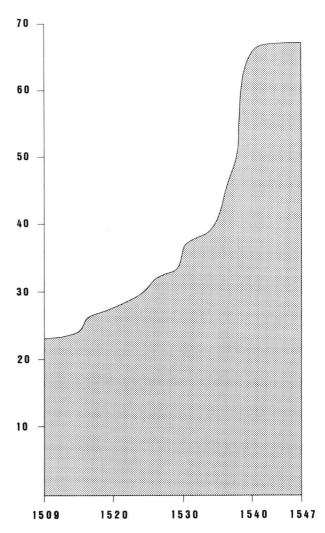

50

were, according to the Spanish ambassador, expressly 'to please the lady who prefers that place for the King's residence to any other'.[64] This preference was due to the fact that York Place, unlike Hampton Court, did not have provision for the Queen's household, and so Anne could stay there alone with Henry. Significantly the push to finish the first phase of works at Whitehall was in order to prepare it for Anne's coronation;[65] the wedding feasts and jousts were held there in May 1533.[66]

The completion of the first phase of work at Whitehall was not, however, the only major work undertaken in preparation for the new Queen's coronation. In accordance with custom, the medieval English monarch spent the eve of his or her coronation at the Tower of London.[67] As Queen Consort Anne Boleyn observed this custom, but the existing royal lodgings were not deemed satisfactory for her use so new lodgings were built (figs 43 and 44). This expensive and extensive building work was undertaken for two reasons. First, the celebrations preceding the coronation involved the Tower being used for two days of almost uninterrupted ceremonies, including the creation, by the King, of no less than eighteen Knights of the Bath, and the dubbing of a further forty-six knights.[68] Second, and more importantly, a fundamental change had taken place in the King's expectations. Henry was not content to live in the lodgings as left by his

father; they were now rearranged and extended to meet his own requirements and those of his wife. This was identical to what was happening at York Place and Hampton Court at the same period. All three places were being altered to make them fit for the use of the Tudor Court of the 1530s, an institution rapidly becoming very different from the one which Henry VIII had found at his accession twenty years earlier.

Whitehall and Hampton Court[69]

Henry's conversion and extension of Wolsey's houses at Hampton Court and Whitehall are inextricably bound up with Wolsey's use of them before 1530. Wolsey held York Place, later Whitehall, by virtue of his incumbency of the Archbishopric of York. It was his town house where he stayed during the legal term which required his presence at the law courts at Westminster. Hampton Court, on the other hand, was his personal property, and it, together with The More, was used in equal measure for entertaining ambassadors and the King.[70] Lack of accommodation at York Place meant that before 1529 the King, as far as is known, only spent one night there,[71] whereas he was lavishly entertained on several occasions at both Hampton Court and The More. Thus, the extensions made after 1530 by the King at

70. Hampton Court, Surrey. Plans showing the principal stages in the development of the building 1529–40. From left to right: 1529–32, A: new kitchens; B: great hall, C: tennis play; D: bayne tower; E: gallery. 1533–6, A: new queen's lodgings; B: refurbishment of king's lodgings; C: construction of the great house of ease; D: king's privy stair; E: communication gallery; F: remodelling of chapel. 1537–40, A: new king's lodgings; B: new queen's gallery; C: new lodgings for prince Edward; D: remodelling of queen's lodgings; E: Queen Catherine Parr's new lodgings.

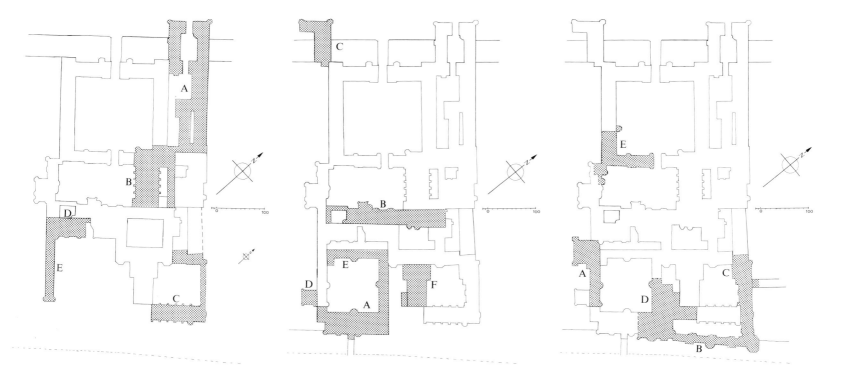

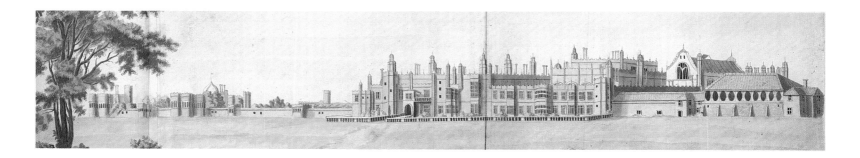

71. Hampton Court, Surrey. A view from the east commissioned by Samuel Pepys sometime in the 1660s. From left to right the view shows the wall of the privy garden, the queen's lodgings facing the park and ending in the long gallery, and another gallery running north to the seventeenth-century tennis-court on the left; behind the gallery towers the great hall.

the two houses differed in character. At York Place, Wolsey's lodgings were turned into the Queen's side, while a new King's side was built from scratch. At Hampton Court there was accommodation for both King and Queen, but this, in various ways, was deemed unsatisfactory and further accommodation was provided.

Henry's buildings at Hampton Court are particularly important, for over 6,000 pages of building accounts survive for the alterations made between 1529 and 1539. Furthermore, apart from St James's, it is the Tudor royal house of which most remains, and about a hundred years of detailed archaeology has revealed almost as much about what is lost as about what survives. In a decade of almost continuous building and after spending about £62,000, Henry had created at Hampton Court what was universally regarded as his most magnificent house after Whitehall. Three major phases can be detected in the development of the plan of the house (fig. 70). The first, which has already been discussed, can be labelled the phase of the stacked lodging. Between 1529 and 1533 the King was content to live in Wolsey's stacked lodging, and indeed to augment it by the addition of a small donjon containing further private rooms for himself. In 1533 there was a drastic turnaround. He decided to abandon the

stacked lodging and, with his new wife Anne, planned a new set of Queen's lodgings on the same level as his own. The two sets were to be linked to the galleries, and the King's lodging was connected to a new privy garden by a grand staircase, which the King and Queen could share. In the final phase, undertaken between 1537 and 1539 (after Jane Seymour's replacement of Anne as Queen) an entirely different principle of design was adopted. What had, for a period of five years been a division between the King's and Queen's lodgings, now became a division between the private lodgings and the more public ones. The old chambers of estate in the west of the palace were now only used for the most formal occasions. Henry ceased to sleep in the bedchamber of 1529, and used the new privy lodgings on both the ground and first floors of the south front for everyday life, the Queen having lodgings mirroring his own on the other side of the courtyard. The King's most private rooms, the 'secret lodgings', were situated on the east front near the Queen's lodgings (figs 71–3, and plans 7 and 8).

Two principal features can be identified in this simplified three-phase development. The first is the abandonment of the stacked lodging after 1533, and the second is the increased desire of the King in the late 1530s to have private quarters. The first phase

of the Henrician conversion of Hampton Court deliberately altered the original arrangement of stacked lodgings. The Queen's lodgings, which had been occupied by Catherine of Aragon and were situated above the King's, were abandoned, and a new courtyard was built to the east of the King's range and to the north of the long gallery.[72] The general abandonment of the stacked lodging at Hampton Court and elsewhere resulted in the houses built under Wolsey's supervision in the early part of the reign becoming outmoded within a few years of their construction. In fact, soon after Wolsey's fall, these houses were completely abandoned. Bridewell, the King's seventh most favoured house before 1530, visited on at least thirteen occasions, was never used again after 1530; Beaulieu likewise fails to feature in the post-1530 itinerary and Richmond, Henry's second most visited house before 1530, fell to his twelfth afterwards. The extraordinary reversal in the fortunes of these early houses can be largely explained by the fact that the stacked lodgings they provided were no longer considered satisfactory by the King.

A similar architectural pattern can be detected in France. The French king, Francis I, built stacked lodgings in the first part of his reign. At Blois, where Francis built a new wing between 1515 and 1524, the King lodged above the Queen, with a *grande vis* connecting their lodgings (fig. 74). This was also the case at Chambord (begun 1519), where the main lodgings were stacked in an enormous donjon. The arrangement was also in operation at Saint-Germain-en-Laye and the Château of Madrid. The King's later works at Fontainebleau during the 1530s do not share this vertical accent; here the lodgings were all on one level, as at Hampton Court after 1530. This change mirrors that in England.[73] For the English the abandonment of the stacked plan was a return to the time-honoured plan of the King's and Queen's lodgings side by side all on one level,[74] but, in France the design of Fontainebleau was innovative, as the French Crown's buildings had been stacked since the early Middle Ages.

Yet, although the stacked lodging lost its previous popularity in England after 1530, its essential adjunct, the processional stair, lived on. In all Henry VIII's later buildings a processional stair was a major element in the plan. It is perhaps because the French also favoured this element that it retained its popularity in England. The staircase in the Cour de l'Ovale at Fontainebleau, begun in 1531, adheres to the same tradition as the staircases by Henry VIII built at the monastic conversions and the later houses (see p. 58). Thus, in terms of plan, Wolsey's

73. Hampton Court, Surrey. A view from the north-east by an anonymous early seventeenth-century artist. From left to right the view shows the queen's lodgings terminating in her gallery; behind can be seen the three-storeyed king's lodgings of the 1520s and the great hall; behind the great orchard are the tiltyard towers.

72. Hampton Court, Surrey. A view from the south by an anonymous early seventeenth-century artist. From left to right the view shows the great gatehouse, the north range of base court (under the stain), the great hall, the king's lodgings with a bowling alley running in the foreground, walls and towers of the privy garden, and the watergate.

74. Blois, Loire-et-Cher. The inner courtyard and the great staircase. Although no English royal house of the 1520s had a stair of equal architectural pretension all had great stairs giving access to the royal lodgings on the upper floors.

Act of Parliament, when it was officially designated as the King's palace, his principal seat and therefore the seat of government.[76] 'Demed reputed called and named the Kynges Paleys at Westminster for ever', Whitehall assumed 'official' functions which the other houses did not have, and these functions not only influenced its development but also its final plan.

Whitehall was divided into two halves by a road, King Street, which linked Westminster and Charing Cross and eventually led to the City of London via The Strand (see plans 13 and 15). The western side of the palace, called the park side, housed the largest recreation centre of any Tudor house. There were four tennis-plays (courts), two bowling-alleys, a cockpit, a pheasant-yard and a gallery for viewing tournaments in a tiltyard (fig. 253). All these were built between 1531 and 1534. They were linked to the main part of the palace by a gatehouse over King Street which has traditionally been called the 'Holbein Gate' — here it will be referred to as the northern gatehouse (fig. 75).

The palace proper was entered from the court gate to the north of the northern gatehouse on the

75 (right) and 76 (facing page top). Whitehall Palace. The northern gatehouse (or 'Holbein Gate') and the King Street Gate, as engraved by George Vertue for the Society of Antiquaries in 1725. The northern gatehouse, built in the early 1530s was richly decorated with flint chequerwork, stone badges and arms and antique terracotta roundels. The King Street Gate, built right at the end of the reign, has circular rather than octagonal turrets, doorcases flanked by pillars and pilasters and busts on the facade. These antique elements sit happily with arms, heraldic beasts and signs of the zodiac.

architectural legacy was the state staircase, a factor which has been consistently underplayed in the discussion of the houses of the early Tudors.[75]

The other concern which influenced the plan of Hampton Court in the 1530s was the King's desire to have a more extensive privy lodging. This is discussed at length below (see p. 135), here it should be noted that the evolution of the King's Privy Chamber as the organisation which looked after his private needs had a major impact on the privy parts of the house. Conversely, as the King occupied the privy lodgings more and more, the outer rooms declined in importance. The full social significance of the tendency to live only in the privy lodgings was not, at first, fully understood, and at Hampton Court a new — and almost immediately obsolete — great hall was built. The same mistake was not repeated elsewhere, where great halls were either not incorporated in the design or otherwise demolished. The two principal themes of the abandonment of the stacked lodging and the expansion of the privy lodgings can be seen equally clearly in the development of Whitehall after 1530.

Henry VIII's Whitehall, like Wolsey's was charged with an administrative as well as a domestic role. This duality received official recognition in 1536 by

THE GATE AT WHITE HALL
Said to be Designed by Hans Holbein.

Sumptibus Societatis Antiquariæ Lond. 1725.

KING STREET GATE WESTMINSTER
demolish'd Anno 1723.

G. Vertue d. et Sculp.

Sumptibus Societatis Antiquariæ Lond: 1725.

east side of King Street. It led to a courtyard, on one side of which was the great hall. From the great hall were reached the King's and Queen's outer rooms and the chapel. Beyond these, all at first-floor level, lay the most extensive privy lodgings at any of the King's houses. They were set in a gallery-like structure running east–west from the river to the northern gatehouse and, like those at Hampton Court, looked out over extensive gardens (the site of which is now occupied by the Ministry of Defence building). The Queen had lodgings in and around another gallery which ran north–south. To build this sprawling palace, which was eventually to cover over twenty-three acres (Hampton Court covered only six) Henry had to evict and compensate the inhabitants of King Street whose lands he required. At a cost of £1,120 and an incalculable degree of human distress, a whole suburb of Westminster was wiped out to make way for the new palace (see plan 15).[77]

If Hampton Court and Whitehall shared the same general development in the 1530s, so did the most visited house of the reign, Greenwich.[78] At Greenwich a large private territory for the King and Queen was developed on the west side of the inner court of the palace (see plan 4). Although present knowledge of the Greenwich privy lodging is limited, it is clear that Henry VII's donjon ceased to house the King's bedchamber and privy lodging,

77. Whitehall Palace. A general view of the excavations of 1939. The area shown is to the west of the privy kitchen.

space being made instead for a whole maze of inner rooms for the King and Queen all on one level.

The building history of Henry's three main houses highlights the changes which took place in the planning of the inner lodgings of the King and Queens of England in the 1530s and 1540s. The development of the outer rooms in royal houses can be best illustrated by examining the King's works converting the monastic houses acquired at the Dissolution.

The monastic conversions

The suppression of the monasteries, which was triggered by two Acts of Parliament in 1536 and 1539, posed a severe problem for the King in terms of accommodation. Both he and his father had relied heavily on the great monastic houses during progresses. Feeding the wayfarer is one of the seven Acts of Charity, and the performance of this fundamental Christian obligation, was one of the few duties being properly performed by the monasteries in the early sixteenth century. The Dissolution presented Henry VIII with a dilemma and he had little choice but to appropriate those monastic houses where he had regularly stayed as a guest. St Augustine's, Canterbury, was visited nine times before he acquired it and four times after, Dunstable six times before and four after and Rochester four times before and a similar number afterwards.[79]

Other monastic houses regularly visited by late medieval kings, but not finally acquired, were also considered by Henry VIII. Abingdon Abbey had

been a particular favourite as a staging post on the way to Woodstock, Langley and Ewelme. Henry VII had stayed there at least seven times and his son at least six.[80] When Sir Richard Rich surveyed the abbey in 1538 he wrote to Cromwell saying that he had 'viewed and seen the plight of the said late monastery', and that he wished Cromwell to 'signify to the King's Majesty that the most part of the houses of office therof be much in ruin and decay except the church . . . and as concerning the abbot's lodging, I think it is not like for an habitation of the King's Majesty, unless his Highness will expend great treasure'.[81] Not only were the buildings unsuitable for the King but 'as I and others can judge no ground thereabout on the northeast side to be conveniently imparked for the King's disport and pleasure' unless, that is, the King imparked certain land which would be 'much to the hindrance of tillage near the town'.[82]

The chance to acquire Abingdon as a royal house was only rejected because Reading Abbey was so close. Reading had, together with Abingdon, been a monastic staging-post to the west. Henry VII had stayed there and Henry VIII frequently stayed when he came from Windsor, it being only a day's ride away. In September 1538, Richard Pollard was reassuring Cromwell that he had left 'the whole house and church' at Reading 'undefaced',[83] pending a decision as to its use. Not long afterwards, Dr London explained to Cromwell how the people of Reading would like to have the church as a town hall.[84] Their petition was not granted and the abbey buildings were defaced except for the 'mansion' which was 'wholly reserved for the king's use'.[85] Another house which had been heavily used by the early Tudors before its suppression was Chertsey Abbey, visited at least six times by Henry VII and a similar number of times by Henry VIII.[86] Because the King had recently acquired the nearby house of Oatlands, Chertsey was not needed and was demolished. A book of accounts details the way the abbey was dismantled and used for materials for the King's new house.[87]

Frequency of royal visits before the Dissolution was not the only criterion, and some houses rarely visited by Henry VIII in the past could be considered for royal appropriation. The report of the Commissioners to Cromwell on the fabulously rich abbey at Glastonbury was glowing: 'We assure your lordship it is the goodliest house of that sort that ever we have seen . . . we doubt not that your lordship would judge it a house meet for the king's majesty'.[88] But, as the King rarely visited Somerset, their advice was not taken. By far the most important group of monastic houses which the King acquired were those situated on roads linking London with Kent and Sussex. Rochester, Guildford and

78. St Augustine's, Canterbury, Kent. Photograph taken from the south showing Henry VIII's work building up the north wall of the nave of the abbey church as the south wall of his royal lodgings.

56

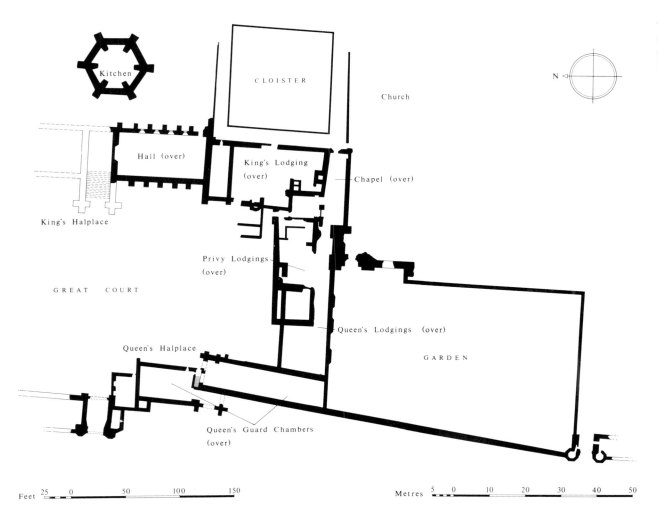

79. St Augustine's Canterbury, Kent. Plan showing layout of the royal lodgings c.1547.

Kitchen

CLOISTER

Church

N

Hall (over)

King's Lodging (over)

Chapel (over)

King's Halplace

Privy Lodgings (over)

GREAT COURT

Queen's Lodgings (over)

Queen's Halplace

GARDEN

Queen's Guard Chambers (over)

Feet 25 0 50 100 150

Metres 5 0 10 20 30 40 50

Canterbury, and to a lesser extent Dartford, were all key staging-posts on the route south both for the King and his ministers.[89] Wolsey, for instance, on his way to France in 1521, had stopped first at Dartford, then at Rochester, next at Faversham and finally at Canterbury.[90] A year later, the Emperor Charles V followed the same route in reverse from Dover to Greenwich, as did Anne of Cleves in 1539.[91]

On account of the frequency of royal visits to these particular religious houses, lodgings were often reserved there for the monarch, and improvements funded by the Crown. For instance, alterations were carried out at Canterbury in 1520 at the King's expense for the visit of the Charles V.[92] At Rochester lodgings had been set aside for royal visits since the fourteenth century.[93] At Guildford Friary the King had built a lodging range with a garden in the 1530s and had held a state reception there.[94] Therefore Henry VIII was not only extremely well acquainted with these houses but they were essential buildings to retain in his own hands. With the construction of the new coastal fortifications in the

1540s, and the increasing regularity of the King's visits to the south coast, they took on an even greater importance.[95] In addition to these monastic staging-houses, Henry VIII acquired a handful of monasteries for other purposes. He acquired Ashridge as a nursery house for Edward and Elizabeth, and Newcastle-upon-Tyne and York for the use of the Council in the North.[96] The acquisition of the Bridgetine convent at Syon was the prelude to its use as a munitions factory.[97]

The fullest information on the King's monastic conversions comes from the three sets of particular books surviving for the conversions at Canterbury, Dartford and Rochester. Between them they give full details of what exactly was involved in the process of converting a former monastic house for royal use. Elsewhere less is known: at Ashridge it seems that few alterations had to be made; similarly, at St Albans, the abbot's house provided adequate accommodation for the King; the nature of the work at Dunstable, Guildford, Reading, Syon and York is unclear, even though a plan of Dunstable survives (fig. 157);[98] at Newcastle the alterations

80. Dartford Priory, Kent. The remains of the gatehouse drawn by ?John Carter, 1783.

Dartford. The usual term for the principal kitchens in the royal house had been the 'hall kitchen'. At Dartford, a house without a great hall, the more pat phrase 'great kitchen' was preferred in the majority of accounts; other references call it the 'new kyttchen for the kyngs howsolde' and 'the lordes kechyng'.[101] This distinction, between the 'hall kitchen' and 'the lord's or household kitchen' is significant. It indicates the final abandonment of the idea that the King should preside over the feeding of his Court in the great hall (see pp. 113–14).

The last building works of Henry VIII

In the last seven years of his reign Henry VIII began three new major building projects, each very different from the others. Of these the grandest and most expensive was the rebuilding of Whitehall, a project which remained unfinished at his death. The hunting lodge at Nonsuch remained equally incomplete, with only the remodelling of the house at Oatlands nearing completion.

Between about 1540 and 1547 Henry VIII built a new east front, gatehouse, banqueting house, 'preaching place', orchard and great garden at Whitehall. A declaration of expenditure by Sir Anthony Denny for the period 1541–8 reveals that the prodigious sum of £28,676 was spent on Whitehall in those years.[102] The total expenditure on Nonsuch in the same period was only £24,500, and the whole of Bridewell cost £22,000.[103] So it is clear that Henry was spending vast sums on improving what was, after all, the principal seat of the English Crown.[104] The campaign was largely an attempt to give an appearance of order to the decidedly haphazard conglomeration of buildings which formed Whitehall Palace. A new southern gatehouse, the King Street Gate (as it later became known), did this by linking the southern part of the palace being developed in the 1540s, with the palace parkside, just as the northern gate linked the royal lodgings with the parkside (see figs 76, 81 and plan 13).

The extension of the palace was only possible through further compulsory purchases from the unfortunate inhabitants of Westminster and the reclamation of about 12,600 square yards of the Thames foreshore by building a massive stone river wall over 700 feet long.[105] The river wall itself was intended to be a foundation for a new gallery running alongside the river for the whole eastern frontage of the palace and for a new privy lodging for Princess Mary. The final effect of this can be seen in two paintings from the royal collection (figs 82, 83). The palace gardens were reorganised. Until 1540 the privy garden had been to the north of the

were for the Council in the North, and not for the King.

Dartford (fig. 80) is an illuminating example of a royal house formed by converting a religious foundation, in this case a house of Dominican nuns. Its plan is obscure, but of interest.[99] The royal lodgings were approached directly from the great court by a processional stair. There was no great hall serving as an entrance to the house, only a chamber at the top of the stair where visitors could wait before being summoned to the guard chamber. The royal lodgings themselves were ranged round the monastic cloisters, with subsidary offices located below. Perhaps the most important feature of this plan is the omission of a great hall. This was far from unique, for as early as 1520 the temporary palace at the Field of Cloth of Gold (fig. 65) had lacked one, as did Bridewell (fig. 54). The royal lodgings at St James's were also approached by a processional stair directly from the outer court without a hall (fig. 110). At Hampton Court in the mid-1530s, Henry built a stair on the south front, enabling most visitors arriving by water to bypass the great hall and enter directly into the long gallery leading to his lodgings (see plan 8).[100] At The More the great hall was actually demolished and the site of the former structure became an ante-room to the guard chambers like that at Dartford (see plan 10).

The shift away from the great hall as the magnificent prelude to royal outward chambers is also reflected in the building of the new kitchen at

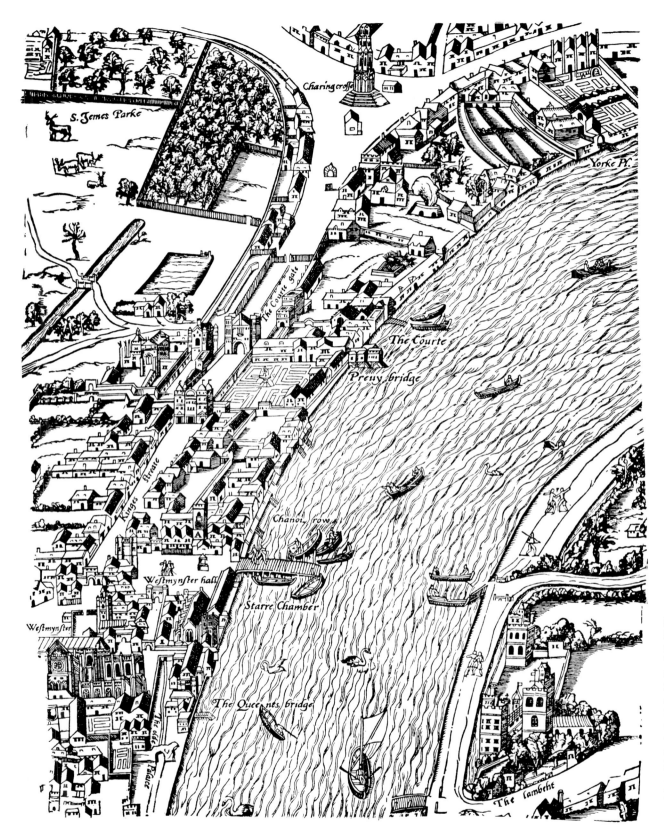

Labels within the image: S. Iemes Parke · Charing croſſe · Yorke Pl. · The Courte gate · The Courte · Preuy bridge · Kinges Streate · Chanoi, row · Westmynster hall · Starre Chamber · Westmynster · The olde Palace · The Queenes bridge · The Lambeht

81. Woodcut plan of London, *c*.1561–6. This is the earliest overall view of Whitehall Palace. The northern gatehouse and King Street Gate can clearly be seen. To the left of King Street is the park side with the great and little close tennis-plays, bowling alley and cockpit. To the right of King Street is the privy gallery range looking out over the privy garden and behind it the rest of the palace.

82. *The Lord Mayor's Procession on the River Thames*, by an unknown artist, mid-seventeenth century (detail). In the background can be seen the river frontage of Whitehall Palace. Surviving Tudor structures include the great hall (right) with a louvre on the roof. In front of the hall is the privy kitchen range. Running left along the river front is the river gallery ending in Princess Mary's lodgings (with two turrets and a bay window between them). Behind the river gallery can be seen new lodgings built by Sir Christopher Wren.

84 (facing page bottom). Nonsuch, Surrey. View from the north-west by an unknown artist, *c*.1620.

privy gallery range, the great garden between the privy gallery and what had been Endive Lane (see plans 13 and 15), and the orchard between Endive Lane and Lamb Alley. The purchase of the extra land enabled each of the gardens to move southward, the orchard being replanted south of Lamb Alley, the great garden on the site of the old orchard, and the privy garden to the south of the privy gallery. This freed the area to the north of the privy gallery for what the accounts call 'the preaching place'. This was one of the most extraordinary structures built in Henry VIII's reign. Extraordinary, not so much in its form but in its function. The preaching place was an outdoor pulpit surrounded by a loggia and overlooked by the King's lodgings (see pp. 199–200, plan 13 and figs 268–9). The importance of this classical loggia in the history of English architecture, and particularly its influence on Inigo Jones when designing the Banqueting House for James I, has gone almost unnoticed.

Nonsuch and Oatlands

Two Acts of Parliament in 1539 and 1540 created the new honour of Hampton Court, the vast tract of royal hunting lands covering eleven parishes along the south side of the Thames, extending some six miles between Weybridge and Thames Ditton, and a similar mileage in breadth (fig. 92).[106] The reason for the creation of this new royal hunting-ground is given in the acts of the Privy Council for 1548, which state, 'the said Chase was but newly and very lately erected in the latter dayes of the King of famous memory, when hys Highnes waxed hevy with sicknes, age and corpulences of body, and might not travayle so readyly abrode, but was constreyned to seke to have hys game and pleasure

ready at hand'.[107] That this was the case is borne out both by the curtailment of royal progresses in the 1540s and by the building accounts. The last time Henry VIII made his favourite progress westwards to Woodstock and Langley (where the hunting was rated best) was in 1543, and from that date onwards the King's activities were mostly confined to the Thames valley. Building accounts furnish details relating to the construction of blocks enabling him to mount his horse at Greenwich and Enfield, while at Oatlands a special ramp was built to allow him to mount his hunters (fig. 88). Other evidence of the King's ill-health can be found in the accounts: special wheelchairs were built for the King's use at Whitehall, and the great royal beds at Hampton Court and Whitehall were extended to take the huge mass of the King's body.[108]

The creation of this suburban hunting-ground involved more than the mere annexation of land, for the intention was to build a new mansion and hunting-lodge in the chase, which would enable him to make 'mini-progresses' around London. A precedent for such a scheme had been established earlier at Woodstock and Langley, and to a more limited extent at Ewelme. Henry had used Woodstock frequently as a progress house.[109] It was a house large enough to accommodate the whole Court. The usual pattern was for the King to leave all the courtiers at Woodstock while going off on a hunting trip with a few close friends, staying at Langley or sometimes Ewelme.[110] Thus, Langley and Ewelme, the two satellites to Woodstock, were lesser houses where he retreated for greater privacy.

The intended purpose of the new honour was identical to that once fulfilled by Woodstock. The new greater house acquired in 1537 was the large and splendid house of Oatlands, and commissioners were immediately employed to find a suitable

adjoining lodge. They settled upon the small but 'well builded' manor house of Cuddington. It was recommended on account of its being 'newly and lately builded . . . in good repair' with 'bay windows cast out, very pleasant in the view and show' and with plentiful supplies both of fresh water and good building stone for extensions.[111] The recommendations made by these commissioners were strikingly similar to those of the surveyors of the monastic properties (see p. 56). But it is clear that either they

were not fully aware of the King's intentions, or else the King's plans changed, for it soon transpired that the existing manor house and village were to be swept away and a new house built. Exactly what motivated Henry to make this decision is unclear, but as the building was started on the thirtieth anniversary of the King's accession it may have been intended as a monument to thirty years of his rule.

Developments in the 1530s had produced planning requirements which demanded the imposition

83. Whitehall Palace from the river, by an unknown artist, c.1700. The riverside gallery and Princess Mary's lodgings can be very clearly seen. Behind Mary's lodgings is the great tennis play on the park side.

85. Nonsuch, Surrey. Conjectural plan of the principal floor, from archaeological and documentary evidence.

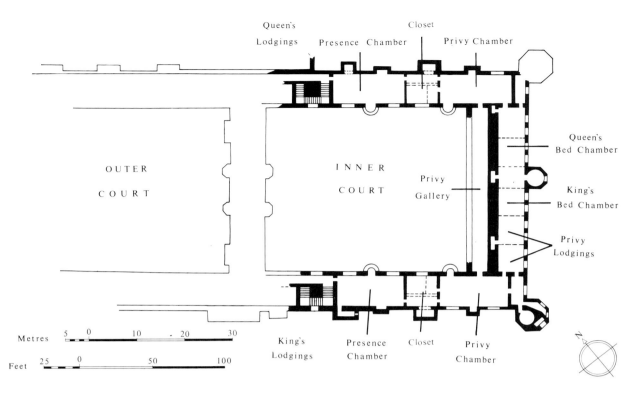

Queen's Lodgings

Presence Chamber

Closet

Privy Chamber

OUTER COURT

INNER COURT

Privy Gallery

Queen's Bed Chamber

King's Bed Chamber

Privy Lodgings

Metres 5 0 10 20 30

Feet 25 0 50 100

King's Lodgings

Presence Chamber

Closet

Privy Chamber

86. Nonsuch, Surrey. Aerial view of the site of Nonsuch during the excavations of 1959. In the foreground are the kitchens; to the right, the outer court; to the left, the inner court. In the middle of the inner court are the footings of the medieval parish church of Coddington, demolished by Henry VIII to make way for his new residence.

Palatium Regium in Angliae Regno Appellatum Noncivtz
Hoc est nusquam simile.

of a standard plan for all the King's houses, and Nonsuch, one of the his last houses, is especially important in providing evidence for this. Unusually, amongst Henry's houses, it was built on a virgin site with no preexisting structure to influence its eventual plan. From this it is reasonable to infer that the plan of Nonsuch represents Henry VIII's mature thoughts on planning. This inference has one rider, however, which should not be forgotten: Nonsuch was a special sort of palace. Royal houses fell into two groups, the greater houses, and the lesser.[112] The greater houses were those where the 'hall was kept', houses in which there were sufficient facilities to accommodate and feed the whole Court, numbering some 1,500 people. In 1526 the Eltham Ordinances had named Windsor, Beaulieu, Richmond, Hampton Court, Eltham and Woodstock as houses where hall should be kept.[113] By comparison with these great houses, Nonsuch was a mere hunting-box annexed to the honour of Hampton Court. It covered no more than about two acres, compared with Hampton Court's six, Oatlands ten and Whitehall's enormous twenty-three. It lacked a series of grand outward chambers for the reception of ambassadors or for great Court festivities. Instead of a conventional great hall it had a 'dining chamber in the outer court', which was designed to feed the King's riding household.[114] Neither did it provide a large number of courtier lodgings; in July 1545, when Henry decided to show off his new house to the Court, a great encampment

of tents had to be provided to accommodate everyone, and furniture and hangings had to be brought from Whitehall.[115] Significantly, the whole Court did not return there in the King's lifetime. To put it simply, Nonsuch was a house for the King and his riding household — an inner group of courtiers comprising his Privy Chamber and favourites — and perhaps a few guests. Nonsuch was, in fact, 'privy palace', the ultimate expression of Henry VIII's quest for privacy. It was the residence expressly built for the King's private entertainment, and this accounts for the lavishness of its decoration.

The King's lodgings were entered by a processional stair from the inner court (fig. 85). In this Nonsuch followed the, by now standard, pattern of houses without halls. Where it differed was that the guard chamber was on the ground floor; why this should have been so is unclear. Possibly it was due to lack of space, if so it reflected badly on the designers. More likely it reflected the nature of the palace, which was never intended for major receptions and only required one reception room, the presence chamber. Entered directly at first-floor level, the presence chamber was the first of the King's lodgings. A short gallery with two closets off it linked the presence chamber with the privy chamber. Once in the privy chamber one door led to the privy gallery, another to the King's privy lodgings and a third to a small room giving on to a tower. Beyond the two chambers of the privy lodging was the King's bedchamber, centrally positioned

87. Nonsuch, Surrey. View from the south by Joris Hoefnagel, 1568. The wall of the privy garden obscures the lower part of the elevation. The central staircase can be seen, and above it the tower on the inner gatehouse. The buildings on the right are the kitchens; the two low roofs on the left are later additions. Also clearly visible are the panels of stucco decoration fitted to the timber frame of the building.

63

88. Oatlands, Surrey, as depicted in a lost Elizabethan drawing from an engraving from Manning and Bray's *History of Surrey*, 1804–14. This shows the house as Henry VIII would have known it except for the buildings on the right in the outer court which were kitchen offices added by Elizabeth I.

89 (facing page top). Oatlands, Surrey, from the west, from a drawing by A. van den Wyngaerde, 1559. The base court is approached via a walled outer courtyard containing service buildings as at Hampton Court and Eltham. As at Knole House, Kent, these outer courts were an addition by Henry VIII. Beyond is the inner court, which the King acquired largely intact. It has two groups of towers to the north and south. These probably contained the king's and queen's lodgings.

90 (facing page bottom). Oatlands, Surrey, from the background of a portrait of Anne of Denmark by Paul van Somer, 1617. The painter shows the house from the south, with the gateway built later by Inigo Jones in the foreground. The prospect tower, one of Oatland's most notable features, closely paralleled by the southern towers at Nonsuch, features in the centre of the view.

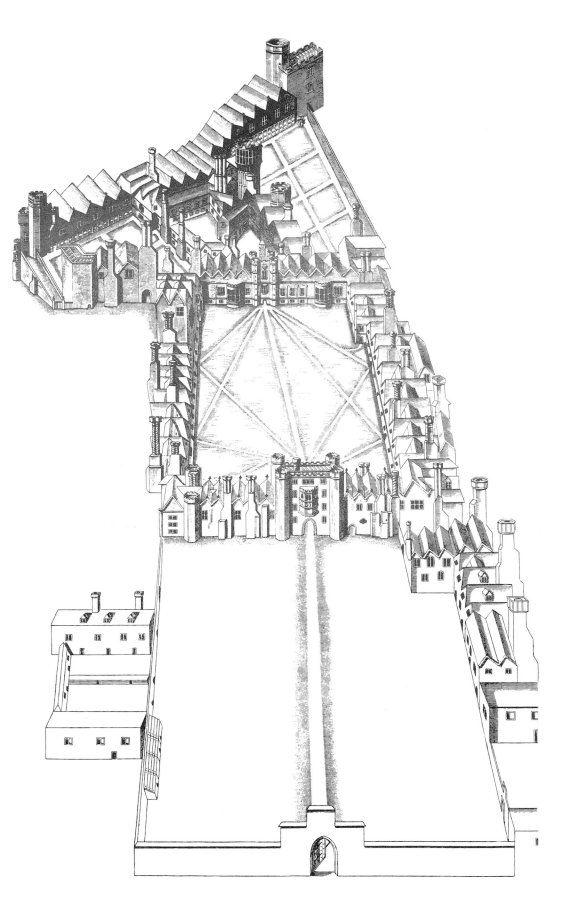

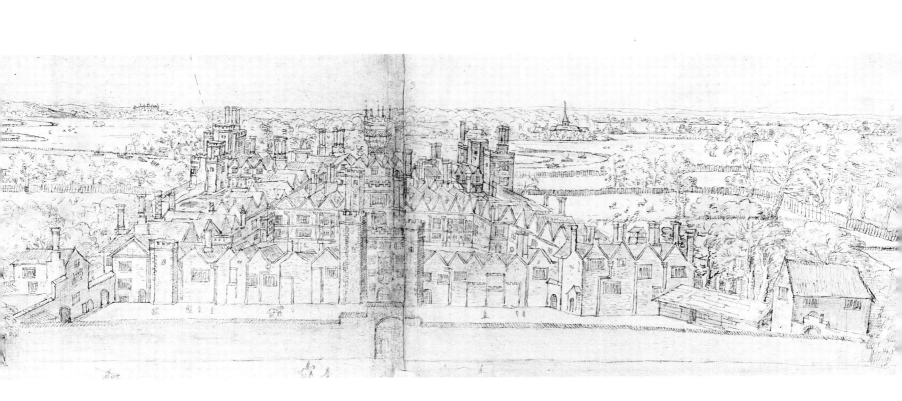

on the south front. The Queen almost certainly had an identical arrangement, except that she had only a single room as her privy lodging on the south front. Her bedroom was separated from the King's by a small room behind the stair turret. This stair turret was positioned off-centre on the south front to allow the King's bedroom to occupy the central position and leave room for his privy lodging.

The plan of Nonsuch reflected the architectural demands of the later part of the reign in microcosm: the absence of a great hall and a privy lodging beyond outer rooms all on one level. So too, within the confines of limited evidence does the house of Oatlands.[116] The original house belonged to Sir Bartholomew Reed, a prosperous merchant and Lord Mayor of London. Reed had built the substantial house shown in surviving views (figs 88, 89–90). Reed's house was a courtyard house with projecting wings on the north front, which at either end incorporated a donjon incorporating a tower with a vice-stair against it. Although nothing can now be said about the layout of lodgings at Oatlands, a parliamentary survey of 1649 leaves no doubt that it did not have a great hall.[117] From a references to 'a new stayre ... servyng for the quenys syde',[118] it appears that a processional stair may have led up to the Queen's guard chamber, much in the same way as at Nonsuch and the other later houses. Thus Oatlands was another late house

without a great hall and in which a stair in the inner court may have given direct access to the royal lodgings.

Chapter 5

PURPOSE AND FUNCTION

ANY STUDY OF THE HOUSES at the disposal of Henry VIII raises a number of questions: Why were there so many? Was there a pattern to their distribution? Were all houses used in the same way? How and why did the Court move between them? How were all the courtiers accommodated? What happened to the houses when they were empty? Who looked after them and where did those people live?

The progress and the itinerant Court

Under Henry VIII, there was an important distinction between the itinerant Court and the royal progress. On a progress the King and Court followed an extended itinerary which had been planned, often months in advance, in contrast with frequent *ad-hoc* moves between houses in the Thames valley. This distinction also had a seasonal aspect: the summer months, the 'grass season' (the time when the hay was cut and the hunting was best, August to October), were progress time;[1] by contrast, the winter months were generally times of random moves between the houses in the vicinity of the capital.

In most years the King's summer travels were defined by the issue of a table of movements known as the 'giests'. These were lists setting out the King's movements from place to place with the number of miles between stops and the time to be spent at each location. In 1521 Bishop Ruthall of Durham told Wolsey that the King was 'entendyng to procede in hys progresse accordyng to the gists'.[2] The King undoubtably had an interest in his future movements, but the work of compiling giests fell to others. The issue of the giests was eagerly awaited, as the personal costs and inconvenience of a progress to most courtiers could be great. In 1543 Thomas Heneage, the King's Chief Gentleman of the Privy Chamber, had to write to Mr Eton, his father-in-law, requesting a loan to 'go on this progress' and promising to repay it at Michaelmas.[3] Giests were not prepared every year, for Hall relates that in 1521 'no great jestes' were appointed, but this seems to be an exception, and the lists survive for several years.[4]

Once issued, giests were regularly adhered to, but adverse weather conditions, food shortages and disease could result in alterations, sometimes at short notice. The best documented incidence of such a change was in 1517 when 'the king appointed his gestes for his pastyme this Sommer, but sodeinly there came a plague of sickenes, called Swetyng sickenes, that turned all his purpose'.[5] Much the same happened in 1528, following the death of one of the Duke of Suffolk's servants at Woodstock. The King 'coulde not oonly a litle marvaille' that the Duke 'advertised not his grace of the deth of his said servant . . . to thentente he might have determyned his giests sum other weye' and ordered revised giests dropping Woodstock from the route.[6]

When the giests were changed, problems were bound to occur. An example is the occasion when, in August 1529, the King was once again fleeing from the sweating sickness in the vicinity of London and was faced with the problem of changing his intended route from a large house to a small one. The plan had been to visit Wolsey's house, The More, but this was cancelled. The King's secretary, Stephen Gardiner, wrote to Wolsey, staying at Tyttenhanger: 'I said I thought Tytenhanger to lyte to recyve his highnes. Whereto his highnes answered that your grace, as he doubted not, ye woulde be removing for the tyme with your company to Saint Albans'.[7] Wolsey complied with Gardiner's request, but his doubts about the suitability of the houses proved well founded. The problem had an unexpected resolution. The King's paranoia about the plague led to his leaving 'some of his chamber in every place where he went', and this thinning-down of the royal household enabled it to fit more comfortably than expected into Tyttenhanger. Servants were sent ahead to check whether the towns through which the Court was to pass were free of sickness[8] and strict regulations in the Black Book of Edward IV provided that 'There ought no perilous sykeman to lodge in this courte, but to avoyde within three dayes, and then by favour, as the soveraynes thinke according to contynewe his lyverey'.[9]

The compilation of geists reflected the two main

91. Detail of fig. 97 showing the great watergate at Hampton Court. There are no accounts for its construction between 1529 and 1539, making it either a work of Cardinal Wolsey's or an addition of the 1540s.

reasons for progresses. First, it served a political function: in an age when general movement was restricted, one of a king's main obligations was to show himself to his people, and progress afforded him an opportunity to do this. Perhaps the most obviously political of Henry VIII's progresses was the great journey that he made north in 1541 in the hope of meeting the King of Scotland at York. But all progresses were meant to increase 'the points of contact' between king and country.[10] On most occasions, however, the primary reason for the progress was not political, it was pleasurable — the pursuit of good hunting.

From the early Middle Ages the distribution of royal houses had to a large extent been determined by the location of the royal parks or forests. A park was an enclosed area of land in private ownership reserved almost exclusively for deer, while a forest was a vast tract of unfenced land upon which deer lived protected by forest laws. Most of the major royal parks, like Woodstock or Devizes, had been established long before 1200, and many of them were attached to a substantial royal house rather than a mere hunting-lodge. Hunting had remained the sport of English kings throughout the Middle Ages, although the number of new emparkments had declined during the fourteenth and fifteenth centuries. In the later Middle Ages, as well as providing recreation, parks were important sources of income, providing six hundred head of venison a year for the royal household as well as offices, fines and dues.[11]

In the late fifteenth century there began to be a steady trickle of new emparkments. Edward IV not only enlarged existing parks but be created additional new ones. At Eltham, for instance, he 'inclosed horne park, one of the three that be here, and enlarged the other tweine'.[12] Henry VII was an even more devoted hunter than the Yorkists.[13] He enlarged the medieval park of Sheen, which adjoined Richmond and enclosed a new park at Greenwich, stocking it with deer brought from the manor of Ditton.[14] At the start of his reign Henry VIII was, like his father, a very keen hunter. His enthusiasm was shared by many of his servants and courtiers who took the opportunity to join him whenever possible. The disorderly assemblies which resulted gave rise for concern, and the Eltham Ordinances tried to rectify this,

> whensomever the King's grace hath gone further in walkeing, hunting, hauking, or other disportes, the most parte of the noblemen and gentlemen of the court have used to passe with his grace, by reason whereof, not only the court hath been left disgarnished, but also the King's said disports lett, hindred, and impeached

and ordered that in future the number of hunting companions should be reduced.[15] After 1526 only a select, hand-picked circle of companions accompanied Henry VIII on such expeditions.

During the 1530s the King's interest in hunting and in emparkments took on a new aspect and Henry set out on what was to be the last great batch of emparkments in England. His increased interest in emparkment is graphically illustrated by what happened at his final meeting with Wolsey at Grafton in 1529. The King, tired, bored and increasingly impatient with his minister, cut the interview short and 'the kyng Rode that mornyng to vewe a ground for a newe parke, whiche is calld at thys day hartwell parke'.[16] In the next fifteen years the King emparked Whitehall (now St James's) Park (1532),[17] Hyde Park (1536), two parks at Nonsuch (1538), Nasing Park, Essex (1542), and Marylebone (now Regent's) Park (1544). In addition he was busy acquiring existing parks for his own use. Some came as the result of forfeitures, as did Penshurst from the Duke of Buckingham, but most were the result of exchanges, often with churchmen, as for instance the seven great Kentish parks of the Archbishop of Canterbury. A list of royal parks in a household book of 1540–41 names eighty-five parks and forests.[18] This extraordinary programme aimed at improving the hunting available to the Crown reached its culmination in 1539 with the establishment of the first new royal forest for over two centuries, centred on Hampton Court. Hampton Court Chase covered an area of 10,000 acres which was more than double the size of any of the existing parks in his possession. The cost in terms of pales alone, was over £15,000.[19]

This sudden resurgence of interest in royal parks influenced the choice, distribution and use of the royal houses. The most important medieval houses such as Clarendon, Windsor and Woodstock had been centred on royal forests; Henry VIII reasserted this trend. In the time of Edward III there were twelve houses and three hunting-lodges in the Thames valley centred on the great park at Windsor. By 1547 there were about twenty-five houses in the same area serving the great band of parks encircling London. Houses further from London were also chosen for their hunting; such an example was Ampthill, bought by Henry VIII in 1524. Ampthill was a modest, but well-appointed house situated at the centre of a wooded park.[20] In 1542 it was promoted to an honour, and several adjoining estates were annexed to it. The establishment of this honour necessitated an improvement and extension to the house.[21]

Another way in which the hunt influenced the distribution of houses was their grouping into clusters of lesser houses serving as hunting-lodges

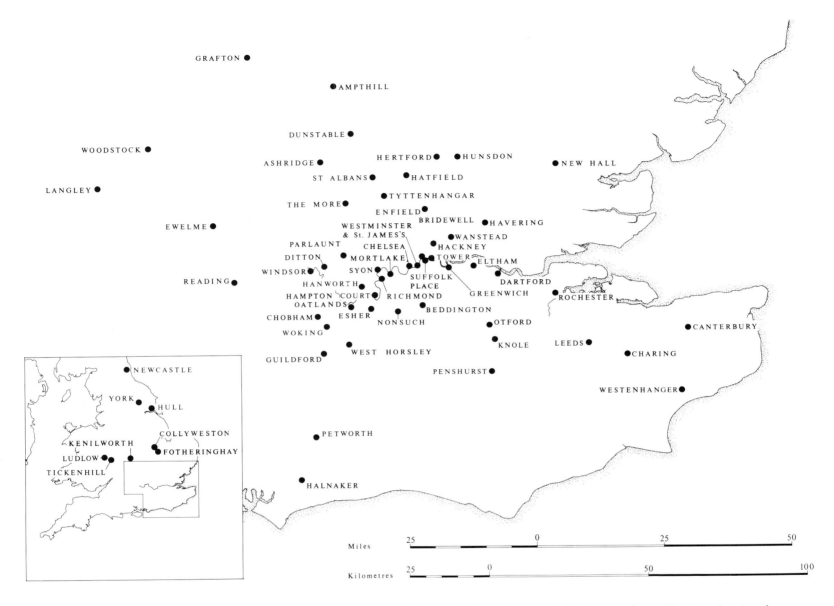

GRAFTON ●

● AMPTHILL

DUNSTABLE ●

WOODSTOCK ●   HERTFORD ● ● HUNSDON   ● NEW HALL

ASHRIDGE ●

LANGLEY ●   ST ALBANS ● ● HATFIELD

EWELME ●   THE MORE ● ● TYTTENHANGAR

                 ENFIELD ●   ● HAVERING

                 WESTMINSTER   BRIDEWELL
PARLAUNT   & St. JAMES'S   ● WANSTEAD
DITTON   CHELSEA ● HACKNEY
WINDSOR ●   MORTLAKE ● TOWER
READING ●   SYON   ● ELTHAM
                 HANWORTH   DARTFORD
                 HAMPTON COURT ●   GREENWICH
                 OATLANDS ● RICHMOND   ● ROCHESTER
CHOBHAM ●   ESHER ● BEDDINGTON
WOKING ●   NONSUCH   OTFORD ●   ● CANTERBURY
                                 KNOLE   LEEDS ●   ● CHARING
GUILDFORD ●   WEST HORSLEY
                        PENSHURST ●   ● WESTENHANGER

NEWCASTLE ●

YORK ● ● HULL

COLLYWESTON ●
KENILWORTH
LUDLOW ● ● FOTHERINGHAY
TICKENHILL

PETWORTH ●

HALNAKER ●

Miles   25   0   25   50

Kilometres   25   0   50   100

and orbiting round greater houses. Thus Woodstock was served by lesser houses at Langley and Ewelme where the King stayed on hunting trips (fig. 92). Oatlands was similarly served by Nonsuch, and Hampton Court by Esher and Hanworth. In 1527, when the French ambassadors were being entertained at Hampton Court, 'the officers caused them to Ride to hanworthe a place and parke of the kynges within ij or iij mylles there to hunt and spend the tyme untill nyght At whiche tyme they retorned agayn to Hampton Court . . .'.[22] Albeit this occurred before Hampton Court entered royal possession, it is a good example of how the lesser houses were used as bases for hunting trips from the greater ones. Although not originally conceived as a lesser house, Eltham became subsidiary to Greenwich during the reign of Henry VIII.[23] Lambarde, in

the *Perambulation of Kent* observes 'this house, by reason of the nearnesse to Greenwiche . . . hath not bene so greatly esteemed: the rather also for that the pleasures of the emparked groundes here, may be in manner as well enjoyed, the court lying at Greenwich, as if it were at this house it selfe'.[24] This arrangement of a greater house and satellites not only allowed the King to set up at one house and continue with short hunting visits to the lesser houses around, but enabled him to make day trips, with somewhere to rest and eat.

Provision for an 'abiding household' and a 'riding household' dated at least from the reign of Edward IV. King Edward's Black Book provided: 'that if the kinges hyghnesse plese to kepe a lesse household than the foresayde grete summe sheweth, here in this boke are deuysed IX other smaller houses . . .

92. Map showing the distribution of royal houses in 1547.

69

wherof the king may cheese suche as shall please hym best'. Wolsey's Ordinances of Eltham also made provision for the occasional reduction in the household as did many noble houses.[25] Henry frequently left the full Court at a greater house and set off, with his riding household, for one of the lesser houses. In August 1530 Henry VIII was reported 'for nearly one month' to have 'given himself entirely to hunting privately and moving from one place to another; a year later, in June 1531, he left 'for Windsor and other places only in his company Anne Boleyn, Sir Nicholas Carew and two others', while in 1541 he was to have 'left his Privy Council here, and is with a small company in the neighbourhood'.[26]

The King's more marked enthusiasm for hunting in the 1530s and 1540s may have been in emulation — as was so much else — of Francis I of France who was, at the same time carrying his own love of hunting to wild extremes, settling in his last years into a continual round of hunts.[27] But age and health are more plausible explanations. Henry VIII's most favoured pastime at Court had been the tournament, but his participation was first curtailed after March 1524 when he forgot to fasten his visor and got a helmet full of splinters, and finally terminated after January 1536 when he lay unconscious for two hours after a fall from his horse.[28] To fill the gap he took up tennis much more seriously and became more interested in bowling and cockfighting (see pp. 181–8). Hunting now became his principal outdoor recreation and, no longer tied to the tiltyard, he could devote more of his time and energy to it. Tilting was a sport associated with the greater houses, and it is thus perhaps no coincidence that, with no other pastime to compete with hunting after his exit from the tiltyard, the lesser houses, with their greater privacy, began to figure larger in the King's life and building works.

The size of the full Court on progress is difficult to estimate. In 1541 the French ambassador believed that four to five the normal number of one thousand horses was used on the progress to York.[29] This estimate would include the horses necessary to pull the carts loaded with household equipment. From the evidence provided by the accounts of the King's visit to the Earl of Hertford in 1539, about eight hundred members of the Court were present.[30] This figure roughly agrees with the ambassador's estimate. As the full winter Court numbered approximately fifteen hundred people, the Court seems to have halved in size during progress time.

However, these figures depend to a great extent on whether any other members of the royal family accompanied the King. His successive wives often had their own itineraries, separate from his. For instance Catherine of Aragon went on her own

pilgrimages at least four times, in 1515, 1517, 1519 and 1521.[31] Sometimes Henry VIII's children, each of whom was eventually to have his or her own, not inconsiderable, household, would accompany their father. More often they too had their own separate itineraries — a list of giests survives for Princess Mary's household for 1518,[32] which comprised sixty-nine servants and officers and their twelve servants; in addition, twenty-one ladies and gentlemen accompanied her. Her household expenses show that in May 1523 she needed twenty-six carts to move her effects between Richmond and Greenwich.[33] So when Princess Mary joined her parents at Court for a religious festival or a state occasion its size was substantially increased.[34]

Transporting these large numbers of people on progress was an enormous task. The principal household officers and courtiers had their own horses, but moving the staff of the Lord Steward's department often required additional transport to be commandeered. A list found amongst the papers of William Thynne, Clerk of the Kitchen from 1526 to 1546, shows how much transport the constables of Ropley in Hampshire had to provide for the King when he moved house. The totals for each village were set out in two columns, one for winter and one for summer; the number of carts needed for the summer removals was higher than that for the winter.[35] However it is clear that most of the departments of the Household had carts or 'chariots' assigned to them for removals. An account of Henry VII's removal from Westminster to Richmond in 1501 illustrates this nicely:

> the kinges officers of Houssold imbuysid themself in all their deligens and pouer to trusse and stuffe ther great and huge standardes, coffers, chestes, clothe sakkes, with all othir vesselles of conveyaunce, every officer with such thinges as he hadde in his governaunce and ruele, and this sent forthe by many cartes and chariattes by lande, and also in dyvers botes and wherys by watir.[36]

The principal way in which such removals affected the architectural components of the King's houses, was in the need for extensive stabling.

All of the King's houses had at least one stable building, and the larger ones had several. Limiting the number of horses at Court was as important as controlling the number of people. In the Eltham Ordinances, Wolsey set down the number of horses each courtier was entitled to stable at the King's cost.[37] For the courtiers' horses, the King's and those of the Household, considerable space was needed. At Greenwich, for example, there were several stables. In 1509, not long after his accession, a new stable was built for the King's coursers.[38] Only four years later another new stable was erected,

COURT

Feet 0   50

93. The Royal Mews,
Hampton Court, Surrey.
The surviving building was
extended by Queen
Elizabeth I.

94. The Royal Mews,
Hampton Court, Surrey.
Plan showing the extent of
the buildings in the reign of
Henry VIII.

this time, for the King's stud mares.[39] In 1537 the King's Master Bricklayer, Christopher Dickenson, built a new stable at Hampton Court at a cost of £130. The building survives, although altered and extended by Elizabeth I in 1570 (figs 93–4).[40] As with the other departments of the Tudor Court, the stable establishment was divided into two wings, one for the King and another for everyone else. At Greenwich there was 'a partition between ye comyn stabyll and ye master of ye horse stabyll'. The common stable housed the horses used for the carriage of the Court when it removed and the horses of the courtiers. The Master of the Horse ran the department which looked after the King's horses. In 1534, the Master of the Horse, Sir Anthony Browne, paid for repairs and alterations to the stable buildings at Greenwich.[41] The Grooms of the Stables, the assistants of the Master of the Horse, lived either above the stables, as at Hampton Court, or in a wing of the stables, as at Greenwich.[42] The Queen had her own Master of the Horse and her own stable buildings.[43]

Some offices, especially those detached from the main palace buildings in any way, had their own independant stables. The houses of offices at Hampton Court, built in 1529, for the scalding-house and baking-house, had their own stables situated at the rear of the building, to allow supplies to be brought in without entering the outer court of the palace (figs 189–90).

Preparations for feeding the Court while it was on the move had to be made in advance. The Black Book required the Clerk of the Market to ride 'in the contries before the kinges commyng to warn the peple to bake, to brewe, and to make redy othyr vytayle and stuff in to theire logginges'.[44] The officers of the Greencloth, who were responsible for the feeding arrangements, needed transport themselves; they had assigned to them 'one charyotte complete, and a sompter horse for the grene coffers'.[45] The buildings belonging to the Lord Steward's department, the kitchens, larders and storehouses, were planned in the same way at every house. This was so that the Household departments could function immediately on arrival at a new destination. Indeed, the Household ordinances stress that 'all manner of officers at thier first cominge to the kynges house that they know the places and offices . . . that they may be expert to got to them when they be comannded for the redy servinge of the kinge'.[46] The uniform planning of the service parts of the houses aided the King's officers in their task (see pp. 156–7).

The officers of the King's Works also went ahead of the Court. Tudor kings, like their medieval predecessors, directed their royal works programmes, to a large extent, by their itineraries.[47] James

Nedeham, the Surveyor of the King's Works, and his teams of workmen were to repair and maintain the houses listed in the King's geists in advance of the King's arrival. To take a single example, at Ampthill in 1543 Lawrence Bradshaw, 'the overseer and setter owte of the works', set out for the workmen the 'reparacions done agaynst the kyngs comyng to the said manor'.[48] James Nedeham's riding costs, presented at the end of each year, tell the same story: 'gevyng attendance his grace removing from place to place to know his graces pleasure as well in surveying the forsaid castles and manors for buyldyng and repairing the same'.[49] Once repairs had been made and the provisions and transport organised, each house had to be cleaned and opened, a highly labour-intensive process (see pp. 74–5).

Following the departure of the Court, another team of Household servants would begin their tasks. Gangs of labourers cleaned the house of all superficial dirt: an account at Whitehall is 'for the swhepyng makyng clene and caryng a waye of all the rusches and duste owte of all the lodgyngs within the manor'. Wooden panelling was also cleaned, as at The More: 'swepyng washyng and makyng clene thold selyngs of waynscott'.[50] The size of Whitehall made it an exception to the standard procedures and by the 1540s there was a permanent cleaning staff of three people 'occupied makyng clene of the palace'.[51] It was not only the Office of Works that cleaned houses on the departure of the Court, but the Chamber staff helped as well. William Lee, Gentleman Usher, was paid for supervising seven men cleaning the outward chamber at Windsor.[52] A stay of longer than a few weeks created more serious problems than just dirt; then, the whole fabric of the building would often need attention. On 11 April 1533 the whole Court removed to Greenwich where it remained until 28 May.[53] The seven-week stay took its toll on the building and necessitated a complete overhaul of the palace. Not only were hearths replaced as usual and minor improvements undertaken, but also thirty yards of matting were renewed, huge numbers of windows were repaired, scuffed paintwork was touched up, locks mended and roofs patched.[54] Spruced up, Greenwich was ready to receive the Court on 8 June, where it stayed for the rest of the month before going on progress.

The need to keep houses clean and repaired was another factor which affected where the King stayed. In 1522 Wolsey was informed that the King

thinketh it not best to change his opinion from the keping off his ester at richmond not only be cause much off his provisions agenst the seyd tym be there now in a rydnesse but allso at his grace departyng from grenewich there was no small suspition of the plage his grace would allso have the howse off grenewiche at the emperor comyng as cleane as it migth.[55]

Thus the King left Greenwich, not only to avoid plague, but to go to another house prepared for him, and to allow Greenwich to be repaired and cleaned for the visit of the Emperor Charles V. Another example is in 1559 when the Venetian ambassador noted that Queen Elizabeth I 'will go to Greenwich to give time for cleansing the palace of Whitehall, where she now is, and then she will return directly'.[56]

Removing, with all the preparations and organisation it involved, was a cumbersome and laborious process, and not one which Henry VIII particularly relished. His anxiety to avoid unnecessary fuss is glimpsed in June 1518, when he was at Woodstock and decided to meet Wolsey at Greenwich secretly. The King's secretary, Richard Pace, wrote to Wolsey that the King

desirith your Grace to commaunde provision to be made there for hys suppar and yours, for he wull departe hense secretly wyth a small numbre off his chiambre wythowte ony suche parsons as schulde make ony provision for hym. Hys pleasor is also that your Grace schulde commaunde suche off his Warderope as be in London to prepare the House for hym, wyth suche hys Graces stuffe as is in the Towre at london.[57]

The months of progress, although mainly centred on the royal houses also made use of the houses of the King's subjects. During his reign Henry VIII is known to have made some 1,150 moves between houses with his Court.[58] Of these, 830 were to his own houses, the rest to ecclesiastical or courtier houses.[59] Thus it can be seen that three-quarters of the moves made by the King were to houses which he owned. Before 1530, out of a total of 556 moves, only 366, or 65 per cent, were to royal properties. After 1530 the figures are much higher: out of a total of 596 moves, all but 52 were to royal houses; or to put it another way, in the second half of the reign nine out of ten of the King's moves were to his own houses. The reason for the change in the figures can be explained not only by the great increase in the number of royal houses after 1530, but also by the fact that a proportion of that increase was to houses which he had been in the habit of visiting long before acquiring the properties themselves. Thus, in reality, the pattern of Henry VIII's visits did not change during the reign.

However, the simple enumeration of moves is only one way of measuring the King's movements. It takes no account of the duration of each visit.

There was, in fact, a significant difference between the length of time which the King spent at one of his own houses and the time spent at a non-royal house. On the whole, the non-royal houses were smaller and less comfortable than royal ones, with the result that part of the Household and Court had to be accommodated nearby, an expensive and uncomfortable operation. Although 35 per cent of moves before 1530 were to non-royal houses the King rarely spent more than 20 per cent of the nights of any one year in them.[60]

Relative brevity did not diminish the honour of a visit from the King and Court. Harrison, in the *Description of England*, noted Queen Elizabeth's policy that 'everie noble mans house is hir palace'[61] and her father's attitude was undoubtably the same. Courtiers seemed to have concurred with their monarch's notions in this respect. Sir Thomas Lovell's provision of a lodging at Enfield for Henry VII[62] was frequently imitated, the most spectacular instance perhaps being Wolsey's provision of splendid lodgings at Hampton Court for Henry VIII and Catherine of Aragon.[63] The Eltham Ordinances took this tacit acceptance one stage further in 1526 when they included Wolsey's Hampton Court in the list of houses at which the full Court could stay.[64]

The itinerant Court and the greater house

There was an important distinction to be made between the houses where 'hall was normally kept' and the others. The keeping of hall meant that the full complement of six hundred or so people who were entitled to eat in the hall, did so communally, in relays, as specified by the ordinances. This was only possible in houses with a great hall and enough lodgings to accommodate the whole Court. During the 1520s, there were six houses in which the whole Court could be accommodated with ease.[65] The Eltham Ordinances specified in 1526 that hall should be kept at Beaulieu, Richmond, Hampton Court, Greenwich, Eltham and Woodstock.[66] These houses may be called the greater houses. Five of them were in the Thames valley and were tightly grouped for easy access during the winter months. Woodstock, which was further afield, was still used during the winter. After the fall of Wolsey the King acquired Whitehall as a seventh greater house but although Whitehall was a gain, three of those specified in 1526 had almost fallen out of use. The King rarely used Beaulieu, Richmond or Eltham, popular houses early in the reign. By the 1540s there were four greater houses; Whitehall, Greenwich, Hampton Court and Woodstock.

The winter was, as much as the summer, a time of continual changes in scene. It is perhaps in the context of the winter removals between the greater houses that the mechanics of setting-up can be discussed. Moving, or 'removing', as it was called, and setting-up elsewhere was like a well co-ordinated military operation, and it had to be planned down to the last detail if it was to be carried out efficiently. Perhaps a more apt analogy is that of the theatre, for at each house the stage — the architectural shell — was fixed, and it remained for the staff of the Wardrobe and Chamber or Privy Chamber to arrange the scenery. The scenery (tapestries) and the props (furniture) were either in store at the house if it was a greater house, or brought in carts if it was a lesser one.

The Wardrobe had primary responsibility for the furnishings of the houses. In the Black Book the officers of the Wardrobe were required, on removing day, to 'sette in all manner of lyveres [liveries] to hepe trusse, and bere the . . . harnys and stuffe, to wayte upon the carryages'.[67] In addition to carts, the Wardrobe had at least one 'little bote' which was used to ferry the King's furniture and hangings between houses.[68] When the destination was reached responsibility was passed on to the Grooms of the Chamber or Privy Chamber. The Grooms of the Chamber were instructed by the Black Book to 'make fyres to sett up tressyls and bourdes, with yeomen of the chamber, and to helpe dresse the beddes of sylke and arras upon the ushers appoyntment . . . help hang the cloathes, and to kepe them clene from dogges and other uncleannes'.[69] The Eltham Ordinances instructed the Grooms of the Privy Chamber to do likewise in the King's privy chamber.[70]

Members of the King's Chamber were responsible for supervising and undertaking the furnishing of his chambers. In 1540 John Harman, Usher of the Chamber, was paid for his work and that of four Yeomen, the Groom Porter, a Groom of the Wardrobe and two Grooms of the Chamber, for setting up Hampton Court before the Court's arrival.[71] A passage in Cavendish's *Life of Wolsey* describes the efforts of Wolsey's grooms in setting up Hampton Court for the reception of ambassadors in 1527:

Then my Lord Cardinal sent me [Cavendish], being gentleman usher, with two other of my fellows, to Hampton Court to forsee all things touching our rooms to be nobly garnished accordingly. Our pains were not small or light, but travailing daily from chamber to chamber . . . the yeomen and grooms of the wardrobes were busied in hanging of the chambers with costly hangings and furnishing the same with beds of silk and other furniture apt for the same in every degree . . . the carpenters, the joiners the masons, the painters and all other artificers necessary to glorify the house and feast were set a work. There was carriage and recarrage of plate, stuff, and other rich impliments so that there was nothing lacking.[72]

This bustle was not peculiar to Wolsey's household, but was typical of the Henrician Court.

In the greater houses there were a variety of stores where furnishings could be kept; the King's and Queen's wardrobe of the beds, the King's standing wardrobe of the beds, the King's and Queen's wardrobe of the robes and the King's and Queen's jewel-houses. The two wardrobes of the beds housed the loose hangings for the beds and testers of state as well as tapestries. However, these were really just repositories where the removing wardrobe, which looked after the furnishings transported with the King, could be housed.[73] There was a removing wardrobe at every house the King owned. These wardrobes could not always cope with the volume of furnishings and often, even at the greater houses, additional space was a necessity. For instance in 1537 Nicholas Newes, a Groom of the Beds to Princess Mary, had to hire houses at Windsor, Esher and Hampton Court to store his 'gaurd stuff' when the Wardrobe officials were unable to help him.[74] In the 1530s an additional wardrobe was set up at the greater houses — the standing wardrobe of the beds. At Greenwich, in March 1533 there was constructed 'a new wardrobe ffor the kyngys standyng beddys'.[75] Three years later at Hampton Court a similar standing wardrobe was erected, two storeys high,[76] and by the end of the reign, one also existed at Whitehall.[77] Standing wardrobes were normally situated in the outer courts away from the royal lodgings. The inventory taken in 1547 shows at which houses there was a standing wardrobe at Henry VIII's death.[78] All the greater houses are included; Greenwich, Whitehall, Hampton Court, Oatlands, Windsor, Woodstock, The More, Richmond and New Hall. In addition wardrobes were maintained at the Tower, where there had been a standing wardrobe since 1509;[79] at Nonsuch and Beddington, two houses where the King had recently been staying, and Nottingham, for some obscure reason, was also included.

The standing wardrobes were fitted with cupboards and storage racks. That at Greenwich had 'longe presses ffor the kyngs arres, grett carpetts, cusshions and hangyngs to lye in with . . . a duble dore to the same'.[80] Another press was made there 55 feet long.[81] These presses were so large on account of the size of the tapestries stored within them. One of the tapestries at Hampton Court, depicting the *History of Abraham*, measured 30 feet by 18 feet. This of course made setting them up very difficult especially as, in addition to their great size, many were shot through with gold and silver thread and were extremely heavy. At Greenwich the standing wardrobe possessed 'vii newe ladders made as well for the wardroppe to hang up clothes of Arras'; but as these were continually stolen they were kept locked up: there was a 'chene for the grome porters with ii staples and a hangyng locke to hang the ledders upon thatt hangs the kyngs chambers'.[82] Once hung, Household regulations decreed that 'no man wipe or robe their hands upon none arras of the kinges wherby they might be hurted',[83] further illustrating the care taken with furnishings of such great value. While the Court was present the Wardrobe was run by the King's officers of the Wardrobe, but special provisions had to be made at the houses with standing wardrobes. Household regulations put this task on to the Keeper of the house, to whom was delivered all the wardrobe stuff at the Court's removing. He had to sign for it and keep it until the next visit.[84]

The wardrobe of the robes contained clothes belonging to the King and Queen, and was invariably situated beneath the King's and Queen's privy chamber with a stair connecting it to the room above (see plans 2 and 3, 7 and 8, and pp. 138–9). The wardrobe of the beds was less well placed, being normally situated in the outer court. The jewel-house contained the small items of value which the King and Queen needed for everyday life, such as combs, mirrors and hawk hoods, and at Greenwich and Whitehall jewels as well. Henry VIII's jewel-house at Hampton Court still retains its barred windows to prevent forcible entry and theft. Such jewel-houses were restricted to the greater houses and the inventory of 1547 gives details of their contents.[85] Their apparent namesakes, the privy or secret jewel-houses, belonged to a different organisation and were under the control of the King's Privy Chamber, their contents being conveyed between houses by the Privy Chamber, and not by the Wardrobe (see plan 13, fig. 174).[86]

The Laundry was an important supporting department to the Wardrobe. It was staffed in the 1540s by five men under a Yeoman Launderer. The Black Book divided the Laundry into the two familiar divisions; one intended only for the King's use and the other for everyone else. 'Everyone else' included the Wardrobe, the Chamber, the Chapel Royal and the Lord Steward's departments. Towels, napkins, table-cloths, surplices, albs, aprons and clothes were all washed. Most articles were boiled and then dried indoors with charcoal braziers, but the finest clothes were never washed, only brushed. The King had his own laundress, in the 1540s a woman named Anne Harris. Mrs Harris was provided with chests for storing the King's linen,

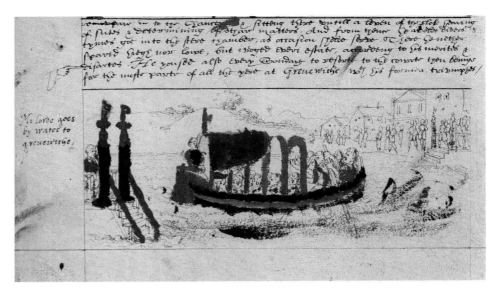

herbs for making it smell sweet and £20 a year to cover the cost of wood, soap and her wages.[87] The drying of washing could be a hazardous operation, and one which in 1698 was to result in the destruction of Whitehall Palace by fire.[88] Each of the King's family, the Queen and their children had their own Privy Laundries, those of the women staffed by women.[89] The only laundry building which can be identified in Henry's reign is that in the outer court of Eltham (see plan 1); it consists of four rooms, two with enormous fireplaces.

An important distinction between the Court on progress and the itinerant Court was the mode of transport employed in transferring the Court between houses. The greater houses around London were all situated on the Thames and transport between them was usually by barge. Each member of the royal family had his or her own barge, as did the more important courtiers (fig. 95).[90] The King was exceptional in owning what amounted to a small flotilla of barges, and in 1522 these formed the nucleus of the thirty barges used to convey the Emperor Charles V and his retinue from Gravesend to Greenwich.[91] A surviving account from the King's Barge Master throws light on how the barges were furnished. 'Swete herbs' were burnt to hide the offensive smells of the river. Each barge had soft furnishings to make the journey as comfortable as possible.[92] The royal barge was often accompanied by the 'king's privy botes', presumably carrying his wardrobe stuff and body-servants.[93] Sometimes the barge was used purely for recreation as when in 1539 'the kyngs grace toke hys barge at whytte-halle and rowyd uppe to lambethe and had hys drumys and fyfes playng and so rowd upe and downe the tems a hour after the evenyng after yvnsong'. Occasionally it was lent by the King as a mark of

95. 'My Lord Goes by Water to Greenwich', from an illustrated copy of George Cavendish's *Life of Wolsey*, by Dr Stephen Batman, 1578. Clearly shown are the privy steps guarded by heraldic beasts and a late sixteenth-century barge on its way to Greenwich, in sketch form in the background.

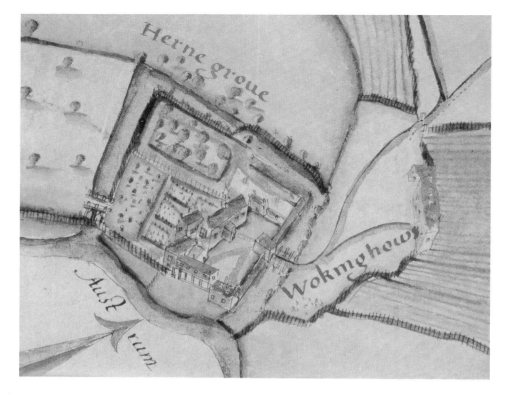

reason of the nearnesse to greenwiche (which . . . is through the benefite of the river, a seate of more commoditie) hath not beene so greatly esteemed'.[96] Eltham was a victim of its landlocked position (fig. 92). A house that did not lie on the River Thames or was not at least accessible by water, could fall from favour. Elsewhere, if access by water could be improved, this was done. For instance at Woking in 1533–4 (fig. 96), considerable effort was expended to upgrade river access: 'takyng downe old wharffes in the mote goying about the said manor and takyng upe a greate grate of tymbar lyng in the said moote with takyng uppe of dyverse pyles in the same to clenche the same moote for the ronnyng water to come throwe for bargs to have passage in the same moote'.[97] The level of the River Wey was raised by building 'a newe damme in the ryver to torne the same ryver into the moote . . . for the kynge to passe into the medys'.[98] The operation was completed with a bridge or landing-stage described as 'a newe brydge made over the ryver for bargys to passe under with a greate gate made and sett in the myddis of the same brydge'.[99]

Such bridges, or landing-stages, were not novelties. St Thomas's Tower at the Tower of London is the most elaborate surviving medieval example (fig. 11); but information survives on several Tudor structures. The bridges at Baynard's Castle (fig. 51) and Whitehall (plan 13) have been excavated and early views of those at Hampton Court (figs 72, 97, and plan 6), Whitehall (see plan 13, fig. 98), Richmond (see plan 11, fig. 43) and Greenwich (fig. 48) survive. At Whitehall there were two bridges, the great bridge and the privy bridge (fig. 99). The privy bridge led directly into the royal lodgings and via a short gallery into the privy gallery (see plan 13). Such a direct link to the privy lodgings leaves no doubt that only the King and Queen used the privy bridge and that everyone else had to enter the palace either by land or at the great bridge. The bridge at Richmond also seems to provide entry into

97 (below). Hampton Court, Surrey, from the south, from a drawing by A. van den Wyngaerde, *c*.1558. A covered gallery linked the watergate to the south-east corner of the king's lodgings.

favour to certain figures, for example the Neapolitan ambassador in 1494.[94]

There are occasional references to the repair and maintenance of the King's barge in the works accounts. In 1535 when £4. 2s. 1d. was spent on its maintenance, the King's principal barge was called the *Lyon*. A new dock was built for mooring the royal barge at Whitehall in the 1540s with a boat-house over it as a shelter.[95] The choice of Whitehall for this dock is a further indication of the palace's primacy towards the end of the reign.

The King used the royal barge to journey between most of the greater houses around London. The exception was Eltham, which Lambarde says 'by

98. Whitehall Palace, from the east (riverside) by A. van den Wyngaerde *c*.1558. Wyngaerde's drawing is very confused and seriously misaligns the parts of the palace. The privy stairs are, however, shown in great detail; immediately behind them the inner court is shown; to its left the northern (or Holbein) gate and behind it the cockpit. The building to the left of the gate is the great close tennis-play. The privy garden occupies the left-hand side of the drawing.

White Hall

Lambeth

99. Whitehall Palace, from a seventeenth-century engraving. The great and privy stairs are shown. The great stairs remained a public right of way through the palace during the reign of Henry VIII.

96 (facing page top). Woking (or Oking), Surrey, from a survey by John Norden, 1607. Both Henry VII and Henry VIII favoured this house. A long gallery can be seen above a cloister facing the river in the south; the only other structures that can be identified are the great hall and the gatehouse. The river, moats and bridges can be clearly seen. The works undertaken in 1533–4 were on the east and so may relate to the small square building (a watergate?) at the bottom right of the house.

the palace at a point which would suggest that only the King and Queen could use it (see plan 11). At Greenwich the river-projection built by Henry VIII on the face of his father's frontage (see plan 3) probably contained a stair and thus he could land and ascend directly into his privy closet. At Hampton Court the river-gate was situated much further from the royal lodgings than at the other greater houses. A long gallery connected the gate with a privy stair situated on the south front of the building allowing direct access from the linking gallery, via the stair, to the privy lodgings (see plan 6).[100]

Henry VIII's extensive use of barges as means of transport allowed him to move with ease directly from privy lodging to privy lodging without entering the public domain at all, except during the harshest winters. Giustinian wrote in 1517 'though I could not go to Greenwich by Water, owing to the very thick ice, the journey by land likewise being difficult on account of the frozen and dangerous roads, I however rode thither'.[101] The King and Queen also, on occasion, were forced to ride, as in December 1536 when 'the Thamis of London al frosen over wherfore the kynges Majestie wyth hys beutifull spouse quene Jane, roade throughout the citie of London to Grenewich'.[102] Ice was not the only drawback to river travel, for the tides always had to be taken into account. In July 1520 'the shiriffes of London made [the French] gentilmen a goodly dyner, and for that the tyde was commodious for theym to Richemount aboute noone . . . were then after conveyed thider in a barge'.[103] The importance of river travel, and the need to know the exact times of the tides explains why Henry VIII, in asking Nicholas Kratzer to install the astronomical clock at Hampton Court in 1541, requested that it should tell the times of high and low tides at London Bridge (fig. 100).[104]

100. Hampton Court, Surrey, the astronomical clock. Designed by Nicholas Kratzer and made by Nicholas Oursain, the clock tells the hour, month, day of the month, position of the sun in the ecliptic, the number of days since the beginning of the year, the phase of the moon, its age in days, the hour of the day at which it crosses the meridian and thence the time of high water at London Bridge. Made before the revelations of Copernicus and Galilleo, the sun moves round the earth. Oursain was subsequently appointed Keeper of the Clock at 4d. a day.

102 (facing page bottom left). Westenhanger, Kent. Henry VIII acquired this house by exchange in 1540 and it was used by him and particularly Princess Mary, who had a large lodging there. An eighteenth-century house now nestles in the remains of the castle.

Specialisation and the lesser house

Henry VIII's lesser houses were divided into those which he regularly used on progress (usually as satellites to greater houses) and those which were set aside for specific uses. Amongst those not on his regular route there were two particular groups; those belonging to his wives and those used by his children. Each of Henry's wives held, in turn, Baynard's Castle (fig. 51).[105] Baynard's Castle was, in effect, the Queen's official residence in London, almost never visited by the King himself. In addition to Baynard's Castle each of Henry's queens was granted lesser houses in the vicinity of London. In

June 1509 Catherine of Aragon received Havering (fig. 103) as her country seat.[106] There in 1519, Catherine invited her husband and other guests and 'for their welcommyng she purveyed all thynges in the moste liberallest maner: and especially she made to the kyng suche a sumpteous banket that the kyng thanked her hartely'.[107] Other than Havering, Catherine had no other houses for her exclusive use.

The situation with Anne Boleyn was markedly different: while still the King's mistress in 1532, Anne obtained the house at Ditton (fig. 104) and another at Hanworth. Hanworth, originally an acquisition of Henry VII's, was a lesser house attached to Hampton Court and was improved at some cost for Anne. The accounts for the alterations, which were carried out at the King's expense, mention her closet and dining chamber, and 'a table for the nether ende of my ladyes great chamber for my ladyes gentilwomen'. On her marriage both Baynard's Castle and Havering passed to Anne, and in early 1536 Collyweston in Northamptonshire was settled on her by Act of Parliament.[108] Both Baynard's Castle and Havering formed part of the jointure of Jane Seymour, but of the two only Baynard's Castle was settled on her three successors. In July 1540 Anne of Cleves obtained, as part of her divorce settlement, The More and Richmond. The adulterous Catherine Howard had only Baynard's Castle. But Catherine Parr was more fortunate, receiving as part of her jointure Chelsea, Hanworth and Mortlake in mid-1544.[109]

In addition to the lesser houses which the King's wives occupied, major additions were carried out at all the greater houses for their convenience. The work done at Hampton Court, Hanworth, the Tower of London and Whitehall for Anne exceeded anything done for the other five; Anne was almost certainly the only wife with a keen interest in architecture. The work done on successive building campaigns in the Queen's lodgings at Hampton Court was the most extensive, the only wife not to derive any real benefit from it being Anne of Cleves. This programme of providing lavish lodgings for his wives reached its culmination when a totally new Queen's lodging was built for Catherine Parr in the east range of the base court, and the previous lodgings abandoned.[110]

The royal children were likewise granted, or at least accommodated at, various of the lesser houses. Princess Mary was the victim of all sorts of machinations over her accommodation. Mary's early upbringing was mainly at Hanworth and Ditton but after her household was fully constituted in 1525 she took up residence at the Worcestershire house of Tickenhill (fig. 101). Closer to London, Wolsey had provided her with lodgings at Hampton Court. During her parents' divorce, when doubt was cast upon her legitimacy, she lived at Beaulieu,[111] but following the judgement at Dunstable she had to move into less desirable property, as was noted by the imperial ambassador in October 1533: 'the king has caused the princess to dislodge from a very fine house [Beaulieu] to a very inconvenient one [Hertford], and has given the former . . . to Lord Rochford the lady's [Anne Boleyn's] brother'.[112] In addition to Hertford, Mary stayed at a variety of houses including The More, Woodstock and Hunsdon. After the death of her mother and the fall of Anne Boleyn in 1536 she made a humiliating submission to the King. As a mark of reconciliation, Jane Seymour persuaded Henry to give Mary lodgings at Hampton Court once more[113] and at Greenwich. Mary's room at Greenwich, for which a breakfast table was made in 1537, overlooked the river, and so cannot have been far from the King's lodging.[114] In the 1540s Mary had lodgings at several of the King's lesser houses, at Ampthill, Enfield, Guildford, Working, Otford and Westenhanger (fig. 107).[115] She also received a splendid river-side lodging at Whitehall, completed in 1543 (see plan 13, fig. 83). Her Whitehall lodging was a small courtyard house which the building accounts describe as 'my lady maries newe lodging'.[116] It was built on the two southernmost bastions of the river wall which were used as bases for two-storey bay

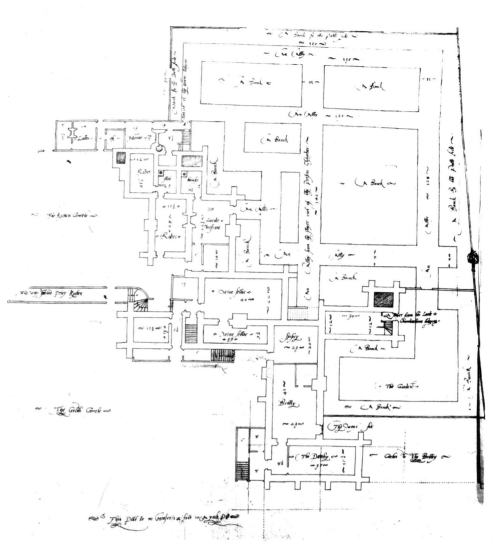

windows and, between these, oriel windows were set at first-floor level. The intervening wall spaces were also filled with windows to make the east wall of the lodging more or less entirely glass on the first floor. Both the luxury and prestige of this lodging accorded with her continuing favour with her father and her position as second in line to the throne.

The history of Princess Elizabeth's accommodation is equally chequered. During her mother's lifetime she was, of course, well provided for. She was born at Greenwich, and the Queen's lodgings at Eltham nearby were converted into a nursery for her. A cradle was set up with an 'irne brase to bayre the canyby over the said cradell'. She was given a great chamber, dining chamber, raying chamber and bedchamber. After Anne Boleyn's execution, Mary and Elizabeth were both bastards in the same boat and were both treated with distance but consideration; Elizabeth had lodgings at Hampton Court

103 (above). Havering, Essex. A plan of the house in 1578 by John Symonds.

101 (left top). Tickenhill House, Worcestershire by William Stukeley, 1721. Built by Henry VII for Prince Arthur as Prince of Wales and subsequently occupied by Princess Mary. The house was the lesser country house in the orbit of Ludlow Castle where the Council of the Marches was based.

104. Ditton House, Buckinghamshire, from John Norden's map of 1607. Early in Henry VIII's reign much was spent on improving this house and the young Princess Mary spent time there. It seems to have been a substantial moated house with a large lodge in the park.

throughout the reign, also permanent lodgings at Greenwich.[117]

It is no matter of surprise that special provision was made for the Prince of Wales. Born on 12 October 1537, he had a household of his own strictly regulated and directed by Sir William Sidney before he was eighteen months old.[118] At Hampton Court a new set of lodgings was built for him (see plan 8, fig. 105). His privy chamber was known as the nursery and his bedchamber 'the rocking chamber' after the task performed by his 'rockers'. Nearby were a garderobe, which still survives, a bathroom and privy kitchen. In addition to these inward rooms the young Prince had a set of outward chambers, a watching chamber and a presence chamber approached by a grand staircase.[119] Hampton Court was the grandest of the lodgings prepared for Edward at the greater houses. At Greenwich he was provided with lodgings next to the King's (see plan 4).[120] Prince Edward also had lodgings at Enfield, Tyttenhanger and Hatfield, and for much of 1546 he lived at Hunsdon, where his portrait was painted (figs 106, 107).[121]

At first sight it seems odd that Edward had no

105. Hampton Court, Surrey. North side of chapel court; although largely rebuilt after a fire of 1886, this range is still mainly that built for Prince Edward by Henry VIII. The projection in the corner on the right was his garderobe.

accommodation provided for him at Whitehall, particularly as his wardrobe seems to have been stored at Durham House adjoining Charing Cross.[122] But there is good reason to believe that St James's Palace, described by the Spanish ambassador in 1553 as a house 'built by the late King Henry VIII as a residence for the royal children'[123] was his official residence, and its proximity to Whitehall made rooms for the prince unnecessary in the palace (figs 108, 110). Certainly, parts of St James's were called the 'princes lodging' as late as 1588–9,[124] and it looks as though James I was following an Henrician precedent when in 1604 he gave St James's to Prince Henry for his official residence as Prince of Wales.[125]

106. Portrait of Prince Edward by an anonymous hand, *c*.1546. The significance of the view of Hunsdon in the background is that the prince spent much time there in his youth.

Henry VIII also provided accommodation for at least one of his illegitimate offspring, Henry Fitzroy, Duke of Richmond. Margaret Beaufort's favourite residence at Collyweston was Richmond's principal house from 1531 to 1536 when he surrendered it in exchange for Baynard's Castle and Durham House, neither of which he lived sufficiently long to enjoy.[126] In the absence of a legitimate male heir to the King in the late 1520s, Richmond had enjoyed an unrivalled position at Court and, interestingly, he lodged at St James's and was eventually to die there on 22 July 1536.[127]

Henry VIII's legitimate children did not always live apart. All three shared Christmas together in 1542 at the lesser house of Enfield. We learn of the Prince's lodging there and of Lady Elizabeth's and Lady Mary's chambers. Edward had his own privy kitchen, and a room was provided for his nurses.[128] After becoming Queen in July 1543 Catherine Parr promoted similar reunions, particularly at her house at Hanworth. Even more than Hanworth the Hertfordshire house of Ashridge fits the appellation 'nursery house' for it became, after 1539, the venue

108 (above). St James's, Westminster from the east, a mid-seventeenth-century view by an unknown artist. In the centre is Inigo Jones's chapel of 1625. To its right is the gatehouse, to its left the chimneys and turrets of the king's lodgings. The tower is a small donjon built on the south front near the king's bedchamber.

107. Detail of fig. 106, showing a view of Hunsdon House, Herts. Recent archaeological work has made the form of Hunsdon clearer, but still little can be made of this sketchy view. On the right, however (and corroborated by documents), is a donjon in which Henry VIII sometimes ate in private.

109. St James's Westminster. An early nineteenth-century drawing from the north by Thomas Shepherd. To the right of the gatehouse is the chapel whose 'east' window can be seen.

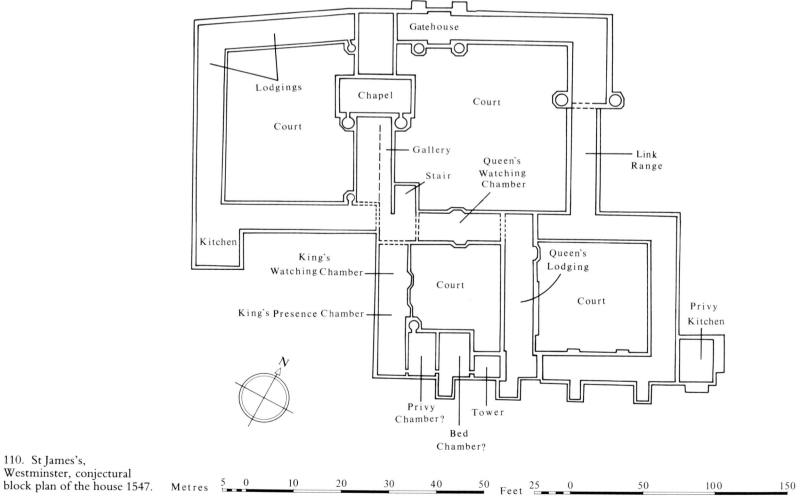

110. St James's, Westminster, conjectural block plan of the house 1547.

Metres

Feet

for a series of prolonged and frequent stays by all Henry's children.[129]

The role of the Keepers

Since earliest times royal manors had had keepers. In the Middle Ages the repair of manors which were not directly administered from the King's Chamber were the responsibility of the Keeper.[130] With the development of the Office of the King's Works the importance of keeperships declined, but still in Henry VIII's reign occasional references indicate that the Keeper undertook minor repairs.[131] Increasingly, his responsibility towards the fabric was confined to housekeeping; Household regulations commanded the Keeper to 'sweepe and make cleane the fflowers, walles wyndowes and roffes . . . before he hath his fee for the keepinge of the said place'.[132]

A list of the King's Keepers from Richard III's reign indicates that the Keeper of a house was only one of several associated with each building. At Havering for instance, in addition to the Keeper of the manor house, there were Keepers of the park, warren and park gate.[133] Although the names of the Ricardian Keepers are not known, from references to the Keepers of houses in the reign of Henry VIII it is clear that they were generally favoured courtiers;[134] Henry VIII's appointee at Byfleet, Chobham and Oatlands, Sir Anthony Browne, is a good example. More significant is the fact that the King's principal houses were kept by the principal courtiers. Whitehall was kept by Sir Anthony Denny and Greenwich by Sir William Compton, both Grooms of the Stole, which accounts for their choice as Keepers of the two most important houses during their tenure as Groom. Evidently it was considered essential for these two with their extensive privy lodgings to be kept by high-ranking members of the Privy Chamber. The keeperships of lesser houses, such as Beaulieu or Wanstead, rarely visited by the King, were used as sinecures, the fees attached to them treated as rewards, and the recipients permitted to use the houses as if their own. For instance the keepership of Beaulieu was held successively by Nicholas Carew, William Carey, George Boleyn, Robert, Earl of Sussex, and the Marquess of Northampton.[135]

The Keeper was generally provided with two lodgings. A fairly substantial lodging in the house itself and a proper house in the park or gardens nearby. At Whitehall, Thomas Alvard had a lodging off the tiltyard gallery[136] and also a lodging within the new park (fig. 81).[137] The Keeper's house at Hampton Court was large and comfortable, it had a hall and a kitchen, a buttery and lodgings over the hall.[138] In 1535 the house of the Keeper at Greenwich had an extra room added to it.[139] A new lodge was built for Sir Francis Bryan the Keeper of Ampthill in 1538 and the same year the Keeper of Oatlands was built a new lodge with a hall and parlour.[140] The Keeper of the house shared with the Cofferer of the Household the official responsibility of keeping the keys.[141] But it was the Keeper alone who kept the keys when the Court was absent. At Enfield carpenters were paid for 'makyng and hangyng of a newe dore in the corner of the brekwall by the hall dore for newell the kepar to laye in hys keys'.[142] When the Court arrived, the Keeper would hand over the keys to the Cofferer. Each door in a royal house had a lock, and the wine-cellars had two.[143] At Hampton Court the King had a special lock put on his reserve store of 'paynted bords' (paintings).[144] Some keys were more important than others, and those to the royal lodgings were of course the most important. The King had his own locksmith, Henry Romains, who travelled around with the Court ensuring that the correct locks were on the correct doors and that the keys were distributed to those eligible. To help him in this task he had two assistants.[145] Sometimes local locksmiths would be called in to reinforce security. Such an occasion was when the baby Prince Edward came to The More. The accounts list 'ii lockis spente on the dores yenste the prynsis comyng' and 'new crokyd boltis for the utter doris of my lorde princis lodging'.[146]

Clearly the critical factor was who should be issued with which keys. Of the two types of keys, called 'masters' and 'by-keys' only Henry and a handful of others held masters — and the King's holding of these often led to master keys being referred to as the 'King's keys'. The Queen would, likewise, have her own set of master keys. This privilege is vividly demonstrated at Queen Catherine Howard's disgrace when she was confined to her chambers, but was allowed to retain her 'privy keys' and thus not be a prisoner in her own lodgings.[147] These privy keys were presumably her masters which gave access to the privy lodgings.

The locks into which these keys fitted were moved around in advance of the King on progress. At Woking two dozen locks were kept in store ready for the King's arrival[148] but at the greater houses they were certainly permanent fixtures. That is not to say that they were not changed. Several times the accounts indicate that all the locks in the royal lodgings were changed and new keys issued. In August 1541 Romains changed all the locks in the King's lodgings to fit 'his new keys'.[149] A single royal lock of the period from Beddington is preserved in the Victoria and Albert Museum, London (fig. 111).[150] The Groom of the Stole was in charge of the distribution of the keys to the King's lodgings.

111. The Beddington Lock. A lock formerly at Beddington Place, Surrey, one of the King's houses inventoried on his death in 1547. The lock has two keyholes which operate two separate bolts. They can be operated at the same time by the insertion of a pin.

Romains delivered all new keys, by-keys and masters, to Henry Norris, and later to Thomas Heneage.[151] The Groom then distributed them, as instructed by the King, to members of the Privy Chamber. In addition to high-ranking members of the Privy Chamber, certain other people were given masters on a 'need for access' basis. In February 1538 James Nedeham was given by-keys to the garden door at Greenwich to enable him to go about his business without inconvenience.[152]

Chapter 6

STYLE AND FORM

IN 1477 THE FORCES OF LOUIS XI destroyed the Burgundian army and its leader, Charles the Bold, at the Battle of Nancy. With Charles the Bold fell the whole great edifice of the Burgundian state founded by his great-grandfather. With the collapse of Burgundian power the way was left open for France to resume continental dominance, first under Charles VIII, then under Louis XII and Francis I. In 1494, Charles VIII, with the biggest army Europe had ever seen, invaded Italy and conquered Naples. It was the start of twenty-one years of French involvement in Italy which sucked almost every state in Europe into a mesh of alliances.[1] For France, at least, the shift in the political and military focus of Europe to the Italian peninsular states caused a cultural shift also. After 1494 soldiers and diplomats, many the richest and most influential men in their own lands, flowed to Italy and on their return helped diffuse Italian ideas throughout Europe. The wealth, power and intellectual curiosity of the north began to draw a steady stream of books, engravings and craftsmen into northern Europe, creating the possibility of a new decorative vocabulary for northern European artists.

As French involvement in Italy helped to bring elements of the Italian Renaissance to France, English intervention in France helped to bring elements of the French Renaissance to England. In June 1513 Henry VIII crossed the Channel at the head of a magnificent army.[2] The war itself was, at least in Henry's terms, a success. But it had an impact unplanned — and certainly not anticipated — by the war leaders. The young King's Court met the Courts of both the Emperor Maximilian I and the Regent of the Netherlands, Margaret of Austria. The three entourages met twice, first for three days of feasting in Lille, and then, at the fall of Tournai, for three weeks of celebratory revels, balls and jousts to mark the capture of the city.[3] These encounters had an impact on the English similar to that of the marriage of Charles the Bold and Margaret of York in 1468. Once again, the English Court had a chance to observe, at close quarters, the most fashionable courtiers in Europe.

In some respects the most important, and certainly the longest lasting, effect of the war was the rekindling of the English Court's love-affair with France. Henry VII had visited the French Court and must have known its buildings. He brought his Household into line with French (and Burgundian) Household organisation by creating a new Household department, the Privy Chamber, in about 1495. He also created the new Yeomen of the Guard in imitation of the French King.[4] The process started under Henry VII accelerated under his son. During the campaign of 1513 Henry, at the 'Battle of the Spurs', captured several important French nobles and treated them with great honour in his camp. The treaty signed after the English withdrawal provided for French hostages to be held in England as guarantors of the peace, and these Frenchmen graced the English Court for several years.[5] Diplomatic connections between the two countries continued and Hall records the behaviour of the King's minions (or playmates) when they went to France in 1518 to ratify the Treaty of London:

> They, with the French kyng roade daily disguysed through Paris throwing egges, stones and other foolish trifles at the people . . . when thay came again to England they were all Frenche, in eating, drynkyng and apparell, yea, and in French vices and bragges, so that all the estates of England were by them laughed at . . . nothing by them was praised, but if it were after French turne.[6]

The final seal upon the influence of France came with the festivals connected with the Field of Cloth of Gold. There the English and French Courts intermingled allowing a full exchange of fashions.

The King himself was equally enamoured of France and all things French, and the English royal household and administration underwent periodic but often short-lived spurts of Frenchification throughout the reign. In 1518, members of the King's Privy Chamber were briefly re-named Gentilhommes de la Chambre, and in 1540 the Lord Chamberlain was re-named the Grand Maistre d'Hostel du Roy after French practice. The Court was largely bilingual and there were close personal connections between the personnel of the Privy Chambers of Francis I and Henry VIII.[7]

Between 1477 and 1520 an important change had been wrought in the cultural alignment of the English Court: the Court of Burgundy was no more and the French Court had won back the cultural influence it had temporarily lost to Burgundy, and France itself was looking south, towards Italy, both in its political and its artistic ambitions and the artistic interests of the English Court swung south with it. These interests were fuelled by direct links between the Court of Henry VIII and several northern Italian courts. Since the reign of Henry VII there had been close ties with the Court of Urbino. In 1474 Federigo da Montefeltro of Urbino had been elected a Knight of the Garter and early in 1504 the King sent ambassadors to offer the same honour to Federigo's son Guidobaldo. Guidobaldo was unable or disinclined to attend the installation himself and sent Baldesar Castiglione, who deputised at the ceremony at Windsor in 1506. Castiglione's *Book of the Courtier*, inspired by his service at the Court of Urbino and eventually published in 1527, influenced such English publications as Sir Thomas Elyot's *The Boke Named the Governor*, published in 1531. Another figure from Urbino who was to be highly influential at the early Tudor Court was Polydore Vergil, who had first come to England as deputy for Adriano Castelli, the Papal collector, and who was invited by Henry VII to compose a history of England in 1506. More direct and wider contact with northern Italy came through the small but significant English contingent at the crucial Battle of Pavia in 1525; both soldiers and eye-witnesses from this event returned to England after a prolonged stay in Italy. Finally, the passage of diplomats and senior churchmen during the King's 'great matter' should be considered — another example of interesting but ultimately unresolvable direct contacts with Italy.[8]

Yet England did not abandon its links with the Netherlands and the German states, who themselves, via another route, were becoming influenced by Italian events and were developing an Italian artistic vocabulary. This was even more the case after the Reformation when the traffic of French craftsmen and designers all but dried up, and the single greatest influence on royal architectural decoration came, in fact, not from France or Italy but from Northern Germany and the Netherlands. One of the first signs of a cultural realignment can be seen in the adoption of new fashions in Court festivals. As early as 1512 Hall records in his chronicle that on Epiphany night 'the Kyng with a .xi other were disguised, after the maner of Italie, called a maske, a thyng not seen afore in Englande'.[9] Hitherto Court festivals had largely taken the form of feats of arms, dominated by entries by pageant cars knights, and elaborate allegories: such entertainments had followed Burgundian precedents. But after the Tournai campaign such semi-drama with its speeches, challenges and disguising was abandoned in favour of an emphasis on heraldry, devices and horse armour.[10]

The change was as sudden as it was permanent and it seems as if the new form of tournament reflected the Court's recent French experiences.[11] The first tournament of the campaign in 1513 was during the Court's three-day stay in Lille. For it, a pavilion was set up for the King and his guests and 'there were only lists of planks and no barrier at the sides', nor were there any pageant cars. But these novelties were small compared to the 'new kind of tournament' held the following day. This event was held indoors in an enormous room paved with black marble, and to prevent them from damaging the floor, the horses were shod with felt.[12] Clearly, the greatest novelty in this event was the fact that it was held indoors, but the forms adopted during the combat also differed from the English custom. Returning to England victorious, with hostages in tow, Henry instituted the new kind of tournament at home. Henceforward the Burgundian-style pageant was replaced by the new form seen in France; less magnificent, in that the ostentatious pageant cars were abandoned, it was more sophisticated and closer to the Renaissance indoor fête.[13]

Court festivals have been taken as one example of the effect of the French war on the English Court. Change could also be seen, from about 1513, in the Revels department which began to adopt a new vocabulary of decoration. The word 'antique' begins to appear in the accounts and not long after in reports of the festivals themselves.[14] 'Antique', throughout the reign of Henry VIII, normally signified grotesque-work but could be applied to any architectural or decorative form with a reference to Italy or ancient Rome. The use of the antique or grotesque in applied decoration had social and political significance, being linked, as it was, with a general growing awareness of 'empire'. It was also the principal new form of decoration adopted in England during Henry's reign.

In the Rome of the 1490s a group of daring painters began to explore the maze of underground passages and caverns which made up the remains of the buried rooms of the Golden House of Nero on the Esquiline Hill. In these buried chambers or *gròtte*, on their hands and knees and by the light of flaming torches, Pinturicchio, Morto da Feltre, Pietro Luzzi and their colleagues began to record ancient Roman decorative schemes. They were eventually to be named after the places in which they were found, *gròtte* or grotesques.[15] Soon painters

In the painting, the inscription reads: NATIVITAS TVA DEI GENITRIX VIRGO GAVDIVM ANNVNTIAVIT VNIVERSO MVNDO

such as Pinturicchio were using the grotesque to great effect on contemporary commissions such as the walls of the Vatican Loggetta and Sala dei Pontefici and the Bathroom of Clement VII in the Castel Sant'Angelo. As a form of decoration it was an instant success and by 1502 Pinturicchio's client for a library in Siena could specify in the contract that he wished the vault to be decorated with grotesque-work.[16] Perhaps the best known Italian example of the grotesque is the private loggia of Pope Leo X in the Vatican Palace in Rome. Here Raphael co-ordinated a scheme of decoration, using as his helpers Giulio Romano and Giovanni da Udine; the latter was, according to Vasari, in charge of the grotesque-work.[17]

The grotesque, in opposition to earlier forms of Renaissance decoration, and those of northern European late Gothic, was generally inorganic and unnatural. Foliage, festoons and garlands were largely banished and in their place came masks, weapons, vessels and plates with inscriptions. These were linked together in an arbitrary manner, usually in strips, often with a spinal candelabrum around which the other motifs were grouped. At first grotesques were used as embellishments in archi-tectural compartments, especially within pilaster strips (figs 112, 113, 115). Gradually the borders of the compartments themselves began to take on an important role and became a sort of twisting, curling climbing frame for the grotesques. In this

112. Domenico Ghirlandaio, *Birth of the Virgin*, S. Maria della Maria, Florence. This Florentine interior of the 1480s shows an early manifestation of the grotesque in interior decoration. The decorated pilasters (see fig. 115), the panels with tablets with mottoes and the painted frieze can all be closely paralleled in English royal work of the 1520s and '30s.

87

are not easily answered. Clearly the knowledge was at first held by a few craftsmen, men who can be identified, and who certainly did not travel as far north as England. The new designs were therefore seen by others who cannot have held the information in their heads but must have turned to portable visual sources. Whether these were Italian pattern-books or sketches taken on site cannot be certain as so very few survive, but it is likely that printed books played an important part in the transmission of new designs to northern Europe and particularly to England.

Printing had made possible the rapid reproduction of decorative motifs and their relatively cheap sale and distribution. Certainly, in the Rome of the late 1490s, men such as Nicoletto da Modena, Antonio da Brescia and Giovanni Pietro da Birago were publishing sheets of decorative motifs derived from the grotesques of the Roman *gròtte*. Probably the best known of these is a sheet by Pierino del Vaga, dated 1532, with a poem explaining that the drawing, taken from a *gròtta*, was intended for the use of artisans (fig. 114).[19] The circulation and availability of such sheets as del Vaga's is almost impossible to document, but that they circulated and were available cannot be doubted. A series of engravings by Pietro da Birago dating from between 1505 and 1515 provided the motifs for woodwork in the chapel of the Cardinal d'Amboise's house at Gaillon (figs 116–17).[20] But in France examples of grotesque-work can be found even earlier than this; the Louis XII wing at Blois, for instance, had grotesque pilaster strips.[21] Indeed, due to French military intervention in Italy and the passage of craftsmen and patrons either way, the development of the antique in France is more akin to that of northern Italy than England or the Netherlands.

War may have facilitated the transmission of ideas northwards but so did trade, and in a much more direct way. Not only did examples of Italian craftsmanship and artistry enter English ports but so did an increasing stream of printed source material. From the late 1460s books printed in Italy had been imported directly into England and by the early sixteenth century it was possible to obtain foreign books in England only months after their publication. John Yonge, a fellow of New College, Oxford, obtained works by Savonarola published in Paris only one month earlier.[22] As the fifteenth century drew to a close, although France and Italy remained important sources of printed materials it was Switzerland, the German states and the Netherlands which were to become the principal channel through which new printed decorative ideas flowed. During the second decade of the sixteenth century, Basle emerged as the centre of printing and the book trade

113. Carlo Crivelli, *Annunciation*, 1486. In figure 112 the grotesque decoration is painted, but here it is carved and moulded. The fashion for strips of grotesque decoration strung on candelabra such as this swept across Europe from the 1480s, reaching England in the first decades of the sixteenth century.

way strapwork was born — a new decorative vocabulary which eventually completely overwhelmed the grotesque itself.[18]

There is still a lingering idea amongst historians that England was a backwater and that these fashions did not reach the Court of Henry VIII until long after they were popular in Italy. Fashions in decoration, however, travelled just as fast as the craftsmen who executed them, and as fast as drawings and woodcuts of them could be transported. But questions about the transmission of the antique and more particularly about the transmission of the grotesque

Il poeta el pittor Vanno di pare
Et nra il lor ardire' tutto ad un segno
Si come espresso in queste' carte appare
Fregiare' dopre' & dartisitio degno

Di questo Roma ci puo essempio dare
Roma ricetto dogni chiaro ingegno
Da le cui grotte oue mai non saggior
Hor tanta luce asi bella arte torna

in Europe and as such became the central dissemination point for some sorts of designs. Johann Froben (d. 1527), led a sizeable group of Basle printers including Adam Petri and Andreas Cratander. Froben, in 1512, published the first Basle title-page in the antique style (fig. 118) designed by Urs Graf, the soldier, goldsmith and glass-painter who had fought in the Italian wars. Later Froben employed Hans Holbein the Younger who designed architectural frontispieces for him, including one dating from 1516 (fig. 119).[23]

English kings had been quick to realise the value of printed books: in an Act of Parliament of 1484 designed to limit the activities of Italian merchants, there had been a special exemption for printed books. Edward IV had been a patron of William Caxton, and Henry VII, who can be claimed to have been the founder of the English royal library, purchased books directly from French and Italian sources.[24] More important, however, was his appointment of Richard Pynson as King's Printer in 1504. It was Pynson who in 1518 produced the first English title-pages in the antique style (figs 120–21). The first was copied from a design by Urs Graf for Froben and the second, also from Froben, was designed by Holbein. Clearer evidence of the

influence of imported foreign woodcuts on English design would be hard to find.

The evidence afforded by books should be treated with some caution, as such title-pages were themselves only reflections of passing fashions, never trend-setters. More important were pattern-books. One published by Heinrich Vogtherr in Strasburg 1538 began by explaining why he assembled such a miscellaneous group of decorative designs, intended to adorn anything from the grandest palace to the head-dress of a merchant's wife: 'I . . . have assembled an anthology of exotic and difficult details that should guide the artists who are burdened with wife and children and those who have not travelled.'[25] The evidence for the use of patterns and pattern-books in the royal works in England, although not overwhelming, is wide enough to be entirely convincing. It is certain that both the client, the King himself, and the craftsmen owned pattern-books of one sort or another. It is unlikely that Henry ever undertook any such concerted search for ideas as Philip II of Spain, who, while he was building and decorating the Escorial, collected a library of ideas which included some 5,000 prints and drawings, in addition to the *Codex Escurialensis*. Henry did, however, own a small collection of patterns and pattern-books, which in 1547 was kept in the King's study at Whitehall:

> one white boxe conteyninge diverse writings
>   and paternes
> itm a booke of parchement conteyninge
>   dyverse paternes
> a gonne of brasse for a paterne
> a booke of paternes for phiosionamyes

The book of 'phiosionamyes' was removed from the study in November 1549 by Edward VI who wanted it for himself.[26] Henry VIII's collection was not restricted to Whitehall: at Greenwich there were two patterns for bridges in a closet by his bedchamber; there were also patterns at Hampton Court.[27] Many of these were probably unexecuted architectural and ornamental designs.

Only one complete royal pattern-book, or more properly a design manual, survives from Henry VIII's reign; it is a French treatise on geometry, handwritten and bound for him at the Greenwich bindery. It does not appear in any surviving inventory, nor does it bear the characteristic mark of the Westminster library. There is no doubt however that it was the personal property of the King.[28] The treatise, which is divided into four sections: 'des lignes', 'des plaines superfices', 'des figures corporelles ayans longueur largeur et profondeur' and 'aucunes questions en la practicque de geometrie' is illustrated with the five orders of architecture (fig. 123). However, it is not likely that this was

114 (previous page left). Perino del Vaga, a pattern-sheet, 1532.

115 (previous page right). Detail of fig. 112 showing a decorated pilaster.

116. Three engravings from a set of twelve giving designs of grotesques assembled as candelabra by Giovanni Pietro da Birago. The middle strip provided the source for the right-hand panel in fig. 117.

117 (facing page). Three carved wooden panels with roundels depicting St George and the Dragon, Cardinal Georges d'Amboise and a hunting scene, sixteenth century. From the chapel of the Château de Gaillon, Normandy, France.

118. Title-page designed by Urs Graf for Johann Froben in 1512. It was the first Basle frontispiece to be designed in the antique style.

119 (far right). Title-page designed by Hans Holbein the Younger for Johann Froben in 1516. It was actually a copy of a Nuremburg title-page, but Holbein added the renaissance detail.

120. Title-page to Thomas Linacre's translation of Galen. The design was undertaken by Urs Graf for Froben in 1518, but was copied by Richard Pynson in 1519.

121 (far right). Title-page designed by Holbein for Froben in Basle in 1516. It was first used in England by Pynson in 1518 and then became the title-page to Henry VIII's *Asserto Septem* in 1521.

representative of other pattern-books in the royal collection; an idea of the sort of book that the 'booke of parchement conteyninge dyverse paternes' at Whitehall was can perhaps be gained from such a book now in Sir John Soane's Museum in London (fig. 124). This book, a volume of designs on vellum, is a copy of a northern Italian pattern-book which might conceivably have been copied by an English craftsman or designer and brought to England.[29] The single sheet shown in figure 122 is Holbein's design for a gold and jewelled cup for Jane Seymour of 1536, and this represents a rare surviving sheet pattern.

Although it is interesting and important that Henry VIII owned such material, it was the patterns which were in the possession of his craftsmen which were more likely to have directly influenced the form of his buildings. Because of the very nature of artisan patterns, they have not survived; heavy use meant that, like herbals and other workmen's manuals, they wore out and were eventually disposed of. Likewise single sheets were often used on site and then thrown away. A· set of patterns which may have been of antiquework was owned by the Neapolitan Vincent Volpe, the King's Painter, who died in 1536. In his will he left a bundle of patterns to John Pegrome, who can probably be identified as a painter employed on the royal revels.[30]

Both extant royal buildings and furniture illustrate the possible use of pattern-books and sheets. The ceiling of the chapel at St James's has a design which is identical to a plate in the fourth book of Serlio's *Regole generali di architettura*, published in Venice in 1537 (figs 125–6). The ceiling is dated 1540 and bears the mottoes and cyphers of Henry and Anne of Cleves (fig. 265). The influence of Serlio, or possibly Peruzzi, may also be detected at Hampton Court in the ceiling of the so-called Wolsey Closet (figs 125, 127), whose design also appears in Serlio's book. In the sphere of furniture there is the small table-desk made of walnut and covered with painted and gilded leather now in the Victoria and Albert Museum (fig. 130): the lid is painted with the arms of Henry VIII held by trumpet-blowing putti, and on either side of the arms are the figures of Mars and Venus which appear to be after woodcuts by Hans Burgkmair.

Prints were not the only type of pattern circulating in the early sixteenth century. Henry VIII had a small brass pattern in his study at Whitehall, and workmen had moulds and templates from which they worked. Such templates had been commonly used throughout the Middle Ages, and during the early sixteenth century were still in common use for late Gothic detailing as much as for grotesque-work. For instance, while Wolsey was building Hampton Court he sent moulds for his mason there from

122. Design for a gold cup for Jane Seymour by Hans Holbein the Younger, 1536.

York Place. They would have been used as templates to cut stone mouldings. At the Field of Cloth of Gold another type of mould was used: Sir Nicholas Vaux wrote to Wolsey explaining that he had been informed that 'the duke of Suffolke hathe manye batons . . . and also divers of the kinges armes and bestes caste in moldes, whiche wold doo great ease

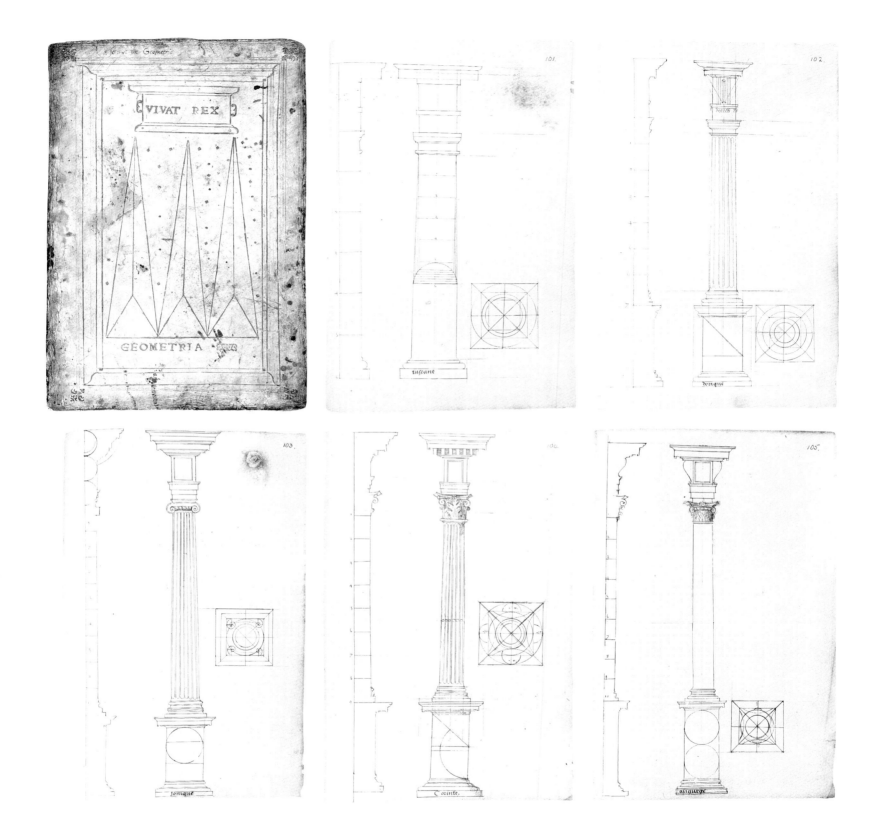

VIVAT REX

GEOMETRIA

tuscane

dorique

ionique

corinte

composite

101.

102.

103.

104.

105.

123 (facing page). Five pages and the cover of a French treatise on geometry owned by Henry VIII. The Tuscan, Doric, Ionic and Corinthian orders are illustrated with the sub-composite order.

124. One page from a vellum pattern-book in Sir John Soane's Museum. A royal connection cannot be proved, but is certainly not impossible. The book may have been copied by an English craftsman from a North Italian original.

125a and b. Sebastiano Serlio, *Regole Generali di Architettura*, Venice, 1537. Details of plates from the fourth book showing designs for ceilings.

and furtheraunce to the kinges busynes',[31] and asked for their loan for use at Guisnes. These were moulds in the modern sense, and once acquired they were a licence to produce huge quantities of decorative moulded-work to a single pattern. Some patterns and moulds lasted for many years. An example of

their longevity can be seen in the ceiling of Wolsey's south range at Hampton Court, decorated in the mid-1520s with a geometrical pattern enriched with moulded grotesque strips (fig. 128). The pattern on those strips is identical to that used on the ceiling of the King's Holyday Closet at Hampton Court,

96

126 (above). The ceiling of St James's chapel from Richardson's *Architectural Remains* (1840). The plate has been reversed.

127. Hampton Court, Surrey. The ceiling of the Wolsey Closet. The Prince of Wales feathers date this ceiling from after the birth of Edward VI in 1537. The ceiling was heavily restored in the 1880s and the room now known as the Wolsey Closet was made around it. It represents a type of moulded ceiling once ubiquitous in Henry VIII's houses.

128. Hampton Court, Surrey. Ceiling of the 'Wolsey rooms'. This fretted wooden ceiling, enriched with moulded strips of grotesque design, dates from c.1526.

129. Hampton Court, Surrey. Ceiling of the King's Holyday Closet, 1536.

130 (facing page). Henry VIII's writing desk; walnut and leather with painted and gilded decoration, made before 1527. The interior has a figure of St George and heads of Christ, Paris and Helen. The inside of the lid has Goliath (or Mars?) and Venus flanking the royal arms.

erected for the King in 1536 (fig. 129). The inference is that the same moulds were still in circulation and were used again up to ten years later.

The significance of heraldry

For a visitor to an early Tudor royal house these new elements of design would have been virtually submerged beneath the tidal wave of heraldic devices, mottoes and badges. Indeed it is the welter of heraldry that strikingly predominates, whatever

the basic design, in the chapel ceiling at St James's Palace, the great watching chamber at Hampton Court or the Wolsey Closet. To the contemporary this was the important part of the scheme which gave the viewer information, information which today has to be decoded, but in the sixteenth century was as easy to read as the year-letter on a car number-plate is today.

The penetration of the antique into England is what most interests art historians looking for progress and equating progression with aesthetic change wrought by the Italian Renaissance. There was no such fascination in the England of the early sixteenth century. The antique merely added a new series of motifs and ideas to the repertory of the late Gothic craftsman. It was novelty which first won the antique a foothold; then fashion entrenched it. From the 1490s the new learning from Italy was increasingly and deliciously mixed with the long-standing and dominant forms of chivalry.

Just as the Renaissance historian Polydore Vergil, who came from North Italy, wrote his *Historiae Anglicae* (1534), so did Edward Hall write his chivalric chronicle *The Union of the two Noble and Illustre Famelies York and Lancaster . . .* (1542). A man who embodied these two approaches and perhaps epitomised their mix was John Tiptoft, Earl of Worcester (1427–70). Tiptoft, the chivalric master of ceremonies who had formulated a set of rules to govern the tournaments of the Yorkist court in 1466, had also studied Latin in Padua and then in Florence and Rome, and had translated Cicero's *De amicitia*. He owned a manuscript, illuminated for him in Padua in c.1460–61, which had its title-page designed as an inscription on a marbled antique monument (fig. 131). There was nothing surprising or uncomfortable about this marriage of interests which, during the late fifteenth century, increasingly began to influence the visual arts.[32]

After 1450, sets of large-scale tapestries woven in Tournai and Brussels increasingly depicted scenes from classical history rendered in a contemporary chivalric mode. A well-documented set is the ten-piece series, the *Trojan Wars*, bought by Henry VII in 1488 (fig. 133); identical sets from the same cartoons were owned by patrons as diverse as Federigo da Montefeltro, Charles the Bold and the King of France. Another set which gained European popularity was the *History of Alexander* which was owned by Edward IV, Henry VII and Philip the Good of Burgundy. Such tapestries were housed in architectural interiors which reflected the same mix of mythologies. At the Field of Cloth of Gold the tapestries were surmounted by a frieze of moulded-work in which figures from classical mythology held the armorial bearings of Henry VIII and his ancestors.[33] A surviving architectural example of this

132. Portrait of a court
official by Hans Holbein the
Younger. This is one of two
portraits of Henrician court
officers by Holbein (this is in
New York, the other is in
Vienna). The officer wears
the Royal initials H[enricus]
R[ex] and may have had
other badges elsewhere on
his coat.

happy mix is the carved panel outside the chapel at
Hampton Court Palace (fig. 134). Probably first
executed for Cardinal Wolsey, the panel was later
altered to encorporate the arms and motto of the
King.

Henry III was the first English king to use architectural heraldic decoration, first at Westminster
Abbey, and then later at his own houses, carved in
stone or wood, cast in metal, fired in enamel, set in
glass and tiles, woven in hangings, painted on walls
or furniture. During the thirteenth century heraldry
became a standard part of the decorative vocabulary
of masons, joiners, painters and glaziers. Part of the
reason for its success was that heraldry provided an
easy repertory of highly decorative and coloured
ready-made motifs which could be repeated at will
by craftsmen. But more important was its ability
to convey messages about the owner of the arms.
The display of coats of arms indicated lordship and
affinity. Henry VIII expected his subjects to show
their allegiance, with great figures like Sir Thomas

131 (right). Manuscript of
Synesius Cyrenensis, *De
Laudibus Calvitii*, Padua,
c.1460–61. Commissioned
by John Tiptoft, it is a very
early appearance of antique
architectural decoration
owned by an Englishman.

More wearing collars of office that incorporated the Tudor emblems (fig. 296), and the King's personal servants dressed in royal livery, for example the grooms of his Privy Chamber wore a uniform with the Tudor rose and Henry's coat of arms (fig. 132). For the monarch such liveries revealed ownership and majesty, for a building heraldic decoration was the architectural equivalent to a livery. It was a livery that was vastly simplified to become instantly recognisable — the rose, the portcullis, the dragon and the greyhound — and one which was a superb vehicle for expressing magnificence, as its very origins lay in the field of rich and instant display.[34]

Heraldic imagery not only proclaimed ownership and allegiance, it carried additional messages; helping to abolish any remaining notion that the Tudors were upstarts by stressing their glorious and well-documented lineage. The use of heraldry thus had not only a decorative but a powerful dynastic and political potential. This led to a series of measures being taken by the early Tudor kings. Henry VII, in 1498–9, licensed two Kings of Arms to undertake a visitation to ensure that arms were not being abused by the gentry. Henry VIII took this further issuing letters patent under the Great Seal in April 1530 proclaiming that Thomas Benolt, Clarenceux King at Arms would undertake a visitation to, where necessary, 'reform all false armory and arms devised without authority, marks unlawfully set or made in scucheons, squares or lozenges, which scucheons, squares or lozenges be tokens of nobleness, and them to deface and take away wheresoever they be set . . . whether it be in stone, windows plate or any other . . .'.[35] Finally in 1542 an Act of Parliament made it a felony for any person to write or utter prophecies relating to the King, or anyone else, based on interpretations of 'Armes, feldes, beastes, fowles or other suche lyke things accustomed in armes cognisaunces badges or signets or by reason of lettres of the name of the King or of any other persone'. That this was taken seriously is borne out by the indictment and conviction of Henry Howard, Earl of Surrey, in 1546–7, whose use of arms and ensigns was considered to be appropriate only to the King and his heir apparent.[36]

The correct use of arms was therefore, almost

133. *The Trojan Wars*, Tournai tapestry of *c*.1480. This was woven from the same cartoons as the ten-piece set purchased by Henry VIII in 1488. Gothic heraldry and classical mythology deliciously combine in the composition.

tural heraldry was the direct consequence of the chivalric values of Henry VII and his son. It was under their patronage and that of their immediate predecessors that the art of chivalry reached its most elaborate external form. The tournaments of the Yorkists and early Tudors were the magnificent death-throes of medieval England. Henry VIII's wars with France were at least half a chivalric crusade.

Chivalric and heraldic imagery dominated the domestic buildings of Henry VII and his son. Today, despite 450 years of alterations, the first thing the visitor to Hampton Court sees is the coat of arms of Henry VIII carved in stone on the outer gatehouse (fig. 63).[41] This is but a faded reminder of a residence whose principal decoration was heraldry; the King's and Queen's badges and arms were carved on the hall roof, set in the windows of the outward rooms, painted on vanes held by beasts, moulded in compound on the ceilings and embroidered on hangings and upholstery (fig. 134). For a king who married as many times as Henry, heraldic decoration could pose a problem, and on each change of spouse glaziers and painters were required to alter all accessible heraldry: 'for xx vanes payntyd and new altered from quene annes armes unto quene janes . . . '.[42] Inaccessible badges remained, like those on the roof of the great hall at Hampton Court (figs 139a–d).

The Doche and other strangers

The intellectual fusion of native and foreign influences was matched, on the building site, by a

134. Hampton Court, Surrey. The royal arms outside the Chapel Royal, carved for Cardinal Wolsey and altered and repainted for Henry VIII after 1529.

literally, a matter of life and death. Royal painters, carvers and other workmen consequently had to ensure that they were using the correct forms in the decoration of the King's houses. Heraldic pattern-books were certainly owned and used by many of Henry VIII's craftsmen. In his will John Browne, Serjeant Painter to Henry VIII, refers to his 'great boke of armys, and my boke of trickys of armes, and my boke of armys and badges in my studye . . . '.[37] During the preparations for the Field of Cloth of Gold, Sir Nicholas Vaux asked Wolsey to give instructions to Sir Thomas Wriothesley, Garter King of Arms that he 'by th'advise of all other the kinges heraudes, do make a boke in picture of all the armes, . . . bestes, fowles, devises, badges and cognisances [of the] kinges highnes, the quenes grace, the Frenche king . . . '.[38] This book has not survived, but a book in Wriothesley's hand recording beasts and banners probably taken from architectural decoration does (fig. 137). Inevitably it is books such as this that do survive and not the patterns used by the painters on site.[39]

Architectural heraldic decoration reached its apogee in the late fifteenth and early sixteenth centuries, not only in England but across Europe. Two of the most significant English heraldic buildings, King's College Chapel, Cambridge, and Henry VII's Chapel, Westminster, date from this period. Both chapels proclaim a single message — the magnificence, permanence and triumph of the Tudor dynasty.[40] This Indian summer of architec-

The lord tho
mas wolsey
cardinall legat
de latere
archebisshop
of yerke
and chan
cellor of
Jngland

L. Roy henry
le viij et
de la comme

The duc of ferrare
hercules kinght of
the garter

137. A record by Sir
Thomas Wriothesley of arms
and beasts, including those
of Henry VIII, Francis I of
France and Cardinal Wolsey.
Such records were
maintained in order to
record architectural
decoration and to give advice
to heraldic painters.

135 (facing page bottom
left). Hampton Court,
Surrey. Fragment of a stone
shield bearing the arms of
Queen Jane Seymour,
originally held by a stone
lion. Jane Seymour's badge,
with its gateway, hawthorn
tree and golden phoenix, is
an excellent example of
Tudor elaboration, pregnant
with dynastic and political
symbolism.

136. (facing page bottom
right). The arms of Henry
VIII, formerly adorning the
outer gatehouse of Beaulieu,
Essex (see fig. 61).

combination of English and continental craftsmen. During the early sixteenth century there were numerous complaints about the infiltration of foreigners. Edward Hall explained how the influence of foreigners, especially from the Low Countries, affected the building and furnishing trades in particular . . .'for the duchmen bring over iron, timber, leather and wainscot ready wrought as nayles, locks, basketts, cupboards, stools, tables, chests, girdles with points, saddels and painted cloths'.[43] Legisla-tion had existed since the fourteenth century to control what were termed 'aliens' in London. During the fifteenth century the alien population of London and the suburbs rose rapidly, and during Henry VIII's reign three Acts of Parliament reinforced the measures to protect English craftsmen. The English attempted to use the monopolistic craft guilds, from which foreigners were generally excluded, to prevent aliens from working their trades, and so foreigners tended to congregate in the suburbs of

138a and b. Richmond, Surrey. Two stone statues formerly from the middle gate of Henry VII's house. Originally these two heralds would have been brightly painted and would have held gilded metal trumpets. Their task was to welcome visitors to Henry VII's principal country residence.

139a–d (below and facing page). Hampton Court, Surrey. Carved and painted badges from the roof of the great hall, *c.*1532.

London to avoid guild scrutiny. Two suburbs were particularly favoured, Westminster and Southwark, and by 1500 both of these contained concentrated pockets of Flemings and Germans who shared the generic name of 'Doche'.[44]

These foreigners were often skilled workmen and artisans, of whom a high proportion were connected with the building trade. These men had little difficulty in finding employment, for contemporary attitudes often favoured them above the English. For instance, since the mid-fifteenth century there had been a preference for Flemish bricklayers. In correspondence relating to the royal manor of Havering-Atte-Bower, the writer expresses a wish to find a 'ducher or a fleming' to cut the bricks for a new chimney.[45]

Evidence as to the degree to which the royal works had been penetrated by aliens only becomes available in the reign of Henry VIII. In the surviving Henrician Office of Works' accounts, there are about 3,500 named workmen whose trades are known. But only occasionally is their nationality mentioned, as in the case of John Delamayne, a French painter who also supplied wainscot to the royal works. More often we know where they lived, as, for example, the matlayer John Amsell, who is always described as being 'of southwark',[46] but this rarely gives any conclusive evidence to nationality.

The most effective way of identifying aliens in the accounts is to compare their names with the letters of denization and naturalisation for the years covering Henry's reign. During the 1540s, in response to tighter legislation against aliens, there were mass denizations: after the declaration of war with France in 1544, for instance, two denization rolls contain over 2,500 names.[47]

Joiners were responsible for much of the internal decoration of the King's houses, and evidence from the reigns of Henry VII and the Yorkists would tend to confirm that this was not a new phenomenon. The joiners were, more than almost any other trade, dominated by the Doche.[48] Accounts divide woodworkers into joiners and carpenters; there is a movement of personnel between the categories, but in general terms the joiners (or enbowers) were specialist carvers and the carpenters structural woodworkers. Of the several hundred joiners in the works accounts, the majority had Doche names. For example the name Johnson, a very common Doche name, appears over twenty times in the accounts: thirteen are joiners, three are bricklayers, there is one glazier, one plasterer, one plumber and a smith. Of the thirteen joiners called Johnson, eight lived in Southwark. Sometimes these trades ran in dynasties.[49] At other times distinct firms can be identified. The head of one such firm seems to have been a joiner named Harmon West who acquired denization in Southwark in 1541. West ran a workshop of joiners who worked for the King at Greenwich, Dartford, Richmond, Enfield and The More. At The More in 1541, there is an entry for 'harmon and his company at ii times to paye their bord 30s'. The 'company' comprised six other joiners — all with Doche names. West was not only involved in architectural joinery but was also commissioned to make furniture. Four joined tables from his workshop cost 8s. a joined form cost 2s. 8d. and stools cost 18d. each. His most important furniture commissions were for the King himself: West was Henry's official close-stool maker, supplying all the timber and ironwork ready-made to the upholsterers.[50]

All this suggests close-knit workshops of Doche joiners, many based in Southwark, working on the King's houses. This is largely confirmed by correspondence between the alien joiners and Wolsey. In the 1520s they petitioned him, stating that in Henry VII's reign during the building of Richmond Henry VII had set up mechanisms to ensure that the alien and native joiners co-operated. Now, they claimed, the Lord Mayor prosecuted them at the instigation of the native joiners.[51]

Another group of workmen dominated by Doche was the glaziers and, as with the joiners, the rot had set in for the English in the reign of Henry VII.

Indeed, from about 1500 all major royal glazing contracts went to foreigners, prompting the English glaziers, like the joiners, to remonstrate. Indeed, the act 'concerning the taking of aprentices by strangers' passed in 1523 was almost certainly a response to the complaints of the glaziers and joiners. Its tenth clause admitted that English craftsmen were incapable of meeting the desire of the King or his richest subjects for high-quality work: 'it shalbe laufulle to any Lorde of the Parliament and every other of the Kynges Subjectes having Londes and Tenementes to the yearly value of oon hundred poundes to take and reteign Estraungers Joyners and Glasyers in their servyce'.[52] This proviso allowed the rich to employ the aliens who possessed styles and possibly skills which the native craftsmen did not. The glaziers continued their fight against the aliens throughout the remainder of Henry's reign, never getting full satisfaction from the courts, which persisted in recognising that there was an important market for the aliens.[53]

Not only were the majority of joiners and glaziers aliens, but so were the other craftsmen who provided decorative finishes for his houses; the painters and moulders are another important example. At Hampton Court in the 1530s there was a decorative partnership between a moulder of antique-work called Robert Shynk and a painter called Henry Blankston. Most of the internal decoration that was not carved in stone or wood was moulded in a quick-setting instant compound called leather-mâché made from shreds of leather, size and brick dust. Shynk, who was evidently a Docheman, was one of the craftsmen with the knowledge to make leather-mâché and prepare the moulds. Shynk's unofficial partner was Henry Blankston who had originated in the Bishopric of Cologne and lived in Southwark. His work ranged widely: in 1529 he was painting heraldic beasts in the garden at Hampton Court, two years later he was painting heraldic decorations on furniture. He also painted targets for the King to shoot at and antique terracotta heads.[54] Both Shynk and Blankston were involved in decorating what was called the 'King's Long Gallery end' at Hampton Court which had a frieze of putti. Part of such a frieze survives at Hampton Court today (fig. 141).

Unfortunately, it is not possible to trace the provenance of the moulds used by Shynk, but their use was not confined to alien craftsmen. A highly successful royal interior decorator called Clement Urmenson must have had a set of moulds, which seem to have been made by him. During the preparations for the Field of Cloth of Gold the records state that 'the duke of Suffolk hathe many batons of Urmenson's making, and also divers of the kinges armes and bestes caste in moldes'.[55] Urmenson was

English, admitted as a freeman of the Grocers' Company in 1502. He subsequently worked for the Duke of Suffolk, possibly on Suffolk Place in Southwark, before playing a major role at the Field of Cloth of Gold where, with John Rastell, he decorated ceilings. In 1527 he worked on the banqueting hall at Greenwich. His next commissions were for Cardinal Wolsey at Esher and York Place, the latter turned into a royal commission when Henry VIII, in 1531, invited him to decorate the ceiling of his new gallery there.[56] It may be that the sort of battens and moulded work found in Wolsey's rooms at Hampton Court were his doing (fig. 128), but he was certainly one of the few natives to work on royal interiors in Henry's reign.

All the above-mentioned craftsmen were closely linked by family ties and friendship. Henry Blankston's will mentions the fact that his daughter married the son of Galyon Hone, the King's Glazier. His will was, perhaps significantly, overseen by Harry Harmanson, a bookseller. John Browne the King's Painter included amongst the beneficiaries of his will Andrew Wright, who was eventually to become Serjeant Painter, and also John Hethe. The remainder were mostly painter-stainers.[57] This network of Doche connections throughout Westminster and Southwark was highly dependent on both work and favour from the King. Indeed, the Acts which restricted their activities had specific exclusions for the royal family; in September 1540 a writ to the mayor and sheriffs of London suspended the execution of the Act against strangers where servants of the King, Queen and royal children were concerned.[58] These exclusions were particularly important bearing in mind that such key royal craftsmen as the King's Blacksmith and Locksmith were Doche.

Although the Doche were, numerically, by far the largest alien influence on the King's building works, the Italians also had a part to play. Indeed their influence may have been out of proportion to their numbers. During Henry VII's reign men such as Guido Mazzoni and Pietro Torrigiano had been commissioned to design royal tombs at Westminster, but the first Italian to play more than an incidental or occasional part in royal building projects was probably Giovanni da Maiano who, in 1521, had supplied Cardinal Wolsey with painted and gilded terracotta roundels to adorn the exterior face of the inner courtyard at Hampton Court (figs 142, 143, 145). Maiano went on to enter the King's service, almost certainly continuing to provide roundels in both terracotta and less durable fabrics such as papiermâché. He also worked with Benedetto da Rovezzano on the King's tomb, possibly as late as 1536. It seems unlikely that Maiano's influence ever

141. Hampton Court, Surrey. Fragments of a leather mâché frieze of 'naked children' or putti from an unknown location in Henry VIII's lodgings of the 1530s. This precious survival is the minutest part of thousands of yards of similar moulded work which formed the principal decoration of friezes and ceilings throughout the royal houses.

extended beyond surface decoration in the King's houses.[59]

The Neapolitan painter Vincent Volpe served as an heraldic painter to the Navy for over thirty years, until his death in 1536. He also performed other minor tasks in the Works department, assisting Holbein, Maiano and Anthony Toto on architectural decoration.[60] Toto was the most important Italian painter employed by the King. He is mentioned by Vasari in his biography of Pierino del Vaga. Vasari recorded that Toto del Nunziata went to England where he entered the service of Henry VIII 'for whom he executed numerous works; some of which were in architecture, more especially the principal palace of that monarch, by whom he was very largely remunerated'. But this summary of Toto's career is not borne out by English documents where evidence points to him being a decorative painter and painter of religious pictures. He enjoyed an annuity of £25 from June 1530 until his death in 1554; in January 1544 his annuity was supplemented by a further £10 a year as Serjeant Painter.[61]

As Serjeant Painter Toto helped to prepare and organise Henry VIII's funeral in February 1547, but curiously he seems not to have attended the funeral itself. However, three other Italian artificers did, and they received a livery of black cloth. The trio were 'Gasparin de Gaffyn, Modena and Johannes de Padua'.[62] Gasparin de Gaffyn is a deeply shadowy character who often appears with Nicholas Bellin of Modena in royal disbursements of the 1540s. He seems to have been a vaulter or saltator. John of Padua entered royal employment in March 1543, and for his services 'in Architectura' he received the extraordinarily high fee of £36. 10s. a year until 1556–7. Variously described as 'architectus', deviser

of buildings, engineer and artificer, he never held an official appointment in the King's Works. His capacity rather seems to have been that of a consultative adviser to Henry VIII, who presumably discussed with him the work of James Nedeham and Sir Richard Lee. John of Padua was equally skilled in music, and it was for his musical accomplishment that he was perhaps better known outside the King's immediate circle.[63]

More evidence survives for the work of Nicholas Bellin of Modena. He first appears in the Chamber accounts in December 1538 and lived in England until his death in 1569. His career in Italy is relatively obscure, but he was taken into the household of Francis I where he remained, on and off, for twenty years before a financial scandal precipitated his flight to England. He worked with Giovanni Battista Rosso and Francesco Primaticcio at Fontainebleau, probably on the Galerie François Ier and on the now lost Chambre de la Grosse Tour. From his transfer to Henry VIII's employment in August 1537 (with an annuity worth £20 and an additional 20s. a year for clothes) until the King's death in 1547, he was responsible for providing decorative architectural elements for the King's houses. After Henry's death his tasks shifted towards the Revels department and evidence of his activities dries up entirely for the last ten years of his life. Unfortunately the evidence which survives to indicate the scope of his works is thin. He was certainly involved at Whitehall Palace where payments were made to him for unspecified works around 1540.[64] In 1541 he was working both on a banqueting house in the garden at Whitehall and on Nonsuch. At both buildings he and his assistants were involved in carving decorative features out of slate, the slate carving at Nonsuch con-

tinuing for at least four years (fig. 144). In 1547 he produced the King's effigy for Henry VIII's funeral where he is described simply as a 'kerver'.[65]

That Bellin had a reputation as more than just a carver can be seen from a letter sent by Sir John Wallop to Henry VIII in November 1540 describing Francis I's gallery at Fontainebleau as 'all antique of suche stuff as the said modon maketh your majesties chemenyes'.[66] The chimneys in the gallery at Fontainebleau were composed of *stucco duro*, and it is this connection which has led to the suggestion that Modena may have been involved in the stucco work at Whitehall and Nonsuch. Another incidental reference connects Modena to the construction of the preaching place at Whitehall. After Modena's death, one Robert Trunckey petitioned Elizabeth I for an annuity, having been an accomplice of Modena at Whitehall whilst building the preaching place there.[67] Modena's sphere of activity can therefore be seen to have been quite wide, and the lack of documentary evidence in the works accounts in the 1540s probably conceals the true extent of his work for the English Crown.

Although Modena was an Italian he was very much an isolated figure, all his helpers were Doche or French and there was no Italian workshop to support him. Three Normans took out patents of denization in 1544 and described their occupations as working with Modena at Whitehall. One of these men lived with Modena in the Tomb House at Westminster with two further strangers with Doche names.[68] Likewise, slate carvers who worked for him at Nonsuch were Frenchmen rather than Italians.

In addition to John of Padua, Henry VIII also retained the services of Girolamo da Treviso as architectural adviser. Treviso's modern reputation rests on his surviving output as a painter: one of his paintings for Henry VIII survives today in the royal collection (fig. 179). He was killed at the Siege of Boulogne whilst acting in the capacity of an engineer and after his death was described as 'Jheronimo the deviser' which would indicate that he had played some sort of architectural role.[69] According to Vasari, Treviso studied under Raphael in Rome before going to Mantua to work for the Gonzagas. At Mantua he worked on the Palazzo del Tè, and presumably became acquainted with Pinturicchio. He may have also have met Nicholas Bellin of Modena there, if his collaborator is identifiable with Nicolò da Milano (Henry VIII believed that Bellin was of Milanese birth, and if correct the designation 'da Milano' suited him as well as 'da Modena').[70] Treviso's involvement in painting the Camera dei Venti (fig. 148) raises an interesting possibility, as the geometric pattern of its ceiling is very similar to that in the Wolsey Closet at Hampton Court (fig. 146). It is doubtful if Treviso was the conveyer of the design to England as he is not known to have arrived until 1542, which probably post-dates the completion of the Hampton Court ceiling by a couple of years. A link between Henry VIII's houses and Mantua should not be lightly dismissed however, as the barrel-vaulted entrance to the Palazzo del Tè and the ceiling of the Stufetta there has a design similar to that of the chapel at St James's (figs 147, 126). This raises the interesting possibility that Henrician designers drew not so much on Serlio's *Regole* as on pattern-sheets from Mantua.[71] Such observations fail to bring us any closer to the sources of antique design in England in Henry's reign; rather they show the variety of sources,

142 (facing page top).
Hampton Court, Surrey.
Fountain court from the
west by A. van den
Wyngaerde, 1558. On the
left, by the buttresses of the
hall, are two of the terracotta
roundels, supplied by
Giovanni da Maiano, in their
original locations. Further to
the right is the conduit or
fountain powered by excess
water from the Coombe
Conduit water-supply
system.

143 (facing page centre).
Hampton Court, Surrey.
Terracotta roundel by
Giovanni de Maiano, re-set
into the face of the inner
gatehouse.

144 (facing page bottom).
Fragment of carved slate
from Nonsuch, Surrey. It is
certain that Nicholas Bellin
supervised the carving of
such work.

145. Hampton Court,
Surrey. This gatehouse was
rebuilt for George II by
William Kent in 1732, but
Giovanni da Maiano's
roundels were re-set in its
turrets where they remain
today.

demand. During the spring of 1538 Clement and Dickinson were reported to be riding from Hampton Court to the King at Greenwich, carrying plans for royal approval. On the way they stopped off to set out work at Nonsuch, Oatlands, Chertsey and Marten Abbey.[75] That year both men were awarded annuities of £25, a sum equal to that awarded to Toto del Nunziata and more than that awarded to Nicholas Bellin. In 1540, Clement was also granted the house of the late Abbot of Glastonbury in Smithfield, but died before he could properly enjoy it.[76]

Some of their platts or those of their assistants survive (figs 153–5, 157, 164) but none shows any more than the overall topography of the buildings. The majority of their drawn output was probably delivered to site, used and disposed of, thus depriving modern historians of an archive equivalent to that produced by the eighteenth-century Office of Works. But one thing is certain and that is that the English master-craftsmen were the dominant force in the king's building works. What then of the aliens?

Undoubtedly the majority of the artificers who were engaged on decorative work in the King's

146. Hampton Court, Surrey. Ceiling of the 'Wolsey Closet'.

148 (right). Palazzo del Tè, Mantua. Ceiling of the Camera dei Venti.

147 (below). Palazzo del Tè, Mantua. The Stufetta ceiling.

craftsmen, artists and advisers who brought influence to bear on the decoration of the King's houses.

None of this discussion of alien participation in the royal works should obscure the important fact that it was still the King's master-craftsmen, all of whom were English, that were responsible for the design of the King's houses.[72] William Vertue, Thomas Redman, John Moulton, Humphrey Coke, James Nedeham, Christopher Dickinson, John Russell and William Clement — the King's Master-masons, Joiners and Bricklayers carried the official responsibility for royal design. On the occasions when architectural plans are mentioned in the documents it is the master-craftsmen who drew them. They had drawing offices (or tracing houses) at all the main centres of work, certainly at Whitehall, Hampton Court and Greenwich. Frequent references to the purchase of paper, parchment and ink for the drawing of platts confirmed that these offices were the centre of design work during the major summer building campaigns.[73] For instance, the king's Master-mason John Moulton, responsible for much of the work at Hampton Court and Whitehall in the 1530s, had 'tracereye roddis' provided for him at his tracing house at Whitehall in October 1531. These rods, or rulers, were for the drawing of platts.[74] He and his colleagues, men like Clement and Dickinson, were at the top of their profession, high in the King's regard and in great houses were aliens, most were Doche, the remainder French; in addition, there were three or four very highly paid Italians who were given retainers to provide specific, and unspecified, design services to the Office of Works, and these Italians relied exclusively on Doche and French labour to achieve their ends. How the interrelation of English master-craftsmen, Italian consultants and Doche specialists was achieved is unknown, but probably the master-craftsmen with their Italian devisers laid out the overall decorative schemes, while the specific execution and decoration of the works was provided by the Doche. For the Doche brought with them technical know-how in terms of manufacturing brick, terracotta, leather-maché, glass and iron, and in the techniques of carving, moulding and painting. They also brought stylistic innovation, particularly in the form of the grotesque, probably gained from patterns and moulds either imported or made from master-copies in England. The final effect was a truly international effort overseen and underpinned by their employer and patron, Henry VIII.

Chapter 7

THE OUTWARD CHAMBERS

THE OUTWARD CHAMBERS OF the King's houses were the public rooms of the house: the hall, the great chamber, the presence chamber and the various lodging ranges. They fell under the jurisdiction of the Lord Chamberlain, a post first occupied by Charles Somerset, 1st Earl of Worcester (1508–26), then by William, Lord Sandys (1526–43), William Paulet, Earl of Wiltshire (1543–6), and Henry FitzAlan, 12th Earl of Arundel (1546–50). Assisting the Chamberlain was his deputy, the Vice-Chamberlain, and also the Captain of the Guard. The outward chambers were staffed by Yeomen Ushers, Yeomen Waiters, pages and the Yeomen of the Guard. Their territory comprised all the rooms which came before the door out of the presence chamber. Normally this included the great hall, or outer chambers, the great (or watching) chamber, the presence chamber and any other chamber of estate which might lie beyond that and before the privy chamber. Those rooms were designed to provide a setting for the public life of the King. Their uses can be broken down into three categories; occasions of estate, Court entertainments and daily use.

During Henry's reign there were six principal occasions of estate: his coronation in 1509, the meeting with Francis I at the Field of Cloth of Gold in 1520, the visit of Charles V in 1522, the meeting with Francis in Calais in 1532, Anne Boleyn's coronation in 1533 and the reception of Anne of Cleves in 1540. These were very much the exception; most occasions of estate were far less glamorous, such as the creation of peers, reception of ambassadors and the courtly etiquette of births, deaths and marriages. Court entertainments likewise comprised great set-pieces but also general entertainment designed to relieve the tedium of everyday Court life. Each year the great feasts were celebrated; Christmas, Easter, New Year, Twelfth Night and the Feast of St John the Baptist (Midsummer's Day). Occasions of estate might often have Court entertainments linked to them; certainly the six major occasions of estate already mentioned were largely made up of entertainments.

As to daily use, the outer rooms were the part of the King's houses where almost anyone was free to move, and when the Court was in residence at a particular house these rooms were busy with courtiers and servants, eating, drinking, talking, dancing and, at night, sleeping. During the Middle Ages the great hall had provided the natural focus for all three types of Court life, being the largest roofed space in the house. During the early sixteenth century this remained broadly true of the greater houses where the Court stayed in the winter months. During the summer, in the lesser houses, a more active outdoor life was led and the hall had a lesser importance.

The great hall: Decline and fall

The first of the outward chambers and the largest and most important room in the house during the Middle Ages was the great hall. For many years now historians have known that there was a decline in the importance of the great hall from as early as the mid-fourteenth century.[1] This decline was noted by William Langland in his *Vision of Piers Plowman*, dating from about 1362:

> Wretched is the Hall . . . each day in the week
> There the lord and lady liketh not to sit.
> Now have the rich a rule to eat by themselves
> In a privy parlour . . . for poor men's sake,
> Or in a chamber with a chimney, and leave
>   the chief hall that was made for meals,
>   for men to eat in.[2]

Observing today the austere enormity of extant medieval halls at Penshurst Place or Haddon Hall (fig. 150), it is no wonder that the great lords who owned these houses preferred to eat in the comfort and warmth of their private parlours. This retreat from the hall by the king and his great lords sounded its death knell as the most important room in the house. For wherever the king or lord was, there was the centre of power, interest and opportunity. In the absence of the monarch the great hall became a

149. Hampton Court, Surrey. The great hall today. The paint was stripped from its roof in the 1920s, thus depriving the room of much of its impact.

communal dining room for the Court. Moreover, senior ranking courtiers availed themselves of opportunities to eat nearer their royal master, in the great chamber and elsewhere, with the result that by 1500 the great hall had become the preserve largely of lesser officials and servants.

A series of articles prepared for the ordering of Henry VII's household make an allowance for keeping a 'day of Estate in the Hall' but seem to indicate that the King remained in the great chamber throughout.[3] This indication that the King had effectively abandoned the great hall by the early sixteenth century is confirmed by contemporary descriptions of Court ceremonial, none of which mention a Tudor king eating in a great hall. But the first administrative blow to the great hall was not dealt until as late as 1526 when, in the Eltham Ordinances, Wolsey effectively ensured the end of the great hall as a major component of the majority of the King's houses. He specified that hall was only to be kept in the greater houses, that is to say Greenwich, Eltham, Richmond, Beaulieu, Woodstock and Hampton Court. In these houses

the lower members of the Court ate communally in the great hall at set times, in the lesser houses other arrangements were made. This directive is very clearly borne out in the subsequent history of the King's building works. Henry VIII was to build only one great hall, that at Hampton Court (figs 149, 151). Elsewhere great halls were systematically removed from the lesser houses and replaced by a second outer chamber approached by a great stair.

The first of the lesser houses where the great hall was removed was The More in Hertfordshire (see plan 10). This building had been one of Wolsey's principal houses acquired by the King on Wolsey's fall.[4] The original great hall, which probably predated Wolsey's ownership, was a ground-floor structure with a stair leading from it to the great chamber. In the spring of 1535 Henry started major works designed to remove the hall by dividing it horizontally with the insertion of a new floor and by heightening the walls of the original structure to give the new upper chamber sufficient head-room. The new room so created was named the 'new chamber' (not the 'new hall') and served as a com-

munal ante-room to both the King's and Queen's watching chambers (see plan 10).[5]

The More was only the first of a series of conversions where the great hall was deliberately removed and replaced by a new outer room. The conversions at Rochester (begun 1540) and at Hull (1541) are particularly illuminating, for at both places there was a change of plan after work had

started. In both cases the builders started work along traditional lines intending to provide a great hall for the King; in both cases, following a visit from him, the plans were changed and a great hall omitted. Rochester Priory (fig. 152) was suppressed on 31 March 1540, and work on converting it for royal use began soon after. The first task faced by the builders was to undertake an emergency

151. Hampton Court, Surrey, from the north by A. van den Wyngaerde c.1558. From left to right the view shows the tiltyard towers, the close tennis-play, the side of the chapel, the great hall, the gabled roofline of the kitchen courts, the great gatehouse before its top two storeys were removed in 1771–3 and the outer courtyard with the houses of offices at the gate.

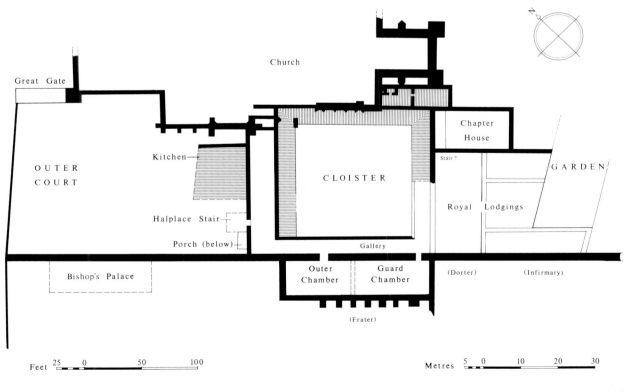

152. Rochester, Kent. Plan indicating the arrangement of the royal lodgings as finally completed.

115

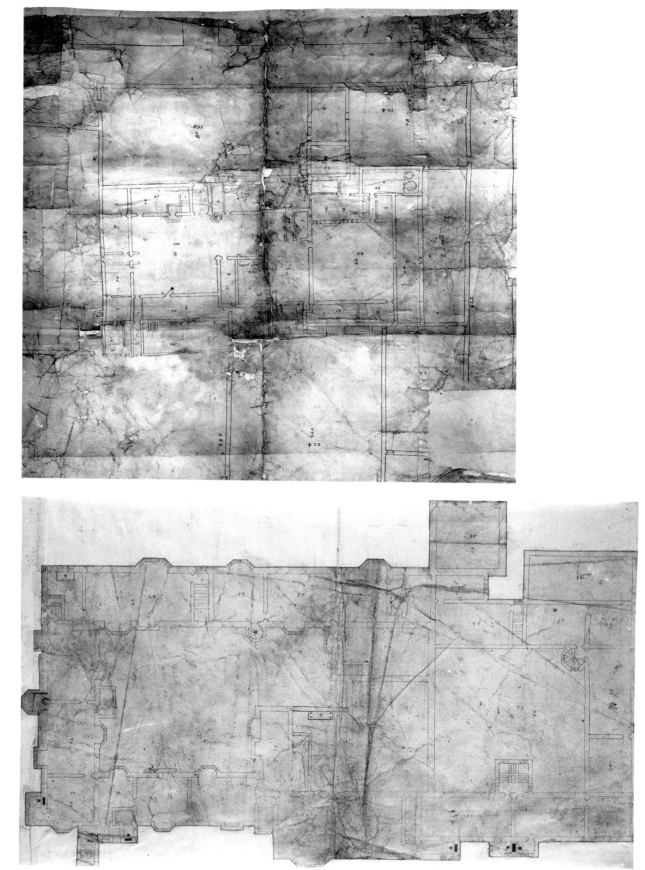

153. Hull Manor, 'platt A', by John Rogers, 1539. A survey of the house before the start of work.

154. Hull Manor, 'platt B', by John Rogers. Rogers's proposals for conversion rejected by Henry VIII.

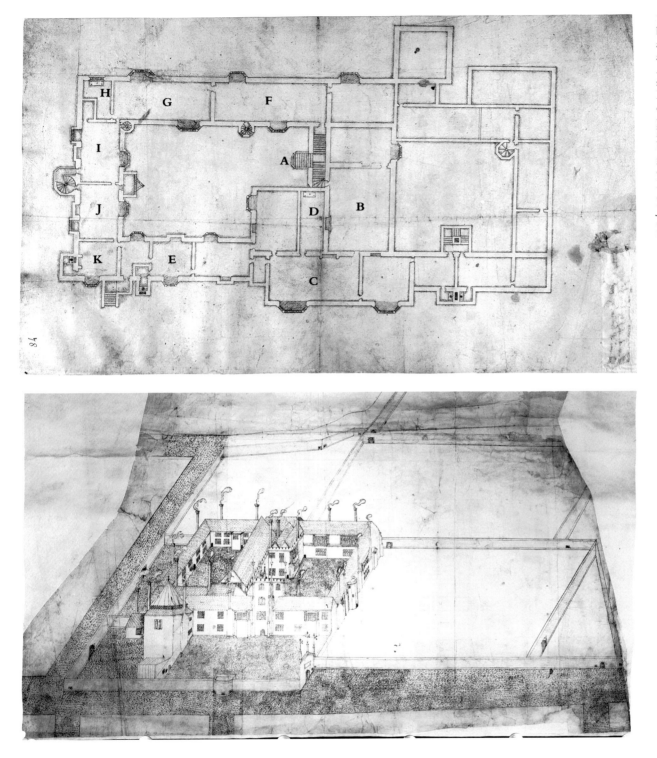

155. Hull Manor, 'platt C', by John Rogers. The manor as finally adapted by Rogers at Henry VIII's request. A: The great T-shaped stair similar to that at Bridewell. B: The king's guard chamber. C: The king's presence chamber. D: The king's closet. E: The king's bedchamber. F: The queen's guard chamber. G: The queen's presence chamber. H: The queen's closet. I: The queen's privy chamber. J: The queen's withdrawing chamber. K: The queen's bedchamber.

156. Hull Manor, 'platt D', by John Rogers. The manor as completed. The kitchen is at bottom left. The corner of the great stair can be seen in the inner court, as can the window of the king's closet placed high over the altar.

campaign to make the new property habitable for the King, who visited on 22 March 1541. This first phase involved creating a great hall in the former monastic frater and linking this by two stairs to a fairly standard, if cramped, set of royal lodgings for both the King and Queen. Henry VIII cannot have been satisfied with either the extent of this work, or more particularly, the end product, for when work started again in February 1542 a change of plan was afoot. The roof of the recently created great hall was

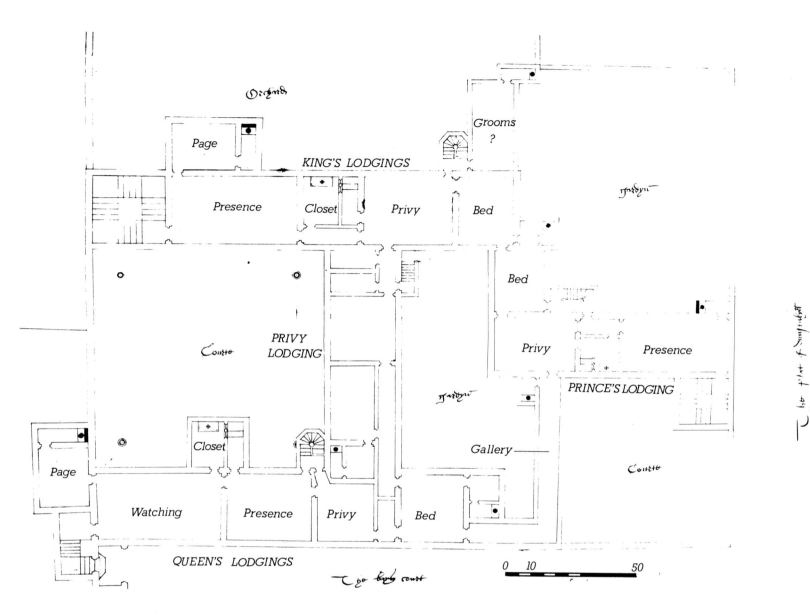

Orchard

Grooms
?

Page

KING'S LODGINGS

Presence   Closet   Privy   Bed   jardyn

PRIVY
LODGING   Bed

Coutto   Privy   Presence

jardyn   PRINCE'S LODGING

Closet

Page   Gallery   Coutto

Watching   Presence   Privy   Bed

QUEEN'S LODGINGS

the plot of Dunstable

the kyng court

0   10   50

157. Dunstable Priory, Bedfordshire, possibly by Lawrence Bradshaw, Master Carpenter to Henry VIII, ?1543–4. Dartford was converted into a residence for Henry VIII between 1543 and 1544. The plan of the building as completed, if indeed that is what is shown by the platt, is typical of Henry's later houses. There is no great hall, and the lodgings are approached directly by a grand stair from an outer court. As at Nonsuch, the guard chamber was on the ground floor.

removed as was that of the adjoining great chamber; windows and walls were demolished, new fireplaces inserted and the building re-roofed. The end product was a building with 'ii gret chambers' and no great hall.[6]

The events which led to the removal of the great hall at Hull Manor House are surprisingly similar to those at Rochester and can be illustrated by a series of surviving contemporary plans. The first of these, 'platt A' (fig. 153), is a survey of the house as it existed in 1538, showing a courtyard house with a conventional hall. The second plan, 'platt B' (fig. 154), is a proposal by John Rogers to alter the house into a royal residence providing a traditional set of royal lodgings. This plan was not acceptable to Henry and another plan was drawn up for him. This, 'platt C' (figs 155–6), involved the elimina-

tion of the old manorial great hall which, as at The More, was divided horizontally and given an approach by a processional staircase.[7] The monastic conversions at Dartford (from 1539, fig. 80) and Dunstable (from 1540, fig. 157) seem never to have envisaged a great hall as part of their design. The extensions at Oatlands (figs 88–90) and St James's (figs 108–10) likewise were hall-less. Dartford and Rochester had outer chambers, but not so Dunstable or St James's, the precise arrangement at Oatlands is unclear.[8] In addition to this list of lesser houses converted or modified to have no great hall, Henry VIII also built one hall-less house from scratch on a virgin site. Of all Henry's houses Nonsuch had the most coherent plan (fig. 85). Indeed it was built on an ideal plan, part of which was the absence of a great hall. Instead, the King's and Queen's lodgings

158. Bridewell, London. The south-west corner of the outer courtyard from an eighteenth-century view. The projection in the corner is the processional stair built by Henry VIII in the 1520s. Other than the stair to the great hall at Hampton Court, this is the only early Tudor processional stair of which there is a detailed record.

were approached by a great staircase and provision for communal dining was made in the outer court. Here there was a room called the 'dining chamber in the outer court' where the lower servants of the Court could eat.

The demise of the great hall in the King's houses after the mid-1530s went hand in hand with the rise of the halpace stair. The halpace — or processional — stair was, in the absence of the stair at the dais end of the great hall, the means of entry to the King's and Queen's lodgings on the first floor. It became a vehicle for architectural display and remained a major element in royal planning right into the nineteenth century. The history of great staircases in royal planning, and indeed in English architecture in general, begins in the reign of Henry VIII and may be traced back to the influence of Cardinal Wolsey. Wolsey's adoption of the stacked lodging has already been noted (see pp. 41–2), and to have a two-storey structure with important rooms on the upper floor, a major stair was required to provide access. Such stairs were built at Hampton Court, Richmond, Bridewell and at the temporary palace at the Field of Cloth of Gold (not in itself a stacked lodging). Wolsey did not, however build great stairs to approach the hall, for at Hampton Court they led directly to the royal lodgings, by-

passing the hall and great chamber (see plan 8). From as early as the 1520s, therefore, an architectural bypass had removed the hall at Hampton Court from the processional route. Henry was to take this further. At each of the hall-less houses discussed above there was a staircase leading directly out of the courtyard into the outer chamber.

One of the best documented halpace stairs was that which provided entry into the royal lodgings at Dartford (fig. 80). The Dartford stair was probably situated centrally on the north side of the great court. At its foot there were a carved stone dragon and lion, each standing on a stone pillar, gilded and holding gilded vanes decorated with the royal arms. The stair was tiled with 9,000 paving tiles and painted.[9] A contemporary plan of the halpace stair at Hull Manor shows it to have been 'T' shaped, similar to but not as complex as that at Bridewell (figs 54, 58, 158). Only the first flight was outside; it then led left and right into the King's and Queen's lodgings. Sometimes, as at Nonsuch (fig. 85) and at Dunstable (fig. 157), the halpace stair was inside. Both of these houses had ground-floor outer chambers and an internal stair leading up to the first floor. At others such as St James's (fig. 110), Bridewell (fig. 54) and Hull (fig. 155), the staircase led directly into the watching chamber. There does not seem to be any great significance attached to whether there was an outer chamber or not; the existence of an outer chamber was evidently determined by the constraints of space.

Despite this wholesale removal of great halls, Henry VIII did build one at Hampton Court (figs 149, 151). Hampton Court was one of the greater houses, one of the buildings where the King and his Court kept full estate, where he was seen in all his magnificence. The hall which Henry inherited from Wolsey in 1529 was probably the work of Giles, the first Lord Daubeney, who had owned the house before Wolsey. This hall was a ground-floor structure of little pretension (see plan 5). Henry's new hall was not merely a replacement of the old one, but was larger and more impressive, and — most importantly — it was on the first floor. By raising the great hall on a basement and making a new approach by a grand staircase, the King had transformed the impact made by the hall. No longer did one go up from the great hall to the King's lodgings; the great hall had become the first and most magnificent room within those lodgings. There was an important architectural consequence to the transfer of the stair from the dais end of the hall to the great chamber: it enabled a new, architecturally pretentious stair to be made, providing a grander entrance to the King's lodgings.[10] The new hall at Hampton Court enabled the King to have his cake and eat it. As with his other houses, the royal lodgings were now approached by a processional stair and an outer chamber. However the 'outer chamber' at Hampton Court was a great hall, fulfilling all the communal functions which were required of it and fulfilling them in the most magnificent manner possible.

By the end of the reign of Henry VIII, therefore, a major change had been wrought in the most fundamental part of the medieval domestic plan. No longer was entry to a house through a porch into a great hall, past a dais, up a stair, through the great chamber to the King. Now entry was from the courtyard, up a great stair, through two outer chambers into the presence chamber. During the reign of Henry VIII the great hall, or the outer chamber, retained two functions — it served as the communal dining-room for the lower members of the Court (see p. 150), and as a venue for Court revels. The great hall had, from the very start of the reign, provided the setting for revels or entertainments as it alone of the components of the house provided sufficient space, its gallery a place for minstrels and the dais a viewing-point for the King. It is highly significant that in the 1620s and 1630s the hall at Hampton Court was set up as a theatre and that in 1665 that at Whitehall was converted permanently into a theatre. Less than a hundred and fifty years after the death of Henry VIII the hall had finally lost the last vestiges of its principal traditional use.

The great, guard or watching chamber

The guard chamber was, as its name implies, the room in which the Guard stood, 'in habits of red'. It was also known as the King's watching chamber, where the guard watched over the King's safety, or as the great chamber, the medieval term for the first of the outward chambers. The Royal Guard had been instituted by Henry VII, and Henry VIII had raised their number. There were 126 at the start of the reign, 200 by 1510; in 1512 it was 300 strong and in 1513, just before the war with France, it numbered 600.[11] In the Eltham Ordinances this increase in the number of the guard was heavily criticized as they 'doe occupie the greatest part of his hall and likewise of his lodgings neere about the court, but also do enterteyne everie of them one or two laddes or symple servants'. To redress such irregularities the Guard were forbidden to have servants and their number reduced. By the early 1540s their numbers had fallen to just over eighty, a number which could have happily been accommodated in the great hall or outer chamber.[12]

They were under the command of the Captain of the Guard who was required to liaise with the Lord Chamberlain about their deployment. The King's expenses show continual payments for the transport of the uniforms of the Guard from one place to another, usually just ahead of the King's arrival.[13] The Yeomen of the Guard had important ceremonial functions within the palace. Their principal daily task was to line the King's route from one part of the building to another. Soon after their creation, at the marriage of Henry VII's son Prince Arthur, they stood 'by the weies and passage upon a rowe in bothe the siddes where the Kinges Highnes shuld from chambre to chambre . . . be remeovid'. At the Field of Cloth of Gold we learn that 'A way is cleared by force. Drawn up in broad ranks, on this side and that, the glittering guard of king Henry makes a wide path, two hundered halberd-bearers in all, gleaming with gold.' On a more domestic occasion we learn of Queen Elizabeth's progress through Hampton Court to the chapel: 'before the Queen marched her life guard, all chosen men, strong and tall . . . then came the gentlemen of rank and the council'.[14]

The Pages were the workaday servants of the outward chambers. It was their job to 'dress, repair and make clean' the room,[15] and, at night, to sleep in a pages' chamber nearby. In all palaces, one or other or both of the outward chambers had Pages' chambers attached. At Hampton Court, for example, we learn of 'the pags chambre adyoneyd to the great watchyng chambre' (see plan 8).[16]

A book of ceremonials, preserved in the British Museum, gives details of how the Pages and their chambers were used on an occasion of estate.[17] Such an occasion was when, on 23 December 1543, Queen Catherine Parr's brother and uncle were ennobled respectively as Earl of Essex and Lord Parr of Horton at Hampton Court:

> ffurste the pagis chamber within the kings greate chamber was well strawed with rusheys, and after the kynges highnes was comen to his closette to here high masse the erle and the baron [entered the page's chamber aforementioned] and immediately after the kings maistie was comen into the chamber of presence his highnes being under the cloth of estate . . .[18]

Thus the Pages' chamber was used on ceremonial occasions as a preparation room.

The Yeomen Ushers of the Chamber performed the important task of regulating who came into the outward chambers. They, or the Yeomen Waiters, were each day to 'take charge of the door of the same [guard] chamber, not permitting or suffring any person to enter, but such as by his discresion shall be seene good and mete for that place'.[19] They had also to prevent people congregating at the King's great chamber door at the top of the stair from the hall. They had to 'avoyde and purge the haute-pace at the king's chamber doore, of all manner of servants, raskalls, boyes, and others so as the same place be not pestered with any greate number of persons'.[20] Theirs was the important task of ensuring the proper forms were observed once people had entered the room; they had to be 'curtious, and glad to receve, teache, and direct every man . . . know all the custumes and ceremonies, used about the kyng'.[21]

Under Henry VIII the principal day-to-day function of the watching chamber was as a dining room for household officials. The Eltham Ordinances specify that 'the lord chamberlyn likewise to keepe his boord in the utter chamber, calling unto him the residue of the barons with other noblemen [who did not dine in the presence chamber]'. In addition the other senior figures of the Household ate in here, the Vice-Chamberlain, the Captain of the Guard, the Master of the Horse, the Lord Steward, the Comptroller, the Cofferer, members of the King's Council of lesser rank and any guests.[22] After their evening meal the Pages of the Chamber would draw the straw mattresses which they and the Esquires of the Chamber would sleep upon. The guard chamber then assumed its nocturnal role as a dormitory for the more junior Chamber staff who slept there until

eight the following morning when they had to rise and clean the room. At eight o'clock the Grooms and Ushers on duty arrived and a waiter took up his place by the door to check that only authorised people entered. Thus started a new day in the outward chambers.[23]

In addition, there were the minstrels whose duty it was to enliven both everyday life and special occasions with fanfares and music (fig. 159). There were a large number of musicians resident at Court. In 1509 Henry VIII had sixteen trumpeters in his service and by 1526 there were ten sackbutts; by 1540 there was a six-man string consort and a twenty-four-strong royal band.[24] These musicians and others would have not only been functionaries at great feasts but would sometimes provide accompaniment for revels or masques which were also held in the great chamber. An example of this is at Greenwich in 1517 when the King caused the great chamber 'to be staged and great lightes to be set on pillers that were gilt, with basons gilt, and the rofe was covered with blewe satyn set full of presses of fyne gold and flowers'.[25] The staging was probably seating for spectators, for few if any plays required scenery.[26] These entertainments were supervised either by officers of the Wardrobe or officers of the Tents until in 1545 the King instituted a permanent Master of the Revels, Sir Thomas Carwarden. The Master of the Revels sometimes worked independently, but he was expected to co-operate closely with both the Lord Chamberlain and the Dean of the Chapel, who also provided musical accompaniment.

Finally, the guard chamber was the preferred

159. Hans Holbein the Younger (attributed), *Musicians on a Balcony*.

160. Hampton Court, Surrey. The great watching chamber. Of the hundreds of outward rooms built by Henry VIII, this is the only one to remain in anything like its original form. Decoratively, however, it has suffered badly. William III, in 1700, removed Henry VIII's cornice, the great moulded-work frieze (in the area above the tapestries and below the ceiling) and his fireplace. In the nineteenth century the gold leaf was stripped from the ceiling battens.

venue for various assorted ceremonies on account of its size; after the hall, it was the largest room in the house. The guard chamber was often used to dine ambassadors, as when in April 1520 both the French and Venetian ambassadors were fed in the guard chamber at Richmond. In April 1542, Henry used the great chamber at Greenwich to distribute the Royal Maundy to a large number of the local poor invited into the house. Indeed, of the outermost chambers, the guard chamber was the most flexible.[27]

Only one of Henry VIII's guard chambers survives, that at Hampton Court (fig. 160) — its ceiling and stained glass are Victorian restorations, its tapestries, however, are part of Henry's collection and the size and overall feel of the room give the modern visitor some idea of the stark magnificence of a Tudor outer chamber.

The presence chamber

Throughout Henry VII's reign, and for almost the whole of Henry VIII's, the presence chamber was the principal ceremonial room of the house. It was otherwise known as the dining chamber or sometimes the chamber of estate.[28] Its most obvious feature was a cloth of estate directly opposite the entrance. No one but the King was entitled to go beneath it as the regulations made clear: 'no manner of whatsoever degree he be of so hardye to come nighe the kings chayre nor stand under the clothe of estate'.[29] The King's public dining took place in

here with great ceremonial and splendour, with the monarch seated beneath his cloth. Under Henry VII the King's public dining-room had often been the guard or watching chamber, but there is no evidence to show that Henry VIII ever publically ate in there.[30]

The Queen's presence chamber was likewise intended for dining and there is plenty of evidence to show that successive queens entertained Henry in their presence chambers. In February 1533 Anne Boleyn treated the King to a banquet in her apartments at Greenwich . . . 'the lady herself sat on the king's right hand whilst the Dowager Duchess [of Norfolk] was lower down on the left, at the end of a cross table joining that of the king were the Chancellor the Duke of Suffolk and several other lords and ladies sat'.[31] Tables were almost always set up in a 'T' shape or that of an inverted 'U'. A seating plan for a banquet at Greenwich in 1517 shows the inverted 'U' and the positions of the King, Queen and Cardinal (fig. 161).[32]

When Henry VIII dined in the presence chamber the ushers and waiters had the task of overseeing the meal and co-ordinating the other serving staff. It was at such times particularly that the device of the hall place came into operation. The hall place was an area before the door to an important room, sometimes at the top of a stair but often merely a space between rooms (see fig. 164). An account at Hampton Court mentions 'the haull pase of the great stayere cumyng up in to the kyngs lodgeyng'. It was a leaning or resting place before the door of a room, to allow dishes to be marshalled at mealtimes and robes to be adjusted during ceremonials. The regulations concerning the ordering of such areas in the Eltham Ordinances attempt to ensure that the area did not become a place where dirty dishes and waste were left. The ushers were to ensure that a hall place should 'be kept clene, soe that noe ale, water, broken meate, or any other thing conveyed out of the king's chamber, be cast or remaine there, to the annoyance and filthynesse of the same'.[33]

As well as dining in the presence chamber, Henry VIII entertained important visitors there. Accounts of ambassadorial visits show that ambassadors were frequently dined in the presence chamber.[34] In July 1517 the Spanish embassy was feasted by the King for seven hours — 'the removal and replacing of dishes the whole time [being] incessant, the hall in every direction being full of fresh viands on their way to the table'.[35] The King, on these occasions, often ate next door in his privy chamber. On the famous occasion in 1527, when the King surprised the Cardinal at dinner at York Place, he withdrew 'to sup in one of the Cardinal's chambers, the rest of the guests continuing in their repast'[36]

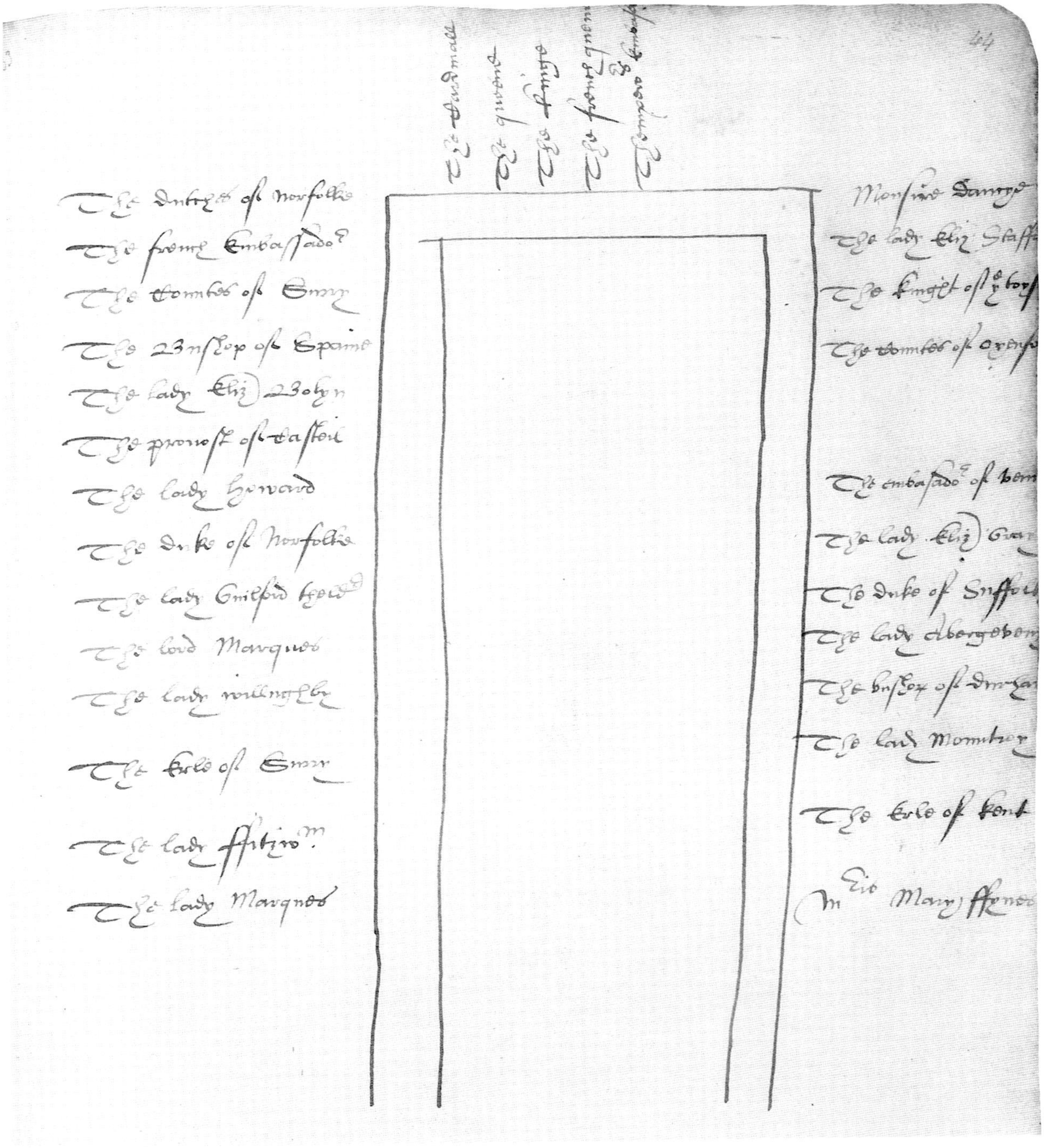

161. A seating plan for a banquet at Greenwich in 1517. At the top of the table sat the King and Queen, with Wolsey to their right. On the King's left were the French queen and the Emperor's ambassador. Most of the major court figures of the early part of the reign sat along the flanks. In all, thirty-one people were seated.

The seating plan (handwritten)

Top of table:
- The Cardinall
- The quene
- The kinge
- The ffrenche quene
- The Emperors Embassador

Left flank (top to bottom):
- The Dutches of norfolke
- The ffrenche Embassador
- The countes of Surry
- The Bishop of Spaine
- The lady Eliz Bolyn
- The provost of Cassel
- The lady Howard
- The Duke of norfolke
- The lady Grifford howard
- The lord Marques
- The lady willughby
- The Erle of Surry
- The lady ffitzwilliam
- The lady Marques

Right flank (top to bottom):
- Monsire Damnye
- The lady Eliz Stafford
- The knight of ye body
- The countes of Oxenford
- The Embassador of Venice
- The lady Eliz Gray
- The Duke of Suffolk
- The lady Abergevenny
- The bishop of Durham
- The lord Mountley
- The Erle of Kent
- Mris Mary ffenes

before returning to the presence chamber to dance. Elizabeth I, according to Paul Hentzner in 1598, 'dines and sups alone with very few attendants; and it is very seldom that any body, foreigner or native is admitted'.[37] However, the presence chamber, although used for public dining by Henry VIII, was not the room where he ate most often. In practice the presence chamber was the dining-room for upper members of the Court. The Eltham Ordinances explain: 'when the King's highnesse shall not dine abroad, in his owne dyning chamber, there shall be a boord in the same furnished with such lords spirituall and temporall, to be served with the service called the King's service'. All of the temporal lords were to be at least above the rank of a baron.[38]

Later in the reign there was a shift in the function of the presence chamber. From the start of the reign there were occasions when Henry only presided

123

long-term consequence in altering the function of the presence chamber.

At Henry VIII's accession the presence chamber was universally used as the reception room for ambassadors, as the room in which audiences were held and in which all major court ceremonial took place. These ceremonies varied from the receipt of new year's gifts by the King to the ennoblement of his mistress Anne Boleyn as Marchioness of Pembroke.[40] From about 1540 several of the functions of the presence chamber were switched to the privy chamber. This shift towards the privy chamber was accelerated by Cromwell's household reforms of 1539 which established a new royal guard, the Band of Gentlemen Pensioners. The new guard comprised fifty Gentlemen Pensioners under the captaincy of Sir Anthony Browne and they made their first public appearance at Greenwich in January 1540 as part of the reception of Anne of Cleves.[41] The Gentlemen Pensioners assumed responsibility for the presence chamber, standing there, and taking precedence over Yeomen of the Guard who still stood in the guard or watching chamber. This immediately made the room more public, with a consequent loss in both privacy and prestige forcing the King to use the privy chamber

162. Whitehall Palace. Sketch by Francis Place. The tall gable in the background is that of the great hall, in front of it the crenellated gable is the north gable of the king's watching chamber, to its right is the west window of the king's presence chamber.

over the meal and dined, in reality, in his privy chamber. Henry VII had probably acted in a similar manner, but Henry VIII from quite early in his reign began to invite people into his privy chamber to watch him dine. These occasions initially caused some comment. The apostolic nuncio considered it 'a very unusual proceeding' when in July 1517 the King had the Spanish ambassadors 'to dine with him privately in his chamber with the Queen', presumably as a mark of favour as the Spanish king was Catherine of Aragon's nephew. On another occasion in May 1527 the King asked the Bishop of Tarbes and the vicomte de Turenne to dine with him, 'the others dining apart'.[39] This occasional use of the privy chamber to entertain important guests had a

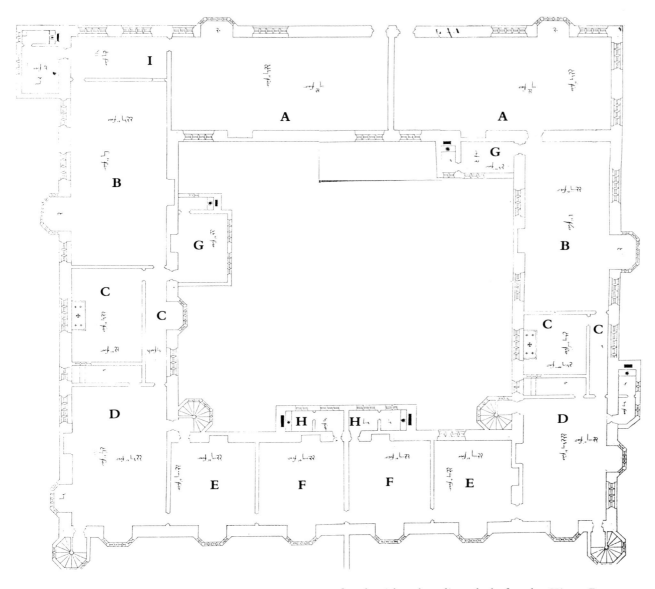

164. Waltham-in-the-Forest. Design for an unexecuted house for Henry VIII. This house, like Nonsuch, was conceived on an ideal plan, as no pre-existing building was present to influence the design. It shows the late Henrician plan at its most sophisticated. The rooms can be identified as A: watching chamber; B: presence chamber; C: gallery-and-closet plan; D: privy chamber; E: withdrawing chamber; F: bedchamber; G: pages' chamber; H: garderobe; I: halplace.

for functions hitherto reserved for the presence chamber.

The gallery-and-closet plan

The junction between the presence chamber and the privy chamber next door was one between the outward and inward parts of the King's lodgings. As such it received special attention. This can be best illustrated by the plans of Whitehall and Hampton Court. At both houses (see plans 8, 13) the arrangement was identical. A short gallery led out of the presence chamber towards the privy chamber; off this gallery were two small rooms, one approached from the gallery and the other from the privy chamber. At both houses the larger room was a closet housing an altar, and the smaller room was

fitted with a kneeling desk for the King. Between the two rooms there was a small wooden window or lattice to enable the King to hear mass said in the adjoining closet (fig. 163). These arrangements can be seen on several contemporary plans (figs 103, 155, 157, 164) and identified at every other house belonging to the King.

The purpose of the plan was both religious and organisational. First, in terms of organisation the junction between the presence chamber and the privy chamber was one between a public room and an exclusively private area. Access to the privy lodgings was, as we have seen, heavily restricted. The physical barrier of a narrow passage or gallery between the two areas was an effective filter between the crush of the Court in one room and the relative tranquility of the privy chamber.[42] The 1526 ordinances required a member of the Privy

163 (facing page bottom). *Henry VIII at Prayer*, from the Black Book of the Garter (1534–41). This illumination shows Henry VIII in a closet. He kneels on a cushion, beneath a rich canopy. Before him on a prie-dieu, resting on another cushion is a prayer book. An altar can be seen to the right. The presence of an altar might suggest that this view does not show a closet in a traditional closet-and-gallery plan.

chamber itself, as at Greenwich (see plan 4). A second stair, likewise sometimes in the gallery and at other times directly leading to the privy chamber, linked it with the privy kitchen below.

An equally important service performed by the closet-and-gallery plan was as an 'air-lock' between the two areas of the palace when the King 'came forth'. It was unreasonable to expect Henry VIII to enter the public arena of the presence chamber directly from his private rooms in such a way as to allow courtiers sight of them. The gallery formed an interim preparation area, an air-lock which allowed the door of the privy chamber to be firmly shut before the King made his ceremonial entry into the presence chamber. There were good religious reasons for the adoption of the gallery-and-closet plan too. Organisationally the religious constitution of the King's household was divided into two parts; the Chapel Royal (the Household chapel) and the Royal Closet (the King's own chapel) — to put it another way the Chapel had a Privy and Household wing. The King was served by the staff of his Closet, who were separate from the Household Chapel. The Black Book of Edward IV charges the clerk of the King's Closet to prepare 'all thinges for the stuffe of the altres to be redy and taking upp the travers; laying the cuysshyns necessary for the kynge and the chapleyns'.[44] At Hampton Court at least, the clerk was given his own lodging.[45]

The King heard mass daily and often several or all of the offices. In 1519 the Venetian ambassador believed that the King heard vespers and compline daily in addition to mass.[46] The evidence of the King's expenses shows him rewarding the clerk of his closet with a frequency which would suggest several daily devotions.[47] For instance, in 1519 Dr Rawson, Clerk of the King's Closet, was paid for 'diverse priests syngyng for his grace'.[48] Even at the major church feasts the King heard mass in his own closet. At Christmas in 1510 and 1518 there are payments 'for the king's offring at taking of his rights in the morning in the closet'.[49] But later in the day the King might perform a more public devotion (see pp. 198–9). Usually the wall between the closet and the kneeling place, as it was known, was only a thin timber partition. An account for alterations at The More illustrates this: 'i barre of iron tynnde ronde with lowpes to stey the wainskots seellyngs betwen the closet and the kyngs knelyng place'.[50] The closet itself had an altar lit from above by a clerestory window.[51] At the Tower of London the altar was particularly splendid: 'in the king's closett an awlter wrought rownde aboute the hedges with antyk and a cofer wt tylles thereto for the preiste to say Masse on'.[52] At Hampton Court there was a painted altarpiece in the closet.[53] The King's kneeling place was furnished in a variety of ways.

165. Hampton Court, Surrey. Stair turret in Clock Court. Built in 1535 to provide access between the ground-floor wardrobe and the first-floor privy chamber. It also contained a pages' chamber at first-floor level (see fig. 166).

Chamber to stand at the door to regulate access, and the gallery provided a waiting place for this. It also provided a waiting place when the King's clothes were brought up from the wardrobe below. This 'no man's land' was, in effect, dominated by the clerks of the Closet and the personnel of the Wardrobe. Frequently the gallery was approached by a vice-stair from the wardrobes below, for example at Hampton Court (figs 165, 166 and see plans 7, 8). The Yeomen of the Wardrobe of the Robes had to bring the King's clothes 'to the kyngs privy chamber door without entring the same, where one of the grooms shall receive the said garments and apparell'.[43] Sometimes the stair did not lead to the gallery but to a hall place in the privy

There was invariably a 'deske for his grace to knelle upon'[54] but at Greenwich there was also a 'stolle of prayers with foldyng fette'.[55] The inventory taken of the King's houses after his death enumerates at length the altar frontals and other fabrics which adorned both closet and kneeling place (figs 163, 262).[56]

Each member of the royal family had his own closet establishment. A surviving inventory of the Duke of Richmond's effects lists in detail the hangings, vestments and equipment in his closet in 1525.[57] In 1518 Catherine of Aragon, perhaps the most devout of Henry's wives, asked Wolsey if her chaplain could remain with her throughout the summer for she 'haith none other to saye matens wyth'.[58] Catherine Parr, in 1544 paid William Harper, Clerk of the Closet for 'the heyre of carts at sundry removings as for the letany and books psalmes for the quenes grace, with other necessars by him doon apperteyning to the closet'.[59]

The planning of the King's closet was difficult to manage. The priest was not a member of the Privy Chamber and it was undesirable that he, together with any servers or singing men, should be admitted into the privy chamber. Equally, it was most undesirable that the King should have to leave the privy chamber to hear mass. The solution to this dilemma was to make the closet part of the outer rooms and the King's oratory part of the domain of the Privy Chamber. This meant that the closet had to be positioned between the presence and privy chambers. Who proposed this practical arrangement and when it was first introduced remains uncertain but it was certainly in existence by 1530. It is also true to say that the organisational requirements which made its adoption necessary (the privacy of the privy chamber) were in existence in the reign of Henry VII. It is therefore likely that the plan was conceived under Henry VII and found its most fullest realisation in his son's reign.

The outward chambers in use

No precise accounts survive showing the King's outward lodgings in use but the reports made by ambassadors are full of incidental references which more than compensate for the gaps in the evidence, as may be seen in the following two examples. The Imperial ambassador Chapuys had a personal interview with the King at Greenwich on 18 April 1536; it was 6 a.m. on Easter Day and Chapuys arrived at Greenwich by barge. The King was still in his inward lodgings and so Chapuys was received by all the Lords of the Council outside in the presence chamber. Cromwell acted as a go-between and won for Chapuys an assurance that after dinner the King

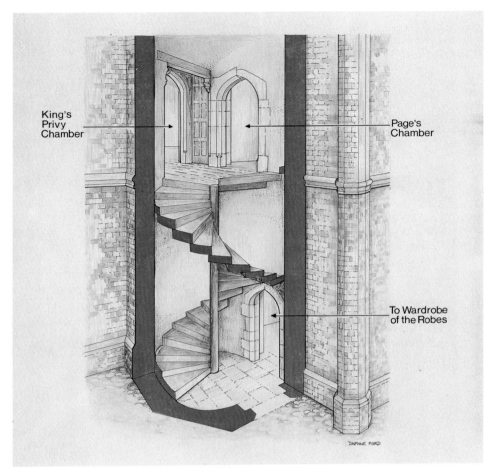

King's Privy Chamber

Page's Chamber

To Wardrobe of the Robes

DAPHNE FORD

166. Cut-away diagram showing the arrangement of the stair serving Henry VIII's privy chamber at Hampton Court. (Drawing Daphne Ford)

would speak to him. Eventually, Henry came forth, acknowleged Chapuys and proceeded to mass. After the service the King went to dine in Anne Boleyn's lodging while Chapuys was taken to eat in the King's presence chamber 'with all the principal men of the court'. After dinner the King 'in passing by where I was made me the same caress as in the morning, and, taking me by the hand, led me into his [privy] chamber, whither only the Chancellor and Cromwell followed. He took me apart to a window', where a discussion about the current international situation ensued. Cromwell in the meantime sat on a coffer and sent for something to drink. In Chapuys's account the importance of the King's coming forth is brought out. Courtiers, ambassadors and suitors waited outside the door to the closet and gallery for the King's appearance and during the time it took for the King to get from there to the chapel, or wherever else he might be going, he was fair game for all.[60] The second illustration dates from 17 February 1544 when the Duke of Najera met Henry VIII at Whitehall:

Before the Duke arrived at the King's chamber he passed through three saloons, hung with tapestry,

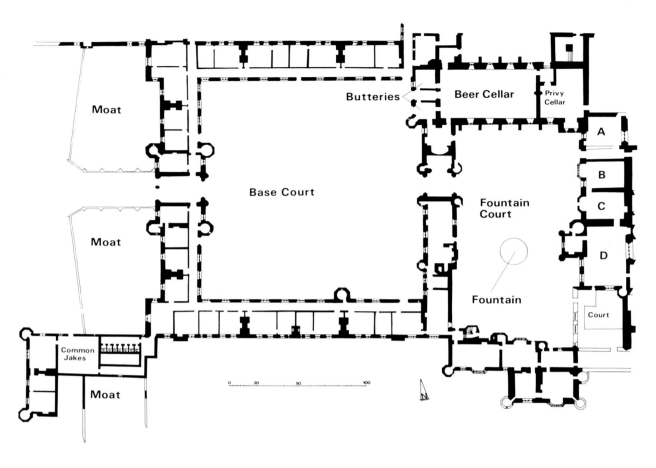

167. Hampton Court, Surrey. Base court. Ground-floor plan, 1547. 1520–6: Rooms A–D comprise Wolsey's reception parlours. 1526–36: Rooms A–D comprise lodgings for Princess Mary. 1536–9: Room A, lodging for courtiers; rooms B and C comprise the queen's wardrobe of the beds; room D, the king's wardrobe of the robes. 1539–47: Courtier lodgings; room A, probably Anthony Denny; rooms B and C, probably Thomas Heneage; room D, another courtier lodging.

in the second of which [the watching chamber] were stationed in order on either side the King's bodyguard, dressed in habits of red, and holding halberds. In the third saloon [the presence chamber] were nobles, knights and gentlemen, and here was a canopy made of rich figured brocade, with a chair of the same material . . . here the brother of the Queen and other noblemen entertained the Duke for a quarter of an hour until it was announced that we should enter the chamber of the King [the privy chamber]. Don Rodrigo de Mendoca and Tello de Guzman entered with him and no one else, nor did they permit us even to see the king.[61]

Lodging the King's Court

The lodgings required by the King and Queen and their family was only one small fraction of the accommodation needed by the Court. The larger amount of accommodation in terms of numbers of people was taken up by the lodgings of the officers of the Court and the King's courtiers.

Of the servants assigned lodgings at Court, those who worked for the Lord Steward's department made up the greatest number. About two hundred people manned the kitchens of the greater houses and as a general rule the officers of any department, whatever their rank, were accommodated either next door to, or above, the offices in which they worked. Figures 187–8 show the ground and first-floor plans of the territory of the Lord Steward's department at Hampton Court. The Officers of the Pastry lived above the pastry house, and the Officers of the Larder above the larder. Even the relatively high-ranking officers such as the Cofferer and the Comptroller lived next to their offices. They, however, had a suite of two or three rooms or individual rooms to themselves. Most of the domestic servants slept communally with their workmates. These servants not only slept in their rooms but they ate there also. Household regulations commanded them 'at every meal to eat their meate togethers in one of the workinghouses of the ketchen'.[62]

Most of the staff of the Privy Chamber had lodgings in Court. When they were on duty they would sleep in the privy chamber and use the latrines and washroom nearby.[63] At other times they would stay in their own lodgings, which can often be iden-

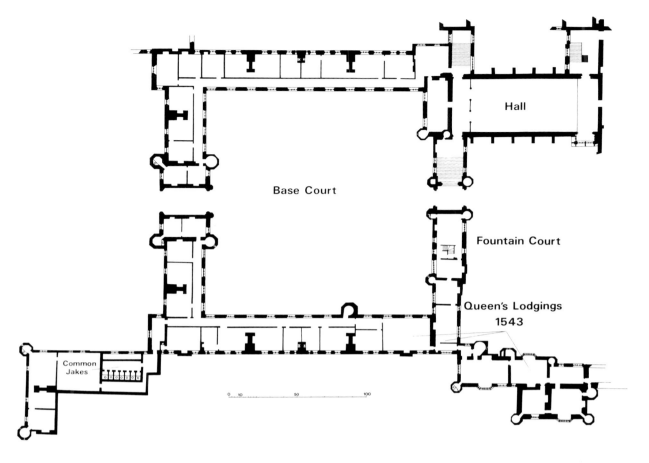

tified in the building accounts. Henry Norris, Groom of the Stole, executed in 1536, had a room directly adjacent to the King's closet at Greenwich; his rooms adjoined the King's at Hampton Court and at Whitehall he stayed in the privy gallery itself. Norris's successor as Groom, Sir Thomas Heneage, was lodged at Hampton Court directly below the King's privy chamber (see plan 7). All these men had lodgings close to the King, as did other favoured courtiers like George Boleyn, Lord Rochford, who had quarters below the King's privy chamber at Greenwich in 1535 (see plan 3), and Thomas Howard, Duke of Norfolk, whose room at Hampton Court was next to the King's bathroom.[64]

In addition to lodgings in the palace itself, many members of the Privy Chamber, peers and officers of state had houses in the grounds of royal houses or nearby. Most is known of the group of courtier town-houses at Greenwich. During the visit of the Emperor Charles V in 1522 a list was made indicating those Greenwich residents who had houses which could accommodate the Emperor's retinue. The names of the Earl of Kent, Nicholas Carew, Henry Norris, Henry Bird, William Cornish and Robert a Lee appear.[65] Other courtiers had houses there, including Sir Christopher Garnishe and Sir

Thomas Carwarden who had a particularly impressive residence which included a garden and an orchard.[66] Henry Norris, Groom of the Stool, was entitled to his own stable near the tiltyard at Greenwich, in addition to his houses there and at Eltham.[67]

At Hampton Court, Thomas Heneage had a large two-storey house next to the carpenter's yard. There was also a house for the Surveyor; his study, bedchamber and hall are mentioned.[68] At Whitehall likewise, many courtiers had houses nearby, Sir Anthony Browne, for instance, had owned property in Westminster from the early 1530s. In the 1540s Sir Anthony Denny, the Keeper of the Palace, owned seven acres of land in nearby Covent Garden. In addition, many lesser Court officials lived in and around Westminster, especially officers of the King's Works. Other residents included a 'yeoman of Prince Edward's household' who had tenements with gardens in Tothill.[69] At Richmond there is a similar story, but there, the house being of lesser stature than Whitehall, Hampton Court or Greenwich, we find only lesser members of the Court: the Sergeant of the Woodyard, Clerk of the Signet, Keeper of the Wardrobe, Yeoman Porter. A few significant courtiers are mentioned though, including Thomas,

129

Lord Darcy, Comptroller of the Household, Sir Henry Guildford and Hugh Denys.[70]

Larger and grander lodgings were often enjoyed by the King's chief ministers. Wolsey was treated with particular favour. Not only did he have lodgings at Eltham (see p. 46), but Cavendish tells us that because Wolsey had built such splendid lodgings for Henry at Hampton Court 'the kyng was well contentyd that he shold remove to Rychemond'. Hall confirms this and reports that Wolsey held open house there for Christmas 1526.[71] Thomas Cromwell likewise had use of the King's houses; Ralph Sadler wrote to Cromwell in 1537 stating that he had 'thanked the king on Cromwell's behalf for the commodity . . . in his houses of The Nete and St James's'. By 1538 Castillion was writing to Francis I to tell him that he would be 'at a house the king has given him [Cromwell] at the end of Westminster park'. Cromwell evidently used St James's, given or loaned, whilst the Court was at Whitehall; it also appears that Cromwell was given the use of Hanworth.[72] Thus for the most favoured of his servants the King was willing not only to devote substantial lodgings within the royal house, but actually to licence the use of one of the less favoured of his manors for private use.

For the King's closest advisers and ministers a lodging at Court was not just a place to sleep, for at Whitehall especially, a lodging was an office too. For officials such as Sir William Paget, Principal Secretary from April 1543, his lodging at Whitehall had to provide him with enough space for his secretaries and clerks as well as room for discussions with suitors and other ministers. Following the reorganisation of the King's secret lodgings at Whitehall in 1545, Paget lost his accommodation and was given in exchange two very small rooms in the northern gatehouse. He wrote from his embassy in France and complained to Sir William Petre:

> the chamber over the gate wil scant receyve my bedde, and a table to write at for myself . . . I have no place nother for my own clerks, nor such others as must serve his Majestie, . . . and His Majesties affayres be not written in every place, but where they may be secret, . . . If I had no more, but my chamber kepers, and the or four of myn own men, the two litle rowmes wer byg inowgh; but you know what a nomber we have alwayes, both of necessary ministeres, and also of suters . . .[73]

If Paget's outburst in November 1545 was provoked by an arbitary reallocation of a lodging, more common were arguments over the maintenance of lodgings. The occupant was the one who was responsible for furnishing and cleaning his chambers at Court, the Office of Works for maintaining the structure. The surviving book of expenses of the Marquess of Exeter from 1525 illustrates vividly how a leading courtier maintained and furnished his rooms at Court. He bought rushes for the floor of his chamber at Bridewell, hooks upon which to hang tapestries and a cord by which to suspend a tester. At Windsor more hooks were bought for his chamber. However, Exeter, like others at Court, occasionally received help from the King: a pallet was brought from the King's wardrobe to Exeter's chamber at Windsor, and at Greenwich in 1535 the Office of Works made him two stools.[74]

Very occasionally the King sanctioned alterations to a courtier's lodging at the Crown's expense. Such an occasion was in 1534 at Greenwich when Lord Rochford's lodging was altered for him, 'carpenters settyng upe of a hihe frame crese panellyd with waynscote mad for a stody in the lorde of Rochefords chamber with makyng of a wyndowe with molyene enbowde forthe same'.[75] Such departures were rare, the reason for Rochford's special treatment was that he was the King's brother-in-law.

In the Eltham Ordinances, Wolsey attempted to lay down strict rules for the allocation of accommodation at Court and included a list of people who were entitled to have lodgings permanently assigned to them. These people were distinct from those who at each house *might* have accommodation allocated by the King's Harbingers. The Harbingers allocated accommodation at each house visited on progress according to rank and availability, and they kept lists or 'books' to help them to perform this task at the Field of Cloth of Gold.[76]

At the lesser houses, where space was limited, once lodgings had been allocated there was no room for latecomers. An example of this is the occasion in 1529 when Campeggio and Wolsey visited the Court which was staying at Grafton.

> Thes ij prelattes beyng come to the Gattes of the Court . . . Supposyng that they shold have byn receyved by the hed officers of the howsse (as they ware wont to be) yet for as myche as Cardynall Campagious was but a straynger in effect the seyd Officers recyved them and conveyed hyme to a lodgyng within the Court which was prepared for hyme oonly. And after my lord had brought hyme thus to his lodgyng he left hyme ther and departed supposyng to have goon directly lyke wyse to his chamber . . . and by the way as he was goyng it was told hyme that he had no lodgyng appoynted for hyme in the court and . . . Sie Herre Norreys . . . came unto hyme . . . and most humbly offered hyme hys chamber for the tyme untill an other myght some where be provyded for hyme.[77]

130

169. Hampton Court, Surrey. Engraving of the base court, c.1800. The base court was built by Wolsey between 1514 and 1521 to accommodate his court and guests. It was later used for the same purpose by Henry VIII.

This is an example distorted by the deliberately humiliating insult being given to Wolsey, but the procedures used to slight him were common practice at Court.

At the greater houses at least, but also at some of the lesser ones, many courtiers had rooms set aside for their own use. About a hundred named individuals are known to have enjoyed the privilege of having their own reserved accommodation. Some, such as Thomas Howard, Duke of Norfolk, had rooms at as many as nine houses, including all the greater houses and lesser ones such as Ampthill and Woking. Others, such as John Skelton the poet, are known to have only had one — at Windsor. Certain conclusions can be drawn from this data.[78] First, lodgings were often permanently assigned to courtiers whether they were at Court or not. Paget wrote anxiously from Calais in 1545 enquiring 'where the king would keep Christmas, and what was to be done about his chamber at Westminster [Whitehall]'.[79] Wolsey, who had lavish provision made at all the greater houses, had a member of his household nominated as the keeper of his chamber in Court.[80] Also, and not surprisingly, it was mainly at the greater houses that lodgings were reserved. Of the total number of known lodgings, 30 per cent are at Greenwich, 31 per cent at Windsor, 19 per cent at Hampton Court and 6 per cent at Richmond and Whitehall. The low figure for Whitehall can be explained by the fact that no repair accounts survive from the 1530s and so there is no evidence about courtier lodgings there. Only the members of the Privy Chamber and high-ranking peers were assigned lodgings in the lesser houses, while large numbers of lesser courtiers could expect reserved lodgings at the greater houses.[81]

The position of these lodgings, and the identity of their occupant, is very difficult to establish. For instance, at Hampton Court there was the large and well-appointed base court (figs 167–9). It had two sorts of lodging, double and single. In the double lodgings there were two large rooms, each with a fireplace, and the inner one, which opened off the outer, had a garderobe in a partitioned closet (fig. 170). The single lodgings comprised a single room with a fireplace. There were twenty-seven double lodgings and thirteen single lodgings. As to the occupants, a lodgings' list from 1540 entitled 'lodginges in hampton courte used to be appointed by the gentleman ussher',[82] provides an invaluable pointer. There the ladies of the Queen's Privy Chamber, Master Heneage (Chief Gentleman of the Privy Chamber), Master Denny (a former and future Chief Gentleman), Lady Margaret Douglas, Princess Mary, Sir Anthony Browne (Master of the Horse) and Thomas Cromwell (Lord Privy Seal) all were assigned double lodgings. A double lodging was therefore a perk of a great officer of state, a royal child or a member of the Privy Chamber. But it was not as simple as that; for, given the choice, a courtier would prefer to lodge in a single room near the King than in a whole suite of rooms in the base court. Unfortunately the 1540 list does not name the assignees of the single lodgings, but presumably they were more minor figures at Court. The living arrangements in these lodgings mirrored those in the main part of the house where the assignee's body-servants slept in the outer chambers.

It is difficult to estimate the capacity of the King's houses to provide courtier lodgings. Calculations have to take on several imponderables such as the number of servants kept by any individual and the pressure on individuals to double-up on certain occasions. Yet we know that the lodgings in

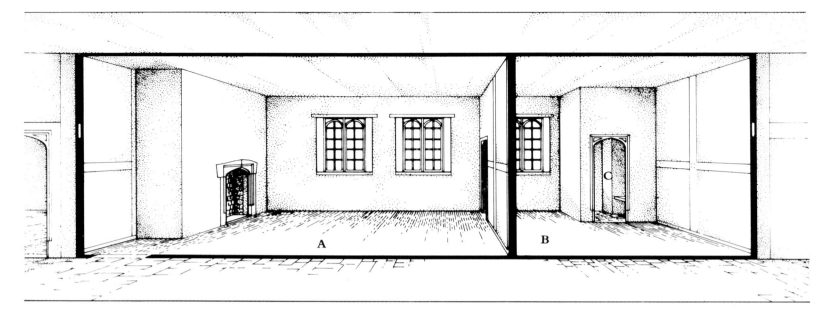

170. Hampton Court, Surrey. Reconstruction diagram showing a double lodging in the base court. A: outer chamber; B: inner chamber; C: garderobe. (Drawing Daphne Ford)

Hampton Court base court could accommodate forty courtiers and their ration of servants. The acute shortage of accommodation can be appreciated. The 1540 lodgings' list has at the end a note to the effect that there were ten lodgings outside the gate in towers in the gardens. The number of lodgings at Greenwich seems to have been much greater. The estimate for the lodging of the retinue of Charles V in 1522 reveals that lodgings for 360 people were available in the palace and town.[83] Subtracting the number of people listed as being accommodated in houses in the town, there were lodgings for 232 people in the palace and four courtier houses. Even if the latter could accommodate 10 people each, the palace itself would still have 192 lodgings, more than double the number available at Hampton Court.

Embassies and ambassadors

The vexatious matter of accommodation was exacerbated during embassies. The most extreme

171. *The Arrival of Charles II at the Banqueting House, Whitehall Palace*, attributed to Issac Fuller, *c.*1660. The gabled range in the centre is a lodging range, part of the Tudor palace. Inigo Jones's Banqueting House (far right) was itself built on the site of a lodging range of Henry VIII's.

132

example of this was the visit of the Emperor Charles V in 1522. There was absolutely no hope of accommodating all the Emperor's retinue in royal buildings and most of the prominent men of the City of London had to provide lodging in their houses.[84] In addition many of the King's own servants were removed from their chambers at Court to provide room for the Emperor's men. Once the visit was over Thomas Compton, a Groom of the King's Chamber, put in a bill for 'the lodgyng of the ymbassytores of the empower for wod in ther chamber and making clene of my howes and wassyng ther sheets with other'.[85] Visits on this scale sent the officers of the Wardrobe scurrying from place to place with beds, hangings and furnishings and involved the Grooms of the Chamber in enormous amounts of overtime setting up and taking down interiors.[86]

All this was exceptional. The usual impact of foreign dignitaries was confined to the resident ambassadors, and the occasional small embassy. On the latter occasions it was often not possible, nor politically desirable, to accommodate them in Court. In 1515 a visiting embassy was lodged in three houses and the Greyhound Inn at Greenwich.[87] Sometimes they were given lodgings in a lesser house if the Court was staying at a greater one nearby. Henry VII lodged ambassadors at Baynard's Castle in 1508.[88] The following year when the Scots ambassadors were in London for Henry VIII's coronation they were put up at the Archbishop of York's house, York Place, and in June 1540, while at Hampton Court, Henry had Hanworth set up for the reception of a visiting delegation.[89]

The first resident ambassador to be accredited to the English Court arrived from Venice in 1483, and the Venetian Republic maintained ambassadors in England throughout the sixteenth century. Ferdinand and Isabella sent their first resident ambassador to England, but it was not until 1528 that the French decided to follow suit.[90] More is known about the housing of the French ambassadors than of their Venetian and Spanish counterparts. In 1531 Gilles de la Pommerage was invited to use Bridewell, and from that date it remained fairly consistently the official residence of the French ambassador until the establishment of Bridewell Hospital in 1553–4. Indeed, it would not be an exaggeration to claim that Bridewell was the first embassy building in England. When the French first moved in, the house was repaired for them at the King's expense. But in 1534 when the question of paying for repairs arose again, William Symons wrote to Cromwell to ask 'whether the provision shalbe made at brydewell at the kyng's charges or elles the ambassaders'. It is not known what was done on that occasion, but in 1538 the King supplied the house with tapestry and furniture for the French.[91]

The tenure privilege of Bridewell depended on the diplomatic situation. In July 1535 during a period of coolness towards Francis I, the Bishop of Tarbes, who had only recently been painted by Holbein standing, apparently securely, in the house, was 'respectfully requested to leave' by Cromwell,[92] but the minister's request was shortly withdrawn. In 1537 the Bishop's successor, the sieur de Castillon found Bridewell too expensive for his needs but was helped out financially by the King the following year.[93] Nevertheless, as only one repair bill survives in the royal accounts, maintenance must have generally been the responsibility of the French.[94] The Spanish ambassadors did not share the same good fortune as the French. Eustace Chapuys referred to 'his apartments' at Hampton Court in July 1538, but this reference seems to be unique.[95] Yet the reference may indicate that ambassadors occupied lodgings at several or all of the greater houses.

172. Hampton Court, Surrey. A view from the east by an unknown artist, *c.*1663–70. The great canal was dug on the orders of Charles I, but the range of buildings behind was built by Henry VIII in the 1530s to contain his, and his queen's, innermost lodgings.

Chapter 8

THE INWARD CHAMBERS

THE INWARD CHAMBERS FROM THE DOOR of the privy chamber onwards, fell under the control of the King's Privy Chamber, the privy chamber being not only a room but the organisation which populated and governed the inward rooms. The inward chambers were divided into an outer and an inner sanctum for the King. The outer part was known as the privy lodging, the innermost part the secret lodging. The inward chambers did not follow a standard layout, and the extent of both the privy and the secret lodging varied with the size of the house. At a large property such as Hampton Court there was a whole range of rooms including studies, libraries, private dining-rooms, drawing-rooms and several bedrooms. At a smaller house such as Nonsuch the inward rooms might be restricted to a closet or two and a bedchamber.

The development of the inward lodgings

The expansion of the inward lodgings is one of the central themes in the evolution of Henry VIII's houses after 1530 until his death. Before 1530 the King's inward rooms were a fairly small group of private rooms usually sited in a donjon containing a study, library, bathroom, garderobe or other private accommodation. However, in the early 1530s, the accommodation provided in the inward lodgings increased dramatically so that they became a complex of private rooms. The actual moment of expansion in the development of the inward rooms at Hampton Court and Whitehall can be pin-pointed. The first royal building account at Hampton Court, dated April 1529, opens with a bill for 'Dyggyng and lyke making other wyed and deipe foundacions where uppon dyvers baynes shall stonde'.[1] These 'baynes' or baths were to be situated in a tower (the bayne tower) immediately beyond the King's privy chamber (figs 173–4, and see plans 7, 8).[2] This tower, three storeys high, contained an office at ground-floor level, a new bedroom, bathroom and study at first-floor level, and on the second floor a library and jewel-house. The tower was squeezed into a small courtyard between the King's bed-

chamber and his long gallery and was intended to make the private accommodation at the house fit for the King.

135

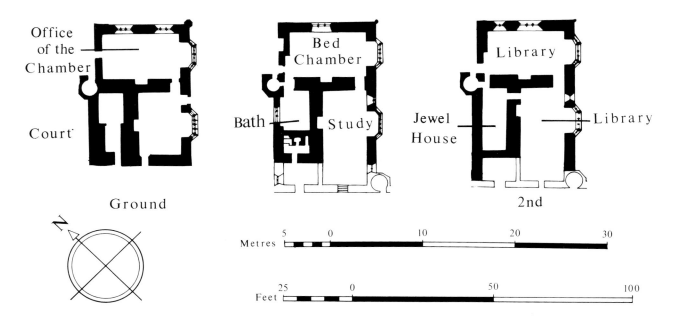

174. Hampton Court, Surrey. Plan of the bayne tower as first built, c.1530.

Office of the Chamber Court

Ground

Bed Chamber

Bath — Study

Library

Jewel House — Library

2nd

Metres 5 0 10 20 30

Feet 25 0 50 100

173 (previous page). Hampton Court, Surrey. The bayne tower today. Although partly refaced and with Victorian windows, the surviving structure gives a good impression of the size of Henry VIII's structure. The first-floor windows in the foreground were originally those of Henry VIII's bedchamber; the windows above were those of his library. Today the bayne tower is a grace-and-favour residence.

The erection of the Hampton Court 'bayne tower' was in the hallowed tradition of building donjons to provide small private rooms for a monarch. But this was to be the last tower lodging built by an English King, for in April 1531, two years later, foundations for a radically different privy lodging were being dug at Whitehall. This was the 'new gallery' or privy gallery (see plan 13)[3] which was to be the equivalent of the bayne tower at Hampton Court; it provided a series of private rooms for Henry VIII. But there were fundamental differences. At Whitehall they were all on one level leading off a gallery, not stacked as previously. They were also far more extensive than the accommodation provided by the bayne tower. At Whitehall the bathroom was situated on the ground floor and on the first floor there were at least ten rooms available for the King's use. More significantly, where the bedchamber had hitherto adjoined the privy chamber there were now four rooms separating the privy chamber from the bedchamber, and beyond the bedchamber came five further rooms and a gallery (see plan 13). This arrangement of privy gallery and lodgings at Whitehall in 1531 was highly innovative and was not only to provide the model for the remaining sixteen years of Henry VIII's reign, but one which was to last well into the eighteenth century. The revolutionary change in the design of Henry VIII's innermost lodgings between 1529 and 1531 was linked directly with changes in the organisation of the King's private attendants, a sub-department of the royal Household known as the King's Privy Chamber.

From 1509 Henry VIII had followed his father's example in appointing a Privy Chamber, which was headed for sixteen years by Henry VIII's child-hood friend and favourite, Sir William Compton, as Groom of the Stole.[4] Until 1518 the Privy Chamber had been a department staffed by socially somewhat insignificant men, but in that year the King changed all that by drafting in a group of young favourites including Edward Neville, Nicholas Carew, Francis Bryan and Henry Norris, whom he renamed *gentilhommes de chambre*, after the French fashion. If the King was enamoured of these new companions of his, popularly nicknamed 'the minions', few others were taken with them. Adverse reactions, costs and the palpable need to define the role of the Privy Chamber resulted in the department being reformed in 1519. Not only were its functions clearly defined, but its finances were regularised and its staff salaried. These reforms produced a sophisticated, autonomous department of the Household staffed with men of rank, money and ability.[5]

The first detailed instructions regarding the duties of the Privy Chamber staff were included in the Eltham Ordinances of 1526. These further defined the department by clearly setting out the function and extent of both the quarters and the personnel of the Privy Chamber. In the good keeping of the privy chamber rested 'the King's quiet, rest, comfort and preservation of his health', therefore 'noe person . . . from henceforth presume, attempt or be . . . admitted to come or repair into the King's privy chamber; other than such only as his grace shall from time to time call for'. Six Gentlemen, two Ushers, four Grooms, a Barber and a Page, each with clearly specified duties, attended the King in his private room. The Groom of the Stole, the man in charge of the organisation, was now to be Henry Norris, a former 'minion' who had escaped the expulsions of 1519. The Groom of the Stole alone had access to the King's 'bedchamber, or any other secret place, unlesse he shall be called and admitted thereunto by his said grace'.[6]

So in architectural terms, the Eltham Ordinances envisaged a graded system. First, the privy chamber, a single room next to the bedchamber,[7] to which the full complement of fifteen staff had access. Second, the bedchamber and secret places to which only the King and Groom of the Stole had access. This graduated system had been introduced to all the royal houses under Henry VII. The donjons at the Tower, Windsor, Greenwich and elsewhere had been his equivalent to the secret places — those privy areas behind the closed privy chamber door. Wolsey in the Eltham Ordinances was only giving written force to the architectural status quo. He had not, however, taken into account the changed nature of the staff of the Privy Chamber, and therefore the changing function of the room itself. Under Henry VII the privy chamber, as a room, was the centre of the King's business and private life — his social and political life was conducted outside the privy chamber in the public rooms. But Henry VIII's privy chamber, filled with his friends and confidants, was the forum of his social life and the field for rivalry between royal favourites. Membership of the Privy Chamber was highly sought after, bringing with it not only personal intimacy with the King but wealth, influence and power.[8] The attractions of Privy Chamber membership were magnetic. Although in 1526 there were the designated fifteen staff, by 1530 the number had risen to twenty, and by 1539 to twenty-eight.[9] This rapid expansion in personnel entailed a corresponding architectural expansion.

The privy lodgings at Whitehall are crucial to an understanding of this enlargement. They were the first of their kind (see plan 13).[10] Here, between 1530 and 1532 the territory of the Privy Chamber was stretched by adding a full four new rooms between the privy chamber and the bedchamber. With this change the Whitehall privy lodging ceased to be a single room as laid down by the ordinance of 1526, and became a suite of five rooms managed, by 1532, by twenty-four staff. The privy chamber itself became the first, and in time the most public, of the King's private rooms. Beyond it, in the direction of the bedchamber, now lay three further rooms in which the life of the Privy Chamber was played out.

However, the King still needed to retain his most private rooms, in other words those situated beyond the bedchamber before 1530. At Whitehall, after passing through the bedchamber one came to a gallery and at the end of that, two more secret rooms in the palace gatehouse. We know about these secret lodgings from two inventories, one

taken in 1543, and the other on the King's death in 1547.[11] The picture they paint is of six rooms filled with the King's most personal and valued possessions. The value of the contents of the secret lodgings was one of the reasons that access to them was even more restricted than to the privy lodgings. The appellations 'private' and 'secret' in the inventories confirm that they were the province of the King only. Access was, as laid down in 1526, controlled by the Groom of the Stole, who in the 1540s was Sir Anthony Denny. These rooms were 'perticulerly charged upon the same anthony denny by the kinges commandement'.[12] However, others clearly had access to the rooms; Philip van Wilder, 'one of the king his gracs privy chamber', and the King's Clerk, Nicholas Bristowe, both received goods in the secret jewel-house in Whitehall in February 1543.[13]

The secret lodgings at Whitehall underwent a two-stage development. In the 1530s there were only a few rooms beyond the King's bedchamber inaccessible from the privy gallery. Indeed, the gallery was used as a thoroughfare early in the reign to obtain access to the gallery beside the tiltyard, and the gatehouse itself was used for viewing the wedding jousts celebrating Henry's union with Anne Boleyn.[14] During the rebuilding of Whitehall in the 1540s the gallery was closed off to the Court and the King's new secret lodgings were set up in it.[15] The reasons for this further expansion of secret accommodation can again be found in the organisation of the departments of the King's Household.

In 1540 the Privy Council was formally constituted.[16] It was a body mainly drawn from the King's Household who met daily at Court, wherever the King might be. At most of the King's houses there were council chambers. Those built early in the reign had been positioned in small square rooms off the King's long gallery. This was the case at the Tower (see fig. 8),[17] at Wolsey's York Place (see plan 15),[18] at Bridewell (see fig. 54)[19] and at Hampton Court (see plan 8).[20] This particular location seems to have been an innovation of Wolsey's, for at the Tower, at least, the position of the council chamber was moved in Henry VIII's reign from its place during his father's reign to a new position in the long gallery.[21] At Whitehall, in 1532, the council chamber was built off the King's long gallery, in line with the plan of the houses built earlier in the reign (see plan 13).[22] It was thus within the King's privy lodging and approached from the privy gallery.

For over two decades of his reign Henry VIII's council was not a formal body and so the location of the council chamber within the privy lodgings was not of great significance. In 1540, however, the Privy Council became a fully-fledged body of state

137

with right of access into the privy lodging. By Cromwell's ordinances of 1540 all the privy councillors had the right to dine in the council chamber — flooding the privy lodging with a further group of courtiers.[23] By 1539, therefore, there was not only a much enlarged Privy Chamber (twenty-eight men), but there was also the Privy Council (with nineteen). So the privy lodgings with a staff of forty-seven people were hardly 'privy' any longer. The King was thus forced to retreat once more, this time into a newly set up and extended secret lodging.

As the privy and secret lodgings become progressively more private, information about them becomes harder to acquire. Yet we know what the plan was like at Hampton Court in the same period, and there, as at Whitehall, the graded private sector of the palace can be seen: the semi-public privy lodgings and the highly restricted secret lodgings.[24] There (see plans 8, 13) the whole south side of the inner court was given over to a second set of public rooms, the east front contained the privy lodgings, and the secret lodgings were on the ground floor. Similarly at Greenwich, the King's secret lodgings occupied the west side of the inner court, while his privy lodgings preceded them on the river front (see plan 4).

The privy lodgings

The privy chamber itself was, during the reign of Henry VII and in the early part of that of Henry VIII, the centre of the King's non-public life. The ordinance of 1526 spells out in some detail the way life was conducted in the room and the topography of the King's houses substantiates this picture. The staff of the Privy Chamber comprised the Gentlemen, Grooms, the Ushers, a Page and the Barber. The Gentlemen were the key servants; two of them slept on 'pallets' on the floor of the chamber at night. They waited on the King, dressed him in the mornings, stood by all day to do the King's bidding, occupied the privy chamber in the King's absence and waited on him while he dined. Below them in rank were the Gentlemen Ushers who were the contact with the outside world. They kept guard at the door to the chamber and may have been based in the gallery between the privy and presence chambers to ensure that only those entitled to enter did so; they also acted as carriers of the King's clothes and at mealtimes passed food in to the Gentlemen who served the King. The Grooms served the Gentlemen and acted as domestic servants. They cleared away the pallets on which the Gentlemen slept, cleaned the room and made the fires. In addition there was at least one Page (the junior 'odd-job-man'), and a Barber to shave and groom the King each day. In charge of them all, and second only to the King in terms of domestic power, was the Groom of the Stole who alone had right of entry into the bedchamber and into the secret places beyond. Additionally, and less formally, there was a fluctuating group of musicians whose task was to entertain the King at his pleasure.

Early in the reign most of Henry VIII's time was spent in the privy chamber. He frequently dined there served by its staff, and detailed regulations set out the way that this was performed. A mid-sixteenth-century view of Henry dining probably shows him in a privy chamber (fig. 175). A large number of Gentlemen and Grooms can be seen serving Henry who is seated, alone, beneath a canopy.[25] Sometimes the King would eat in greater seclusion than that afforded by his privy chamber, and retire to a spot in the secret lodgings. At Hunsdon, in 1528, the King was said to be in secret communication with his physician, William Chambers, in 'a chamber within a towre where his hignes sometyme useth to suppe aparte' (figs 106–7).[26]

The area around the privy chamber was designed to ensure its smooth operation. The privy kitchen where the King's food was prepared was normally sited beneath the privy lodgings (see pp. 160–1). At both Greenwich and Hampton Court the King's wardrobe of the robes, which stored the King's and Queen's personal clothes, was positioned directly

175. Henry VIII dining, by an unknown, late sixteenth-century artist (larger than actual size). The form of the windows and wall panelling suggest a late sixteenth-century date for this drawing. It is unlikely to be representative of a real interior as there is no door on the far wall. The scene shown may be representative of the King's dining habits in the 1540s. He is seated in his privy chamber and being served by his Gentlemen; on the right there is a buffet.

beneath his privy chamber and a vice-stair linked it with the privy chamber above (see plans 3, 7). This enabled the Yeoman of the Wardrobe to bring the clothes up to the privy chamber door and hand them over to the Usher without going in. Nearby were also stationed the lodgings of the Privy Chamber staff. The Grooms, Waiters and Barber were assigned lodgings at Court as were the Gentlemen, who might be given substantial accommodation (see pp. 128–32). The Groom of the Stole was given a room directly adjacent to the King's within the privy lodging; at Greenwich this communicated directly with the King's bedchamber.

During the 1520s and early 1530s the privy chamber was in its heyday, but the expansion in personnel and territory which occurred after 1530 heralded its decay. The success of the organisation undermined the very thing it had been invented to protect — the King's privacy. From about 1540 the privy chamber had been opened up to admit others than those who were strictly the members of the Privy Chamber and gradually several of the functions previously held in the presence chamber were switched to it. Whereas elevations to the peerage had hitherto been performed in the presence chamber, the ennoblement of Sir John Dudley as Viscount Lisle in March 1542 was carried out in the privy chamber at Whitehall. In May 1544 it was from the throne in the privy chamber at Whitehall that Henry VIII conferred the Great Seal on Lord Wriothesley, and in February 1544 the Duke of Najera was received in the privy chamber. The same process occurred on the Queen's side, in April 1544 Queen Catherine Parr distributed maundy money in her privy chamber.[27]

This invasion of the privy lodgings by large numbers of courtiers participating in state ceremonial made the privy chamber more of an ante-room to the privy lodgings. It should be noted that at Whitehall by 1547 there was a room beyond the privy chamber, between it and the privy gallery; this room has every appearance of having been a withdrawing room, which acted, like the closet-and-gallery, as a break between the now rather more public privy chamber and the privy lodgings. At Woodstock there is reference to the 'utter prevy chambre', which might indicate that, as at Whitehall, there was a graded series of rooms rather than just one privy chamber.[28]

Parallels with later developments in the royal Household would suggest that this was the case. By the time of Charles II the Household ordinances stated: 'For our Privy Chamber, though We find it much changed from the ancient institution, both in number of gentlemen and their service; neverthelesse we are pleased to continue a fitt number . . .'.[29] It was certainly much changed, for James I had formalised what seems first to have taken place in

the reign of Henry VIII: the replacement of the Privy Chamber with a new sub-department — the Bedchamber. Because the privy chamber, and the privy lodgings, had become so populous the King's true private life had retreated to the bedchamber; no longer was membership of the Privy Chamber the prize it had once been. Access to the secret lodgings was now the most coveted prize. To formalise this situation James I established an organisation modelled on the Tudor Privy Chamber, but focused on the new centre of the King's private life, the bedchamber.[30] The one remaining link with the past was the Groom of the Stole, the Tudor head of the Privy Chamber and the only person whose entry into the secret lodgings during Henry VIII's reign was assured by ordinance. Around him collected a group of 'inner' Privy Chamber members, the men who in James I's reign became the Gentlemen of the Bedchamber.[31]

The secret lodgings

The secret lodgings adhered to no set plan other than that they began with a bedchamber. In this they differed very much from the outward rooms and to a degree from the privy lodgings, both of which followed an unvarying sequence. The extent of the secret lodgings varied from a single closet at a small lesser house to the extensive lodgings of Whitehall or Hampton Court. Something is known of the Whitehall secret lodgings described in an inventory of 1547: 'the king's secrete wardrope at Westminster the stuffe lefte in the kings secrete juelhouse, in the studye at the nether ende of the long gallerye, in the chaierhouse and the studie next the kinges olde bedchamber'. Most of these rooms can be identified (see plan 13).[32]

The study at the 'nether' end of the gallery was presumably the room at the western end of the privy gallery range, beyond the library. The chairhouse (also called the King's secret study) was probably in the northern gatehouse. It acquired this unlikely name from 'two chaires called trammes for the kings maiesty to sitt in to be carried to and fro in his galleries and chambers'.[33] These were wheelchairs, designed to move the King during the bouts of disablement caused by his ulcerated leg. Above the chair-house was the King's upper library; an account describes it as being 'over the porter's lodge'.[34] Then there was the secret jewel-house, which faced the great garden, and so must have been situated off the privy gallery. Finally, there was the King's secret wardrobe, described as 'the kings owne wardrobe house in the long gallery at Westminster'.[35] This may have been situated on the ground floor beneath the King's lodgings, being part of the wardrobe of the robes.

The bedchamber

In very few houses did the King or the Queen have only a single bedchamber; by 1547 in all of the greater houses, the King had at least two, if not three. First there was the formal official bedchamber, the room which came after the privy chamber or immediately after the privy lodgings. This room housed the bed of estate, in which the King officially slept during the night. Sometimes this bed was not designed for slumber, for the King often had a lesser bedchamber next door or close by where he was actually accustomed to sleep. This was the case at Hampton Court, for instance (see p. 52). By the 1540s a third bedchamber was normally provided on the Queen's side, and this, presumably, was where he went if he desired to sleep with his wife. The plans of Hampton Court (see plan 8) and Greenwich (see plan 4) fit this pattern.[36] Almost everywhere the bedchamber had a garderobe or stool-room attached.

References to occurrences in Henry VIII's bedchamber are rare. This, given its innate privacy, is not all that surprising, but it is in total contrast to what is known of the bedchamber of Francis I of France. Sir Richard Wingfield wrote to Wolsey in 1520 stating of Francis that 'after dinner assembled all the great personages of the realm in his bedchamber'.[37] Nothing of this sort would have ever taken place in an English king's private bedroom. Great occasions of state did take place in bedchambers, but only those of a special nature. Each of these events was surrounded by careful procedures, many of which were written down in Household regulations.

Only one account of a royal consummation survives from the sixteenth century, that of Henry VIII's elder brother Prince Arthur with Catherine of Aragon, an event, or non-event, which was to have enormous consequences. After the newly-wed couple had finished their dinner at about five in the afternoon, Henry VII sent the Lord Chamberlain to the Duchess of Norfolk, the Countess of Cabra (for Catherine) and the Prince and Princess's 'mistresses' with instructions to prepare their bedchamber, which took about three hours. After the Lord Chamberlain had ensured that all was well the Princess was escorted to the bed, shortly to be followed by the Prince, the King and many of the Court. At this point the wedding service was resumed and the bed and bedchamber were blessed by the priests and bishops present. Wine and spices were then served before the assembled company left and 'thise worthy persones concludid and consummat theffecte and complement of the sacrement of matrimony' or, perhaps, as Catherine later claimed and Henry was forced to admit, did not.[38]

Details of where the King and Queen slept together after marriage are less fully recorded, but evidence cited during Henry VIII's attempts to divorce Catherine of Aragon suggest that in the 1520s Henry went to Catherine's lodgings when he wanted to sleep with her. These occasions were sometimes preceded by a meal together, and it seems likely that the dinners given by all the King's wives in their apartments ended — or were intended to end — with their joint withdrawal into the Queen's bedchamber.[39] Household regulations only once break silence on the subject, and that is to outline the historical precedents for the king being accompanied by servants during intercourse with his wife. Henry V, we learn, had his Chamberlain and Steward in the room, but in latter days they were 'removed in a short season' while outside the door lay squires.[40]

To facilitate the King's infidelities special arrangements were made. Thus in May 1510 William Compton, the King's Groom of the Stole, was involved in arranging an intrigue between the King and the sisters of the Duke of Buckingham. Unfortunately Buckingham caught Compton in one of their rooms and the matter came to the notice of Catherine of Aragon. Mistress Amadas, wife of Robert Amadas, sometime Master of the Jewelhouse, was given to prophecy, hallucinations and had a sharp tongue: she claimed to be one of three virtuous women in England, yet she broadcast how, to mask her affair with the King from the Court, Compton arranged liaisons at his own house in Thames Street.[41] The fact that the King and Queen kept their own separate households and itineraries facilitated such liaisons, a fact which Henry used unscrupulously in his pursuit of Anne Boleyn.

The result of Henry's legitimate liaisons was expected to be the production of an heir. The birth of a royal child was surrounded by detailed Court etiquette. The Queen retired to her bedchamber four to six weeks before confinement, her bedchamber was carefully prepared and hung, its floors carpeted and a bed specially made. Just as she went into labour the Queen made a final public appearance, first going to chapel followed by the lords and ladies of the Court, then taking spice and wine in the great chamber before bidding farewell to the men and entering the exclusively female world of her bedchamber. There, attended by her servants, she would wait to be delivered, whilst outside waited priests in preparation for a hasty baptism, if needed, and courtiers ready to dispatch news to the King.[42] Details of the confinement of Anne Boleyn at Greenwich before the birth of Princess Elizabeth survive. In August 1533 carpenters were busy laying of 'a ffalse rooffe in the quenes bede chamb ffor to seyle and hange yt wth clothe of ares and makyng off a cubborde of state with an alpace with iii shelves ffor the quenes plate to stonde upon'. Meanwhile her presence chamber was divided in two by an arras and a second great bed was made in it in which the Queen could receive female visitors.[43] On 26 August Anne took her confinement and on 7 September the Queen was delivered of a Princess. Henry's next surviving child, Prince Edward, was delivered at Hampton Court and there equally lavish provisions were made. Jane Seymour's bedchamber was fitted with curtains around the bay window, an internal wooden porch was made round the door, the chimney-piece painted and a screen put round her bed.[44] Prince Edward was soon moved to his own bedchamber (see p. 80) where special provisions were made: 'making a fframe of skaffolde polis over the prynsis bed to kepe a waye the hete of the sonne'.[45] These are rare glimpses into the Queen's and Prince's apartments of which otherwise little is known.

Like birth, death was a feature of the bedchamber. On 24 October 1537, following the birth of Prince Edward, Jane Seymour died in the Queen's bedchamber at Hampton Court, where she was later embalmed before being laid out in state. Not much more is known about the King's own death on 28 January 1547 in the bedchamber at Whitehall. Late in December 1546 the King had been very unwell and had almost completely retreated to his secret lodgings. It was generally noted that 'few persons have access to his lodging and his chamber'. Not even Queen Catherine or Princess Mary was allowed in to see him. After his death it was reported: 'Three days afterwards I learnt from a very confidential source that the king . . . had departed this life, although not the slightest signs of such a thing were to be seen at court, and even the usual ceremony of bearing in the royal dishes to the sounds of trumpets was continued without interruption'. The efficacy of Henry's secret lodgings as developed by 1547 was thus proved by the fact that he did not have to be alive for Court etiquette to continue.[46]

The closet

The term closet signifies either a small private room for secular use, usually business, or an oratory with or without an altar. Generally, apart from the oratory in the closet-and-gallery, the type of closet found in the privy lodgings was of the business type. A detailed description of the King's closet or 'privy closet' at Hampton Court survives. In this lavishly decorated room Henry VIII had all the paraphernalia of an early sixteenth-century office with cupboards, tables, boxes, chests and

a clock.[47] Not all closets were so functional, for many were more like the seventeenth-century cabinet of curiosities, indeed they were sometimes called cabinets and had cases, possibly glazed, round the walls containing curios, antiques and precious items. A closet at Greenwich in 1547 contained everything from tennis-rackets to a box of needlework samples, another closet had coffers and chests piled up, a cupboard wired to the wall and a press over that cupboard — all were filled with curiosities.[48]

A refinement of the closet was the jewel-house, one of which formed part of the King's 'bayne tower' at Hampton Court in 1529 (figs 173–4), another of the privy gallery at Whitehall. The jewel-houses normally had more valuable items than mere closets, either jewellery, plate or considerable sums of cash — the privy coffers. The privy coffers at Whitehall often contained as much as £50,000, and those at Greenwich held similarly large sums. At Greenwich 'gret trussyng coffers ffor the kyngs plate' were kept in the privy chamber. These were possibly the 'removing coffers' rather than a permanent store of plate. At Whitehall there were certainly 'removing coffers' which were used to carry money about with the King.[49]

Closets and libraries sometimes overlapped in the lesser houses although at the greater ones they were usually distinct rooms. Although Edward IV had been a keen collector of books he carried books from place to place and there was no permanent establishment.[50] It was Henry VII who added to his household the office of Librarian, first held by a naturalised Frenchman named Quentin Poulet. He and his successors began to build up a library which was eventually to total several thousand volumes. Henry VIII continued the tradition, appointing another Frenchman, Giles Duwes.

Henry VII had certainly built a library at Richmond and at the Tower, and there was also one at Westminster. His son created new libraries at Whitehall, Hampton Court and Greenwich, although there were several subsidiary ones. The King's burgeoning collection was considerably augmented at the dissolution of the monasteries and the expansion of the Hampton Court and Whitehall libraries coincide with this.[51] In the absence of a complete set of catalogues from Henry VIII's library it is impossible to estimate its exact size, but the inventory for Whitehall in 1547 lists 910 volumes in the 'upper library' there.

The gallery

One of Henry VIII's first alterations to Wolsey's house at Hampton Court was to build a second

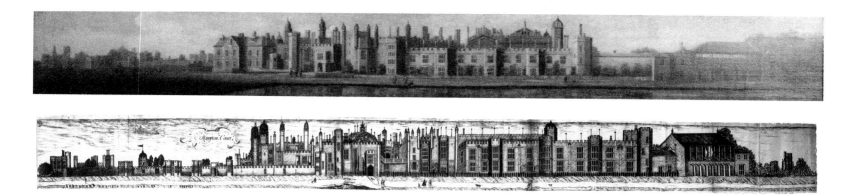

176 (top). Hampton Court, Surrey. View from the east by an unknown artist, c.1673–88. The view shows (from left to right) the east wall of the privy garden, the new block built by Charles II in 1671–3, the queen's lodgings and the queen's gallery, behind which are the hall and chapel. On the far right is the Stuart tennis-court.

177 (above). Hampton Court, Surrey. View from the east by an unknown artist, c.1656–70. Although rather a confusing drawing, the queen's lodgings can be clearly seen, including (centre) a balcony from which the queen and her ladies could watch the chase. The diaper-work on the external brickwork can just be made out, as can the painted grotesque-work on the exterior wall of the queen's bedchamber.

storey, on top of the long gallery.[52] Both the new 'privy story' and Wolsey's old gallery were approached from the King's bayne tower, his innermost sanctum. The gallery was therefore truly 'privy' (see plans 5, 8). When a gallery was built for the Queen at Hampton Court in 1537 it led directly from her bedchamber (figs 176–8 and see plan 8). The Hampton Court galleries were by no means unique in being part of the privy lodging. The gallery at the Tower of London led directly off the Lanthorn Tower, which was probably the King's bedchamber (see fig. 8). At Whitehall likewise, both the King's and Queen's galleries led off their bedchambers (see plan 13). These examples suggest that the royal gallery of the 1530s was designed for private royal use.

As with other parts of the secret lodging, the use of the gallery is best illustrated by considering its furnishings. Most galleries were furnished with a few tables, forms and stools, but were principally for hanging pictures, tapestries, mirrors and other 'tables', carved, fired or moulded (fig. 179). They were located in positions with good views. The second-floor Hampton Court gallery overlooked the gardens and the Thames, while the Whitehall privy gallery, originally had a prospect of the privy garden. Galleries were havens of calm and beauty with views within and without. They were places for the King and Queen and carefully invited guests to walk and talk in confidence and comfort. They were not part of the general public domain of the house but more like a stretch-closet, a place where curiosities and conversation could be combined.

The privy gallery at Hampton Court, like that at Nonsuch, Greenwich and Whitehall, was connected directly by a vice-stair to the privy garden, an extension of the King's privy lodgings. The gardens were walled off from the rest of the grounds and entered through locked doors to which only Privy Chamber members had keys.[53] Access from the building itself was only from the King's privy lodgings and so total privacy for the King could be assured. In a sense the gallery was a garden for wintertime, for in the summer the state papers show how those private conversations and strolls with ministers and courtiers happened outside rather than in.

Privy lodgings of the royal family

The privy and secret lodgings of the royal family presumably paralleled Henry VIII's. Evidence is, however, very thin on the ground. The only occasions when the veil is lifted are during the trials of Anne Boleyn and Catherine Howard, and the dirty washing hung out during those occasions would shame the modern tabloid press. In reply to questions by her interrogators Anne Boleyn said

that Mark Smeaton 'wase never in my chamber but at winchester' and there she sent for 'hym to play on the virginals for there my lodginge was above the kings . . . for I never spake with hym syns bot upon saterday before mayday; and then I fond hym standyng in the ronde wyndo in my chambr of presens'.[54] Six years later Queen Catherine Howard testified as to the steps taken to discover the layout of her privy lodgings at each house visited on progress: 'Item she seyth that my lady Rocheford wold at eevery lodgyng serche the bak doores and tell hir of them if there were eny'.[55] Once the back service ways into the Queen's privy lodgings were located, they were allegedly used to admit Queen Catherine's paramour Thomas Culpeper. Her testimony suggests that the extent of the privy and secret lodgings of the Queen were as considerable as those of the King himself.

179. Girolamo da Treviso the Younger, *The Four Evangelists Stoning the Pope*, *c*.1540. This is the only surviving work of art the location of which can be identified in any of Henry VIII's houses. It hung in his gallery at Hampton Court.

178 (facing page bottom). Hampton Court, Surrey. Detail of fig. 172. Obscured by a low paling, immediately in front of the east front was a moat. The bridge giving access into the park can be seen in front of the main doorway.

Chapter 9

THE TUDOR ROYAL KITCHEN: FEEDING THE COURT

THE HOUSEHOLD DEPARTMENTS WHICH fed Henry VIII, his family and Court, had grown in size but otherwise had evolved imperceptibly from the early Middle Ages. Scrutiny of the household ordinance of 1318 reveals very little different from Edward IV's regulations as set out in the Black Book. The changes which did occur in the early 1470s were more in the sphere of ceremony than organisation. The arrangements described in the Black Book survived unaltered into the reign of Henry VIII;[1] these were confirmed and reinforced in the Eltham Ordinances of 1526 by Cardinal Wolsey and somewhat modified in the Greenwich Ordinances by Lord Cromwell during 1539–40.

Until 1540 the department was headed by the Lord Steward of the Household, and thereafter by the Lord Great Master. The onus of the administration fell on the Treasurer, the Cofferer and the Comptroller (each with a white stave to designate his authority); they ran the domestic economy of the Court from the Board of the Greencloth. In this they were assisted by three Clerks of the Greencloth and several Clerks Comptroller.[2] The Lord Steward was a highly prestigious appointment, held successively by George Talbot, 1st Earl of Shrewsbury (to 1538), by Charles Brandon, Duke of Suffolk (1540–45) and William Paulet, Lord St John of Basing (1545–1550). As these men had numerous other commitments, in practice it was the Cofferer who had the day-to-day responsibility. He was the chief financial officer of the Household and dispensed money to the various offices. Under Lord Cromwell's reforms of 1539–40 the Office of the Greencloth assumed the task of paying the wages of the entire Court and thus became the primary financial body in the Household. Help was given to the existing staff in the guise of four Masters of the Household who were to help in the regulation of lodgings at Court 'whereby the King's house shall be the lesse pestered, and the lodgings easier for the king's traine'.[3]

Unlike the buildings of the Lord Chamberlain's department, the 'upstairs' part of the royal house,

the architectural form of Henry VIII's kitchens and offices was not susceptible to every subtle change in the political, economic and social life of the King. For, as the essential duties of the Lord Steward's department remained the same — feeding the Court and supplying it with all the comestibles required for everyday life — so did the form of its buildings. Any alterations to the plan of the service departments of the English royal house took place in the mid-fifteenth century, not in the reign of Henry VIII.

Royal kitchens before 1500

In contrast to the full administrative records surviving for the Lord Steward's department in the Middle Ages, information regarding the buildings managed by him is scanty. No royal kitchen survives from the Middle Ages, and the arrangement of most of them is lost. However, at two of the principal medieval houses, Westminster and Clarendon, there are some clues. At Westminster (see plan 12) the kitchen seems to have been a free-standing structure on the south end of the great hall's west side; while at Clarendon (fig. 181), the original kitchen stood directly behind the hall beyond the pantry, buttery and larder. However, in 1245–6 Henry III built a new kitchen at Clarendon to the north of the hall, leaving its predecessor as the privy kitchen, providing food only for the King's table. Both of these kitchens were square and had grouped around them the saucery, larder and an office called the 'herlebecheria'.[4]

The two principal factors governing kitchen design until Edward IV's reign are discernible at Clarendon. The first is the positioning of the kitchen on an axis with the great hall at its lower end beyond the screens' passage and a buttery and pantry. The second is the division between the Household kitchen (later the great kitchen) and the privy kitchen for the King's table. For the Kitchen, in common with the Chamber, the Wardrobe and

180. Detail of fig. 202.

181. Clarendon, Wiltshire. Plan showing the layout of the royal lodgings from excavated evidence. A: the king's kitchen; B: the household kitchen; C: the cloister; D: the larder; E: the great hall; F: the king's chambers; G: the queen's chambers; H: the chapel; I: the wine cellar.

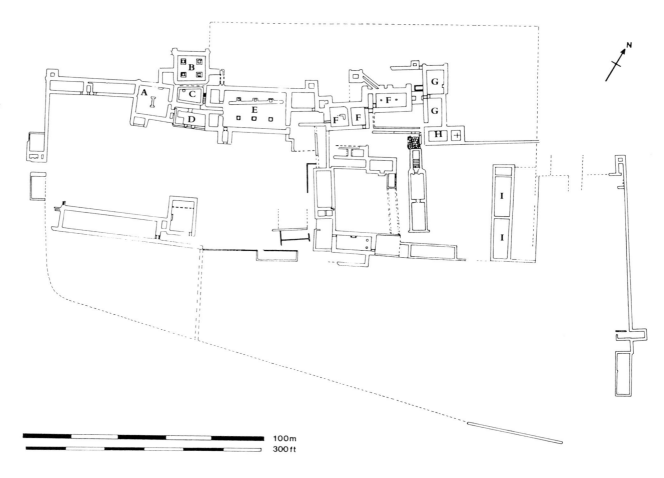

100m
300ft

184 (facing page bottom right). The *domus providencie* from the Black Book, 1472. It shows the Board of the Greencloth meeting in the counting-house: the Lord Steward and the Treasurer sit at the board holding their white staves of office; they are helped by the Clerks of the Greencloth and the Comptroller. Above their heads are the virtues of their office: Reason, Circumspection, Intelligence etc.; before them on the table are check rolls, counters and a till.

several other Household departments, had a Privy and a Household wing. These features applied to courtier houses as much as royal houses, although only in the grandest buildings was a separate kitchen reserved for the master of the house.[5] By the accession of Henry VIII, many courtier houses and most royal ones had developed a plan significantly different: they still provided two kitchens, one for the King and another for the Household, but the relation of the kitchen to the hall had altered.

The first royal building where the relationship of the kitchen to hall is known to have differed from the traditional medieval arrangement was Edward IV's new house at Eltham.[6] There Edward demolished Bishop Bek's hall and kitchen in 1475 and built himself a new one at right-angles to the great hall, linked to the screens' passage, the buttery and the pantry by a corridor (fig. 23, and see plan 1). The kitchen itself had a traditional square plan with two fireplaces, but its traditional position was occupied by a new buttery and pantry, the kitchen itself being sited on the south side of the hall. This plan was duplicated at Richmond by Henry VII from 1498 where the square kitchen with its louvred roof can be seen on Wyngaerde's view (fig. 182, and see plan 11) rising above the ridges of the subsidiary kitchens. The court nearest the hall contained the larders and the pastry-house, to the east of which were the poultry-house, scalding-house and ale-buttery; furthest west was the woodyard.

The kitchens at Richmond presumably provided the model for those begun at Hampton Court by Wolsey sometime after 1514 and then massively expanded under Henry VIII from 1529. There, the great kitchen was sited to one side of the great hall and was approached by two courts surrounded by subsidiary offices (figs 185–8). This arrangement survives almost intact today.

The reasons for the realignment of royal kitchens in the late fifteenth century can be found in the development of Court etiquette during Edward IV's reign. These were set out in the Black Book, and had two basic aims. The first was to control the expenditure of a profligate department of the royal household, the *domus providencie*, by subjecting it to the scrutiny of the Board of the Greencloth. This was achieved by a series of checks and controls including the introduction of 'surveyors of the dressers' who were to ensure that food leaving the kitchens only went to authorised destinations. The

146

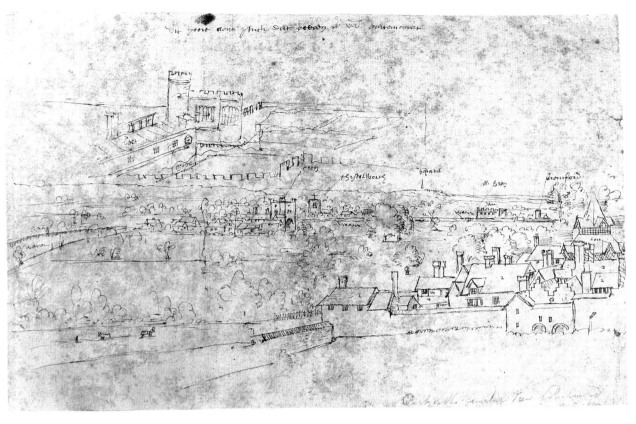

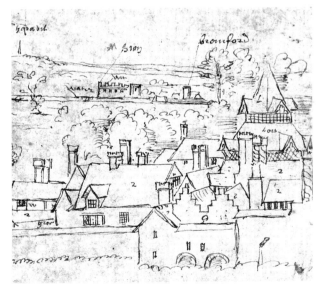

182 (left). Richmond and Hampton Court, Surrey. Site sketch by A. van den Wyngaerde c.1558. Bottom right Wyngaerde shows the kitchens at Richmond.

183 (below left). Detail of fig. 182 showing the kitchens at Richmond. The vegetation in the foreground conceals the moat; the overflow of the great cisterns can be seen running into it. The great kitchen is the structure with the louvre.

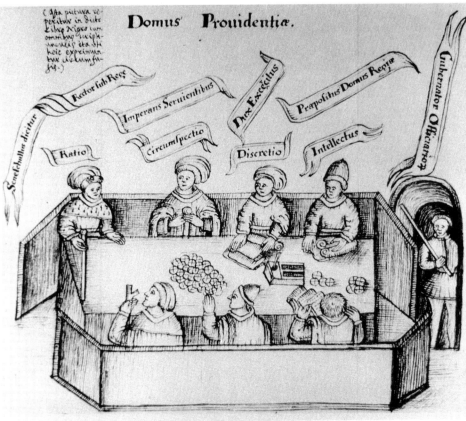

second aim was to formalise the ceremonial of eating along Burgundian lines. The task of the *domus providencie* was to facilitate the magnificence of the other part of the household which was from then on to be actually titled the *domus magnificencie* (fig. 184).[7]

If Edward IV failed to impose financial discipline in his household he succeeded in his other purpose

147

185. Hampton Court, Surrey. A view from the north by A. van den Wyngaerde, *c*.1558. The houses of offices can be seen on the far right and behind, the tiltyard; in the foreground, the gabled range of the kitchen, with its three chimneys, is immediately in front of the great hall.

186. Hampton Court, Surrey. Plan showing location of the kitchen areas. A: the Household kitchens; B: the houses of offices; C: the queen's privy kitchen; D: 1520–36, the king's privy kitchen; E: from 1536, the king's privy kitchen.

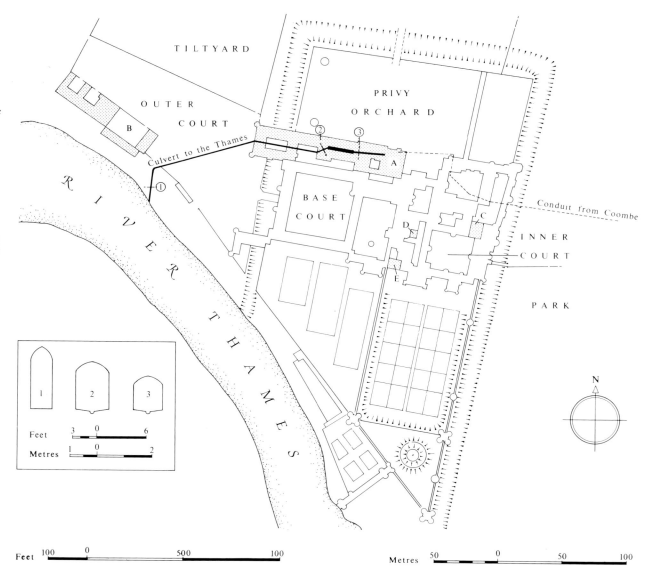

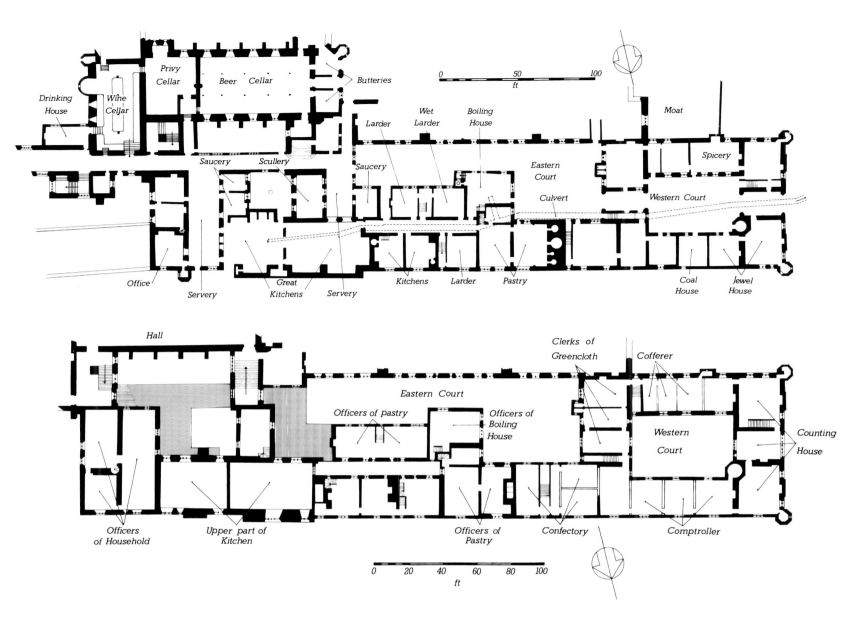

Hall

Privy
Cellar

Beer Cellar

Butteries

Drinking
House

Wine
Cellar

Larder

Wet
Larder

Boiling
House

Moat

Saucery

Scullery

Saucery

Spicery

Eastern
Court

Culvert

Western Court

Office

Servery

Great
Kitchens

Servery

Kitchens

Larder

Pastry

Coal
House

Jewel
House

0   50   100
ft

Hall

Clerks of
Greencloth

Cofferer

Eastern Court

Officers of pastry

Officers of
Boiling
House

Western
Court

Counting
House

Officers
of Household

Upper part of
Kitchen

Officers of
Pastry

Confectory

Comptroller

0   20   40   60   80   100
ft

of creating magnificence. The feasts of the Yorkist Court are legendary; one Christmas his new kitchens at Eltham fed over 2,000 people and a visitor to his Court in 1466 described a royal banquet:

> My lord and his gentlemen were placed in an alcove so that my lord could observe the great splendour . . . the meal lasted for three hours. The food which was served to the queen, the queen's mother, the King's sister and others was most costly. Much might be written of it.[8]

Feasts were not an innovation of Edward IV: what was new was the degree of ceremony that surrounded them. Not only did the Black Book itself specify the degree of ceremony to be adopted in serving, but a whole rash of etiquette manuals

were written at the same period providing guidance on the correct way to behave. One of the earliest of these manuals was *The Book of Nurture* written around 1440 by John Russell; later came such books as *The Boke of Curtasye* (1460) and *The Boke of Kervynge* (1508) by Wynkyn de Worde.[9] By far the largest part of all these manuals was devoted to service at table. At Court this elaboration of etiquette had an enormous impact: from Edward IV's reign an army of servers, ushers, sewers, carvers and cupbearers ceremoniously conveyed food into the hall and the King's lodgings, and then served it with great pomp, in accordance with precise written instructions.[10] This increase in ceremony was complemented by a parallel elaboration of dishes consumed, and to prepare these delicacies the number

187 (top). Hampton Court, Surrey. Ground-floor plan of the kitchens, *c.*1547.

188. Hampton Court, Surrey. First-floor plan of the kitchens, *c.*1547.

149

and variety of subsidiary kitchens was greatly extended.

These changes in the logistics of eating inevitably produced a change in the plan of the kitchens themselves. No longer was it sufficient for a few servants to collect dishes from the kitchen, to traverse a narrow screens' passage and to enter the hall. The larger number of servers needed so much more space for marshalling and circulating that the screens' passage was unable to meet the demand and became obsolete. The new kitchens at Eltham, Richmond and Hampton Court made good this omission by providing a spacious serving place which allowed large numbers of serving staff to congregate, collect dishes and assemble in the correct order before processing into the hall (see plans 1, 7, 11). The serving-place had the added advantage of providing space for the surveyors of the dresser to check what was coming out of the kitchens and supervise its distribution to the correct carriers. Economy and magnificence were thus both well served.

The Lord Steward's department at the Court of Henry VIII

The Lord Steward's department was made up of about nineteen offices. These were the bakehouse, pantry, cellar, buttery, pitcher-house, spicery, chaundry, ewrye, boiling-house, larder, accatary, poultry, scalding-house, squillery, pastry, waffrey, confectary, woodyard and the only office actually called a kitchen, the great kitchen itself. Only in the greater houses were all the departments fully represented. During progress time the kitchen organisation was slimmed down to the minimum, leaving the rest of the staff at a greater house, possibly with the staff on leave. At the greater houses each kitchen office was assigned a particular set of rooms; at the lesser houses offices probably doubled-up and made do in the available accommodation. In both cases, however, the plan of the building was carefully tailored to the efficient production of meals.

In general there were two meals a day, one at midday, the other at about four in the afternoon. Not everyone at Court was entitled to eat at the King's expense and those who were allowed to were set out in a list called the 'bouche of Court'. This list also specified how much a particular courtier was entitled to and where he could eat. In 1526 there were about 600 people who were entitled to eat in the hall and the outward rooms and about 230 domestic servants to eat elsewhere. Each day at a greater house meals would have been prepared for some 800 people.

Food was allocated to offices or officers in 'messes'.

A mess was an allocation of food designed to be split between four people. Therefore when the household lists state that a particular office, say the officers of the Pastry, were to be allocated two messes, food would be provided for eight men. Food was taken to the hall or wherever it was to be consumed in messes and then was divided at table by the senior officer responsible.[11]

The location in which any courtier ate was one of the principal indicators of status, or 'degree' at Court. The lowest ranks were probably the kitchen staff themselves, of whom there were approximately 230. The largest office was the Great Kitchen which had a staff of a little over fifty headed by the Clerk of the Kitchen and three master cooks, one for the Household and one each for the King's and Queen's sides. They ate in the great kitchen at the tables on which they had prepared the food. Other large offices were the Cellar with fifteen staff, the Bakehouse with thirteen and the Pantry with ten. All these dined and supped in their places of work.

Next up from the kitchen staff were those entitled to sit in the great hall: these included the Yeomen of the Guard and the majority of the lower servants of the Court. The great hall, during the reign of Henry VIII, was still the principal recipient of food from the kitchens; although neither the King, nor his highest ranking nobles, ever ate in there (see pp. 113–20), the Eltham Ordinances specified that 'hall should be kept at the greater houses'. This was primarily for economic reasons, as keeping all those who were entitled to eat together in one place at one time ensured greater economy than a free-for-all 'self-service' approach. Later in the reign, in houses built without a great hall or where the great hall had been converted, the outer guard chamber served as the Court 'cafeteria'. The unwritten rule of Court status for the ambitious courtier must have been 'don't eat in the great hall unless forced'. Most ambitious courtiers would have had their eye on eating in the guard chamber next door.

The kitchens of Henry VIII

In an economic sense the efficent planning of the buildings in the Lord Steward's department was more important than that of the royal lodgings; the extent and plan of royal kitchens varied with the type of house. Clearly the greater houses had substantial kitchen complexes to cater for their 1,000 or so occupants. The smaller lesser houses had much reduced kitchen capacity. The common denominator shared by the kitchens in either type of house however, was the ability to produce food efficiently for a large number of people.

An entire kitchen complex belonging to a greater

189. Hampton Court, Surrey, the houses of offices from a photograph of 1860–70. The buildings shown are (from the background to the foreground) the Mitre Inn (not part of the royal estate), the scalding-house and bakehouse, and early nineteenth-century buildings in the woodyard with the low, ruined wall of the stables before them. On the waterfront are the mouths of the Tudor culverts.

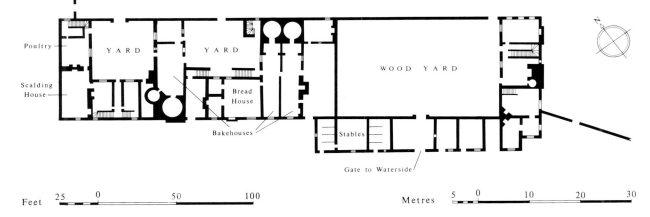

Poultry

Scalding House

YARD   YARD

Bread House

Bakehouses

WOOD YARD

Stables

Gate to Waterside

Feet 25   0   50   100

Metres 5   0   10   20   30

190. Hampton Court, Surrey. Plan of the houses of offices, c.1547.

house survives at Hampton Court (figs 186–7) and can be taken as representative of the greater kitchens.[12] In such houses the kitchens were geographically divided into two zones. Often there

was a group of buildings in the outermost court in which were isolated the most hazardous or noxious kitchen activities. The offices most commonly isolated were the bakehouses, where fire was always a hazard, and the noxious scalding-houses where poultry was plucked. The largest outer court of which there is a record was at Eltham (fig. 191, and see plan 1). There the scalding-house, privy and great bakehouses, spicery, pastry, coal-house and laundry were sited. There was a similar outer court at Dartford and another at Oatlands (figs 88–9).[13] At Hampton Court there was a small, compact group of buildings known as the houses of offices (figs 189–90). They comprised the bakehouses, scalding-house, poultry, rush-house and the woodyard.

At Hampton Court the kitchens proper were approached by a separate gatehouse which led to three courtyards all ranged along the north side

191. Eltham, Kent, surviving buildings in the outer court. By 1603 these particular buildings had become the Lord Chancellor's lodgings. In Henry VIII's reign they were probably the residence of the Keeper of the manor.

151

192. Hampton Court, Surrey. The gatehouse to Henry VIII's kitchens seen from the west today. The window over the archway was that of the counting-house. In the background are parts which have been heightened in the late nineteenth century.

of the house. Most kitchens were sited on the cooler north side of the house, the sunny south side generally being reserved for the royal lodgings and gardens.[14] The first courtyard at Hampton Court was surrounded by offices which stored non-perishable items or were purely administrative. Above the gatehouse was the counting-house where the Cofferer and his assistants, the Clerks of the Greencloth, kept careful tally of the cost of feeding the Court (fig. 192). The counting-house was ideally placed to monitor the arrival of supplies and staff. The Cofferer, the Clerks of the Greencloth and the Comptroller all had rooms at first-floor level round the courtyard. A late fifteenth-century woodcut shows the Board of the Greencloth meeting in the counting-house (fig. 184): its members sit on high-backed settles at a table which would have been covered in green baize. The Hampton Court accounts describe the construction of the

table: 'A pair of trestles for a table in the newe counting house . . . for an irne trestle for the same table . . . for 2 locks for the same table . . . for heart rings for tills in the same table . . .'.[15] The Tudor interiors of these rooms have been altered but physical evidence of the work of the counting-house has been found in the form of a purveyor's note and a counter.

Elsewhere in the western court was the spicery, where spices imported from the Far East and the Mediterranean jostled with English ones such as mustard. Some of the commoner herbs and spices were grown in palace gardens — at Hampton Court there was a herb garden at the riverside.[16] The office of the Spicery was also responsible for the huge quantities of fruit produced each year by the orchards which surrounded most of the greater houses; at Hampton Court there were two orchards planted with apples and pears (see plan 6). Next door to

152

the spicery, and under the control of the Clerk of the Spicery, was the chandlery where wax for candles and tapers and the diaper and other linen cloths for the tables of the upper courtiers were stored. Across the courtyard from the chandlery was the coal-house. It was a store for charcoal for cooking and the expensive 'sea-coal' destined for the rooms of the King and Queen and their children. Charcoal provided an alternative source of heat to the fierce wood fires which the Tudor cooks most commonly used.

on the same principle as provincial Greek or North African ovens today. Bundles of brushwood were lit outside the oven and thrust inside with long forks.

194 (above). Woodcut by Hans Burgkmair, showing a kitchen of 1542, similar to the royal kitchens of Henry VIII. The cook is preparing a sauce on a charcoal-fired boiling range.

The confectionery and the pastry-house were approached from the second kitchen court. The Confectionery prepared the delicate sweet dishes which formed part of the higher courtiers' diet. In this office worked the 'wife who makes the king's puddings', the only woman recorded as working in the kitchen complex. Delicate cooking such as this was done on brick-built charcoal-burning ranges rather like a modern barbecue (fig. 194) or on portable charcoal braziers called chafing dishes. The confectionery, therefore, had no fireplaces.[17] The palace pastry-house prepared pastry coffins (or cases) for both sweet and savoury pestles (or pies) and pasties. It had four ovens (the largest of which was 12 feet 6 inches in diameter) and they worked

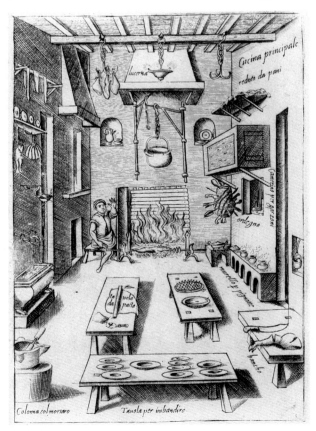

193 (far left). Woodcut by Hans Burgkmair, showing a cook gutting a hare, 1510. In the background can be seen a typical range of cooking utensils.

195. Italian woodcut c.1570 showing a large kitchen in operation. The great kitchens of Henry's houses were very similar to this. But the great fireplace is characteristically Italian, not English.

153

196. Miniature showing a fifteenth-century bakery; Henry VIII's ovens were similar to that shown here, and the method of introducing and removing bread to the ovens on long handled peels was the same as that used by his bakers.

197. Diagram showing how the boiling-house at Hampton Court worked. The cauldron was set into a ventilated alcove approached by four steps; beneath it was the fire on an iron grate closed off by fire doors. The actual copper has been omitted from this drawing to show how the hot gases from the fire circulated round the cauldron providing a steady direct heat.

198. Hampton Court, Surrey. Fish Court from the east. In Henry VIII's time the doors on the left would have led to the larders and boiling-house, the door at the end of the court to the pastry-house and the doors on the right to the dry larder and speciality kitchens. The whole courtyard was remodelled and 'Tudorised' in the nineteenth century.

The flames warmed the brickwork and, on removal of the ashes, the dough was placed inside. The oven was closed with an iron door, sealed with mud, and the bakers knew exactly how long to leave the dough to make the pastry (fig. 196). To extract smoke from the ovens their mouths were covered by an external smoke-hood very similar to the surviving one at Gainsborough Old Hall, Lincolnshire.[18] The pastry-house was approached from the eastern court and comprised three rooms: one room contained the ovens and smoke-hood and must have been enormously hot; next door was a second room fitted with wooden troughs in which the dough was kneaded; the third room was a store for flour and was windowless.

At its eastern end the pastry-house led out on to the narrow central court of the kitchens which was the spine of the kitchen operation (figs 187, 198). Off this courtyard were also sited the boiling-house, wet, dry, and flesh larders, two working houses and the great kitchen. Unlike the pastry-house, all of these had access only from the central court, itself entered only by a single lockable door. The provision of single entries to each of these offices from this central courtyard was a measure to prevent theft and tampering with the stores. No item of food could leave the courtyard without passing through the great kitchen from where it could be distributed to the expectant diners.

The boiling-house was a single room with a stone sump in the centre and a great boiling-copper on its east wall. The copper, which contained about seventy-five gallons, was set into a ventilated brick alcove with a vaulted ceiling which still survives (fig. 197). In it were prepared both boiled meat

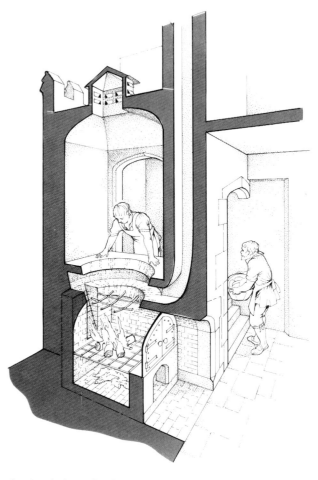

destined directly for the table, and stock, a critical component of both hot and cold sauces.

154

199. The pond gardens built by Henry VIII in 1536 were fed by the excess water from the fountain in the inner court, itself brought by conduit from Coombe Hill three miles away. Originally each pond was surrounded by striped poles supporting heraldic beasts. The ponds have now been much altered, but the low stone-capped walls date from 1536.

There were three larders at Hampton Court. Meat was hung in the flesh larder, venison hanging as long as six weeks before consumption. The royal parks provided the majority of venison eaten by the Court; only a little of this was killed for sport, most was culled by the staff of the park's Keeper. Both Whitehall and Hampton Court (as well as other palaces) had pheasant yards and at both payments for grain often appear in the building accounts.[19] At Hampton Court there was a warren, dating back to the fourteenth century.[20]

The sort of fittings found in a flesh larder may be discovered from an account of the Tower larder, where there were 'planks rownde by the walls and stancions wt pyns and hoks to hange fleshe on'.[21] There was a certain amount of preserved meat in the flesh larder at Greenwich in 1534, where a range was made for a cauldron to boil brine for preserving.[22]

The wet larder, supplied by a cistern, was for the storage of fish. Although the Tudor diet was largely meat-based, fish was eaten on Fridays and during the forty days of Lent; both freshwater and saltwater fish were eaten. At Hampton Court there was a pond garden which contained three ponds supplied with fresh water which overflowed from the fountain in the fountain court (fig. 142). Other houses had similar arrangements, The More, for instance (see plan 9), and Ewelme where there were nine ponds fed by a stream.[23] Fish-ponds were generally divided into two types, breeding ponds and holding ponds for keeping fish which were ready for consumption. The large Hampton Court pond (see plan 6 and

fig. 199) was perhaps an example of a breeding pond, the smaller ones were almost certainly holding ponds.[24] The existence of holding ponds at Hampton Court suggests that the wet larder was used mainly to store saltwater fish brought from the coast packed in seaweed and that freshwater fish were probably eaten on the day that they were caught. However at York Place in 1515 fish were being kept alive in the fish-house by piped running water until the last moment.[25]

All this shows that the greater houses were partially self-sufficient in fresh meat and fish and had rarely to rely on dried or salted foods. In the summer and autumn they would also be self-sufficient in apples and pears and also strawberries, peaches and figs, all of which grew in the gardens.[26] The dry larder stored pulses and nuts, generally in bins.

At the eastern end of the central court at Hampton Court was the great kitchen with its six great fireplaces (fig. 200). Only one of these fireplaces retains its spit-racks, but the other five openings would have had similar spit-holding arrangements. All the flagstone floors slope down to a central sump which led to a drain serving all the other offices (fig. 186). At each end of the kitchen were hatches connected to the two serving-places where liveried serving men received the food and took it to the great hall (figs 192–3). Some of the food destined for the great chamber and other outward rooms where the more important courtiers dined underwent a final stage of preparation in the dressers. These were small rooms near the serving hatches where the most elaborate dishes were finally dressed before being served at table (figs 201, 202). There were two serving places at Hampton Court, one at the east end and another at the west. The eastern one had the offices of the Clerk of the Kitchen adjacent to it.

Almost all the great kitchens, in greater and lesser houses alike, were similar in design to the one at Hampton Court, only their size varied. The specification for a totally new great kitchen survives amongst the accounts at Dartford. There were to be three great fireplaces — one 18 feet wide, the second 16 feet wide and the third 14 feet wide — each was to have a 10-foot-high chimney.[27] A door and three serving hatches were to lead from here to the serving place. A pastry-house, larders, scullery and pantry were built nearby, all serviced by three new drains. Later, carpenters provided trestles and dresser boards for the scullery and kitchen.[28] The great kitchen at Richmond, another for which some evidence exists, was surprisingly primitive, however; like the surviving kitchen at Stanton Harcourt it was without chimneys or stacks and the smoke escaped though a louvre in the roof (fig. 183).

During 1533–4 this louvre was 'lathed' to keep
doves from flying in.[29] Perhaps, like the great stone
donjon, the kitchen was a remnant of the Lancastrian
house and not of Henry VII's time at all.[30]

Occasionally the kitchen facilities were not sufficient to meet the demands made on them, and
temporary structures were erected on special occasions. At Greenwich a special new working-house
was built for the Master Cooks to prepare the
Twelfth Night banquet in 1533. This was not a
unique instance at Greenwich; almost every year
new ranges were put up at Christmas for the
'seythyng and boylyng of brawnes'. At lesser houses

extra provision was often made for the Court; at
Grafton a new 'shead ffor a Rostyng place' was
made with 'Rostyng rakks' inside it.[31]

Washing-up was undertaken in the scullery which,
at Hampton Court, was carefully placed between
the bottom of the steps from the great hall and the
great kitchen (fig. 187). It was a small two-up, two-
down building with its own courtyard. The scullery
at Enfield had a brick-built boiler with a pan in
it to provide hot water for washing, and that at
Greenwich was provided with shelves and benches
for piling up dirty and washed pans.[32]

There were three cellars at Hampton Court,

200. Hampton Court,
Surrey. The great kitchen
today, after restoration in
1978 and 1991.

201 (right). Hampton Court, Surrey. The serving-place. Built by Cardinal Wolsey, the serving-place allowed the King's serving men to collect food from the great kitchen and take it to the hall. A second, nearly identical, serving-place was built by Henry VIII at the west end of the great kitchen. The bare brickwork was originally plastered.

202. A fifteenth-century manuscript illumination showing a great lord dining. Artistic licence has enabled the illuminator to show the serving hatch and a glimpse into the great kitchen. A cook is serving up food for the serving men to take to the high table. In reality, serving-hatches never opened directly into a dining area.

two beneath the hall and one under the watching chamber. The wine cellar (figs 187, 204), had a 'drinking house' attached which was presumably for tasting the wine. The Hampton Court cellars stored some of the 300 casks of wine drunk by the Court each year. The casks belonged to the King and were filled by local brewers who marked their cask with a brewer's mark for accounting and quality control. Next to the wine cellar was the privy cellar containing wine and ale for the King and Queen. Underneath the great hall was the great cellar, its floor sprinkled with sand, where the ale for the majority of the Court was stored (fig. 187). The Tudor Court drank some 600,000 gallons of ale a year and, as with the food, its consumption was carefully monitored by controlling access to the cellars. All the wine and ale passed through the buttery at the west end of the hall before being taken upstairs. Security was tight and the ordinance of 1539–40 was careful to specify that the door to the cellar was to have two locks, the key to one kept in the counting-house, the other by the Keeper of the Cellar (rather like launching a nuclear missile, both keys had to be turned for a successful mission). Such precautions were necessary because the cellar was virtually the only office where provisions continued to be stored between visits by the Court. When the Court removed, the cellar doors would be locked until the Court returned.[33]

At most royal houses the pantry and buttery were at the lower end of the hall. At Hampton Court this was still the case although the buttery was on the ground floor and the pantry on the first. The pantry at Greenwich had timber bins similar to those which survive at Haddon Hall for the storage of bread. There was also a counter for slicing the bread on.[34]

The only reliable view showing early Tudor royal kitchens at work is the painting of the camp kitchen at the Field of Cloth of Gold in 1520 (fig. 206), where the temporary boiling-house, roasting ranges and bread-ovens can be clearly seen. A table has been set up from which to serve; on one side are the kitchen staff, on the other the serving staff. A more grandly dressed official, possibly a Surveyor of the Dresser, supervises. Equally interesting is the description of the royal kitchens by an anonymous Spaniard who accompanied Philip of Spain to

203 (facing page top right). Hampton Court, Surrey. A dresser. Built by Cardinal Wolsey in the 1520s, this room is one of the two dressers that opened on to the serving-place. The photograph shows a typical, high-class dish, 'Peacock Royal', being prepared for the lords sitting in the king's watching chamber. The peacock itself would have been roasted in the great kitchen, then passed through a hatch into this room to be 'dressed' for table.

204. Hampton Court, Surrey. The king's wine cellar. Built in 1536 beneath the king's watching chamber, it housed some of the 300 casks of wine drunk every year by the Tudor Court. Architecturally it is identical to the vaulted cellar built by Cardinal Wolsey at York Place soon after 1515.

England in 1554. This colourful account is the only one to convey any notion of the kitchens in operation and is worth quoting in full.

> The Queen [Mary I] spends over 300,000 ducats a year on her table, for all the thirteen councillors eat in the palace, as well as the household officers, the master of the horse, the master of the household, the Queen's as well as our own . . . and the wives of all these gentlemen into the bargain. The Queen's ladies also eat by themselves in the palace, and their servants, as well as all the councillors, governors and household officials. And then there are the 200 men of the guard . . . There are usually eighteen kitchens in full blast

205. Nonsuch, Surrey. The wine cellar as excavated 1959. The cellar at Nonsuch lay east–west beneath the central inner gatehouse range. The photograph is taken from the east and the steps are in the foregound.

159

206. *The Field of Cloth of Gold*, by an unknown artist, *c.*1545 (detail). At The Field of Cloth of Gold a complete royal kitchen was set up in temporary accommodation. Only the bakehouse (right) was built of brick. The boiling-house, in a tent (centre), can be seen with its vast copper; there were vents in the roof of the tent which served as chimneys. Next to it, in another tent, is the great kitchen with its roasting ranges. Long tables in the foreground act as the serving-place.

and they seem veritable hells, such is the stir and bustle in them . . . The usual daily consumption is eighty to one hundred sheep — and the sheep here are very big and fat — a dozen fat beeves, a dozen and a half calves, without mentioning poultry, game, deer, boars and great numbers of rabbits. There is plenty of beer here, and they drink more than would fill the Valladolid river. In the summer the ladies and some gentlemen put sugar in their wine, with the result that there are great goings on in the palace.[35]

Although some parts of his account are spoiled by inaccuracies and hyperbole, this Spanish observer did not exaggerate the quantities consumed. A list from Elizabeth's reign, reveals the quantity of meat cooked by the royal kitchens in one year: amongst it are 1,240 oxen, 8,200 sheep, 2,330 deer, 760 calves, 1,870 pigs and 53 wild boar.[36]

The privy kitchen

The privy kitchen for the King, Queen and their children was no Tudor innovation. At Clarendon, for example, there had been a privy kitchen from 1245 (fig. 181). Yet both Henry VII and Henry VIII added privy kitchens to existing buildings, which might suggest that by the early sixteenth century one was an essential requisite of any royal house. Henry VII, for instance, converted a building near the great hall into a new privy kitchen at the Tower of London in 1500–02 and Henry VIII built a new one at Greenwich for the Queen in 1516 (see plan 4 and fig. 207).[37]

The need for a privy kitchen stemmed from the monarch's reluctance to be bound by the highly rigid timetable imposed by the great kitchen. A typical day in the great kitchen began at 5.30 a.m.

when preparations for the midday meal would begin, and thereafter its staff followed a strict routine which, on account of the demands made on them, allowed for little or no alteration. The King required an organisation which operated on a smaller scale and a shorter timetable. He needed the flexibility to come and go as he pleased, so the privy kitchen was prepared so 'that in case the King's grace returne not soone, upon the time prefixed for dinner and souper within the chamber . . .' food would be ready for him. In addition, a smaller establishment guaranteed a quality and variety not maintainable in the Household kitchens as well as meeting any culinary demands made by Henry VIII. The smaller establishment also reduced the possibilities of interference by poisoners.[38]

The privy kitchen was able to cater for the special dietary needs of other members of the royal family. In March 1535 when Princess Mary was suffering from a menstrual disorder it was reported that 'the lady Mary . . . was much desirous to have her meat immediately after she was ready in the morning, or else she should be in danger eftsoons to return to her said infirmity' and so on medical advice she dispensed with breakfast and dined between nine and ten in the morning. While she was staying at Hatfield with her half-sister Elizabeth, she found that the latter did not dine before eleven so she 'desired to have her breakfast somewhat the later, to the intent that she would eat little more meat unto supper to the continuance and preservation of her health'.[39] The privy kitchen of Prince Edward, was especially strictly supervised. His household instructions made it clear that he was to receive food only from his own privy kitchen, and the servants of that kitchen had to be specially sworn in to his service.[40] All these tricky little alterations in the routine and diet of the royal family were made possible only by the use of the privy kitchen.

Privy kitchens were often located below the King's most private lodgings. At Dartford a staircase connected the privy kitchen with the King's dining chamber, at Eltham the privy kitchen was directly below the King's closet, as was also the case at Woking, and at Bridewell and Hampton Court the Queen's privy kitchens were directly beneath her privy lodging.[41] In 1567 Lord Treasurer Winchester drew attention to the fact that, because the privy kitchen at Hampton Court was immediately below the Queen's privy closet, the din and the smell of cooking 'reboundeth uppe into the closette [so] that hir highness cannot sytt quiet nor without ill saver'. The Lord Chamberlain expressed his surprise at this juxtaposition, but in doing this Darcy showed somewhat inexplicable ignorance of contemporary building layout and an equal lack of awareness about the heating advantages to the accommodation above. Notwithstanding, a new privy kitchen was built at some distance from the Queen's lodging.[42]

An exception to the otherwise traditional juxtaposition occurred at Greenwich where the King's privy kitchen was not below his lodging but occupied a single-story building at the end of the river range. It was separated from the Queen's privy kitchen by a small gravelled yard (fig. 207). Precautions were taken there when in 1543 a false ceiling was inserted 'for the sauving the kyngs meate from duste'; at the same time carpenters provided a table to set 'vessells' upon.[43] The privy kitchen at Dartford was one of the more elaborate ones, for not only did the King's Master Cook lodge next door but it had its own privy larder and its own water cistern.[44]

The close proximity of the privy kitchen and the flexibility of its staff did not reduce or curtail the formality or ritual of the King's dining. Even food prepared in the King's privy kitchen was taken up to his privy chamber with a fanfare of trumpets and much ceremony, and Henry VIII was personally served by the Gentlemen and Ushers of his Privy Chamber.[45]

207. Greenwich, Kent, as excavated in 1971. View from the south-west. In the centre is a gravelled yard; this separates the king's privy kitchen (left) and the queen's (right).

Chapter 10

HYGIENE AND SANITATION

ONE OF THE MISCONCEPTIONS OF popular history is that concern for hygiene and sanitation is a recent — and decidedly modern — phenomenon. This view has no basis in fact, for such issues had long been considerations for owners, occupiers and builders. Sixteenth-century royal builders were as much alive to these issues as builders today.

Water-supply

The water-supply determined how long the Court could stay in any one place. A good clean supply of water had been a requirement of builders since earliest times. Next to defensibility, it was the principal locational factor for most castles in the Middle Ages and considerable ingenuity was spent on supplying water to buildings such as the Tower of London and Dover Castle.[1]

During the Middle Ages the greatest practitioners of domestic water-supply were the engineers who developed the supply systems of the monasteries. At St Augustine's, Canterbury, for instance, there was an elaborate conduit system with tanks and reservoirs. It even had a back-up system whereby if the conduit failed, water could be drawn from a well and poured into cisterns which would feed the pipework. Other conduits existed at Bury St Edmunds where the water was piped for two miles, at Chester where it was piped three miles and at Gloucester and Reading where some of the water was used to flush the sewers. The first royal conduit of which anything is known was the one which served Westminster Palace built, or possibly rebuilt, by Henry III in 1234. It seems likely that this system brought water from the area of Hyde Park — few other of the medieval houses seem to have been so well provided for.[2]

During the reign of Henry VIII there was a major overhaul of the water-supply systems of all his greater houses. The reasons which prompted this programme were the increased size of the Court and the King's desire to stay for longer periods of time at any one house. If the Court was to remain in residence for any length of time a conduit system would be essential. However, many of the lesser houses were only served by wells; these included Halnaker in Sussex, acquired by Henry VIII in 1539, which was supplied by two wells — one in the house and the other in the outbuildings nearby. The house which Henry acquired at Ashridge as a nursery house for his children was also served by wells. There water was raised not by hand but by a pump worked by dogs. At Rochester there was a 'common well for the kitchen'.[3]

Only two new conduit systems were built by Henry at lesser houses. The first was at St James's, where it was one of the first additions to the pre-existing building. The pipe trenches were dug in 1531–2 by thirty-seven labourers; ten bricklayers were working on the conduit-house and four plumbers on the pipework. The final bill came to over £60.[4] The conduit-house was situated to the north of the house more or less where St James's Church, Piccadilly, is today (figs 209–10).[5] The second conduit built at a lesser house was at Nonsuch: when the King was looking for a site upon which to build the palace in 1537 his commissioners recommended the village of Cuddington because there was a suitable spring which could be tapped for the palace water-supply.[6] A huge lead cistern was built in the south-west tower of the palace from which water was distributed all over the building (fig. 211). Unfortunately there were troubles with the supply from the start and it seems that the pressure was not great enough to fill the tank. Despite the efforts of the German engineer Stefan von Haschenperg, the system never worked properly in Henry's lifetime.[7]

Eltham, one of the stock of large royal houses inherited by Henry VIII, already had a conduit system in 1509, which seems to have been built by his father, and one of its conduit-houses still survives (fig. 212).[8] Many of the larger houses acquired by Henry from his courtiers were already provided with conduits. This was true of Hatfield, Enfield and Otford. At Otford, the house built by Archbishop William Wareham and acquired by

208. Hampton Court, Surrey, the great house of ease.

163

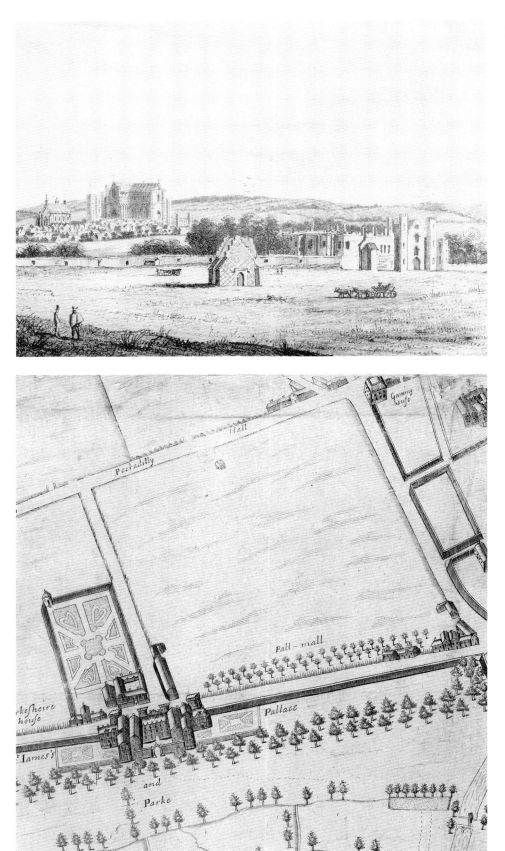

Henry VIII, not only did a conduit supply the house but excess water from the system flushed out the sewers beneath the building.[9]

Not surprisingly it was at the greater houses where most attention was paid to the water-supply. In these enormous rambling palaces as many as 1,500 people had to be supplied for periods of two months or more, and an efficient supply system was essential. Where necessary, earlier systems no longer capable of meeting increased demand were replaced. This is what happened at Greenwich when in 1515 Henry VIII ordered the construction of a new system.[10] This conduit continued to serve the palace until its demolition, when the rights to the spring waters were granted to the Royal Hospital for Seamen. For this purpose a survey of the conduit was taken in 1695 and seven out of the eight tunnels were recorded. The surviving passages under Greenwich Park are almost certainly the remains of the system. At Beaulieu, another of the greater houses, a new conduit was installed by Henry VIII in 1522, although nothing is known about it.[11]

At Woodstock, the furthest-flung great house, Henry VII built a new conduit in 1499. This was clearly not sufficient for the needs of Henry VIII, as in 1532–3 a new and elaborate conduit was built with the water channelled to the house from Rosamund's Spring 800 feet away. The collection chamber was a large sunken stone cistern with access via steps to allow it to be cleaned. This structure may be one of those shown on John Aubrey's seventeenth-century drawing of Rosamund's Bower (fig. 215). Because of the uneven lie of the ground between this cistern and the house itself the pipes were conducted across the 'low vallies' in the park on stone pillars.[12] In the same years at Windsor a different sort of water-collection system was being installed. A new terrace was built on the south side of the castle, and under it was a series of massive brick vaults or cisterns (see plan 14). These were filled with rainwater from the extensive lead flats of the castle above. This supply system was augmented in Edward VI's reign by a new conduit designed to supply the castle from a spring in Blackmore Park.[13] Finally, at Hampton Court in 1543 Henry VIII constructed the most sophisticated of his new conduits. Thus between 1516 and 1543 Henry VIII had built or rebuilt a new conduit system for each of his greater houses which allowed the entire Court to have running water throughout its stay.

The sole surviving example of Henry's work is at Hampton Court. One of the previous owners, either Sir Giles Daubeney or Thomas Wolsey, had built conduits to provide the house with water. There were at least two conduit-heads, one in Hampton village and another in the upper park, and repair accounts from the 1530s indicate that

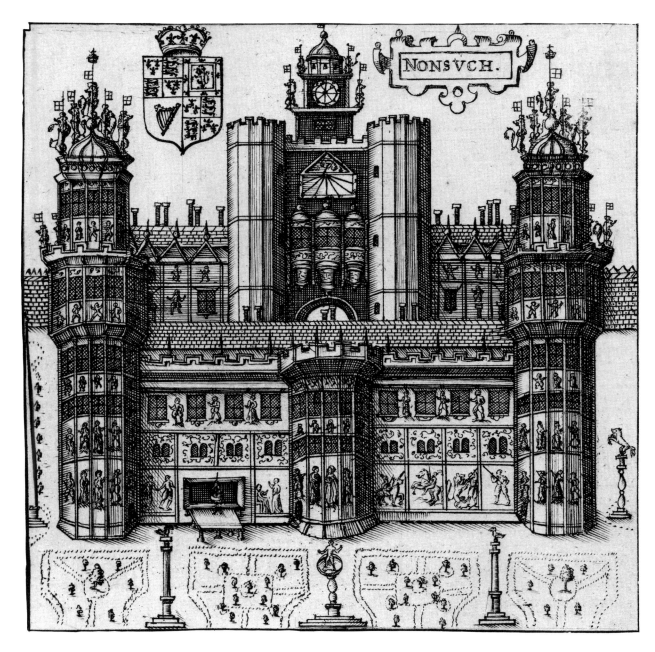

NONSVCH.

209 (facing page top). St James's Westminster. A view of the house and the Henrician conduit-houses by a seventeenth-century artist. Whitehall Park can be seen lying between St James's and Westminster.

210 (facing page bottom). Map of Westminster, St James's and Charing Cross by Faithorne and Newcourt. Clearly shown near Piccadilly is the St James's conduit-house. St James's tennis-court is immediately above the house, by its mews.

211. Nonsuch, Surrey. Engraving of the south front, from John Speed's map of Surrey, 1610. An important view of the house showing in some detail the stucco decorations and the heraldic beasts, and giving a glimpse of the inner court. The tower on the left contained the water cisterns that supplied the whole house with running water.

these were brick conduit-houses with doors and windows.[14] Nevertheless, this system, like the conduit systems at the other greater houses, was insufficient to meet Henry VIII's growing needs. Following the suppression of Merton Priory in 1538, land in upper Kingston with several fresh-water springs was set aside for Henry's new water-supply. A summary account covering the period 1538–45 mentions 'charges of the condyte from Combhill' and also a sum of £100 spent on the construction of the conduit.[15] There were three spring-heads, and at each one a conduit-house was built; lead piping three miles in length linked the conduits with Hampton Court (fig. 214), where, at one point, the pipes had to run under the Thames. The submerged length was strengthened with iron.

One of the frequent problems with conduit systems was burst or leaking pipes. The accounts of the Office of Works are filled with references to workmen digging up pipes to find leaks and this inevitably meant great expense and disruption.[16] To minimise the length of pipe to be searched when loss of pressure occurred, the pipeline was punctuated by tampkins. These were small brick buildings with stopcocks and expansion tanks (fig. 213). They enabled sections of pipe to be isolated and leaks to be identified and repaired.

212. Eltham, Kent. One of the sixteenth-century conduit-houses that supplied the manor with water.

213. The surviving tampkin on Coombe Hill golf course, Kingston, Surrey. There were originally four tampkins on the pipeline from Coombe to Hampton Court.

makyng off divers dressers, maletts, levells and rollers'.[19] The total amount of lead used in the 18,000-foot length of pipeline at Hampton Court was over 150 tons. Further proof of the effectiveness of Henry's thick pipes and his tampkin system was that Coombe Conduit continued to supply Hampton Court with water until 1876. In that year supply was discontinued due to pollution by sewage and continual damage to the submerged section of piping by barges on the Thames.[20]

The conduit-heads at Coombe and at the other houses were, of necessity, sited far from the houses themselves. This created a security problem, as the Court was vulnerable to poisoning of the water supply at source. To help prevent this the conduit heads were built very solidly, with thick walls and doors with double locks, and the area immediately around them was planted with barriers of thistles and thorns.[21] Not only this, but the King further increased protection by securing the ownership of the land upon which the conduits lay. At Coombe, although he let the land surrounding the conduits, there were clauses in the lease which made the lessee responsible for safeguarding the conduit-heads. Likewise at Whitehall Palace the King bought the land surrounding the conduit-houses to prevent people building houses and latrine pits nearby. A map of 1585 shows the conduit-heads on land called Cunditt Meadows, bought by the King for the safeguard of the palace's water supply (fig. 221).[22]

On reaching a royal house the piped water was channelled directly into a series of cisterns, the principal one being in the kitchens, from whence all the domestic offices were supplied with water. Many offices had taps (fig. 222) and the fish-house (or wet larder) and boiling-house had their own subsidiary cisterns. At Hampton Court, at least, and probably at other houses, a second pipeline led to another cistern situated near the King's and Queen's

The three conduit-heads survive today. Ivy Conduit has only a single chamber with a collection tank and an exit pipe. Both Gallows and Coombe Conduits were more elaborate; less survives of Gallows Conduit, and since it has been turned into a gazebo its workings cannot be deduced (fig. 216). Coombe Conduit, however, is still in working condition (fig. 217).[17] The original building comprised an upper and a lower chamber connected by an underground passage (fig. 218). Water flowed into the upper chamber and settled in the upper tank. A pipe at a high level in the upper tank took water to the lower chamber where more sediment was allowed to settle. From the lower chamber water was piped to the palace. In later years, as the surrounding water-table fell, additional upper chambers were dug at lower levels and there are now three upper chambers.[18]

This late Henrician conduit was technically most sophisticated and its use of high pressure an innovation. The measure of the engineering achievement can be gauged by comparison with Henry VII's earlier conduit at Eltham (fig. 219). The fall of the Coombe system was 129 feet and even over a length of 18,000 feet the pressure in the three-inch-diameter pipes was high enough to produce running water in the house at second-floor level. The Eltham system had a fall of merely 55 feet, barely enough to reach the house's cisterns. The high pressure of Coombe Conduit was made possible by the strength of the pipes, the walls of which were over half-an-inch thick (fig. 220). Accounts at Woodstock describe the manufacture of the pipes: 'makyng a new castyng mold to cast scheats of lead uppon and a double hole mould of tymbre to make rounde pyppes . . . as

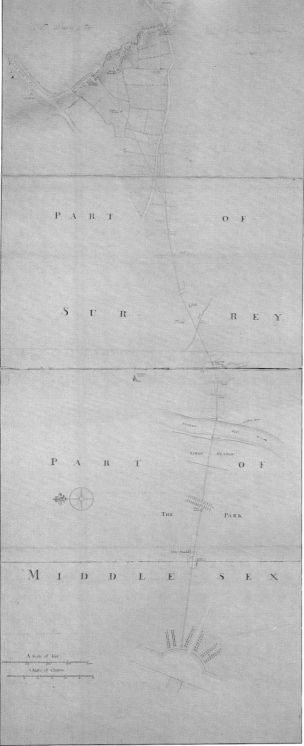

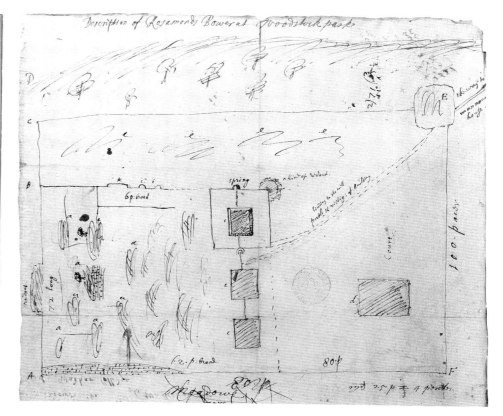

of Henry VIII was the regulation of supply from source. The conduits continued to supply water whether there was a demand or not and so provision had to be made for the overflow from the cisterns. There were several solutions to this problem. The simplest was the one adopted at Richmond where the overflow drained directly into the moat (fig. 183). An alternative measure for disposing of the excess water was the provision of a fountain. At both Greenwich and Hampton Court there were fountains in the inner courts which presumably ran on the excess water from the conduit system (see plan 6). At Hampton Court the overflow water from the fountain was then piped to the King's pond gardens where it provided clean water for his fish.

215. Woodstock, Oxfordshire. Rosamund's Bower, as sketched by John Aubrey. The ruins of the medieval water garden of Woodstock. E is the ruin of the gatehouse and there are three baths in a row in the centre; to the right is a pond; k was a seat and i and i indicate two niches. The whole adds up to a pleasure-ground of baths and seats in a walled enclosure. Henry VIII used the water supply for his new conduit in 1532.

Baths and bathing

Improvements in the supply of water enabled Henry VIII to improve the facilities for bathing. Many of his forbears' houses had boasted bathrooms, and of these perhaps the most luxurious had been Edward III's bathroom at Westminster which had been supplied with '2 large bronze taps for the kings bath to bring hot and cold water into the baths'. Others are documented at Easthampstead, Eltham and Sheen. In most of these the bath was a wooden tub

214 (left). Hampton Court, Surrey. An eighteenth-century map showing the path of the conduit from Coombe Hill to Hampton Court.

lodgings and supplied their bathrooms. Occasionally courtiers had running water in their own rooms; Sir Thomas Heneage had this privilege in his lodging at Greenwich.[23] A problem which the Hampton Court conduit shared with the others built in the reign

167

216. Gallows Conduit, Coombe Hill, Kingston, Surrey.

217 (far right). Coombe Conduit, Coombe Hill, Kingston, Surrey, the lower chamber. The upper chamber was largely destroyed by the fall of a tree caused by an exploding flying bomb in 1943.

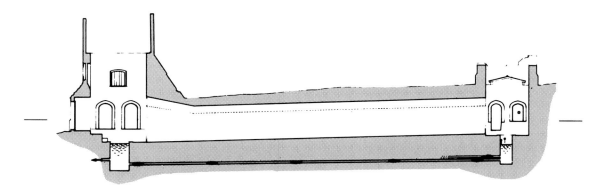

SECTION Y-Y

Lower House

Upper House

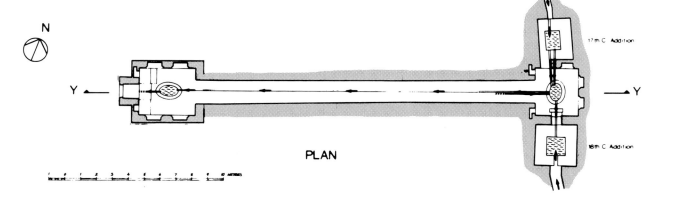

N

218. Coombe Conduit, Coombe Hill, Kingston, Surrey. Cross-section of the upper and lower chambers. The tanks acted as both collection chambers and as recepticles for sediment. (Drawing Daphne Ford)

Y

Y

17th C. Addition

18th C. Addition

PLAN

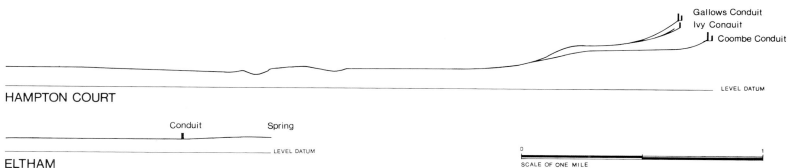

Gallows Conduit
Ivy Conduit
Coombe Conduit

LEVEL DATUM

HAMPTON COURT

Conduit   Spring

LEVEL DATUM

ELTHAM

0   1
SCALE OF ONE MILE

filled by water boiled elsewhere and brought in by bucket.[24] In September 1508 Henry VII had ordered just such a bathtub at the cost of 20 shillings.[25] A set of fifteenth-century instructions describes how the bathtubs were lined with cloth and sponges and a tent was constructed over the top (fig. 223):

> Hang sheets round about ye roof, do thus as ye mean every sheet full of flowers and herbs soote and green and look you have sponges 5 or 6 thereon to sit or lean look there be a great sponge theron your soverign to sit thereon a sheet and so he may bathe hym there to fit.[26]

Because of the difficulty of carrying 30 gallons of hot water weighing some 330 lbs, baths were often

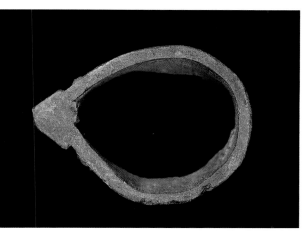

219 (above). Comparative diagram contrasting the fall of the conduits supplying Eltham and Hampton Court.

220. A section of lead pipe from Coombe Conduit.

221. Map of Charing Cross and part of St James's Field, 1585. Much of this area is part of the land Henry VIII acquired to control the water supply to Whitehall and St James's. The conduit-houses are clearly visible.

169

shared or several baths were set up in one room. The Seigneur de Gruuthuse on his visit to England in 1472 was entertained by Edward IV at Windsor; after dinner Gruuthuse was taken to his lodgings and in 'the iiirde chamber was ordeined a bayne or ii whiche were covered with tentes of whyt cloths'. He, and the Lord Chamberlain of England 'went bothe together to the bayne' and remained there 'as long as was their pleasure' before going to bed.[27]

At his accession Henry VIII was bathing in sophisticated, but old-fashioned bathtubs; by the end of the reign he was able to relax in sunken stone sauna-baths. This change in taste was achieved in the bathrooms built for him from 1529 onwards. In 1529 the King ordered a new bathroom at Hampton Court to be sited on the first floor of his new 'bayne tower'. The tower was the King's own private luxury suite on three levels (figs 173–4). On the ground floor

223. Medieval bath. A king is helped out of a typical medieval bathtub by his queen. It has been set up in his bedchamber.

was an office and a strong-room for his Treasurer and officers of his Privy Chamber. The floor above contained his bedroom, a bathroom and a private study. The top floor contained his library and jewel-house. The bathroom had deep window-seats with cupboards beneath and a ceiling decorated with gold battens on a white background. The baths were made by a cooper and were attached to the wall; they were supplied by two taps, one for cold water and one for hot. Directly behind the bathroom, in another small room, was a charcoal-fired stove, or boiler, fed from a cistern on the second floor which was filled by the Coombe conduit (fig. 224).[28]

Hampton Court was not unique amongst Henry VIII's houses in having a bathroom of this sort. Similar baths were also provided at the Tower of London, Windsor Castle, New Hall and even at quite small houses such as Ewelme.[29] An unexplained reference also mentions Henry VIII and Charles V playing 'tennis at the bayne' at Bridewell; whether this indicated that they both bathed afterwards is unknown.[30] In general terms all these bathrooms seem to have been on the first floor, next to or close to the King's bedroom. In France too this was the case: in Francis I's bathroom at Chambord, which still exists, water had to be brought up from the kitchens to fill his bath as, unlike Hampton Court, there was no boiler. Later in his reign the French king built a new kind of bath at Fontainebleau. This was situated on the ground floor beneath Francis's gallery, and comprised a suite of six rooms, the first of which contained a large boiler. The baths were rectangular in shape and sunk into the floor, the largest measuring 14 feet in length by 10 feet in width and 3 feet 6 inches in depth.[31] Later in his reign, Henry VIII built similar bathrooms — the one at Woodstock was described by the late sixteenth-century traveller Thomas Platter: 'we were shown King Henry VIII's bathing-tub and bathing room, also a large square lead cistern full of water in which he bathed; the water comes from Rosamund spring, is cold in summer and warm in winter.'[32] Evidently in addition to the 'tub' there was a sunken pool. At Whitehall Palace there is more concrete evidence for sunken baths. During the excavations of the 1930s a large square sunken bath was found, together with the fragments of a highly elaborate green-glazed stove which must have heated the rooms (figs 226–8). The inventory taken at Whitehall in 1543 lists the contents of the bathroom there. It had thirty-five towels of holland linen and a selection of bathrobes, curtains and a variety of cloths called 'coffins', 'pailes', 'stomachers' and 'sloppes'.[33] From this it would appear that the practice of lining baths with linen might have been continued. Furniture was not neglected either — at Beaulieu in 1547 we learn that 'the 4 baynes are furnished with floors of deale boards, floors with holes, forms, ladders and trussing beds in the walls, one of the beds furnished with curtains'.[34] Very similar equipment was found in the bathroom at Greenwich, where there was a 'trussing bedstedde in the walle for the bayne having a ceeler and a tester of blewe and yellow'.[35] The presence of beds is highly suggestive of Turkish baths and indeed contemporary engravings illustrate sunken baths, bathtubs and beds, all together in a single room (fig. 229).

The Whitehall bath installed in the 1540s far surpassed the Hampton Court bath of 1529 in sophistication, luxury and convenience. Indeed, we know from the Hampton Court accounts of the late 1530s that the 1529 bath there was abandoned and replaced by a new bathroom situated, like Francis I's, under the King's long gallery.[36] During Henry's reign a new sort of bathroom was introduced in the greater houses. It was a development which can be seen as part of the gradual process of making luxury and comfort more permanent and not something which had to be set up to order.

It is one thing to show that Henry VIII's houses had bathrooms but quite a different matter to prove that he took baths. It is known that on medical advice the King took medicinal herbal baths each winter, and also that he avoided baths when the sweating sickness was about.[37] This avoidance possibly reflected a school of thought that rated bathing as a dangerous activity which 'allowed the venomous airs to enter and destroyeth the lively spirits in man and enfeebleth the body'.[38]

As for the courtiers, there were no courtier bathrooms nor were there communal palace baths. Yet it was an easy matter to bring movable tubs into lodgings and set them up in front of the fire (fig. 225). The purchase of large numbers of earthenware pots bought for the stewes (a euphemism for the baths) was probably a provision for courtier bathing.[39]

Sewers and garderobes

An enormous amount of effluent and waste was generated in the royal Household, and how to deal with it had been a fundamental household problem since the early Middle Ages. As the Eltham Ordinances of 1526 succinctly put it, there was an irrefutable necessity 'for the better avoyding of corruption and all uncleanesse out of the King's house, which doth ingender danger of infection, and is very noisome and displeasant'. Henry VIII's master cooks were instructed to clothe kitchen scullions properly so that they should not 'goe naked or in garments of such vileness'. The scullions

were commanded to sweep and clean the courts of 'filthe or uncleannesse' and those who had lodging and bouche of Court were strictly warned not to leave half-eaten food or dirty dishes lying around, or to feed waste food to dogs. On the first offence they would be warned, on the second their allowances suspended and on the third they would loose all their allowances, lodging and bouche of Court for good.[40]

By 1500 it had become standard practice that 'the buttery, cellar, the kitchen, the larder howse be kept

224. Hampton Court, Surrey. Photograph of the remains of the furnace Henry VIII built to heat the water for his bathroom in 1530. The structure was demolished to make way for a lift shaft in the late 1950s.

225. A bathtub set up in a lodging before the fire.

226. Whitehall Palace. Henrician sunken bath or water cistern on the ground floor of the privy gallery range, as excavated in 1939.

227 and 228 (right and above right). Whitehall Palace. Drawings of stove-tiles found during the excavation of the area below the Tudor privy gallery in 1939.

clene that there be no filth in them but good and odyferous savours'. But the problem was less how to keep a room spick and span than what to do with the waste. Rivers were always useful as they were self-flushing and free, and during the early Middle Ages moats were often likewise used. But the dangers of using moats as open sewers were recognised long before the 1540s when Andrew Boorde advised 'in no wyse let not the filth of the kytchen descende into the moote'.[41] Moats were rarely fast-flowing and filling them with waste made a house an island in a sea of garbage. Most of Henry VIII's houses were moated and were, in fact, far from being sewers. They were very regularly cleaned out and great care was taken to ensure that no contamination took place. Indeed, the moats of many of his houses were actually sources of food as carp and other fish were bred there.[42]

The importance of keeping moats clean meant that all sewers and drains from the moated platform of a house had to run either over or under the moat and away from the house. The drains at Hampton Court for instance started in sumps in the floor of the kitchens, ran down the centre of the kitchen court picking up waste from the subsidiary buildings, and then out under the moat. After running across the forecourt they collected more waste from

172

229. *Psyche Served in her Bath*, after Francesco Salviati, *c*.1530. This engraving gives a good idea of the appearance of Henry VIII's later bathrooms, with their combinations of sunken baths, tubs, stoves and beds. Such combinations existed at all the greater houses.

outbuildings before emptying into the river. The drains were 3 feet wide and rose from 5 feet high at source to 7 feet high at mouth (fig. 186). They continued to serve the palace until 1871 when new regulations prohibited the discharge of effluent into the river. The system for disposing of kitchen waste at Whitehall was different. The King's privy kitchen there was built out over the river on brick arches (fig. 230). In the centre of the kitchen was a sump and waste fell through this into channels formed by the arches and was flushed by the tides. At Eltham a system of conduits, which still survives, did a similar job (see plan 1). At The More kitchen waste was conveyed over the moat in pipes rather than under it.[43] If there was no problem with flushing the drains at a riverside house like Whitehall this was not the case elsewhere. Many houses used the overflow from cisterns to do this job, but a house like Enfield had cisterns filled with rainwater to clean the drains.[44] Even flushing was not really sufficient to ensure complete cleanliness, and in 1536 one John Wylkynson was appointed to clean the kitchen drains of all the greater houses. His reward was to be 26s. 8d., plus a coat of red cloth worth 5s. 8d.[45]

The arrangements to dispose of sewage were more complex. Everyone was aware of the danger sewage posed to health and of its unpleasant smell. Andrew Boorde voiced a commonly received opinion:

> Beware of pissing in draughts and permit no common pyssyng place be about the mansion and let the common howse of easement be over some water or elles elongated from the house. And beware of emptyinge of pysse pottes and pyssing in chimneys so that all evill and contagious airs may be expelled and clean air kept unputrified.[46]

But unfortunately practice did not always follow sense. In September 1547, seven months after the death of Henry VIII the Privy Council had to issue a proclamation 'forbidding nuuisance in court': 'no person of what degree soever shall make water or cast any annoyance within the precinct of the court, within the gates of the porter's lodge, whereby corruption may breed and tend to the prejudice of his royal person'.[47]

Greenwich, the largest and most used of the greater houses, seems to have had a particular problem with courtiers relieving themselves against the

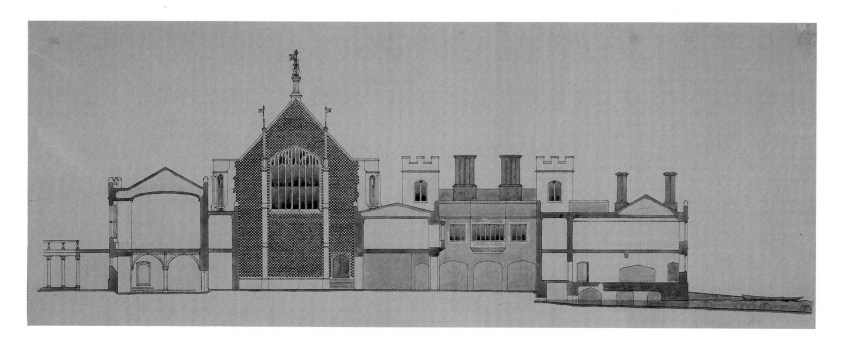

230. Whitehall Palace. Reconstructed cross-section of the Tudor palace, 1939. On the right is the privy kitchen built on arches, with its sump giving access, to the river-flushed channels. To the left of this is the ante-chapel and on the far left, the gable of the great hall with its painted chequerwork. Drawn in 1939, after the excavation of the site.

walls of the many courtyards. Two measures were taken to prevent this. First, repair accounts describe 'Plasterers whiting the walls of the inner court as also making of divers red crosses upon the said walls that none should piss against them'.[48] Crosses were probably used, as it was calculated that courtiers would not wish to dishonour a crucifix by urinating against it. These 'no pissing' signs were augmented by a series of specially allocated pissing places. These were essentially outdoor urinals of stone and lead which drained into the palace sewers. They were placed strategically around the courtyards. Two were specially placed at the foot of the stairs to the King's and Queen's lodgings to reduce the pressure for use of their majesties' own latrines. To ensure these pissing places remained effective the Deputy Keeper of Greenwich was paid for 'keping and scowring of the urin pottes of lede'.[49]

In addition to these pissing places most royal houses — and certainly all the greater ones — were provided with multiple garderobes for the use of courtiers; these were called the common 'jakes', or 'common house of easement'. The concept of vast communal lavatories was neither new nor peculiar to royal houses; there were several in the City of London, the best known of which was the public privy with sixty-four seats called Whittington's Longhouse, erected using money bequeathed for that purpose by Sir Richard Whittington. Monastic buildings had similar multi-seated latrines, that at Christchurch, Canterbury, seating fifty-five.[50] The house of ease built at Hampton Court in 1536 was situated in a wing of the palace built out over the moat (figs 168–9, 208). The discharge from the

latrines fell into shafts running vertically through the building and emptying into great drains which were flushed with water from the moat. This ensured that the moat itself was not polluted and that the waste was washed promptly into the nearby river. A cross-section of the building (fig. 232) shows that the seats of the latrine were arranged on two levels allowing fourteen people to use it at once.[51]

In addition to these communal facilities, all the King's houses were amply served by individual garderobes both in private lodgings and more public areas. This had been the case since at least the fourteenth century and by the early sixteenth century it was standard practice to provide a courtier's lodging with its own latrine. Both the plans of the outer courts at Eltham and Hampton Court show this ample provision (figs 168–9 and plan 1). The outer court at Eltham, built as lodgings by Edward IV after 1460, has external garderobe stacks shared between lodgings. In contrast Hampton Court had integral garderobes with shafts running inside the building into pits.

There were two ways of emptying garderobes or latrines. The first was by an underground drain which was periodically flushed. The second was by an underground pit (what we should call a septic tank) which was emptied by hand. The evacuation method adopted depended very much on the situation of the garderobe. Those ranged round the base court at Hampton Court all emptied into collection chambers which were connected, via a short length of culvert, to the main palace drains (fig. 234), and thence to the river.

174

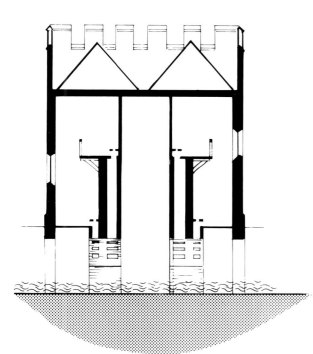

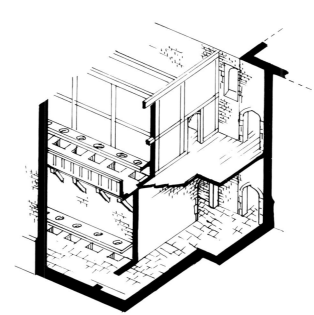

233. Hampton Court, Surrey. Isometric view of the great house of ease, showing probable arrangement of seats. (Drawing Daphne Ford)

234. Hampton Court, Surrey. Cross-sections and plans of garderobes in Cardinal Wolsey's base court. The garderobes in separate lodgings share brick shafts and collection chambers on two levels.

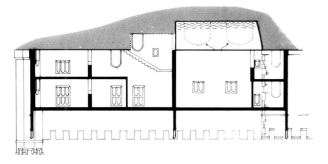

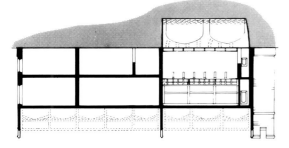

231 (top). Hampton Court, Surrey. North/south section across the great house of ease, showing seats on ground-floor level and on first-floor level. The first-floor seats were on a walkway and were part of the same two-storey room as the seats below. (Drawing Daphne Ford)

232 (above). Hampton Court, Surrey. Sections of the great house of ease, showing how the seats were positioned over two brick culverts. (Drawing Daphne Ford)

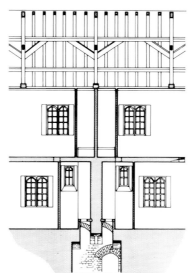

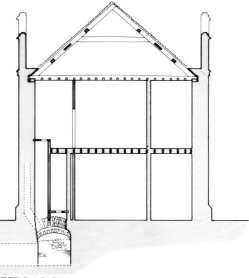

SECTION A-A

SECTION B-B

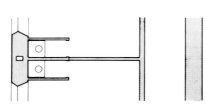

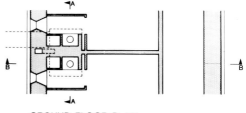

FIRST FLOOR PLAN

GROUND FLOOR PLAN

236. A mid-seventeenth-century close-stool from Hampton Court. Henry VIII's close-stools must have been very similar to this.

At Eltham there was a flushing garderobe: a large lead cistern supplied by water from a brick channel was placed to one side of the bottom of the garderobe shaft; after use the garderobe could be flushed by the activation of a sluice in the cistern. The waste was then washed out under the moat and off into the park (plan 1).[52] At St James's, sited far from the river, there were garderobes serviced by underground chambers which required regular emptying (fig. 235).

Garderobes which discharged into pits were cleaned out by workmen called 'gong scourers' or 'gong fermours' ('gong' was one of the many euphemisms for latrine current in the sixteenth century). Where there was no opening, labourers dug a hole to expose the side of the pit enabling bricklayers to remove enough masonry to allow access. The gong scourers then removed the accumulated filth and scrubbed the pits by candlelight. The operation was completed by re-bricking the opening and backfilling the excavation. For much of Henry's reign the royal gong scourer was Phillip Long. Long's team comprised a master scourer, often himself, and several boys or small men. Small, as the only way to clean the pits and shafts properly was to climb inside them with a scrubbing brush.

The upper part of even quite a grand garderobe was merely a plank of wood with a hole in it (fig. 237) which cannot have been particularly comfortable. Even with regular cleaning and flushing brick gardrobes must have been smelly and unhygienic. For these reasons the King had his own Rolls Royce latrine called a close-stool. A close-stool was a large wooden box with a hole in the top. Inside was a pot, usually made of pewter, into which the seated owner would relieve himself (fig. 236). These close-stools were richly upholstered. One at Greenwich had a padded black velvet seat trimmed with black ribbons and silk. Its sides were covered in scarlet, its edges had a gilt fringe and it had a leather case for protection when it was carried from house to house. The pot inside was of pewter and there was also a cistern which held water for

flushing. Two stools were made for the King at Ampthill which had backs.[53]

The official function of the Groom of the Stole was to look after the close-stool and attend the King while he was seated on it.[54] A fifteenth-century regulation laying down the duties of a great lord's chamberlain outlines some of the duties:

235. St James's, Westminster. Henrician garderobe pit, as excavated in 1990.

237 (far right). Sixteenth-century garderobe with original seat and lid, from a house in Newark, Nottinghamshire.

See the privy house for easement be fair, soot, and clean; and that the boards thereon be covered with cloth fair and green; and the hole himself, look there no board be seen; thereon a fair cushion, the ordure no man to teen. Look there be blanket, cotton, or linen to wipe the nether end, and ever he clepith, wait ready and entende, basin and ewer, and on your shoulder a towel.[55]

The Groom of the Stole or a subordinate was invariably present whenever Henry VIII relieved himself. In March 1528 Thomas Heneage, a member of the Privy Chamber, excused his failure to await on Wolsey on the grounds that 'there is none here but Master Norris [the Groom of the Stole] and I to give attendance upon the King's highness when he goeth to make water in his bedchamber'. And in September 1539 Heneage, now a knight and Groom of the Stole advised Lord Cromwell that after a laxative pill and a clyster the King had 'slept unto two of the clock in the morning and then his Grace rose to go to the stool, which, by working of the pills and glyster that his Highness had taken before, had a very fair seige'.[56]

The close-stool itself was normally kept in a small room called the stool-room by the King's bedchamber. Few details survive of such chambers, the one at Greenwich had 'a picture and certayne cases' in it, the cases might have been shelves for books or papers like those in a surviving garderobe at Hampton Court. Not only the King but some of the higher courtiers had close-stools, an account from 1538–9 is for 'makyng off vi close stollys to stande in the chambre where as the ladys and also the gentyll women doth lye'. These may have been for the Queen's privy chamber where her attendants were sleeping.[57]

All these improvements were part of an overall development — the fact that the Tudor Court was more and more devoted to luxury and pleasure, and less and less a collection of soldiers surrounding a soldier king. The King's houses were no longer temporary stops on the merry-go-round of a peripatetic Court. The King wanted to be able to stay in one place in comfort and cleanliness for longer periods of time. Thus improvements were made to the infrastructure of the King's houses to increase comfort and decrease the danger of disease from insanitary conditions. Interestingly the sanitary advances of Henry VIII's reign remained unaltered for over two centuries and were not superseded until the reign of Queen Victoria.

Chapter 11

SPORT AND RECREATION

The prototypes of the English royal recreational buildings of the early sixteenth century were the buildings of the dukes of Burgundy. At both Princenhof (fig. 16) and Ghent (fig. 17) there were groups of buildings set aside for Court recreation. In the surviving view of Princenhof the tennis-courts and bowling-alley can be seen beyond the palace proper. At Ghent the area before the palace was designated as a tiltyard and further recreation buildings were clustered by the gatehouse.

Curiously, Edward IV, who emulated the dukes of Burgundy in so much, is not known to have erected permanent recreational buildings even though he encouraged similar sports. Thus it was Henry VII's achievement to build the first 'sports complex' at an English royal house (fig. 239). This was at Richmond, where it was described in 1501 by a witness to the marriage of Prince Arthur with Catherine of Aragon:

> In the lougher end of this gardeyn beth pleesaunt galerys, and housis of pleasure to disporte inn at chesse, tables, dise, cardes, bylys, bowling aleys, butts for archers, and goodly tenes plays, as well as to use the seid plays and disports as to behold them so disporting.[1]

This complex, the father of all subsequent English royal recreation centres, was clearly based on the Burgundian model.

Part of Henry VIII's education was vigorous participation in 'all such convenient sports and exercises as behoveth his estate to have experience in'[2], and when he became King in 1509 his Court was launched into an almost incessant round of sport. Hunting and jousting were the most popular and frequent sports of the King's youth, although he also engaged in indoor games like tennis and bowls. After 1528 jousting suffered a sudden eclipse, and although jousts continued after 1536 the King was a spectator not a participant.[3] Instead, from 1530 indoor sports and hunting gained the ascendancy. After 1530 Henry created areas set aside for indoor recreations at the principal greater houses — Hampton Court, Greenwich and Whitehall[4] — and provided many lesser houses with recreational buildings.

The idea and purpose of sport

A revival of interest in physical fitness began in fifteenth-century Italy, and Castiglione, in his *Book of the Courtier* (1527), was among the first to give expression to it. Castiglione justified sports like tennis, swimming and riding in terms other than those of military benefit to the state, which had hitherto been the sole justification for exercising the body. Indeed, turning away from the medieval idea of 'sport' for war's sake, he advocated it in terms of social benefit, to be played in a gentlemanly manner as one of the accomplishments of a courtier. The English, whilst taking up Castiglione's idea of the courtly amateur sportsman, gave it a characteristically practical interpretation by emphasising the health-giving properties of exercise. Sir Thomas Elyot in *The Boke Named the Governour* (1531) recommended sport to the nobleman because 'by exercise, whiche

238. Detail of fig. 241.

239. Richmond, Surrey. View of the gardens and recreation centre by A. van den Wyngaerde, c.1558–62. The tennis play is in the right-hand corner. Some of the galleries were used as bowling alleys. The partially unroofed structure on the right is the church of the Friars Observant.

is vehement motion . . . the helthe of a man is preserved and his strength increased'. Elyot had been profoundly influenced by Galen's *De Sanitate Tuenda*, the great classical work on physical education, translated by Henry VIII's physician Thomas Linacre in 1517. Elyot's recommendation of sport rested entirely on the fact that strenuous motion (Galen's definition of exercise) was essential for man's physical well-being; there was no suggestion that it would also enhance his social standing.[5] Other English writers who were busy advertising sport in the reign of Henry VIII, concentrated exclusively on the health aspect. Andrew Boorde in *A Compendyous Regyment or a Dyetary of Health* (1642) suggested that after prayers in the morning, whether private devotions or hearing mass, a man should 'moderatly exercyse' his body 'with some labour, or playing at the tennys, or castyng a bowle, or payryng wayghtes or plomettes of ledde in your handes'.[6]

Boorde recommended tennis, bowls and weight-lifting as suitable sports, while Elyot tells us that 'shootinge in the longe bowe . . . incomparably excelleth all other exercise', but that 'tenese, seldome used, and for a little space, is a good exercise for yonge men'.[7] Neither writer commends these recreations in terms other than those of health. To these streams of theorising, native and foreign, must be added a simple fact. Days at Court with little to do could be long, and the hours needed filling somehow. The Black Book of Edward IV required the squires of the Household

> wynter and somer, in after nonys and in euenynges, to drawe to lordez chambrez within courte, there to kepe hinest company after theyre cunyng, in talkyng of cronycles of kinges and of other polycyez, or in pypyng, or harpyng, synging, other actez marclablez, to help occupy the court and acompany straungers, tyll the tym require of departing.[8]

In the Court of the early Tudors, the need to amuse the monarch became a thing of the past. The first Tudor king was one of 'distance', who left the Court to entertain itself. This precedent was followed by his son, especially after 1530, when much of his socialising was restricted to the confines of the Privy Chamber. The Privy Chamber, with its privy sub-departments, provided for Henry VIII independently of the rest of the Court, and on some days he might not 'come forth' from the privy lodgings at all. On such days the focus of the Court, the King's presence, was removed and the Court had to entertain itself.[9]

Early in Henry VIII's reign it was necessary to provide indoor and house-based entertainments in the spring because hunting and hawking and the other sports of the grass season were not ready until May or June. So for the 'eschewing of idleness, the ground of all vice, and to exercise that thing that shall be honorable and to the body healthful and profitable' feats of arms, jousts, revels and tournaments were held.[10] All but four of the forty-four tournaments of the reign took place before 1530. By 1530 Henry was middle-aged, in love with a younger woman and acquiring new-found interests. In short the King was no longer 'one of the boys'. The boys now had to entertain themselves — and the King had the good sense to provide them with a means of doing this. This explains the motivation behind the great recreational building boom of the early 1530s. It was for the Court as much as for its master that these buildings were erected. Courtiers were able to entertain themselves in the absence of the King, and indeed, they took every advantage of the facilities provided.

Despite medical advice to take exercise, supported by writers like Boorde and Elyot, there were reservations about the hooliganism and disturbances linked with some games, particularly with football. Thus in 1388 and 1410 Parliament had tried to distinguish between archery and 'idle games',[11] and in 1536 the Act regulating vagabonds and beggars banned, amongst other things, 'open playeing House[s] . . . for commen bowling dysyng carding closhe tenys'. A later parliamentary measure of 1542 promoting archery also tried controlling other games including bowls, quoits and tennis, while exempting noblemen, gentlemen and their households provided they played in their own houses and grounds.[12] Prosecution was not merely a threat, for in 1510 an Oxford man was fined for keeping a tennis-court.[13] These seemingly harmless games were banned because the recreation of the populace was supposed to be archery for the provision of archers in time of war. The medieval nobility were likewise engaged in recreations which doubled as military exercises, the tournament being the principal of these. The late fifteenth century saw a change in this; thenceforward it was no longer sufficient merely to be a fine soldier; now that soldier had to have other accomplishments, to read and to write, to compose verse and music, to sing and dance as well as to wrestle and play bowls and tennis. The criteria which enabled a man to be a fashionable courtier were expanded to include a range of luxury pursuits which a more settled political situation made possible. This was further reinforced and consolidated around 1530 when Henry VIII's personal retirement from the tiltyard, the single measure of courtly excellence early in the reign, signalled a widening of the criteria of excellence at the Henrician Court.

Tilting

For over sixty years up to 1530 tilting was the principal organised entertainment at Court.[14] Tilting involved two mounted knights, in full armour, each with a lance in his right hand, charging towards the other, either side of a timber barrier, 'the lists'. Points could be scored by breaking the opponent's lance or making body contact with him.[15] The arrangements made for the tournaments of the Yorkists and Henry VII were *ad hoc* and did not involve any permanent structures. They are perhaps best exemplified by the famous tournament between Lord Scales and the Bastard of Burgundy in 1467. The tiltyard was a railed-off area measuring 270 feet by 240 feet and overlooked by Edward IV's royal box. Beneath the King's seat sat the scorers and then on platforms either side of a staircase were the courtiers. Opposite were further tiered platforms for eminent Londoners; the common people simply leant against the rails (fig. 240).[16] This method of creating elaborate but temporary tiltyards was continued by Henry VII. During the jousts to celebrate the marriage of Prince Arthur and Catherine of Aragon a large tiltyard was set up on the north side of the Palace of Westminster. It was overlooked by two grandstands, one for the King and the other for the Spanish party.[17]

As a young man Henry VIII was a champion tilter, and his enthusiasm for the sport is borne out by the fact that one of the first payments of the reign, to Henry Smith, was for a tilt at the Tower of London.[18] But neither this tilt, nor any of the others of the very first years of the reign seem to have taken place in anything other than the ephemeral structures of previous reigns (fig. 241). All this changed when, in 1514, Henry began to construct permanent structures for jousting at Greenwich, including a viewing gallery and two viewing towers (figs 242–4 and see plan 2).[19] This had become necessary because tilting was now not just an occasional diversion but a regular activity. Between 1510 and 1520 there were at least fifteen tournaments at Greenwich alone,[20] justification enough for the construction of such elaborate structures. With the acquisition of Hampton Court and Whitehall, further tiltyards were built, first at Whitehall where, as at Greenwich, the structure that was created was more or less a permanent rendering of the temporary structures of previous reigns. The timber grandstand to house the King became the tiltyard gallery (fig. 246 and see plan 2).[21] That at Hampton Court was constructed much later (see plan 6); it was only in May 1537 that William Clement and Christopher Dickinson were paid for 'rydyng to greneweche by the kyngs commandement to tak messur of the tylte and the tylteyard',[22] and it was

not until the following year that 258,000 second-hand bricks could be spared for its walls.[23] For the construction of the towers, which were to replace the tiltyard gallery as the principal grandstand at Hampton Court, the King had to wait still longer.[24] By the time the Hampton Court tiltyard was finished so was the King's tilting career and the yard was never used in his lifetime. Indeed its first recorded use was in 1604 when James I held a running at the ring there.[25]

Early in his reign the King took great interest in

240. Drawing showing the joust on the occasion of the marriage of Henry IV with Joan of Navarre, Duchess of Brittany. Taken from the Beauchamp Pageant, 1485–90. It shows the arrangement of the spectators and a joust in progress.

241. In February 1511 Henry VIII held a two-day tournament at Westminster to celebrate the birth of a son to Catherine of Aragon. This section of the Westminster Tournament Roll shows the temporary grandstand erected for the occasion.

the design of tiltyards. For the Field of Cloth of Gold he drew a platt of the tiltyard as he wished it to be. The King's plan was not, however, a great success: the lists had been positioned off-centre, 88 feet away from one viewing gallery and 208 feet away from the other; instead of rails he proposed ditches, but these were in danger of undermining the foundations of the galleries.[26] The painting of the event shows the arrangements which the Earl of Worcester finally persuaded the King to adopt (fig. 247).[27]

It is difficult to generalise about the size of Henry's tiltyards for they varied widely. The one at Greenwich measured approximately 650 feet by 250 feet, the Whitehall version 480 feet by 80 feet, the tilt at Hampton Court 450 feet by 1,000 feet, that at the Field of Cloth of Gold 900 feet by 328 feet and the one at Eltham approximately 250 feet by 420 feet (see plans 2, 6, 1). The reason for this disparity is that a tiltyard was really only an enclosure within which the lists were set up. Accounts at Greenwich indicate that the area for the actual tilt, including the same sort of rails as used in 1467, was plotted out within the walls.[28] Another account mentions 'making of a newe standyng agaynst the tylte'.[29]

Work on the maintenance of the Greenwich tiltyard gives some details of its surface treatment. An account in 1536 is for 'dyging of gravell a bout the tylte wer as the plaster ys lede and in fyllyng of cartts with the said gravell and also in levylyng of the gravell ayen a bout the said tylte upon the plaster and in sandyng of the same for to kep the hours fette from the plaster'.[30] Several other accounts

confirm that gravel was laid on a thick layer of plaster to form a sort of macadam, and on top of this was laid sand.[31] The sand must have been quite deep as it was raked by labourers.[32] Another detail which emerges is the construction of 'a new stole for the tylte with sterres for them to get upon ther horses'.[33]

The tiltyard galleries seem simply to have been straightforward fenestrated galleries. The towers, however, were something different. In 1465 Lord Scales proclaimed that the purpose of the tournament was the 'augmentacion of knyghthode and recommendacion of nobley; also for the gloriouse scoole and study of Armes',[34] a sentiment which Henry VIII almost certainly shared. For him the tournament was the most graphic expression of the chivalric bent of his Court.[35] The tiltyard buildings with their castellar overtones emphasised the chivalric values underlying jousting. Thus, the tiltyard towers at Greenwich (figs 242–4) resembled diminutive castles, designed as octagonal towers with octagonal stair-turrets surmounted with fanciful wimple-like, pencil-pointed pinnacles — a make-believe backdrop to the mock-warfare of the Tudor Court.

Tennis

In 1527 Castiglione had stated that tennis was a 'noble sport which is very suitable for the courtier to play . . . for this shows how well he is built physically, how quick and agile he is in every member'.[36] But nearly three decades had to pass

242. Greenwich, Kent. View from the north by A. van den Wyngaerde, 1558. The tiltyard towers are clearly seen with the tiltyard itself to its left.

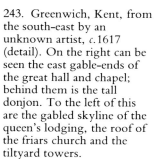

243. Greenwich, Kent, from the south-east by an unknown artist, *c.*1617 (detail). On the right can be seen the east gable-ends of the great hall and chapel; behind them is the tall donjon. To the left of this are the gabled skyline of the queen's lodging, the roof of the friars church and the tiltyard towers.

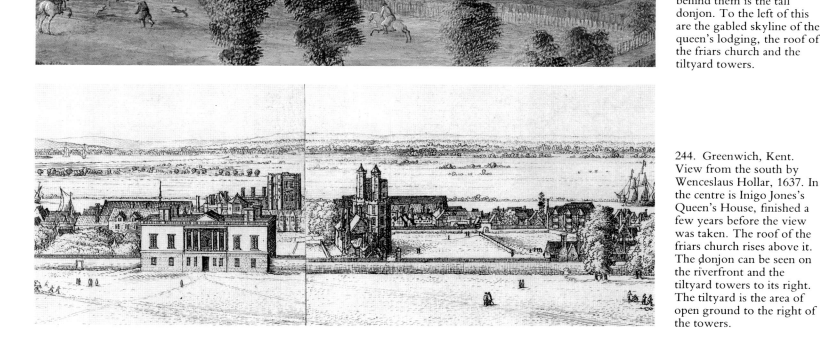

244. Greenwich, Kent. View from the south by Wenceslaus Hollar, 1637. In the centre is Inigo Jones's Queen's House, finished a few years before the view was taken. The roof of the friars church rises above it. The donjon can be seen on the riverfront and the tiltyard towers to its right. The tiltyard is the area of open ground to the right of the towers.

before the game found its first apologist, when in 1553 the Italian Antonio Scaino wrote *Trattato del Giuoco della Palla di Messer*. He began his book by claiming that 'this game has been created for a good purpose, namely, to keep our bodies healthy, to make our young men stronger and more robust, chasing idleness, virtue's most mortal enemy, far from them and thus making them of a stronger and more excellent nature'.[37] Both Castiglione and Scanio emphasised the wholesome, health-giving

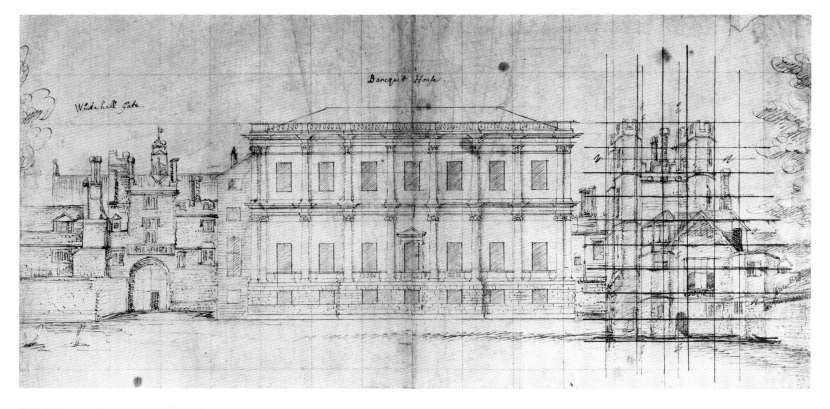

Whitehall Gate

Bancquit House

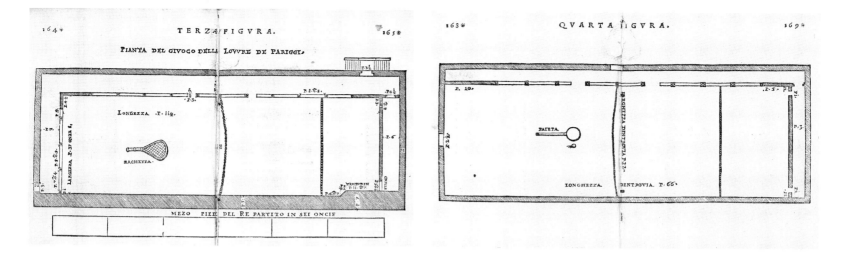

PIANTA DEL GIVOCO DELLA LOVVRE DE PARIGGI.

LONGEZZA .T. 114.

RACHETTA.

MEZO PIEDE DEL RE PARTITO IN SEI ONCIE

PALETA.

LONGHEZZA DENTROVIA .T. 66.

qualities of the game, and Castiglione also saw it as an ideal vehicle for courtly elegance.

There were two versions of the game current in the early sixteenth century and each had a differing type of court (fig. 248). The first version was the quarre court (or what Scaino called the minor court) which took its name from a small hole, one foot square, in one wall. This was the older form of the game which eventually died out at the end of the seventeenth century. The court had penthouses on the long wall and on the side opposite the service end (the hazard side), it also had a 'grille' which was a netted opening above the penthouse. This sort of court was the smaller of the two: Scaino suggests 22 feet by 66 feet as a guideline.[38] The other form of court was called the dedans or major court. It took its name from the dedans — a third penthouse replacing the quarre at the service end of the court. On account of this extra penthouse the court needed to be slightly larger, perhaps 100 feet by 38 feet. Both games were played by serving the ball on to the penthouse and then returning it across the net, or cord, until one or other player failed to return the ball. Points were scored according to how far from the net an unreturned ball came to rest (the chase) and also by hitting the grille, dedans or quarre — if there was one. Balls were not to hit the wall above the 'play line' — 18 feet up — but were allowed to hit the ceiling.[39]

Although the origins of tennis are still disputed, it is certain that from the twelfth century onwards it was popular throughout France and Spain: astonishingly, two French kings, Louis X and Charles VIII, and two Spanish kings, Henry I of Castile and Philip the Handsome, all died as a direct result of their participation.[40] The game seems to have been taken up quite early in England; although forbidden in royal ordinances between 1305 and 1388, it was probably played at Court as early as the

reign of Henry V.[41] There is no evidence to show that tennis was played at Court in mid-fifteenth-century England; Henry VI was not known for his prowess at sport. Meanwhile in France and Burgundy the game was reaching a peak of popularity. The tennis-plays of the Burgundian Court have already been mentioned (see figs 16–17); Philip the Good was an excellent player and during the celebrations for the wedding of Charles the Bold and Margaret of York the wedding feast was held in an open tennis-play at Princenhof. In France, by 1500, the university town of Orleans had forty courts and by the end of the century Paris had over two hundred and fifty.[42]

There are a few clues which indicate that under Edward IV the game was re-introduced into Court circles. In 1470 one Richard Sterys, a Yeoman of the Chamber to the Duke of Exeter, was put to death; the *Great Chronicle of London* describes him as 'oon of the Cunnyngest players at the Tenys in England, for he was so delyver that he wold stand In a Tubb that should be nere brest hye and lepe owth of the same, bothe standyng at the hows and at the Rechase and wyn of a good player, . . .'.[43] During the reign of Henry VII tennis became popular at Court when, in about 1494 at the age of thirty-seven, the King suddenly took up the game seriously. The first hint of Henry's growing interest is in a Chamber account of June 1494 when a payment of £4 was made to 'a Spaynyard the tenes pleyer', followed by payments for tennis-balls.[44] A portent of this interest was perhaps the making of a tennis-play during 1492–3 at Kenilworth, and in the next fifteen years Henry VII constructed courts at Richmond, Wycombe, Woodstock, Windsor and Westminster.[45]

The King's career is recorded in the Chamber accounts in the sums that he lost whilst playing against various courtiers. One of the principal

248a and b. A. Scaino, *Trattato del Giuoco della Palla di Messer*, 1555, showing the recommended size and plan of major and minor tennis-plays.

245 (facing page top). Hampton Court, Surrey. Detail of a view commissioned by Cosimo III de'Medici in 1669. It shows the tiltyard and tiltyard towers on the left.

246 (facing page centre). Whitehall Palace. Drawing for the masque *Time Vindicated to Himself and to his Honours* by Inigo Jones, 1623. On the right, in front of the northern gatehouse, can be seen the bargeboarded end of the tiltyard gallery. The walls of the tiltyard have been omitted to gain a clear view of the Banqueting House. On the left is the Court gate, giving land access into the palace.

247 (facing page bottom). *The Field of Cloth of Gold*, by an unknown artist, *c.*1545 (detail). The tiltyard was designed by Henry VIII. The documents do not fully agree with the arrangement shown here.

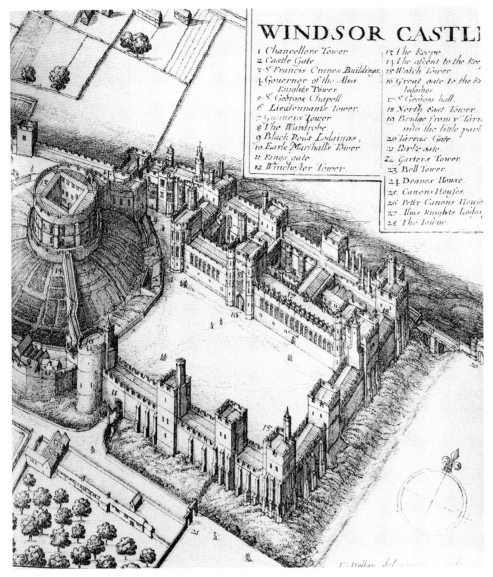

WINDSOR CASTL[
1 Chancellors Tower
2 Castle Gate
3 S. Francis Cranes Buildings
4 Gouernor of the Alms Knights Tower
5 S. Georges Chapell
6 Lieutennants Tower
7 Gunners Tower
8 The Wardrobe
9 Black Rods Lodgings
10 Earle Marshalls Tower
11 Kings gate
12 Winchester Tower
13 The Keepe
14 The ascent to the Kee
15 Watch Tower
16 Great gate to the K. lodgings
17 S. Georges hall
18 North East Tower
19 Bridge from y. Kar. into the little park
20 Tarras Gate
21 Parke gate
22 Garters Tower
23 Bell Tower
24 Deanes House
25 Canons Houses
26 Petty Canons House
27 Alms Knights Lodgi.
28 The Towne

249. Windsor Castle, Berkshire. Detail of a view from the south by Wenceslaus Hollar, 1672. The tennis-court can be seen in the ditch around the round tower. The royal lodgings are grouped around the two courtyards immediately behind it.

250 (facing page left). Whitehall Palace. Remains of one of the west windows of the great close tennis-play, as revealed in 1962.

protect them from stray balls.[47] At Windsor a detailed account describes the tennis-match played on the occasion of the enforced visit of the Infante Philip in 1506. Here the viewing gallery seems to have been a well-furnished room:

After the horse was bated bothe kinges wente to the tenes playe and in the upper gallery theare was layed ii cushens of clothe of gold for the ii kyngs and the rome was honestly hanged wyth [. . . text missing . . .] where played my lorde marques, the lord Howard and two other knights together and after the kyng of Casteelle had seen them play a whylle he made parlye wyth the lord marques of Dorset the kyng lookyng one them but the kyng of casteel played wyth the racket and gave the lord marques xv.[48]

Norden's view of Windsor dated 1607 shows a tennis-play at the base of the great tower and Hollar's later view shows it in more detail (fig. 249) but this need not have been Henry VIII's play which seems to have been a more sophisticated structure.

Henry VIII played tennis from an early age and it formed part of his education, along with hunting and archery. Indeed, one of the first buildings of his reign was the new 'tenys playe' at Westminster.[49] Edward Hall describes how, in 1510–11, 'The kynge was muche entysed to playe at tennys and at dice, whiche appetite, certain craftie persons about him perceiving, brought in Frenchmen and Lombards to like wagers with hym, and so he lost much money', indicating that perhaps it was still the foreigners who were the best players. In 1519 the ambassador Giustinian claimed that it was 'the prettiest thing in the world to see him play; his fair skin glowing through a shirt of finest texture'.[50]

Under Henry VIII the number of tennis-plays in his ownership doubled; after completing the new tennis-play at Westminster he went on build plays at Beaulieu and Bridewell. That at Beaulieu can be seen on an early plan of the house (fig. 63) built, but not as a free-standing structure, in the centre of the building. As far as is known it was the only tennis-play of the reign to be built on this pattern, as all others seem to have been free-standing. That at Bridewell was completed on the eve of the reception of the Emperor Charles V in 1522, when King and Emperor played a match reaching, after eleven games, a diplomatic draw.[51] A further group of tennis-plays was built between 1532 and 1535; in three years Henry built one at Hampton Court, one at St James's, one at Greenwich, one at Calais and five at Whitehall.

The most pretentious of Henry VIII's tennis-plays were the great covered courts at Hampton Court and Whitehall built in 1532–3. The play at Hampton Court (fig. 251) was under construction

attractions of tennis was that it was a spectator sport, and Castiglione commends the game for this reason. Bets were always laid on the outcome, not only by the spectators but also by the players: Charles VI of France lost 300 francs at tennis in 1394 and Henry VII's losses, although not so great, amounted to over £20 between 1493 and 1499, when he is last recorded as playing.[46]

In architectural terms the King's plays at Richmond and Windsor Castle are the best documented. The play at Richmond formed part of the complex of recreational facilities situated at the end of the garden. Later accounts for repairs show that the spectators were able to watch the tennis from 'wyndowes lokyng oute of the gallarii into the tennys playe' which were covered with wire to by March 1532 when staybars were bought for the windows. In May 1534 carpenters were paid overtime for 'makyng the hasserds in the closse tennys play agaynst the kinges cumyng', and as Henry visited the house the following month it was probably then that the play was first used. Work on the Whitehall play started as the land upon which it was built was cleared in early 1532. It was probably complete by April 1533 when Thomas Alvard, the Keeper of the House was also appointed Keeper of the Tennis-plays there.[52] Enough survives of both of these buildings to reconstruct their original appearance (fig. 252). Both buildings were five bays long and buttressed to the string course, above which rose crenellations. The windows, of which an almost complete example survives at Whitehall (fig. 250), were positioned about 20 feet above ground and a lower range of windows lit the penthouses. The form these buildings took was wholly dictated by their function and then rendered into traditional Tudor architectural vocabulary; the hall at Hampton Court was built at exactly the same period as the tennis-play and in an identical idiom.

Both of these courts were part of a recreational 'complex'. At Hampton Court a gallery linked the play with an earlier open tennis-play in the west built by Wolsey. At Whitehall there were three other courts (fig. 253). A small close (or closed) tennis-play was built to the west with a small open

play next to it, and to the north of the great close play was a large open play. On the large plays dedans or major tennis was probably played, the courts measuring 83 feet by 26 feet; the small courts measured 60 feet by 23 feet and were for the minor or quarre game.

The play at Greenwich was far less substantial; it was timber framed and approached by a gallery which was probably used for viewing. Its windows were protected by wire frames, and its floor tiled.

Repair accounts suggest that it may have been sited at the south-west corner of the main courtyard, but it is not possible to identify the structure on any of the early views. A new wooden frame was made for it in 1534 but it was used so heavily that carpenters were again employed in 1536 for 'cawkyng of tenes playe wher as the bords be rent and wynd shakyn'.[53] A considerable effort went into running and maintaining the royal tennis-plays and the King had a

251 (above). Hampton Court, Surrey. The great close tennis-play today after being converted into lodgings for the Duke and Duchess of York in 1670.

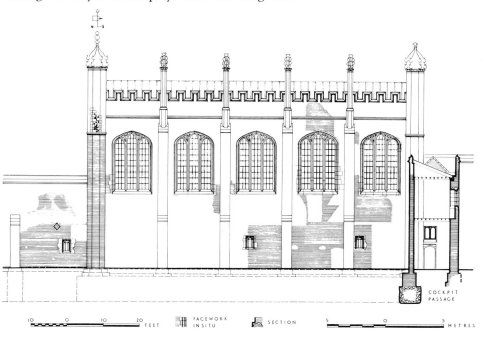

FEET   FACEWORK INSITU   SECTION   METRES

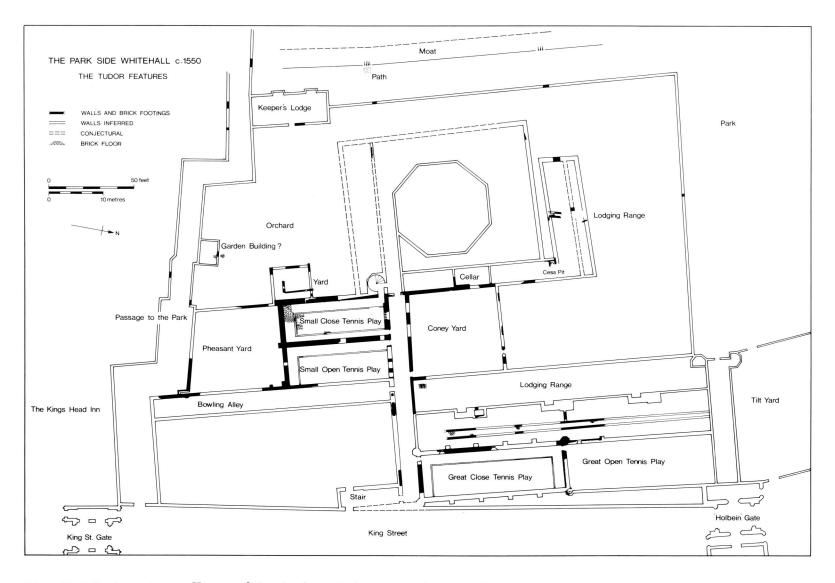

THE PARK SIDE WHITEHALL c.1550

THE TUDOR FEATURES

— WALLS AND BRICK FOOTINGS
— WALLS INFERRED
=== CONJECTURAL
▒▒▒ BRICK FLOOR

0 ____ 50 feet

0 ____ 10 metres

N

Moat

Path

Keeper's Lodge

Park

Orchard

Garden Building ?

Lodging Range

Yard

Cellar

Cess Pit

Small Close Tennis Play

Coney Yard

Passage to the Park

Pheasant Yard

Small Open Tennis Play

Lodging Range

Tilt Yard

The Kings Head Inn

Bowling Alley

Great Open Tennis Play

Great Close Tennis Play

Stair

King St. Gate

King Street

'Holbein' Gate

253. Whitehall Palace. The parkside. Ground-floor plan, *c*.1547, based on excavation and documentary evidence.

252 (previous page bottom right). Whitehall Palace. Elevation of the great close tennis-play, as reconstructed after archaeological investigation in 1962.

Keeper of Tennis-plays, Anthony Annesley, as early as 1528. He was succeeded by one Oliver Kelly, upon whose death in 1543 Thomas Johns was appointed. At Hampton Court there was a lodging for the Keeper of the Play at its north end and a similar building was set aside for the Keeper at Greenwich. The Keeper was responsible for providing balls which were made by the Company of Ironmongers in the City.[54] He may also have acted as the Marker, or umpire. The maintenance of the courts was also his responsibility, although the structural repairs were undertaken by the Office of Works. The most frequent item was the renewal of the wiring protecting the windows; the wires were usually painted red, as were the windows, whereas the internal walls were black.[55]

On the King's death in 1547 'vii rackettes for the tenys' were found in the closet next to the privy chamber at Greenwich. The inventory of Henry's

wardrobe taken in 1517 lists 'blacke velwete for a tenes cote for the kings grace', and when, in 1527, Henry injured his foot as the result of a game of tennis he wore a black velvet slipper to match the coat. It seems as if courtiers had to pay either the Keeper or the Crown to use the courts and that the going rate at Richmond in 1519 was as much as 2s. 6d. a day. Many courtiers played the game, including Lords Rochford and Ros, the Dukes of Suffolk and Buckingham, Henry Courtenay, Earl of Devon, and Anthony Knyvet.[56]

Bowling

The origin and history of the game of bowls, as played in the English Court in the late fifteenth and early sixteenth century is deeply obscure, yet from the ample evidence as to the form of Tudor bowling-alleys it seems to have resembled Flemish bowls as played today in some parts of France; the aim of the game was to place a flattened cheese-shaped bowl as close as possible to the jack using the concave sides of the alley.

But, as with tennis, bowling was a game reserved for the rich, and their social inferiors were prohibited from playing. Andrew Boorde includes in his list of structures to be built at a nobleman's house a bowling-alley for 'a great man, necessary it is for to passe his tyme with bowles in an aly'. Others, though, took a dimmer view of the game's merits: Elyot asked 'why sholde nat boulynge, claisshe, pynnes, and koytyng be as moche recommended? Verily as for the two the laste, be utterly abjected of al noble men . . . classhe is employed to little strength; in boulyng often times to moche'.[57]

Bowling-alleys are mentioned at Richmond in 1501. Their exact whereabouts have not been established, but it is likely that several of the galleries surrounding the gardens housed alleys (fig. 239). If only one example is documented from the reign of Henry VII, six royal houses, in addition to Richmond, possessed them under Henry VIII. These included the three greater houses at Greenwich, Hampton Court and Whitehall as well as Eltham, Grafton and Woking, and work on the earliest of these at Hampton Court and Whitehall did not start until 1532. By 1547 there were three alleys at Hampton Court, one on the north side of the house and two by the river.[58] The latter were brick and stone buildings with flat lead roofs which can be seen in several early views (figs 72, 97), and one wall of which survives as the south wall of the pond garden. The Whitehall alleys built in 1532 were more substantial than their exact contemporaries at Hampton Court. They are shown on the 'Agas' view of the palace (fig. 81) as long narrow buildings, regularly fenestrated and very similar to that shown on the Kip view of Hampton Court (fig. 254). Although less prestigious, the bowling-alleys built at Woking and Grafton are important because information about their structure and function survives in repair accounts. At Woking the alleys were open-air. The accounts of 1536–7 describe 'digging of ii new boullyng alles thon in the kyngs gardyn made wyth banks of cley for the kyng to boullein and thother in thorchard for the kyng and the quene to walke in'. One of the alleys was therefore only a walk. The other, however, was certainly intended for bowling: 'settyng up of sertyn raills and posts att both ends of the same new boullyng alle with bordyng of the same for the bullys to mak a jompe oon'.[59] The alley at Grafton was a more substantial structure. It was built on the north side of the orchard:

for his grace to bowle in as also upon bryngyng up of other walles to enclose too wyde placs for servents waiters the one upon the este syde of the bowlyng aley . . . thother at the weste ende . . . wythe lyke enclosyng the said aley at bothe ends severall ffrom the said waytyng placs with lik walles.[60]

This alley had places at each end for people to wait in. More is revealed by the following account:

makyng and dryvyng of staks drawyng of bords redy for bothe syds of the bowlyng aleye to beare therthe bankwyse a slope for bowles to playe upon, furthermore nat only makyng of seats within the said bowlyng aley for the kyngs grace to rest on closyng up brest heigh thest and west end of the bowlyng aley with borde for gentylmen to leane on.[61]

The carefully prepared boards supported by stakes were covered with potter's clay, and the banks outside the building were turfed to walk on.

All these bowling-alleys were about 20 feet wide. Less is known about their length, but the alleys at Hampton Court measured respectively 230 feet and 210 feet and that at Whitehall 160 feet. There were waiting areas at either end, one where the players assembled and the other where the servants collected the balls. This arrangement can be seen in a late fifteenth-century manuscript illumination which shows a bowling-alley in the background (fig. 255) As far as internal features are concerned, the most important element was the provision of sloping sides, but benches and leaning boards were also fitted for the convenience of both spectators and players. The surface of the alley itself seems to have been of soap ash and/or 'founder's earth' (spoil from furnaces).[62]

The equipment needed for the game was simple. At Hampton Court there was a house 'wher the kyngs bowlls be turned',[63] likewise at Greenwich

254. Hampton Court, Surrey. Detail of Johannes Kip's 1705 engraving showing the Tudor bowling-alley.

255. *Imagination and the Knight in a Walled Garden*, illumination by an anonymous Flemish artist, 1496. Behind the archers shooting at a butt is a bowling-alley. Like Henry VII's at Richmond, it is in a covered cloister; like Henry VIII's alleys, it has an L-shaped plan.

258 (facing page top). Whitehall Palace. An east–west cross-section of the parkside.

256. A fossilised bowling ball found sealed beneath the floor of the Henrician bowling-alley at Whitehall in the excavations of 1962.

257. Frontispiece to *The Royall Pastime of Cocking* by Richard Howlett, 1709.

259 (facing page bottom). Whitehall Palace. The cockpit from a drawing by John Thorpe of 1606. The photograph is an X-ray of a paste-down on a drawing of another subject.

there was a shed for 'the kyngs tourner to mends the kyngs grace boulls in'.[64] During the Whitehall Palace excavations one of these wooden bowling balls was found (fig. 256). The privy purse expenses of Henry VIII show that the King played frequently, and that as with tennis, a major element was betting on the outcome of the match.[65]

Cockfighting

Cockfighting was enjoyed amongst the populace at large; when it was first adopted at Court is unknown, but by 1709 it could be called with confidence 'the Royal Pastime of Cockfighting'.[66] This royal pastime seems to have originated with Henry VIII, at least he was the first king to build cockpits – one at Whitehall and another at Greenwich in 1533–4. The more elaborate of the two, the Whitehall cockpit, was an octagonal building built in three stages surmounted with an elaborate lantern (figs 258–9). It was decorated with flint chequerwork and beasts holding iron standards and gilt vanes. It was the Tudor fantasy building *par excellence*, heavier with chivalric overtones even than the tiltyard towers at Greenwich. A similar structure can be seen in the background of the *Family of Henry VIII with St George and the Dragon* (fig. 266).[67] The Greenwich building, though less spectacular, shared the same features. It was begun in April 1533 and had three tiers of seats for spectators and the King had a special seat which acted as a cage 'ffor dores of partycons ffor cocks to stande in within the kyngs

seytt'.[68] Anne Boleyn may not have wholly shared her husband's enthusiasm and had a more detached viewing-point in her gallery overlooking the pit.[69] An idea of the internal appearance of these two cockpits can probably be gained from a much later frontispiece to the *Royal Pastime of Cockfighting* by 'RH' (1709) (fig. 257) which shows a tiered amphitheatre of seats.

Exactly how a royal cockfight was staged is known from a full account of one fought at Whitehall in 1539:

King Henry the Eighth of that name had had a sumptuous amphitheatre of fine workmanship built, designed like a colosseum and intended exclusively for fights and matches between these little animals [cocks]. Round about the circumference of the enclosure there were innumerable coops, belonging to many princes and lords of the kingdom. In the centre of this colosseum . . . stood a sort of short, upright, truncated column about a span and a half from the ground . . . very heavy bets were made on the mettle and valour of

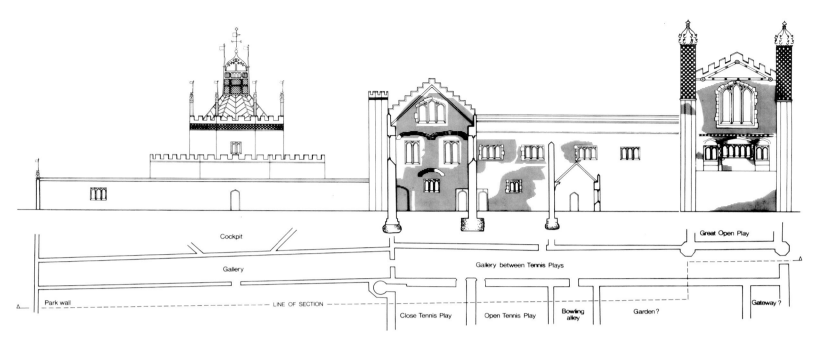

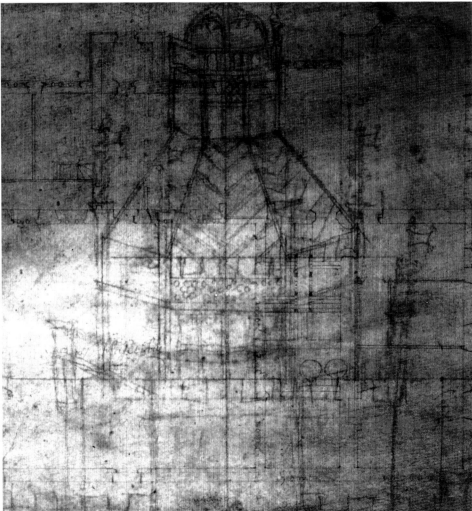

the cocks . . . they are placed two at a time on the column in full view of the great numbers of spectators. The jewels and valuables which are bet on them are placed in the middle. These are taken by whoever's cock wins.[70]

The King housed his own cocks in special coops at both Whitehall and Greenwich. In 1533 'a cocke cope in theste lane for the kyngs cocks with vi roumes in the same' was constructed at Greenwich for the King's prize-fighters. However they did not stay there long because an account the next year is for 'iii cowpes . . . for the kyngs cocks and hens of the game made at the kyngs commandement through the quenes desyre at master norres place in the towne for the avoyding of the said fooles out of the kings gardyne by cause the quenes grace could nott take hir reste in mornyngs for the noise of the same'. The Keeper of Greenwich fed and tended the birds.[71]

Hunting, shooting, fishing and other pastimes

A book about the architectural setting of the early Tudor Court need not dwell long on many of the lesser, but still popular, entertainments of the Court. Yet some sports and games did have an impact on the King's houses, and those were the sports that are still today essentially upper-class recreations. Of these the most important was certainly hunting.

All his life Henry VIII was a keen huntsman. In 1520 he was said to rise 'daily, except on holy days, at 4 or 5 o'clock, and hunts till 9 or 10 at night. He

191

spares no pains to convert the sport of hunting into a martyrdom'.[72] Towards the end of his reign this regime became even more frantic, the King moving from house to house hunting all day.[73] The principal and most prestigious type of hunting was riding for a hart with hounds. The hunt would begin at the break of day before the King rose. A specific beast would be chosen and then a few selected huntsmen with two or three couples of hounds were strategically placed round the hunting area. The main hunting party would then arrive with their dogs and the hart be roused; at this point the chase began, the huntsmen sounding horns to inform each other of the progress of the beast. Once it was cornered by the dogs the hunters gathered round to watch the kill before ceremonially jointing and dissecting the animal. On other occasions a less sportsman-like use of the dogs was made – they could be let loose on enclosures of two hundred to three hundred deer in order to provide first sport and then food for local magnates and gentry.[74] Each house had stabling for horses that included provision for hunters. At some houses there was kennelling for dogs. The kennels at Greenwich were so extensive that the dogs were accommodated a mile away at Deptford. In 1539 a 230 foot-long pale was built around the kennels. Closer to the house four new kennels were made in 1532 behind the banqueting house in the tiltyard. In 1534–5 a new park was made at Eltham and the lodge built in it had kennels provided. At lesser houses other provision would have to be made: the Master of the Buckhounds, Sir Richard Long, who transported the hounds by cart on progress, presumably had to make special arrangements at the lesser houses without kennels.[75]

Although a superb horseman, Henry VIII was not exempt from his share of riding accidents and these increased with age. To try and avoid these his favourite hunting grounds were made safer and easier to ride: at Eltham carpenters were instructed to make bridges and causeways over boggy areas and streams: at The More even more drastic measures were taken in 1539 when a branch of the moat was filled in at the cost of £8 in order to make a clear way for the coursing.[76] After a serious fall in 1536 Henry gave up riding to hounds and instead shot from a platform called 'a standing'. Such a standing was built in the park at The More in 1538. It was timber-framed and plastered externally, of two storeys with an attic and an external stair, and on the first floor it had a 'double pentice' round it. Inside there were fitted benches and 'formes for seates' as well as five stools. Shooting from a standing was a sociable affair and often ladies from the Court would join the King and his male companions. Another standing was built at The More in

1542, it measured 20 feet long by 18 feet wide and 20 feet high. Several others are recorded in works accounts but only one such structure survives, now in Epping Forest (fig. 260).[77]

In this type of hunt a small band of huntsmen and hounds would flush out the hart and chase it past the standing. As well as the skill of the hunters, nets on poles or 'toiles' were used to confine the path of a fleeing beast so that it passed the waiting hunters. This more static form of hunting was ideally suited to the paled parks which surrounded most of Henry's houses (fig. 261). There are frequent references to mending of toils and to the appointment of Keepers of Toils. These bulky items required storage, and some were stored under the long gallery at Hampton Court.[78]

Henry VII was as devoted to hawking as he was hunting, and this love was passed on to his son. In September 1533 Sir William Kingston told Lord Lisle that 'the king hawks every day with goshawks and others . . . vix., Leyners, sparhowkes, and merlions, both before noon and after'.[79] On the whole hawking was a recreation of the late summer and autumn, in December 1540 the French ambassadors reported that the King was 'engaged in hawking, now that the season for hunting deer is passed'.[80] Sometimes this meant the stocks of game were low and in September 1543 a proclamation was made to prevent people hawking pheasant or

260. 'Queen Elizabeth's Hunting Lodge', Chingford, Essex. The sole surviving such lodge of the many dozens built by Henry VIII. In plan it is L-shaped, the short arm being a staircase. There are two floors and originally there were no windows, only gaps between the timber studs. The second-floor room was the principal viewing gallery and has a fine open timber roof.

partridge within four miles of the King's houses while he was on progress.[81] It may be that some of the pheasants kept in the pheasant-yards at the greater houses were destined for the royal table only after being released and hunted.

On the face of it hawking was far safer than coursing. Despite this there was a nasty accident in 1525 when the King, chasing his hawk, pole-vaulted over a stream, broke the pole and landed head-first in the mud; had not a footman leapt into the water and 'lift up his head, whiche was fast in the clay' he would have been drowned.[82] Nevertheless, hawking was not always so hazardous and on more sedentary occasions Henry was joined by Anne Boleyn.[83]

The architectural impact of the sport was the construction of hawks' mews such as the one made in the park at The More in 1542 and that made at Hunsdon in the summer of 1537.[84] The most extraordinary mews was that at Greenwich where one side of the inner court was devoted to a mews nicknamed 'the cage'. It was set up in 1533, probably at second-floor-level as it was approached by a stair and had dormer windows. The windows had double timber-latticed openings and no glass. The King had a bedchamber and privy chamber in the cage; the Queen's bedchamber was only separated from it by one room.[85] The idea of keeping hawks so close to the King's bedroom was not altogether new or unique, Margaret of Burgundy had kept her hawks actually in her bedchamber.[86]

There were also butts for archery at most royal houses; Henry VII had enjoyed archery and had had butts made for him at Woking in 1502.[87] Henry VIII, talented in all sports, was a superb archer; John Taylor noted that during archery practice with the archers of his Guard in Calais in July 1513 the King 'cleft the mark in the middle and surpassed them all'.[88] It was far from uncommon for the king to practice archery indoors – in his youth he had shot in the great hall much to the disquiet of older courtiers and the works glaziers.[89] At The More in 1542 carpenters constructed a great frame with wheels for a butt to stand in the king's gallery. The gallery at The More, almost 300 feet long must have been an ideal place for archery.[90]

Firing handguns was a varient form of shooting, but a novelty available only to a small circle near

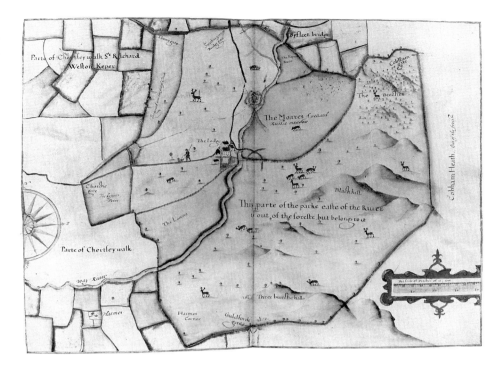

the King who enjoyed shooting duck in Plumstead marshes near Greenwich. In 1538 Richard Ridge, one of the King's joiners made a target in the shape of a man for this group.[91] Sometimes the guns used were larger and more powerful than mere handguns; this was the cause of an unfortunate accident at Greenwich when the king blasted off the roof of Henry Norris's house in the park.[92]

Fishing was another courtly activity. Although the fishponds at Hampton Court were designed to supply the kitchens, at The More mowers were paid for 'clensyng of gresse and weeds in and about the pownds and in the moote for the kyngs grace to fysche', and a special boat was bought to enable the cleaners to keep the water free from weed.[93] Less common recreations, references to which appear in the works accounts, are those which show the King labouring; carpenters provided two trestles to enable him to saw up blocks of wood in 1542 and even more surprising was the provision of two steel hammers for him to make quatts or cobbles.[94]

261. Chobham, Surrey. The house was formally acquired from Chertsey Abbey in 1535, but as early as 1533 Henry VIII had spent money on paling the park there. John Norden's map of 1610 shows the house in the centre of a paled park, in which Henry often enjoyed hunting in the late 1530s and 1540s. His last hunting trip there was only five months before his death in January 1547.

Chapter 12

THE HOUSEHOLD CHAPEL:
THE RELIGIOUS LIFE OF THE COURT

Chapels had been an essential adjunct to any royal residence from the conversion of the earliest English kings to Christianity, but the earliest royal chapel to survive is the Chapel of St John in the White Tower of the Tower of London. This was positioned directly next to the King's inner chamber and separate entrances enabled the King and his chaplain to enter from their respective parts of the building (see pp. 3–4 and figs 6, 7).

It was not, however, until the thirteenth century that a permanent and distinct religious body within the King's *domus*, the Chapel Royal, was formed. The Chapel Royal was not based at any one residence, but like the other departments of the Household accompanied the King wherever he went. The staff of the Chapel during the fourteenth century comprised between five and ten clerks under the Dean of the Chapel; mass was said for the Household every day in the chapel and the King heard it daily in his own private closet.[1] The Chapel Royal was free from any episcopal jurisdiction and appointments were in the gift of the King. The Dean was subject only to the King and the Lord Chamberlain.

The story of the Chapel Royal as an institution can be more fully written in the reign of Henry VI, whose Dean wrote a description of it for presentation to Alfonso V of Portugal in 1449. The workings of the Chapel and its duties are described in detail as are its staff and the financial arrangements to support them.[2] By the reign of Edward IV the religious constitution of the Household had formed into two parts; for himself Edward had at least four chaplains whose duties were to sit in the chamber and hall to say grace at meals and also to give 'attendaunce for mattines, masses, and other devotions, to be ready at such season and place as the king will be disposed'.[3]

In addition to these was the Household chapel under the Dean of the Chapel and his deputy — the Sub-Dean. Just as the King's private chaplains catered for the spiritual needs of the King, the Household chapel tended to the needs of his Court;

the Dean of the Chapel appointed the thirty-eight members of the chapel and oversaw their life at Court. The majority of the chapel staff comprised the twenty-six chaplains and clerks who were 'men of worshipp, endowed with vertue, morall and speculatiff, as of theyre musicke, shewing in descant clene voysed, well releesed and pronouncynge, eloquent in reding, sufficiaunt in organes pleyyng and modestiall in all other manner of behaving'.[4] In addition, there were two Yeomen or Pistellers who were singing men, and eight children of the chapel, boys under the age of eighteen, who made up the choir (pistellers, or pistolers, were those who sang the epistle). The Clerk of the Closet prepared the chapel and altars for service including 'taking up the travers; laying the cuysshyns necessary for the kynge and the chapleyns'.[5] Finally there was the Yeoman of the Vestry assisted by one or more Grooms who oversaw the 'sacred stuff' belonging to the chapel.

Like the other major Household departments, the Chapel Royal was assigned an architectural territory within the King's house — the king's domestic chapel. Royal chapels took their medieval form from those built in the reign of Henry III, royal chapel builder *par excellence*. It was in his reign that the royal chapel became a two-storey building with access at first-floor level for the royal family and at ground-floor level for the clergy and sometimes the Household.[6] The only detailed surviving record of such a chapel is the plan of the royal house at Havering-att-Bower dated *c.* 1578 (fig. 103). This shows a slightly different arrangement, the chapel being entirely on the first-floor approached by separate stairs for the clergy and for the laity.

The upper part of the chapel was usually accessible directly from the King's and Queen's chambers, as was the case at Clarendon and Havering-att-Bower, but at Westminster, where the palace's status demanded a more elaborate chapel, indeed an *Eigenkirche* — St Stephen's Chapel was situated next to the hall and the King and Queen had large private chapels of their own (see plan 12). The

262. Rowland Lockey, *Lady Margaret Beaufort, c.*1598. This is an important painting giving excellent visual evidence for the furnishing of a royal closet. The floor of the closet is either tiled or painted plaster, but the King's mother herself is kneeling on a carpet. Over her head is a canopy of state and to her side rich hangings screen her from the rest of the closet. The table in front of her is covered in cloth of gold.

lower part of St Stephen's Chapel, divided by a screen, was principally devoted to the clergy but space was available at the west end for the Court.

There was very little change to these arrangements during the late Middle Ages and little detail is known of royal chapel buildings until the construction of Richmond and Greenwich by Henry VII. At both houses the location of the chapel broke new ground in terms of the planning of royal houses. The chapels were symmetrically placed across the inner courtyard facing the hall (see plans 3, 11). This plan was at variance with the traditional arrangement which placed the hall opposite the entrance, but had close parallels in contemporary collegiate architecture;[7] it was copied once only by Henry VIII (at Beaulieu), but seems to have had no lasting influence in the planning of royal chapels. Only in the reign of Henry VIII, with a change in the structure of the Chapel Royal and in the King's attitude to attendance in the Household chapel, was a permanent change in the form of domestic royal chapels wrought.

The Chapel Royal in the reign of Henry VIII

By 1509 the Chapel Royal had reached a stable size, one at which it was to remain throughout Henry VIII's reign. It comprised the Dean, thirty gentlemen (normally the Sub-Dean and nine other chaplains, plus twenty lay clerks) and ten choristers.[8] In size it exceeded the choirs of the largest cathedrals at York, St Paul's in London and Salisbury; in quality it was judged amongst the finest in Europe.[9] During the first few years of Henry VIII's reign there was little alteration in the constitution of the Chapel Royal, but Wolsey's Household reforms of 1526, in an attempt to control the cost of the King's Court, reduced the number of chapel staff permanently in attendance on the King. Hitherto the whole Household chapel had travelled with the Court on progress at all times. This was a cumbersome and expensive business and one that was ultimately unnecessary; while the Court was itinerant in the winter months, moving between the greater houses, there was a clear need for the whole Chapel, but in the summer months, with the Court much reduced in size, this was not as important and so Wolsey decreed that only the Master of the Children and six men with an officer of the Vestry should permanently attend the Court. When this reduced Chapel was in attendance they were to have: 'a masse of our lady before noon, and on sundayes and holydayes, masse of the day, besides our lady masse, and an anthem in the afternoon; for which

purpose no great carriage either of vestments or books shall be required.'[10]

This reduction in the services performed by the Chapel Royal had architectural consequences; there now was no need for a major Household chapel at the lesser houses. Just as the King's later lesser houses lacked halls where the whole Court could dine so did they lack chapels where the whole Court could worship. Of course, some lesser houses built earlier in the reign already had chapels, but, other than at St James's (which it should be remembered was the official residence of the heir apparent) Henry did not build a major chapel at any of the lesser houses after 1526.

Before 1530 Henry built, or rebuilt, four domestic chapels, at Greenwich, Eltham, Hampton Court and Beaulieu. The nature of work on the Greenwich chapel is unclear, but it probably entailed a complete rebuilding — the finished structure appears in all views of the house (fig. 264).[11] Between 1519 and 1522 a new chapel was built nearby at Eltham to a specification probably set out by Wolsey. The new chapel at Eltham was closer to the hall than its predecessor and was to have two first-floor closets, each linked to the body of the chapel by a spiral stair (see plan 1). In these staircases Eltham imitated the new chapel at Greenwich, which was similarly provided for. These staircases allowed the King and Queen direct access to the body of the chapel on occasions when the importance of the feast demanded their presence. At both sites the principal difference between the old and new chapels seems to have been the introduction of these staircases. Otherwise there was nothing unusual or remarkable about them.

At Beaulieu, one of the greater houses designated by the Eltham Ordinances, the Richmond and Greenwich plan was followed, whereby the chapel was positioned across the outer court facing the

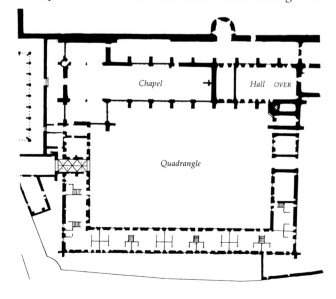

263. New College, Oxford. Ground plan. Either intentionally, or inadvertently, owing to a failure to complete an intended nave, William of Wykeham established the naveless chapel was a model both for future Oxford colleges and for royal domestic residences.

great hall. More important than the imitation of this layout was an innovation in the form of the chapel itself, for the new chapel at Beaulieu had a large ante-chapel crossing the body of the chapel proper at right angles. The royal pews with their symmetrically placed staircases were situated above the ante-chapel and not over the west end of the chancel. A plan of the house of *c*. 1700 (fig. 63) seems to indicate that the screen was not positioned in the body of the chapel but between the ante-chapel and chancel. The origins of this type of plan can be traced back to the chapel built by William of Wykeham at New College, Oxford, in 1380–87 (fig. 263), later followed at All Souls (consecrated 1442) and Magdalen (1474–80).[12] There was no need for a chapel at Bridewell as it was connected to the house of Blackfriars by a gallery.

Henry built only one other chapel: sometime in the early 1530s the chapel of St James's was begun, also on a Wykehamite plan (fig. 110). It is unknown when the building was finished, but its ceiling has the date 1540 (figs 265, 267) and this provides a *terminus ante quem* for the building. The chapel here was the only one built at a lesser house during Henry's reign and was presumably intended to serve the needs of the future Court of a prince of Wales. At Hampton Court Henry made Wolsey's chapel more magnificent by the addition of the roof which graces its interior today without otherwise changing it.

The chapels at Hampton Court and Whitehall were both built by Wolsey and both had Wykehamite ante-chapels, and here lies the clue to the change in the form of the royal chapel. Wolsey seems to have felt a special affinity with this layout developed at Oxford. Not only was Wolsey an Oxonian by education, his administrative career began at Magdalen College where, as a fellow, he had been appointed bursar in the late 1490s. Magdalen College, as has already been remarked, possessed a recently constructed chapel with a Wykehamite ante-chapel. Wolsey's experience of this chapel seems to have influenced him, and when he founded his own Oxford college, Cardinal College (now Christ Church) a Wykehamite ante-chapel was almost certainly planned.[13] Wolsey's household was functionally a similar organisation to an Oxford college, as was any household of a leading ecclesiastic, and the collegiate plan must have been very attractive to him.

The Wykehamite plan was also attractive to Wolsey in terms of his own requirements as a leading churchman. The officers of his chapel comprised a Dean, Sub-Dean, Repeater, Gospeller, Pistoler, twelve singing priests, twelve singing children and seventeen singing men, not including additional singing men hired for great feasts.[14] This large complement of staff would have occupied the whole of the body of the chapel, leaving little or no room for the six hundred or so lay members of Wolsey's household; for this reason Wolsey adopted a Wykehamite plan at both Hampton Court and York Place.

The chapel royal was larger and even more

264. Greenwich, Kent. View from the north by A. van den Wyngaerde, 1558. The view shows, from the left, the chapel with the great hall behind, the king's outward chambers with the tiltyard and tiltyard towers behind, the great donjon, the privy kitchen and, on the right, the friars' church.

197

265. St James's, Westminster. The chapel ceiling. The painted timber ceiling incorporates the mottoes and badges of Anne of Cleves and the date 1540. It must, therefore, have been painted during the short-lived marriage of Anne and Henry, January to April 1540. The grotesque ornament on the battens intersecting the ceiling are cast in lead and gilded.

266. *The Family of Henry VII with St George and the Dragon*, by an unknown artist, *c*.1505–9. There is evidence to suggest that this may have been an altarpiece painted for Henry VII's new chapel at Richmond. It shows two tents with their hangings drawn aside to reveal Henry VII with three sons (the middle one is probably Prince Henry) and Elizabeth of York with three daughters. The elaborately draped prie-dieux are probably similar to those which Henry VII and his queens would have used in the chapel closets at Richmond. Note the fantastic building in the background which bears an uncanny resemblence to the Whitehall Palace cockpit.

prestigious than Wolsey's household chapel and so for reasons of space alone the Wykehamite plan suited its purposes well. But there was another reason also. As has been noted (see pp. 126–7) the King heard mass privately in the closet next to his privy chamber; his real devotions were carried out in private and not in the Household chapel. Yet he would hear mass celebrated in the chapel on most days, often after his private devotions. At Christmas 1512, for example, he heard mass in his own closet before going to the closet of the Household chapel.

It was rare for him to take part in the services there, except at Christmas or Easter, and when he did so the apostolic nuncio noted that it was a 'very unusual proceeding'. The lack of spiritual purpose to these forays to the Household chapel meant that the King would take any excuse to avoid them, on St Andrew's Eve 1534, the King was reported to prefer playing tennis with the French admiral rather than attending vespers.[15] Indeed the King's appearance at chapel had very little to do with his faith, it was much more important as a display of his magnificence.

As the area of the privy chamber developed and the King became more reliant on the privy departments (notably the Privy Kitchen and the Clerk of the Closet) and as he made use of covered galleries to move around the greater houses, it would be possible for several days to pass without the King entering the outward chambers at all. However it was vitally important for Henry to be seen by the whole Court and not just by his private attendants and ministers of state. A formal daily procession to the chapel gave the King a chance to proceed through the outer rooms of his palace showing himself to his Court. As it was the show which really mattered, very often, on arrival, he would attend to business, signing letters and papers and reading correspondence. Just as for the King this daily excursion was an opportunity to see to business, so was it an important occasion for the courtier, ambassador or supplicant to petition the King; the King's route to the chapel and back was lined with people wanting his attention and seeking favours, justice or simply recognition.[16]

The holyday closets in the greater houses were never intended for private devotion, rather they were part of the theatre of Court life. Placed directly above the ante-chapel these closets were spacious well lit and lavishly decorated; the King and his entourage could rest within undisturbed by the Court and probably the clergy below. It is likely that all Henry heard on these occasions were the singing voices of the Chapel Royal and notes from the organ. A staircase allowed the King and Queen to descend to the body of the chapel for important parts of the liturgy such as the traditional Good Friday 'creeping to the cross'. On such occasions the King would be attended by his secular servants who would prepare his way and lay cushions for him.[17]

Holyday closets had not been conceived simply as places for executing royal business. Without doubt they had originally performed a liturgical purpose, in Henry VII's reign the holyday closet at Richmond had been furnished with an altar (fig. 266). The closet can, perhaps, be partially visualised from a painting of Henry VII's mother, Lady Margaret Beaufort, in a holyday closet (fig. 262). Surrounded by rich hangings, and kneeling beneath a canopy, she has a book of hours before her resting on the rich cloth covering her prie-dieu. Occasionally during Henry VIII's reign the closet was used for a liturgical purpose. On 12 July 1543, Stephen Gardiner, Bishop of Winchester, married Henry and Catherine Parr in the holyday closet at Hampton Court; they were attended by about twenty people who would have comfortably filled the small closet there.[18]

Henry VIII's reign saw radical changes in the relations between Church and State and presumably the staff of the Chapel Royal, particularly the King's own personal chaplains, played a significant — even if undocumented — part in the course of the English Reformation. These men, like their master, seem to have been of a conservative disposition, and it is interesting to note that there were no major changes in the personnel or liturgy of the Chapel Royal during Henry's lifetime. A letter from John Worth to Lord Lisle in May 1539 makes the point vividly: 'I was told by those of the king's chapel . . . that on Good Friday last the king crept to the cross from the chapel door upwards and served the priest to mass that same day his own person kneeling on his graces knees'.[19] Divine service continued to be said in Latin and there is no evidence that Bibles in English were introduced there even after the publication of the Great Bible in 1539 with an introduction by Archbishop Cranmer and printed by the King's Printer, Thomas Berthelet. Henry VIII showed no interest in iconoclasm: painted

and carved images adorned all his chapels.[20] Notwithstanding the religious convictions of Thomas Cromwell and Archbishop Cranmer and the pronounced beliefs of Anne Boleyn and Catherine Parr, the Chapel Royal reflected the King's sincerely felt but traditional piety which he shared with two of his wives, Catherine of Aragon and Jane Seymour.[21]

The most significant religious innovation at Court under Henry VIII was the erection of the preaching place at Whitehall (figs 268–9). However, the significance of this should not be exaggerated, as in reality the preaching place did little more than cater for the contemporary passion for sermons which had necessarily gone unsated following the suppres-

267, St James's, Westminster. The interior of the Chapel Royal as drawn in 1816. Stripped of its tapestries and with the introduction of box pews, the interior has lost much of its grandeur and space.

for the patron and founder of the house and his family. At Westminster Henry III constructed the largest and most important *Eigenkloster*, Westminster Abbey — a project entirely sponsored by the King, destined to be the burial place for himself and his successors (see plan 12). In a similar manner Henry V founded a monastery for Carthusian monks by his new manor house at Sheen, the foundation stone for which was laid in 1415.[24] Edward IV, as well as setting out to rebuild the chapel of St George at Windsor, thus creating the grandest of all royal chapels, gave land next to his house at Greenwich to the Observant Friars. This lead was followed by Henry VII who also preferred the now more fashionable Franciscan Observants and built them a friary next to his house at Richmond (fig. 239).[25]

Although both Henry VIII and his first wife favoured the friars, no new house was built in his reign. However Bridewell was built hard by the house of Blackfriars and linked to it by a covered gallery (fig. 53). These *Eigenklostern* did not surplant the role of the Chapel Royal at the houses where they were sited, but complemented it. For instance the Greenwich friary played an important role in Court life at Greenwich. Both Henry VIII and his daughter Princess Elizabeth were christened in the Observant Friars' church (in 1491 and 1533), and Easter 1532 is known to have been celebrated there rather than in the chapel royal.[26] It seems as if the royal lodgings there were linked directly to the friars' church by a gallery so that the King and Queen could visit at will (see plan 4).

*   *   *

268. Whitehall Palace. The preaching place as depicted in John Foxe's *Acts and Monuments*, 1563. The view shows Edward VI listening to a sermon by Bishop Latimer from a casement in the council chamber. There is no reason to doubt that the woodcut shows the actual structures erected at Whitehall.

269. Whitehall Palace. The preaching place and the banqueting house of 1606–9, by Robert Smythson, 1609. Henry VIII's preaching place can be seen in the centre of the courtyard; immediately to its right the projection is the palace council chamber.

270 (facing page). Hampton Court, Surrey. The Chapel Royal. It was begun by Cardinal Wolsey in the late 1520s and completed by the addition of the ceiling in 1536. In 1714 it was remodelled by Queen Anne, when the floor, reredos and pews were introduced. The top of the original east window can be seen peeping above the pediment of the reredos.

sion of the friaries adjoining the greater houses. The preaching place was formed around 1540 to the north of the royal lodgings in an area formerly occupied by the privy garden. It was a cobbled courtyard surrounded by an antique loggia, in the centre of which was erected a square pulpit with a canopy. The great advantage of this open forum was that not only could more attend there than in the chapel royal, but courtiers who would otherwise have been tempted by the rival attraction at St Paul's Cross (in the City of London) remained at Court. For the Henrician regime it meant that a closer surveillance could be kept on the subject-matter of sermons. This is borne out by the second author of Stow's *Chronicle* who noted that the pulpit at Whitehall was 'set up in the king's privie garden at Westminster, and therin Dr Latimer preached before the king, where he might be heard of foure times so many people as could have stoode in the king's chappell'.[22] The King seems to have listened from a chamber above, an account from 1549 mentions 'xx fote of new glasse in the chamber agenst the pulpet in the prevey garden'.[23] From an engraving in Foxe's *Acts and Monuments* it appears that the chamber was the council chamber off the privy gallery (fig. 268).

Not only did royal manors have their own chapels, their *Eigenkirchen*, but from earliest times many were attached to houses of Benedictine orders, winning for their owners the greater spiritual possession of an *Eigenkloster*; the monastery so founded would have been expected to offer prayers

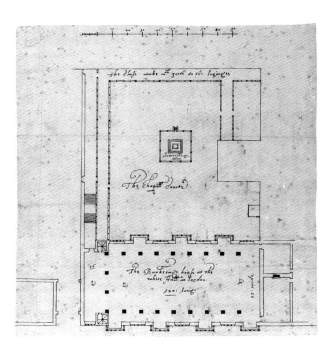

200

271a–c. Designs for the left-hand side of the lower register of the east window of the chapel at Hampton Court, Surrey, by Erhard Schön or his workshop, 1520–29. The designs were commissioned by Cardinal Wolsey and probably executed by James Nicholson. The figures probably represent (from left to right) St Katherine, St Henry, St George, a kneeling girl (Princess Mary), a queen (Catherine of Aragon) and a king (Henry VIII).

Decoration and internal fittings

Little survives of the Tudor interiors of the chapels at Hampton Court (fig. 270) and St James's (figs 265, 267) apart from their ceilings, but two descriptions of the interiors of royal chapels survive and are particularly valuable in giving an impression of their original decoration and furnishing. In 1501 Henry VII's newly built chapel at Richmond was described as being:

weell paved glasid, and hangyd with cloth of Arres, the body and the quere with cloth of golde and the autirs sett with many relikkes, juelles, and full riche plate. In the wallys of this devoute and pleasaunt chapell is picture of kynges of this realme, of thoes whoes lif and vertue was so abundaunt . . . In the right side of the chapell is a goodly and privy closett for the Kyng, richely hangid with silke and travasse carpet and cusshons for his noble Grace; the aultier is also hangid and platid with riche relikes of gold and precious

stone . . . In the othir sid of the chapell othir by the like closettes for the quens grace, . . .[27]

The second describes the temporary chapel at the Field of Cloth of Gold in 1520:

Wooden tribunes with carved stalls rise up on either side, and the desks loaded with mighty tomes above these tapestries with golden figures shine radiantly, overhung on every side with giftes worthy of Phidias. After that the chapel is glazed on every side with stain glass windows, . . . Adorned with embossed images, the elevated vault of the nave glows with gold . . . at the far end of the sanctury a costly altar, such as no human wit could describe.[28]

In both chapels the decoration was lavish; as in secular space there was a hierarchy of decoration, the high altars being adorned with the richest and most valuable materials. Both buildings had clerestory windows beneath which hung either tapestry or rich hangings. Both buildings were provided with choir-stalls and presumably a wooden screen. Such woodwork is described in the specification for the new chapel at Eltham in the 1520s as '. . . a partclose, stalls and setts convenyent within it . . .'.[29] At Hampton Court and Whitehall this meant pews in the choir and benches in the body of the chapel. Those at Hampton Court were carved by Richard Ridge and Henry Corrant, the men who had undertaken the majority of the carving on the hall and chapel ceilings respectively.[30] The other major piece of woodwork in the chapel was the screen; the Eltham specification mentions a parclose and at Richmond the screen had the organ positioned above it as at King's College, Cambridge.[31]

Although little of the original flooring remains in the surviving royal chapels, a small area of sixteenth-century tiling at Hampton Court suggests that it was floored in a white and black chequerboard pattern. The chapel windows, in line with those elsewhere, were filled with stained glass. The east window at Hampton Court, installed by Cardinal Wolsey, is known through a surviving vidimus, or cartoon (fig. 271);[32] it was subject to several important modifications by the King, who removed the image of the Cardinal and after the fall of Anne Boleyn in May 1536 ordered the removal of the image of St Anne: 'for the translatyng and the removsyng of a ymage off saynt anna and other of saynt tomas in the hye alter wyndowo off the chappell'.[33] Only one chapel window from any of Henry's houses survives; it depicts the Crucifixion with Henry VIII, Catherine of Aragon and their patron saints in attendance (fig. 272). The window was the gift of the King to Waltham Abbey in the 1520s, where lodgings were reserved for royal use during progresses, but at the Suppression (notwithstanding the figure of Catherine of Aragon) it was moved, with modifications, to the chapel at Beaulieu. It survived two more moves and an eighteenth-century repainting and refiring to end up in the church of St Margaret's Westminster.[34]

Occasionally the building accounts furnish details of other items in the royal chapels. For instance at Eltham there was a clock.[35] At Hampton Court we learn of a 'branche of irne curyously wrought standyng over the high aulter to hold the canaby and pyx over the blessyd sacrament'.[36] But perhaps the most interesting installations at all the greater houses during the reign were the organs. (Large chapel organs were virtually the only musical instruments to be made in England at the time, the finest smaller instruments normally being imported.) They seem to have been used to play voluntaries at prescribed times in the liturgy or to alternate with voices during plainsong pieces, but were not yet used to accompany voices.[37] The Chapel Royal was the leading choir under Henry VIII, and much of its music, both for voice and organ, was composed by its members, such well-known names as William Cornish, Robert Fairfax and Thomas Tallis.

Organs were major fixtures in all the great houses by the early sixteenth century, and it is likely that they had probably been present much earlier. In 1503 an organ was transferred from Westminster to Richmond and installed in the chapel there for Henry VII. This organ, or its successor, was replaced by Henry VIII in 1511.[38] The new Richmond organ was by no means Henry's first interest in organs, for in July 1509, three months after his accession, he had bought a pair of organs.[39] Henry VIII placed great value on organists and their music. From at least 1514 he retained an organ-maker named William Lewes, and the same year a Master Giles was rewarded for playing the organ in the chapel on Easter Day.[40] In 1517 the Dean of the Chapel found the organ at Woodstock in disrepair, and for the feast of St George — both the guardian saint for England and the patron of the Order of the Garter — he sent to London for two men before resorting to borrowing the organ from Woodstock parish church for the service.[41] In the mid-1520s, a workshop was set up at Bridewell for a royal organ-maker, and it was he who delivered the new organs to Hampton Court in 1538.[42] During Wolsey's ownership of Hampton Court there had been not only 'a grete paire of Organs' but also two smaller pairs. The great pair was almost certainly a permanent fixture in the chapel.[43] The King's virtual reconstruction of the chapel between 1533 and 1536 involved the installation of a new pair in a newly constructed organ loft or organ house, but the new organs made at the Bridewell workshop were not transported down-river until June 1538 when John Bytton and his servants installed them in the new house.[44] Organs at this date were pumped manually: the bellows needed constant attention and both the metalwork and the sheepskin bags needed regular replacement; this was sometimes done by the Office of Works, as in 1534–5 when 6s. 8d. was spent on the Greenwich organ, but more often it was done by specialists like William Bytton and his son. At Greenwich in 1536 a lectern was made for the organist's music books.[45]

As a rule chapels did not have fonts, as this was a mark of parochial status, but on several occasions royal chapels played host to more unusual events such as a christening. In 1515 a silver font was brought from the priory of Christchurch, Canterbury, to Greenwich in preparation for the christening of a child which was prematurely stillborn.[46] The most famous royal christening of the reign was that of Prince Edward, who was baptised in the Hampton Court chapel in 1537. For the occasion a platform was set up on which a silver font

272. St Margaret's Church,
Westminster, the east
window. Engraved for the
Society of Antiquaries in
1758.

was placed. The font was covered by an elaborate canopy and surrounded by screens covered with cloth of gold; charcoal braziers nearby kept both water and infant warm during the ceremony.[47] Ten days later the same chapel played host to the lying-in-state of Queen Jane Seymour who had died shortly after giving birth to the Prince. Her body rested in the chapel for a fortnight while requiem masses were said.[48]

Births, deaths and marriages were not the only occasions when the royal chapels were specially furnished. They were frequently used during diplomatic missions for entertainment. A splendidly executed, beautifully sung High Mass in an impressive chapel was an excellent way to re-emphasise the magnificence of the King's Court. Henry took the Venetian ambassadors to mass at Richmond in 1515 and two years later the Spanish ambassadors at Greenwich.[49] At these times the chapels were re-hung with the finest tapestries, altarcloths and plate.

Not only did the chapel provide a magnificent setting for international events, it served as a fine setting for the meeting of the Order of the Garter. Henry VIII broke with the tradition of holding the yearly chapter of the Knights of St George in St George's Chapel, Windsor, instead convening it wherever he happened to be staying. In practice this was most often Greenwich,[50] and for the meeting of the Order special pews and seats were set up in the Greenwich chapel. In April 1537 even more elaborate preparations were made; eight tables and forms were constructed to replace the Gentlemen of the Chapel's usual stalls and a new altar was made 'to stande in the saide chappell before the kyngs grace for the dene of the said chappell to saye masse by foure the kyng.'[51]

All these occasions were exceptional, however, and the normal regime for the Chapel Royal was the daily celebration of mass for the Court and the magnificent liturgies which accompanied the five principal feasts of the year. For daily work the Chapel Royal was provided with a group of ancilliary buildings. All the major chapels had at least one vestry. At Eltham two rooms were provided on the north side of the chancel, both with fireplaces and one two storeys high (see plan 1). The vestry at Hampton Court was on the south side (see plans 7, 8) and at Beaulieu (fig. 63), Whitehall (see plan 13) and Richmond (see plan 11) there were similar arrangements. In the Greenwich vestry there were 'ii great pressys made with racks to hang vestments and coopes in',[52] and in Wolsey's time there was a long table in the vestry at York Place.[53] These fittings are the same as those of the chapels at Hampton Court and St James's today. Whatever the changing requirements of the kings and queens of England, those of their clergy have remained remarkably consistent.

Chapter 13

THE TUDOR ROYAL INTERIOR

The abiding principle behind the early Tudor royal interior was that of magnificence. It was axiomatic that no surface whatsoever was to be unadorned, but the nature and extent of the adornment was controlled and tempered by two considerations: hierarchy and harmony. There existed a hierarchy of materials; gold came at the top of this list — solid gold, cloth of gold made with real metal, through various gradients down to gold leaf — followed by the less valued silver. Beneath gold, but somewhere above silver, came the very best tapestries, themselves shot through with gold and silver threads. Several gradients of lesser fabrics, lower quality tapestries, carpets, embroideries and velvets were next. Lower down the scale came paintings, furniture, etc. There was an equally strong sense of hierarchy of internal spaces, the status of the room dictating the status of the material used within. By this rule the most important rooms were hung with cloth of gold and lesser rooms with decreasing qualities of tapestry. Perhaps the most vivid contemporary record of this is the list of furnishings required for the proposed marriage between Henry VII's daughter Princess Mary, and Ferdinand and Isabella's son, the Prince of Castile in 1508.[1] The list specifies the manner in which the Princess's lodgings were to be hung and it seems as if the specification was altered by Henry VII, revealing his attitude towards the hierarchy of materials. Princess Mary was to have four chambers with the first, her bedchamber, hung in cloth of gold with a border embroidered with her badges. There was also a large bed hung with matching cloth and a chair likewise upholstered, carpets to cover the floor, crimson velvet coverings for the table, cupboards and window seats and five cushions of cloth of gold. The second chamber was to have been slightly less magnificent, being hung with tapestry of gold and silk threads and furnished with upholstery of gold and purple. In the third chamber the arras was not to be 'so fyne as is the seconde chambur' while the fourth chamber was simply to have 'good and fyne tapicery'. Thus her rooms were furnished in a way that was suitable to the importance of activities to take place within. The more private rooms were the more richly furnished, the outer rooms less richly adorned.

The second important idea underlying the Tudor interior was harmony. A magnificent interior had to be harmonious to the eye, and this involved a co-ordination of textiles and furniture to achieve a unified whole. This point is quite clearly brought out in the list of furnishings for Princess Mary's bridal chambers. If her bedchamber was to be hung in cloth of gold, so was her bed, her chair, her cushions and any other textile or furnishing would have to blend in with the trimmings on the cloth of gold.

Walls

Interior walls were either brick or were stud partitions. Both were plastered with hair plaster and regardless of their composition required adornment of some sort. The choices were few; the plaster could be painted, with a single colour in a utilitarian area, or with a more complicated scheme in a more important one. Timber cladding could be provided for panelling, either to a room's full height, or as wainscot (to two-thirds of the height). Or textile hanging could be used — tapestry, cloth of gold, silks or some lesser material. Whichever of the options was chosen, the wall could be completed with a decorative cornice which might be conceived as part of the ceiling decoration or the wall treatment. Finally, pictures or other objects could be hung against whichever treatment was settled upon.

Almost all the service parts of a royal house were plastered with lime hair plaster and whitewashed. The fad for bare brick is relatively modern and spaces such as the north cloister at Hampton Court would originally have been plastered and painted (fig. 275). Stairwells, communication galleries and courtier lodgings would be treated likewise.[2] The really grand painted effects were reserved for the King's inward lodgings. There had been a long tradition of decorating royal houses with mural cycles: Henry III, for example, had decorated the walls of the Antioch chamber at Clarendon with

273. Panel from a painted oak bed-head (fig. 318), probably made for Henry VIII and Anne of Cleves.

275 (right). Hampton Court, Surrey. The north cloister. Begun by Cardinal Wolsey and completed by Henry VIII as the arterial northern service passage, the cloister would have originally been plastered and painted white.

Crusader subjects.[3] The early part of Henry VIII's reign saw the completion of several major murals. The largest of these was painted on the walls of the low gallery at Whitehall where painters were paid for 'drawing and settyng owte wyth colours the coronacion of our seide soverigne lorde with the circumstance of the same as also certayne other works upon the walles'.[4] At Windsor a room next to his bedchamber was called the Siege of Rhodes chamber after a series of murals which probably depicted the heroic defence of Rhodes in 1480 rather than its unsuccessful defence and capitulation to the Turks in 1522. At Whitehall there was a room known as the Adam and Eve room which was presumably painted with the story of the Temptation and Fall. At Greenwich the King's closet by the waterside was painted with the story of St John.[5]

Although the exact nature of these murals cannot now be ascertained, some pointers can be gained from the Wolsey Closet at Hampton Court (fig. 274). Although the paintings have been brought from elsewhere in the palace and have been several times overpainted there is no reason to think that they came from anywhere else but an early sixteenth-century decorative scheme in the building, perhaps even Henry's study of 1529, where joiners worked upon five 'tables of waynscotting to be paynted'.[6] Two other pointers can be gained from the paintings entitled the *Field of Cloth of Gold* (fig. 66) and *The Embarkation* (unknown artist *c.*1540–7) which remain in the Royal Collection and record important contemporary events. Those two paintings may originally have been intended as part of an *in situ* painted scheme at Whitehall.[7]

The most important mural of the reign, and the only one for which any visual reference exists was undoubtedly the Whitehall Mural painted by Hans Holbein the Younger in the privy chamber at Whitehall. Although this mural was destroyed by fire in 1698 the composition is known through a copy made in the seventeenth century for Charles II by Remigius van Leemput (fig. 278) and from the surviving left-hand section of Holbein's cartoon used for transferring the composition to the wall (fig. 277). The Whitehall Mural had a different function from any other commissioned by Henry

In the image: CESOLECORODEMENT SEINTEDEVVARD

VIII. It belonged to a tradition of royal murals probably stemming from that done in the late 1260s for Henry III in the painted chamber at Westminster Palace. Destroyed in the Westminster fire of 1834, but mercifully recorded in 1793 and 1819, it is the only royal medieval wall-painting for which there is any visual record (figs 10, 276). The mural had been painted for Henry III's bedchamber and the central image depicting the coronation of St Edward was situated directly over the bed itself. Therefore the image was placed in the most important place in the King's house: the most intimate, inner sanctum of the King's principal palace. It was not a public image but one designed to identify Henry with his saintly Anglo-Saxon predecessor, making an important declaration about the nature of Plantagenet kingship.[8]

The Whitehall Mural was similar in purpose. It was located in the King's private chamber in his principal residence. It was a manifesto in paint of Henry's kingship, and it communicated on two levels. Henry's father, Henry VII, in building Richmond began the communication of the first message, a dynastic one. In his great hall he had placed, between the windows, depictions of the kings of England culminating 'In the higher parte, upon the left hond' with 'the seemly picture and personage of our moost excellent and heyghe Suffrayn . . . Kyng Henry the VIIth'.[9] The point that Henry VII emphasised was that he was the latest and greatest in a long line of noble kings. If the iconography of Richmond proclaimed the legitimacy of the dynasty, the Whitehall Mural celebrated its continuation, as father, son and grandson all stood before the beholder. The second message of the mural was that Henry VIII not only saw himself as simple heir to the great monarch but as the son who brought to completion what his father had begun: Henry VII had brought peace, law and order, his son had achieved an even greater victory, that of driving the power of the papacy out of the realm. Yet underlying the iconographic significance of the mural it was, at heart, principally a display of magnificence, forming a backdrop to the King's physical presence in the privy chamber. The priviliged few who saw the mural reported that the figure of Henry VIII left viewers feeling 'abashed and annihilated'; the mural was designed to transform Henry's physical presence on to a supernatural plane.

Last in the category of painted wall decoration, comes the evidence of painted grotesquework

276. *The Coronation of St Edward*, copy by C.A. Stothard (1819) after the mural (1263–72) in the painted chamber, Westminster Palace.

274 (facing page bottom). Hampton Court, Surrey. The Wolsey Closet. Neither originally a closet, nor decorated by Wolsey, this room, largely created in the 1880s, is still the only surviving Tudor royal interior to convey anything of the oppressive magnificence of any of Henry VIII's most important residences. The panelling is sixteenth-century but imported, and the paintings are from elsewhere in the building. Yet there is enough evidence to suggest that the corner of the room illustrated here is a good representation of a typical high-class closet of the 1530s.

277 (far left). Hans Holbein the Younger, *Henry VII and Henry VIII*, 1537. Based on this surviving fragment of the cartoon for the Whitehall Mural which measures 257 by 137 cm, the whole mural can be estimated as measuring approximately 270 by 360 cm. The main difference between the cartoon and the finished version, as shown by Leemput, is the King's face which, in the finished version, is turned towards the viewer.

278. The Whitehall Mural, copy by Remigius van Leemput after Hans Holbein the Younger, 1667. On the left stand Henry VII and Henry VIII; on the right, Elizabeth of York and Jane Seymour, the mother of Henry VIII's heir. The interior in which they stand cannot have been untypical of those of Henry VIII's later houses, although the actual composition has affinities with an engraving of 1481 by Bramante.

279. Whitehall Palace. Plaster painted with grotesque decoration found on the walls leading to Cardinal Wolsey's privy kitchen. The surface was later mutilated to take over-plastering.

recovered in the Whitehall excavations of the 1930s (fig. 279). The whole of the exterior of Whitehall Palace was painted. The hall was painted with imitation chequerwork, while the outside of the privy gallery was painted with black and white grotesques.[10] A projecting wing of the palace with its painting can be seen in the background of the *Family of Henry VIII* (fig. 281). This decoration seems to have extended indoors and the excavated examples of painted grotesquework come from a back stair near the privy kitchen.

Wall-paintings covered a tiny fraction of the wall space of royal houses. Far more important, at least in terms of square yards, was panelling; plain, linenfold or carved with grotesquework. Little of any of this survives today; even the rooms at Hampton Court were repanelled in the nineteenth century with panelling brought from elsewhere (fig. 274). Details in paintings and miniatures do much to redress this loss. Thus, in the background of the *Family of Henry VIII* there is carved panelling of a grotesque design highlighted with paint and gold

280. Whitehall Palace. Design of grotesque decoration found on the walls leading to Wolsey's privy kitchen.

281. Detail of fig. 282.

282. *The Family of Henry VIII*, by an unknown artist, *c.*1545. This painting is a crucial document in the study of early Tudor style and interiors. The setting, on the ground floor of the king's lodgings at Whitehall Palace, very probably represents a real interior set up for the portrait. Apart from the figure of Jane Seymour, who was dead by the mid-1540s, the figures appear to have been painted from life. The view through the archways show the privy garden in the south, with its low rails and beasts on poles. The left-hand archway shows part of Princess Mary's lodging painted externally with grotesques (see fig. 281). Through the right-hand archway part of the parkside can be seen, including a turret of the great close tennis-play. The floor of the room is plastered and painted, but the king's chair stands on a rug. The canopy is a single piece of embroidery suspended from the ceiling. The ceiling is divided up by battens into squares, each with a royal badge. The panelling and pillars are carved with grotesques and highlighted with gold.

283. The Black Book of the Garter, recording the garter ceremonies of 1534. Anticlockwise from top left: Henry VIII enthroned, surrounded by knights, in a panelled room with a typical fretted ceiling; he is seated on a carpeted dais, but the rest of the floor is plastered and painted. Next, the knights process to the chapel down a long tiled corridor, with panelling decorated with grotesques. In the third section the ground of the fretted ceiling is also painted and decorated. The final illustration shows the arrival of three new junior knights in a relatively plain tiled chapel.

leaf. Illustrations from the Black Book of the Garter show painted and carved panelling with the ceiling rising above it (fig. 283). Evidence for the most elaborate scheme of panelling and wall cladding recorded comes from a design for one wall of an unidentified royal house, dating from the 1540s and possibly intended for Whitehall (fig. 284). The closest surviving parallel for this drawing is certainly the Galerie François Ier at Fontainebleau, although a fireplace at Broughton Castle, Oxfordshire, displays similar features.[11] Nothing from any royal house today comes anywhere close to this highly mannered design. However, one should not doubt that it was built, for the background to the Whitehall Mural is not far removed from it in style.

This design was clearly intended to be a three-dimensional wall cladding and of this sort of treatment there is plenty of evidence. Engaged and free-standing columns appear in the *Family of Henry VIII*, in *Henry VIII in his Bedchamber* (fig. 287) and

in Holbein's miniature *Henry VIII as Solomon* (fig. 288), for example. A more detailed view of such a column appears in the background of Holbein's portrait of Lady Guildford (fig. 290). The column's inclusion here is clearly to make a point about the Guildfords' patronage of fashionable antique interior design. The only surviving capitals in this style are the well-known ones in the Sir Thomas More Chapel in Chelsea Old Church (fig. 285), but very similar carved decorations have been recovered in excavation at Hampton Court (fig. 286). These, from the surviving traces of paint and gilt, can be identified as interior features.

The most extreme manifestations of this sort of Mannerist decoration were probably largely confined to the greater houses. Painted panelling such as the fragments which survive at Loseley Park, Surrey (fig. 291), and the ceiling panels at Ightham Mote, Kent, were commoner. Those at Loseley are on canvas, and depict pagan divinities and the Christian

216

virtues in grotesque compositions. Royal devices incorporated in the design date them to the four years following Henry VIII's marriage to Catherine Parr in 1543. The provenance of these panels is uncertain but they would seem to have been perquisites of Sir Thomas Carwarden as Master of the Revels. A Revels provenance also seems likely for the ceiling panels at Ightham, they are much cruder in execution and their royal provenance is less secure. Both of these examples, although neither certainly from a royal house, seem to have been architectural products from the Court of Henry VIII and help envisage the type of painted panelling used in the royal interiors.[12]

Easel-paintings executed on panel or canvas were important decorative elements in certain specific areas. Galleries were the most common location for large numbers of pictures and in 1547 there were at least twenty in the gallery at Hampton Court. At Whitehall there were 167 paintings and 11 'stained cloths'. The subjects of these paintings were predominantly religious, such as the 'table of our ladie with St Elizabeth' and a large number of them were triptychs. Few survive today, but those that do (fig. 179) give a good idea of the King's tastes. Most

pictures stayed *in situ* whilst the house was empty and, partly to protect them on such occasions, they were furnished with curtains. But these curtains tell us as much about veneration of the subject-matter as they do about contemporary attitudes to the conservation of works of art. Curtain-rods were bought at Whitehall to 'hange curteynes upon before tables of imagerye'.[13] The curtains could be quite vividly coloured; almost all of the paintings in the long gallery at Hampton Court in 1547 had green and yellow curtains covering them.[14] The paintings had eyes attached to the backs and were hooked on to the walls and so could be transported if need be, packed in tailored leather cases. Some of the more valuable ones were taken down and stored in special picture stores.[15]

In addition to easel-paintings, maps and plans were also popular. In 1547 the short gallery next to the withdrawing chamber at Hampton Court contained a map of England and Scotland, a separate one of Wales and a map of Normandy.[16] There were as many as thirty-five maps hanging at Whitehall in 1547. In the closet next to the King's bedchamber at Greenwich hung two framed plans for bridges.[17] Mirrors came next in popularity —

284. Design for an interior for Henry VIII, by an unknown artist, *c*.1545. The only surviving architectural drawing of an interior for Henry VIII, this highly sophisticated drawing must have referred to a room at least fifteen feet high and under construction in the late 1540s; as such, it is likely to have been intended for Whitehall. Its affinities with the Galerie François Ier at Fontainebleau suggest that the drawing could be connected with decorative work undertaken by French craftsmen at Whitehall in the 1540s.

285. Chelsea Old Church. A capital from the St Thomas More Chapel. No complete royal example survives of this type of capital, once common throughout Henry VIII's houses.

286. Hampton Court, Surrey. Fragment of a carved Reigate stone pendant with grotesque decoration. Found in 1912 in the infill of the moat, this fragment is the sole survivor of the richly carved stone interiors of Hampton Court.

287 (right). Henry VIII's Psalter, *Henry VIII Reading in his Bedchamber*, 1540. The interior shown is totally imaginary but does plausibly show tiling, a chair and a bed of the 1540s.

288 (above right). Hans Holbein the Younger, *Solomon and the Queen of Sheba*, c.1535. The figure of Solomon is a portrait of Henry VIII. The miniature shows the King in a typical royal interior of the mid-1530s, with a fretted ceiling with pendants, a moulded frieze, wall pilasters and rich embroidered hangings. Only the throne and possibly parts of its alcove are totally imaginary.

289 (far right). Henry VIII enthroned, as depicted in the 1563 edition of Foxe's *Acts and Monuments*. An Elizabethan rendering of a mid-Henrician royal interior. The ceiling and frieze can be paralleled by surviving elements at Hampton Court. The wall-hangings are very similar to those shown in figure 288, and the throne canopy similar to that shown in *The Family of Henry VIII* (fig. 282). Once again, the floor is plastered and painted, and the King sits on a carpeted dais.

290 (facing page). Hans Holbein the Younger, *Mary Wotton, Lady Guildford*, 1527. This painting shows the use of free-standing pillars with grotesque decoration and capitals during the 1520s.

Minor had been a major exporter. Cloth of gold always featured a pomegranate, artichoke, pineapple or rosebud encircled by a wreath of leaves, rosettes or carnations (fig. 292). Later in the century crowns and vases began to appear.[19] Sets of such Italian silk and gold hangings were amongst the King's two or three most expensive possessions. When, in January 1532 the King wanted to give Anne Boleyn a lavish present he chose to give her a complete room-setting with 'rich hangings for one room, and a bed covered with gold and silver cloth, crimson sattin, and embroidery richer than all the rest'.[20] Generally such hangings were restricted to the King's and Queen's bedchambers. At Hampton Court in 1547 there were eight pieces of cloth of gold with white, blue, red and green velvet figuring paned (or pieced) together, with borders of crimson velvet embroidered with imperial crowns, roses, fleurs-de-lis and portcullises.[21] Next in costliness were cut-velvet and silk wall-hangings without silver or gold yarns. A set of nine hangings, again at Hampton Court, were satin figured with velvet coloured crimson, blue, purple, tawny, muzzey ('mosslike'), green and orange, paned together, with a border of crimson velvet embroidered with crowns and the King's badges.

291a and b (above). Loseley Park, Guildford. Painted decoration, possibly from a royal house, with the initials of Catherine Parr, the Prince of Wales's feathers and the King's motto.

there were four in the long gallery at Hampton Court and fourteen at Whitehall on the King's death. Generally made of steel, they required occasional polishing by workmen. Mirrors were either framed in gilded wood or in wood covered in fabric, often crimson satin.[18]

Textiles were the most common form of wall treatment in the King's outward and inward chambers. Cloth of gold was the richest, most prestigious and most valuable wall-hanging available; it is a generic term for silks, either velvets or damasks, which have gilt yarns as a major component. By Henry VIII's time almost all cloth of gold was imported from Italy, but during the fifteenth century Asia

220

293. Hans Holbein the Younger, *Jean de Dinteville and Georges de Selve, ('The Ambassadors')*, 1533. Like figure 282, this portrait probably depicts an identifiable royal interior. However, the only architectural element shown is the plastered and painted floor. In the background is a very rich damask and on the table a beautiful carpet.

On the very greatest occasions of state these fabrics adorned even the outer rooms. In 1520 the temporary palace at the Field of Cloth of Gold was largely hung with cloth of gold and silver: 'The walls are everywhere cloaked with golden hangings, or else with every variety of embroidery an embroiderer has fashioned with skilfull needle. With cloth of silk in lattice work, interspersed with golden rivetts . . .'.[22] The only contemporary depiction of rich fabrics in the interior of a Henrician residence is Hans Holbein the Younger's double portrait of Jean de Dinteville and Georges de Selve (*'The Ambassadors'*) which shows rich green silk damask loose-hung in an outer chamber almost certainly at Bridewell Palace in 1533 (fig. 293). A view of an Elizabethan royal house shows Elizabeth I receiving ambassadors in a room hung with embroidery (fig. 294). An imaginary Elizabethan view of Henry VIII enthroned depicts him surrounded by richly embroidered silks (fig. 289); he appears also in the Barber-surgeons' portrait, sitting before a heavy embroidery (fig. 299).

Notwithstanding these occasional and extraordinary uses, gold, silver and silk were normally found in smaller, more private rooms. Holbein's portrait of Archbishop Wareham with its loose-hung fabric in the background shows such a room, although almost certainly not in a royal setting (fig.

292 (facing page bottom). Italian furnishing fabric, 1475–1525. A rare surviving piece of cloth of gold; the fragment has a pattern rendered in crimson pile against a yellow silk ground which was originally covered with real gold yarn. For illustrations of such fabric in a Tudor interior, see figures 262 and 311.

221

294. German school, *Queen Elizabeth Receiving Dutch Emissaries*, c.1585. Although the windows indicate an Elizabethan rather than a Henrician interior, the decoration is perfectly acceptable for the 1530s. The floor is matted, and beneath the canopy and the Queen is a special mat. The walls are hung with embroidery, except beneath the canopy, which is hung with cloth of gold. Note the damask hanging in the outer chamber and the bird-cages in the windows. Henry VIII is known to have had cages of this sort at Hampton Court.

295). It is tempting to see Holbein's portrait of Thomas Cromwell (fig. 297) as one painted in a royal house, here again the wall behind Cromwell is covered in a silk damask or cut velvet, but in this case it is tight-hung.[23] Another type of silk wall-covering, possibly a curtain, appears in the background of Holbein's portrait of Sir Thomas More (fig. 296) and recurs in the background of the More family group (fig. 298). A very similar fabric appears draped over the tablet in the centre of the Whitehall Mural (fig. 278). In both these last pictures silks are plain with fringes and are loosely hung, the one on the mural appears to be lined, and thus intended for heavier wear. It is likely that such cloths had a variety of uses as covers, curtains, hangings and even carpets.

Without doubt, tapestry was the most important non-architectural internal decorative element in the Tudor royal house.[24] Henry VIII inherited a substantial tapestry collection, perhaps amounting to four hundred pieces, from his father and his grandfather, but this inheritance was dwarfed by the extent of his own purchases over the next forty years. He shared a passion for the finest tapestries with Francis I, Charles V and Philip II. On his death he owned nearly two thousand pieces, a third of which were major high-quality works containing high proportions of gold and silver thread. A single major set like the ten pieces depicting the *Story of David*, acquired in 1528, cost £1,500.[25]

These highly valuable pieces were neither for regular use nor for just any room, there was a strict hierarchy of both occasion and hang. This is vividly demonstrated in the description of the hanging at Hampton Court for the French ambassadors in 1527, where George Cavendish observed that 'the first waiting chamber was hanged with fine arras, and so was all the rest, one better than another . . .'[26] The innermost rooms were hung with the best hangings. Equally, the finest pieces were only brought out for the most important occasions; for everyday use outer rooms and guest rooms would be hung with lower-quality wool tapestry.

In general tapestries were hung just below the clerestory windows, as in the great watching chamber at Hampton Court today (fig. 160).

295 (far left). Hans Holbein the Younger, *William Wareham, Archbishop of Canterbury*, 1527. This portrait makes much of the use of rich and valuable fabrics, the wall-hangings, the cushion, the carpets and even the Archbishop's gown.

297 (left). Hans Holbein the Younger, *Thomas Cromwell*, 1542–3. Cromwell is sitting on an oak settle at a table covered in characteristic fringed green cloth. Royal accounts survive detailing the provision of such table cloths for court offices. Another table by his side is covered in a table carpet. A piece of paper on the table refers to his mastership of the jewel-house, and the sitter may have been attending to official business in an office provided for him in a royal house.

296. Hans Holbein the Younger, *Sir Thomas More*, 1527. More leans on what was probably a table, unusually uncovered—but perhaps only to allow the painter to inscribe the date on it. The curtain behind him has been held aside by a silk cord.

298. Hans Holbein the Younger, *The Family of Sir Thomas More*. Not a royal interior but one of a sophisticated member of the Court. The principal features of interest are in the background: (from left to right) the hooded oak buffet with plate on display; the wall-hanging or curtain, with a clock on a bracket in the middle; and the internal timber porch. Although perhaps a little old-fashioned and plain in the 1530s, this interior must have been typical of the royal interiors early in the reign.

ENRICO OCTAVO OPT MAX REGI ANGLIÆ
FRANCIÆ ET HIBERNIÆ EIDEI DEFENSO
RI AC ANGLICANÆ HIBERNICÆQ.
ECCLESIÆ PROXIME A CHRISTO SVPREMO
CAPITI SOCIETAS CHIRVRGORVM
COMMVNIBVS VOTIS HÆC CONSECRAT.

TRISTIOR ANGLORVM PESTIS VIOLAVERAT ORBEM
INFESTANS ANIMOS CORPORIBVSQVE SEDENS
HANC DEVS INSIGNEM CLADEM MISERATVS AB ALTO
TE MEDICI MVNVS IVSSIT OBIRE BONI
LVMEN EVANGELII TVLVIS CIRCVMVOLAT ALIIS
PHARMACON ADFECTIS MENTIBVS ILLVD ERIT
CONSILIOQ. TVO CELEBRANT MONVMENTA CALENI
ET SELERI MORBVS PELLITVR OMNIS OPE
NOS IGITVRSVPLEX MEDICORVM TVRBA TVORVM
HANC TIBI SACRAMVS RELIGIONE DOMVM
MVNERIS ET MEMORES QVO NOS HENRICE BEASTI
IMPERIO OPTAMVS MAXIMA QVÆQVE TVO

299. Hans Holbein the Younger, *Henry VIII and the Barber-surgeons*, 1540. This painting, commissioned by the Barber-surgeons, has been damaged and altered, and its original form is now doubtful. However, it does show the king enthroned beneath a throne canopy, depicted in much detail, and seated on a chair which can be closely paralleled with one in the inventory taken on Henry's death.

They were suspended by one of two methods. One method was to use battens fastened to the walls with the hangings nailed to them,[27] as was done at Ampthill: 'for ii dosen of gret hokes for ye kyngs chamber to fasten quarters into the walls for hangyngs'.[28] A second, more frequently adopted and less damaging method, was to use hooks and eyes. This was the method favoured by the Marquess of Exeter who, in 1525, bought one hundred hooks and three hundred tenterhooks for his room at Windsor and one hundred hooks for that at Bridewell.[29]

Nearly all the King's tapestries came from the Netherlands, mostly near Brussels, and their import was regulated by special licences from the Crown.[30] As with the cloth of gold, sets of tapestries were ordered by Henry VIII for use in specific rooms, and it is known that Cardinal Wolsey ordered tapestries specially for the great gatehouse at Hampton Court. Although none of these survive *in situ*, a set almost certainly ordered by the King for the great hall at Hampton Court does. The *History of Abraham* tapestries hanging today in the Great Hall make that room the most important surviving royal interior of the Tudor age, by preserving, in

faded terms, the decorative scheme of its builder (fig. 149).

When not on display these valuable tapestries were taken down and stored in great cupboards or 'presses' in the houses' wardrobes (see pp. 74–5). Occasionally the works accounts refer to their transfer; in Greenwich in 1535 a chain and a hanging lock were bought for the Groom Porter's rooms 'to hang the ladders upon that hangs the kyngs chambers'.[31]

During the king's 37-year-long reign the design of tapestry underwent a radical change which reflected the contemporary swing in taste from late Gothic to modish antique. The designs favoured in the collection inherited by Henry VIII were traditional, but his acquisition of a set of the *Acts of the Apostles*, designed by Raphael and woven in Brussels, reveals a royal awareness of the very latest in Italian design. The subsequent purchase of a set, the *Triumph of the Gods* for his new lodgings at Whitehall in 1542, and probably ordered three years earlier, represented a complete acceptance of Italian Mannerist design (fig. 300). These tapestries adorned interiors decorated in the manner of the design for an unidentified royal house in figure 284.

Combined, they helped to make the interiors of Henry's houses in the 1540s as sophisticated as anything in France, Spain or northern Italy.

Windows and chimney-pieces

Windows in the sixteenth century were usually of stone, although rubbed brick, terracotta and timber were sometimes preferred. They were mostly of plain chamfered mouldings and those in important rooms sometimes had elaborately carved and moulded jambs. Internally the stone was painted, usually with whitewash, and the window bars were painted red or black.[32] Sills sometimes had mottoes or badges inset in lead and gilded. In the privy chamber at Greenwich the jambs seem to have been painted with antiquework.[33] Windows were covered either by shutters or with curtains, the more important rooms having both. The King's bedchamber at Greenwich had shutters fitted in 1533 which were carved on the inside and plain on the outside. This

was evidently unusual, as the clerk recorded that they were after the manner of a cupboard. These shutters were right by 'the kyngs bedsyde' which looked out over the river.[34]

It was usually the innermost rooms that had curtains, as in the privy chamber at Greenwich, for example.[35] They were mostly of satin or sarsenet (silks) and lined with buckram (linen). Most of the curtains would be regarded as being very gaudy by modern standards, as the following example demonstrates . . . 'two curtains of purple, white and black satten of bridge paned togethers thone conte vii panes and thother vi panes di either of them conte in depthe two yerde di lines with buckram'.[36] Other favoured colour combinations included green with yellow and crimson with yellow. Even quite big windows had curtains, for at Whitehall in 1532 a long pole was made for drawing tall curtains.[37] Sometimes heavier materials like tapestry or carpet were used. At Eltham instructions were given to furnish all the bay windows in the King's new lodgings with rings and hooks 'for to hange tappetts

300. *The Triumph of Bacchus*, from the Brussels series *The Triumph of the Gods*, woven for Whitehall Palace in the early 1540s. The sophistication of this tapestry should not be seen as anything unusual or surprising in the interiors of the late 1530s or 1540s.

301 (following page). Stained-glass roundel bearing the Tudor royal arms, *c.*1540. Not from a royal building but certainly typical of the heraldic decoration found in the King's houses.

225

mottoes and devices, in the field of the window were invariably the arms of the King and his consort (fig. 301). Each time Henry remarried the glaziers had to work overtime to substitute the arms in the windows; notwithstanding the expense, this was done at houses great and small — even at a relatively small house like Ampthill, Queen Anne Boleyn's badges were inserted in 1533.[40]

Chimney-pieces also provided structural vehicles for exuberant and elaborate decoration. Little evidence survives of royal chimney-pieces before 1509, but an engraving of one chimney in Henry VII's tower at Windsor shows it to have been quite plain (fig. 303). There is no reason to believe that this chimney-piece was important or typical. There is evidence for chimneys built for Henry VIII at St

on theym'.[38] It may be that these heavier hangings were used in winter, the lighter fabrics being kept for summer. A curtain, although probably not a window curtain, appears in the background of the portrait of Sir Henry Guildford (fig. 302); it is suspended by gilded rings from a rod. In a portrait of Thomas Cranmer a window curtain does appear, but the details of its fixings are not included.[39]

The quality of glass used to glaze the windows throughout royal houses varied according to the social importance of the room. Windows were generally given a border containing the King's

302 (left). Hans Holbein the Younger, *Sir Henry Guildford*, 1527. Guildford is here seen proudly bearing the white staff of the Comptroller of the Household and wearing the collar of the Order of the Garter, with which he had been invested in 1526. The curtain behind him could have been a room divider, to cover a painting or a window.

303 (far left bottom). A chimney piece from Henry VII's tower at Windsor Castle (1500–2), engraved before its destruction. The now lost top section of an important fireplace at Hampton Court (fig. 107) was probably similar to this one.

304 and 305. St James's, Westminster. The fireplace dates from the 1530s and was revealed in 1822 in the guard chamber. All internal stonework was originally painted, as it is today.

Chimney piece lately discovered in the guard Room at St James's Palace. May 24th 1822

227

306a–c. Three engravings recording the visit of Marie de' Medici to the English court in 1638. These engravings, done about ninety years after Henry VIII's death, are the earliest depictions of the interior of St James's. They show the use of terracotta roundels above the fireplaces, the comparative sparsity of the furnishings in the outward rooms, the use of wall sconces for lighting and the interesting use of canopies over fireplaces, possibly denoting the positioning of the dining chair.

COMME LE MY LORD MAIOR ACOMPAIGNEDE SES COLLEGVES VIENT SALVER LA REYNE LVY FAIRE SES PRESENS

LE CERCLE DE LEVRS MAGESTES DANS LA CHAMBRE DE PRESENCE A S. IAMES

COMME MESSIEVRS DV CONSEIL PRIVE VIENNENT SALVER LA REYNE DANS SA CHAMBRE

James's where several survive (fig. 305). In their present state the openings with their flat arches, decorated spandrels and quatrefoils fail to impress, but the chimneys there, as at most of the King's houses had brightly painted and gilded terracotta

228

308. Design for a fireplace, attributed to Hans Holbein the Younger, *c*.1540.

307 (facing page bottom left). Hampton Court, Surrey. This fireplace was built by Cardinal Wolsey and installed in the presence chamber of Catherine of Aragon's lodging on the second floor of the Tudor fountain court. It bears Wolsey's badges and mottoes and has lost a shallow projecting overmantle moulding (see fig. 303).

roundels set into the chimney-breast (fig. 306).[41] The chimney-pieces at Whitehall, Greenwich and Hampton Court were certainly grander (fig. 307). A design for one such piece survives, attributed by some to Holbein, although the case for his involvement in the Royal Works is slight (fig. 308). The

229

309. Sixteenth-century rush matting from Hampton Court, Surrey. This example was found beneath floorboards and may date from Henry VIII's reign. It was laid on a plastered timber floor in a first-floor courtier lodging. The matting, made from rushes woven into strips, was delivered in 3-strip wide sections. These were sewn together with twine on site.

310 (facing page left). Westminster Palace. Wooden patera from the ceiling of the painted chamber. Originally it would have been painted and the relief filled with coloured glass.

311 (facing page right). *Henry VIII*, attributed to Hans Eworth, *c*.1545. Henry VIII stands in the post-Whitehall Mural pose, in front of a niche with a shell head, and on a Turkey rug, with cloth of gold hanging to his left.

substantial two-storey chimney is bounded by a Tuscan and an Ionic order and enriched with grotesques and royal badges. The pillars have a strong affinity with those shown in the *Family of Henry VIII*, painted towards the close of the reign and this, together with the strapwork and the general Mannerist tone of the decoration would suggest a date in the 1540s. Assuming that the fireplace opening measured approximately 4 feet by 6 feet, the overall size of the structure would have been about 14 feet high by 9 feet 6 inches wide, suitable only for a great outward room. There were only two projects in the 1540s which could have accommodated such a chimneypiece, Whitehall and Oatlands.

During the modifications undertaken at the Tower of London for the coronation of Anne Boleyn, most of the King's rooms were stripped out and new ceilings; doors and fireplaces were installed in the antique fashion. The 'mantell of wainscott with antyk' installed in the dining chamber there was one of the first antique chimney-pieces to be installed anywhere and soon fireplaces were being replaced at Greenwich and elsewhere. At Whitehall, Wolsey's former presence chamber was taken over by the King and carvers set up the royal arms over the chimney. A few years later the chimney in the next room, again probably dating from Wolsey's time, was being replaced by 'frenchmen' — a reference which may indicate an elaborate antique design.[42]

Floors

Some floors were intended to be covered, others were not. Generally rooms on the ground floor did not have suspended timber floors and therefore they were floored with tiles, bricks set on edge or flagstones. Occasionally rooms on the first floor were tiled, but this relied on the existence of a substantial timber sub-floor. The Great Hall at Hampton Court is one such exception to the rule — it was paved with tiles in October 1532.[43]

More generally floors were boarded with oak boards and then covered with plaster of Paris, sometimes painted to simulate marble (figs 282, 293) or otherwise covered.[44] The most simple, and least hygienic of these coverings was a sprinkling of rushes, but this became increasingly rare as the sixteenth century wore on.[45] Much more common was the laying of rush mats, mostly made in Southwark, in strips sewn together and close fitted. Mat-laying was an endless task which appears in every set of works' accounts. With an almost insatiable demand for new mats and replacements their provision in royal houses was a lucrative business; in October 1539 John Cradocke obtained a monopoly for life to

provide mats for use in all the royal 'places and lodgyns' within twenty miles of London.[46] Fully intact early sixteenth-century matting has been found beneath later boards at Hampton Court (fig. 309), identical matting appears on the floor of the room in which Queen Elizabeth I is shown receiving ambassadors (fig. 294).

In important rooms and on important occasions, carpets were laid on top of mats. The word carpet in the early sixteenth century embraced a range of covering fabrics including velvets, needlework, tapestry and embroidery, as well as the knotted pile fabrics regarded as carpets today. Sixteenth-century inventories usually classify carpets under functional headings such as foot carpets, table carpets, cupboard carpets, window carpets and carpet cushions. Thus carpets (hard wearing fabrics) were used for covering two classes of object: architectural surfaces — floors, window-seats and other ledges — and furniture.

Both inventories and paintings indicate that the largest part of the king's gigantic collection of over eight hundred carpets was of Turkey work (figs 278, 299, 311). Henry also owned significant numbers of Ushak and Chintamani rugs. Of the Turkey rugs listed in the inventory of 1547 about fifty or sixty were described as being 'great' which meant that they measured about 15 feet by 30 feet. Clearly these were foot carpets; there were seventeen such great carpets at Hampton Court and so a fair number of rooms must have been carpeted. Smaller carpets, which formed the bulk of the collection, cannot be positively identified as floor carpets.[47] Certainly, wherever a carpet was laid on a floor it was a sign of status and in his full-length portraits Henry VIII is always shown bestriding one. There is also some evidence to suggest that Henry was responsible for introducing the carpet to the throne canopy ensemble, a tradition which appears earlier in England than elsewhere in Europe.[48]

Ceilings

Ceilings were either flat, with or without some decoration, or had their structural members exposed and decorated. Generally it was only the very largest rooms which had exposed structures, such as great halls and chapels. The structural and decorative principles which governed Henrician flat ceilings had been set in the Middle Ages. The ceiling in the Painted Chamber at Westminster, dating from the 1260s, exemplifies these principles. The underside of the ceiling joists was boarded and to the boards were fixed, in symmetrical lines, two sizes of wooden paterae (shallow bosses) enriched with a coloured composition, possibly glass (fig. 310). The intervening ground was decorated with painted gesso. The effect must have been very rich while relatively easy to achieve, and other early medieval ceilings are mostly variations on the Westminster model. Thus sometimes, instead of wooden paterae, leaden decorations were popular; at Clarendon the flat ceiling was painted with bise (blue) and spangled with gilded lead stars.[49]

This type of flat decorated ceiling remained the principal way of decorating the royal lodgings throughout the early Tudor period. The hall at Richmond, completed by Henry VII, had a 'rof of tymber, not beamyd ne brasid but propir knottes, sraftly corven, joyned and shett toguyders with mortes and pynned, hangyng pendaunt from the sede roff into the growned and floure, aftir the moost new invencion and crafte, of the pure practif of gementri...'[50] This was in contrast to the previous great hall built by an English king at

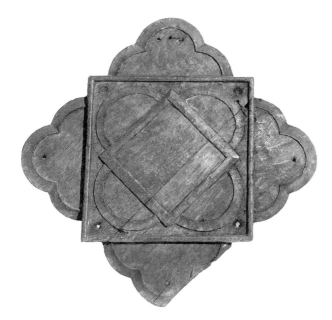

312. Windsor Castle, Berkshire. Ceiling from Henry VII's tower (1500–2). This drawing, together with that of the fireplace (fig. 303), gives a good impression of the gothic richness of Henry VII's interiors. The ceiling, which has had an eighteenth-century box cornice added, is made up of oak ribs with decorated rose bosses and richly carved grounds. It was probably painted and gilded.

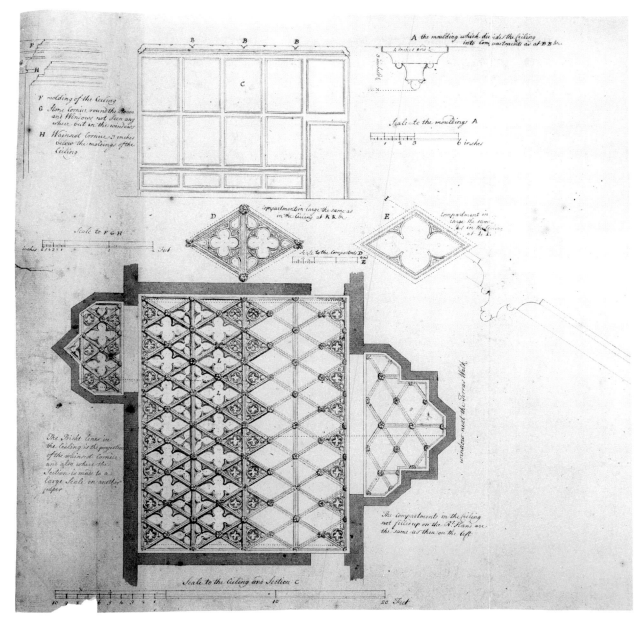

Eltham. There Edward IV had built a hammerbeam roof along the lines of Westminster Great Hall. This sort of flat ceiling was also used by Henry VII in his new tower at Windsor where flat battens were enriched by quatrefoils (fig. 312). More usual was the insertion of badges and devices in the ground between the battens as in the chapel at Richmond: 'the rofe is celyd and whiight lymyd and chekeryd with tymber losengewise, payntid with colour of asure, havyng betwene every chekir a rede rose of golde or a portculles'.[51]

In the King's privy chamber at Greenwich one of Henry VII's ceilings survived until 1537, but had, by that date, become hopelessly old-fashioned.

So Henry VIII ordered Richard Ridge, one of the principal carvers of the great hall roof at Hampton Court, to fit up a new ceiling and cornice after the antique fashion.[52] The *Family of Henry VIII* (fig. 282) shows such an antique flat-battened ceiling of the 1540s with royal badges in the ground. This type of ceiling can be seen today in the great watching chamber at Hampton Court (fig. 160). The flat bosses are made up of leather-mâché elements nailed to a circular timber disc which is itself nailed to the ceiling (fig. 313). The watching chamber has been heavily restored, but the ceiling of the holyday closet dating from 1536 is in excellent condition and it shows how the battens were embellished by the

232

313. Hampton Court, Surrey. Leather-mâché roundels from the ceiling of the watching chamber, 1536. These were taken down from the ceiling in the late nineteenth century and preserve their original decoration. The entire roundel was gilded and then parts of it were picked out, with a coloured glaze. The whole ceiling originally had 130 such roundels representing the badges of both Henry VIII and Jane Seymour. They were placed in the whitewashed ground between the gilded ceiling battens.

use of moulded strips of grotesquework slotted into their sides. An alternative method of embellishment was adopted on the ceiling of the chapel at St James's: there the antique motifs were cast out of lead, gilded and nailed to the battens. Occasionally the whole ground between the battens was enriched as in the Wolsey Closet at Hampton Court where the ground is a separate leather-mâché panel (fig. 274).

The chapel and hall ceilings at Hampton Court are of a different type to the flat ceilings examined above. The hall has its structural members exposed and carved (figs 139, 140, 149). It is an old-fashioned design — hammerbeam roofs being common from the fourteenth century — but enriched with fashionable motifs of the 1530s. The chapel ceiling, however, is far more ambitious: none of the exposed beams is structural and the weathertight roof above is an independant structure (figs 314, 315), thus giving Henry's carvers freedom to create a ceiling on purely decorative grounds. The design, although enriched with antique motifs and embellished with putti, is still a late medieval vaulted ceiling; it embodies that mix of styles that so characterises the Henrician period.

*　　*　　*

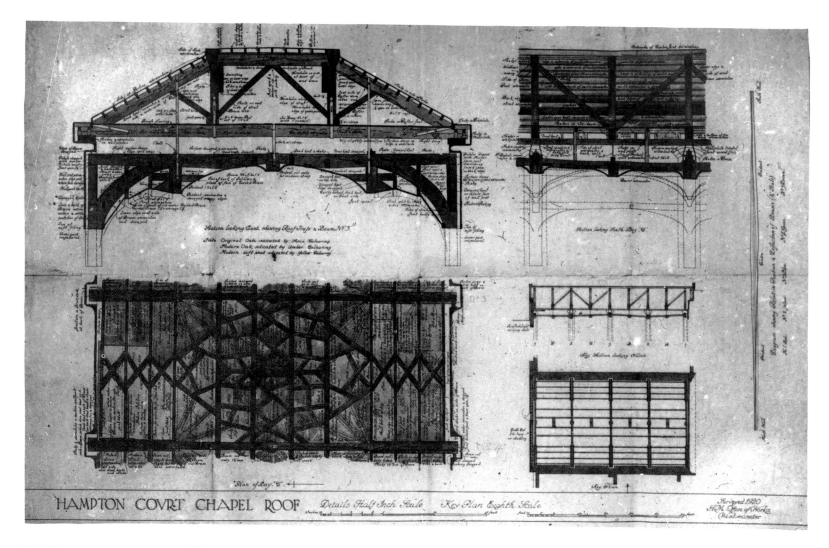

HAMPTON COVRT CHAPEL ROOF *Details Half Inch Scale Key Plan Eighth Scale*

314. Hampton Court, Surrey. Diagrams of the chapel ceiling, from the Office of Works, 1920. The section on the top left shows how the decorative ceiling is suspended from a typical queen post truss by iron straps. The plan beneath shows the bracing above the decorative ceiling.

Furniture

The rooms of the Henrician palaces may be seen as a stage set, an architectural shell, albeit with some built-in decorative features, mainly around doors and chimney-pieces and on the ceiling. However, the rooms of Henry's houses were also furnished with movable objects. As textiles and plate were by far the most significant, valuable and sought-after elements of internal furnishing, freestanding timber furniture was fairly poorly rated. What made furniture important was not what it was, nor what it was made from, but what it was used for. Most of the furniture in the King's houses was utilitarian, everyday stuff, but additionally there was the King's own furniture of estate. Furniture of estate denoted the social estate of the person using it; a courtier could immediately place the user of the furniture in the correct social bracket by assessing what he saw. This had nothing to do with wealth, for a man like Cardinal Wolsey could have afforded furniture identical to the King's. What counted was 'degree' in the hierarchy of Tudor social order.

The three pieces of furniture of estate were the bed, the seat of authority and the buffet. All three were specially singled out in Household regulations: 'no manner of what soever degree he be of be so hardye to come nighe the kings chayre nor stand under the clothe of estate nor to leane upon the kings bedd nor to approthe the cupborde where the kings cushion is layd nor to stand upon his carpet'.[53]

Without doubt the King's bed was the most valuable piece of furniture he owned. Lower down the social scale a bed could be the single most valuable possession of a merchant or yeoman because of the value of its hangings. Such beds were often thought suitable gifts, and in 1529 Henry VIII received a 'rich bed' from Francis I of France.[54] From the Middle Ages English kings had had bed enclosures; evidence from Edward I's reign indicates that there was a canvas outer bed around the inner bed.[55] By the time of the Yorkists, however, the

234

royal bed stood alone as a separate piece of furniture within a room, acquiring a ceremonial and spiritual significance.[56] The earliest surviving set of regulations for the preparation of a royal bed date from the time of Henry VII. His grooms, yeomen and pages of the Wardrobe were expected to strip the bed down daily and, after shaking the mattresses, to remake it with sheets and blankets. They then were to sprinkle it with holy water before drawing the curtains.[57]

The wooden frames of early beds were quite simple, lacking any elaboration. All the richness was reserved for the hangings. Later the frame itself became a subject for decoration, the posts, headboard and other components being elaborately carved and painted. Although no complete royal bed of this type survives, a very grand painted and carved bed does (fig. 316).[58] This belonged either to Henry VII's stepfather, the first Earl of Derby (*d.* 1504) or more probably to the first Earl's grandson the second Earl (*d.* 1521). Even in its unpainted state this bed with royal connections gives a good

315. Hampton Court, Surrey. The chapel ceiling. Carved at Sonning in Berkshire and floated down river in sections before being assembled on site, Henry VIII's ceiling replaced a much plainer one erected by Wolsey. It was redecorated in the late nineteenth century on the advice of A.W. Pugin.

235

ing health and his ulcerated leg which increasingly confined him to his bed.[60]

The framework of the Whitehall bed was the cheaper of its two parts and there can be no doubt that the hangings were costlier. The cost would be significantly increased when a bed had summer and winter hangings, such as the set designed by Queen Jane Seymour herself.[61] The hangings of the King's bed at Hampton Court are listed in 1547: The bed was 8 feet long and 7 feet 6 inches wide with posts and head carved, painted and gilded, and the posts had four gilt balls topped with iron vanes painted with the King's arms. The celer (canopy) and tester (headboard) were of cloth of silver and cloth of gold paned together. There were double valences with gold, silver and silk fringes over a foot deep. The whole was edged with a purple velvet ribbon. Both the celer and tester were decorated with the royal arms in a garland set against a ground spangled with fleurs-de-lis and roses. There were five curtains with twenty-three panes of purple and white taffeta,

316. Joined tester bedstead, English oak, 1500–21. Royal beds early in the reign of Henry VIII were very similar to this.

317. Hanging cradle, *c.*1500. This very grand cradle was originally painted and gilded, and must have been very similar to the cradles described in the works accounts.

impression of the type of bed owned by Henry VII, or by Henry VIII early in his reign. Details of the construction of the 'king's greate bedde of walnuttree' built for the King's new house of Whitehall in the early 1530s survive:[59] two pieces of walnut tree were bought from the Master of Horse and were then transported and seasoned; other materials — eighteen wainscots, three deal boards (for the bottom of the bed), ironwork and glue were bought; a house was hired in the parish of St Lawrence Poultney, where six carvers worked for ten months on the frame before it was gilded by Andrew Wright. Making just the frame came to the enormous figure of £86 3s. 10d. This particular bed has an interesting history, for in 1542 it was enlarged to measure 7 feet 6 inches long and 7 feet wide. This may have been due to the King's declin-

edged with gold ribbon. The counterpane was of taffeta embroidered with the royal arms.

This was probably the most spectacular bed in the kingdom, even the King's wives did not have beds of that richness. The tester of Queen Anne Boleyn's bed was walnut grained and gilded, Jane Seymour's bed had a painted wooden roundel with her arms on it.[62] Part of such a painted royal bed survives in the Burrell Collection in Glasgow (figs 273, 318) it contains the arms of Anne of Cleves and may have been one of those made for her reception in England. These very elaborate beds were not for sleeping in, they were used for the daily ritual of going to bed in the evening and rising in the morning. In fact the King slept in smaller and more comfortable beds, and bedrooms elsewhere. At both Greenwich and Hampton Court Henry VIII had

two bedchambers in his own lodgings and a third in the Queen's apartments.[63]

The royal children, as infants, had carefully made cradles: in 1535–6 a new cradle was made for Princess Elizabeth which must have resembled the surviving cradle shown in figure 317. Elizabeth's cradle was lined in crimson satin with a crimson silk fringe and, as was usual, a leather travelling case was made for it.[64]

The King also provided beds and bedding for courtiers and visitors at all the royal houses. During

318a–d. Painted oak bedhead, 1539. The importance of this fragment of bed can be hardly overstated; it is the only surviving piece of furniture that can be certainly ascribed to Henry VIII's Court. The bedhead retains its original polychrome decoration with the date 1539 and the initials HA. This is highly significant as Henry and Anne of Cleves were married on the last day of 1539, or the first day of 1540. This bed must have therefore been made in anticipation of the event. Either side of the headboard are male and female figures in armour. Above the male figure is a licentious putto, and above the female is a pregnant one. In the case of Henry's marriage to Anne, neither the bed nor its suggestive carvings were to be enough to bring about marital bliss.

237

320. The Winchester Chair, reputedly used at the marriage of Queen Mary I. This chair is a precious survival of a royal X-frame seat of authority.

the early part of 1532 ten 'riche bedds' were specially made for Whitehall. Of these ten, three were to have gilded bedheads and all but two were to have cups with vanes painted with the King's arms placed on the pillars of the bedsteads.[65] These beds were presumably destined for the richest courtier lodgings or guest rooms. In 1525 the accounts of the Marquess of Exeter record that the King lent him two beds while he lay at Bishop's Hatfield; all Exeter had to do was pay 2d. for the carriage. However at Windsor in the same year he was lent a humble pallet from the King's wardrobe and at Bridewell he bought a whipcord to hang the tester of his bed there.[66] Simpler beds were sometimes provided for other Household officials. At Woodstock in 1538 eight new bedsteads were made for the lodgings of the head officers of the Household, along with various other pieces of furniture.[67]

Seat furniture

Some chairs also had special significance. The most important of these chairs were the seats of authority or thrones which were designed to elevate the sitter and should be considered as an ensemble with a canopy, dais, footstool, cushion and rug. The exact combination, size and elaboration of these items varied with the estate of the sitter. Westminster Hall was furnished for Henry VII in 1501 according to his importance: 'in the uppar parte orderyd a Clothe of Estate for the Kinges Highnes with cusshons and carpettes and all othir goodly requysites unto his

319. Edward IV enthroned, from a mid-fifteenth-century Flemish manuscript. The King sits on a boarded seat raised up on two steps. The chair is covered in rich crimson fabric and is surmounted by a canopy suspended from the ceiling. The floor is painted and the walls hung with painted wall hangings. The figure on the left with a garter may be the future Richard III.

noble person and estate'.[68] Henry VII specified the degrees of estate for throne settings in his Household regulations, determining the height of the canopy and whether the backcloth was rolled or hanging loose; the canopy of the Queen was, for instance, to be lower than that of the King by the depth of the valence.[69]

During the Middle Ages there had been two principal types of throne, the post and boarded seat (fig. 319) and the X-frame stool (fig. 320). What converted a seat into a throne, however was the ensemble, not any particular type of seat itself. Kings of England sitting in majesty have been depicted on the Great Seal of England since the reign of Edward the Confessor. From 1340 monarchs appear on raised, canopied platforms which, in 1542, ceased to be Gothic in design and became exuberantly antique (fig. 321). The Great Seals do not show the kings' seat in any detail, but the two at Whitehall in 1547 are described in an inventory: they were timber covered in yellow cloth of gold, fringed with Venice gold and with four balls of silver and gilt. Similar chairs can be seen in contemporary paintings where they are clearly meant to be chairs of authority (figs 322, 324, 325).

The canopy beneath which the seat was placed was of the highest elaboration. The dais was suf-

321a and b. Left: the Great Seal of Henry VII. Right: the third Great Seal of Henry VIII (1542). The transformation in design between the throne of Henry VII and that of his son is clearly seen.

ficiently large to enable a king to be joined by his wife and children. At the marriage of Prince Arthur and Princess Catherine in 1501, a herald observed how, at a reception at Baynard's Castle 'in the hed and uppar parte of this large chambre a sete regall covered over with a cloth of estate precious and riche costly, where undre is magestie was settyng upon cusshons of cloth of golde . . . is dere and wilbeloved sons, the Lord Prince on the right hand and the Duke of York on hys left hand'.[70] Henry VIII possessed a number of such canopies. One at Whitehall in 1547 had a celer and a tester with double valences of purple, black and green with seams decorated in gold braid. Both the celer and tester had the King's arms and supporters richly embroidered on them. The edges of the tester were deeply fringed in gold and purple silk and the whole was lined with black buckram. The canopy measured 6¾ yards long and 2¾ yards wide. Reference to the painting of the *Family of Henry VIII* suggests that celer and tester were not always

separate pieces and therefore 6¾ yards was not the true height of the canopy. Other depictions of throne canopies seem to indicate that celer and tester could be separate (figs 294, 323). Both the *Family of Henry VIII* and *Henry VIII Presenting a Charter to the Company of Barber-surgeons* show heavily embroidered testers, either edged with gold braid or fringe, and this was the type common by the end of the reign.

Another essential part of the ensemble were the cushions. In 1508 Princess Mary was to have 'v. cossions of fyne clothe of golde, i. rycher then the other, iii. longe and ii shorte'.[71] Cushions were placed on seats but were also strewn on the floor as in the Middle and Far East. The King in procession might have his cushion carried before him and placing this on a seat designated it a seat of authority.[72]

The canopy of state was not reserved for audiences and receptions, it was also an essential feature of the theatre of the royal table. The King's seat at table would be indicated by a celer as can be seen in

323 (following page bottom). Part of a seating plan for Anne Boleyn's coronation. Above the canopy are the words 'for the quene', beside her, 'Archebusshop of Canterbury'. The canopy is supported by strings to the ceiling. The sides of the canopy are delineated by posts.

239

322. The Great Bible, detail of frontispiece, 1541. Henry VIII sits on a post-and-boarded seat with a segmental pediment and ball finials.

324 (right). *Henry VIII Enthroned*, from a Plea Roll, Trinity term 1517. The King is seated on a very plain post-and-boarded seat.

contemporary illustrations of Henry VIII and Queen Anne Boleyn dining (figs 175, 323).

For courtiers, forms and stools were the principal means of seating. If the King did sit on a stool it would have been specially upholstered like the one at Greenwich in 1539.[73] The privy chamber at Greenwich had three joined forms and three stools and the withdrawing chamber a form and a stool, the privy chamber at Hampton Court had two joined forms and four stools.[74] Twenty stools were made all at one time for the painted gallery at Whitehall and they presumably lined the walls.[75] Stools were mainly restricted to the inward chambers while forms were the standard means of seating the Household in the outer chambers. More important courtiers were provided with settles which were benches with deep seats and a back and which were more prestigious pieces of furniture than forms or stools. In the Greenwich privy chamber there was a fitted settle with a cupboard in it.[76] Holbein's portrait of Thomas Cromwell (fig. 297) shows quite clearly the back of an oak settle which must have been similar to that at Greenwich.

Cupboards and buffets

Originally the term cupboard meant a board upon which to display plate or other valuables, but it gradually became a term to denote the enclosed wooden box fronted by doors, now known by that name. Often the terminology used in the royal accounts indicates the transitional nature of the cupboard from a surface for display to a container for storage. Sometimes a clerk remembered to clarify the situation, as at Greenwich where two cupboards in the withdrawing chamber are described as being

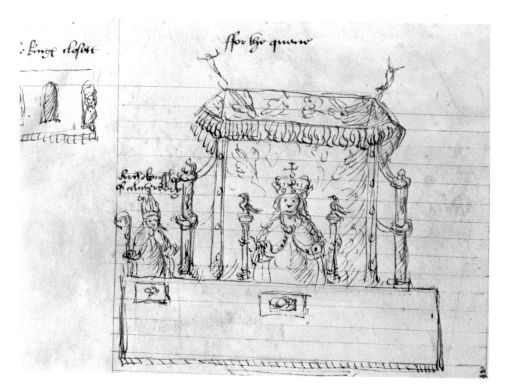

MARYE the QUENE.

Antonio Mor, *Mary I*, 1554.
The Queen sits on a typical
X-frame seat of authority,
upholstered in rich fabric
closely nailed with gilt nails
and fringed in gold. Many
such chairs are listed in
Henry VIII's 1547 inventory.

'with aumbries'[77] (i.e. having boxes with doors attached). The difference was mainly a functional one; the display sort of cupboard can more conveniently be called a buffet or dressoir; the storage type called cupboard.[78]

The inventories taken on Henry's death at Greenwich and Hampton Court identify rooms with cupboards and buffets. The buffet was far more common, both privy chambers had buffets of wainscot. These would have certainly been covered by a carpet or cloth. In 1508 Princess Mary was to have in her bedchamber 'smale carpettes for windowes, borde and cobordes, v. at the lest, of velet of cramosyne, and as many carpettes of wolle for every day'.[79] One of the cupboard cloths belonging to the King, her brother, in 1547 was of 'velvet figured redde borderd about with clothe of tissue hanginge iiii bottomes with tassells of red silke and golde'.[80] Holbein's *Ambassadors* shows this sort of buffet (fig. 293); a tall plain wainscot table covered in a rich carpet. It was leaning against such a buffet that Henry VIII received his New Year's gifts in the Greenwich presence chamber in 1538. The gifts would have then been displayed on the buffet for all the Court to see.[81]

Buffets were also sited in the King's bedchambers. At both Hampton Court and Greenwich there were two buffets in the King's great bedchamber — those at Hampton Court were covered in green cloth. One can only suppose that these were used for supporting candlesticks and plate and possibly a pitcher and ewer by the King's bed. Such a utilitarian buffet can be seen in the background of Holbein's family group of Sir Thomas More (fig. 298). More suprisingly buffets seem to have been positioned in the many entries, lobbies and galleries around the maze of the secret lodgings. There were buffets in the 'entry to the closet to the bedchamber' and in the 'little chamber next the gallery' at Greenwich and at Hampton Court they were in the 'little gallery' in the 'short gallery' where there were two covered, and in the 'lobby'. Only in the case of the 'lobby' can we suggest what it was used to display, for there a clock is mentioned.

However, buffets had an importance beyond their everyday role in dining occasions of state: the Burgundian dukes had transformed the act of dining into an art and the function of the buffet into an indicator of degree (fig. 202). The buffet in this context was a simple stepped structure designed to receive the display of plate. The more steps and the higher the display, the greater the importance of the diner. Tudor chroniclers never omit the number of stages, or tiers, a buffet had; a description from 1501 enthused 'The cuppbord also of vij shelvys and stages of hight, furnysshid and fulfilled with precious and sumptuous plate of moost pleasaunt

fachion . . . The plate wherof were great and massy pottes, flagons, stondyng cuppis goodly bollys, and peces . . .'.[82]

On occasions of state Henry VIII had twelve stages — a buffet fit for a king. Cardinal Wolsey at Hampton Court in 1527 had only six, in accordance with his lesser estate. The value and quantity of plate also varied according to a person's rank. At the marriage of Prince Arthur in 1501, Henry VII provided cupboards for the guests in their own lodgings. The plate intended for the Archbishop was worth 600–700 marks, for the bishops 500, for the earls 500, and for their younger brothers 300.[83] The height of the buffet was not the only factor which advertised the diner's estate, equally important was his ability to complete the banquet without using the plate on display. It was noted of a feast held by Henry VII in Westminster Hall that 'The nombre of the spice plates and cuppis were goodly and marvellous and yet the more to be wondered, for that the cuppbord was nothyng towchid but stode complet, garnysshid, and fulfillyd, nott oonys dimynyssid'.[84] The truly great would give away items from the buffet to their guests as presents,[85] but such display was reserved for the most magnificent Court festivals. More private occasions demanded more practical buffets which could double as sideboards for the serving of wine, as can be seen from the late medieval buffet in the house of Sir Thomas More (fig. 298), a sort which occasionally survives today.[86] More unusual and antique in form is the one shown in figure 175, but the drawing may date from after Henry's death (see p. 138). A more ordinary everyday buffet can dimly be seen in the recesses of a tent at the Field of Cloth of Gold (fig. 326).

Each of the outward rooms in a Henrician house apparently had a ceremonial buffet and by the end of the reign the privy chamber may also have had one; at least, by 1541–2 an eight-tier buffet was set up in the privy chamber at Greenwich.[87] These were usually placed to one side of the King, often in a bay window, and during very grand feasts there would have been two buffets, one for show and the other from which he was served.

Whereas the buffet was furniture of estate like a bed or a tester, a cupboard was totally utilitarian. A cupboard of this type was made for the long gallery at Hampton Court in 1530: 'paid to henry Currunt carver for xii square dores for cupbords and vi dores for tills withe xxiiii panells for the same cupborde standyng in the kings new gallery'. Once carved the cupboard was painted.[88] Such furniture was not only sited in galleries, the 1547 inventory mentions two cupboards in the King's withdrawing chamber at Greenwich and one in the King's inner bedchamber at Hampton Court. These fairly humdrum

326. *The Field of Cloth of Gold*, by an unknown artist, *c.*1545 (detail). Courtiers dine in a tent at the Field of Cloth of Gold; in the recesses of the tent is a simple buffet piled with gilt plate.

pieces of royal furniture have not survived and were never of such a status to appear in the background of paintings. Very often, indeed, they were covered with a carpet or cloth to enhance their dignity. Such pieces were often made by the Office of Works — not by furniture-makers — so accounts for them appear together with those for the buildings. The metalwork for the cupboards, and also for tables and chairs, was made by the works smith. The most popular form for handles was the heart ring.[89]

Tables

Tables were generally of two sorts, those designed with an eye for show and those meant to be covered (normally called boards). An example of the first type was the 'table wyth foldyng leves for here grace to brek here faste upon'.[90] This particular table was required with such urgency that a carver was employed to work all night by candlelight in order to finish it. More unusual was the folding table of 'irne with chens ocuppyd for a burde' which was made for Anne Boleyn at Whitehall.[91] Other display tables included tables 'to play on' presumably dice and other games. These were usually richly carved, most often with antique work.[92] For the majority of the Court the trestle tables and forms in the hall would have been the most familiar sights. The tables in the great hall at The More were set into the ground.[93]

Other movable furniture

Joiners in the Office of Works and city coffer-makers supplied the King with a diversity of pieces. One Grene 'the coffermaker' was a regular royal supplier[94] who made chests or coffers, often with tills or drawers covered in fabric or leather. All his pieces were provided with an outer case, normally of leather. Another item much in demand were screens to cover fireplaces in summer. Office of Works' joiners carved four of these with the King's arms and feet of lions, dragons and greyhounds. Together they cost Henry £10.[95] Most pieces produced by the Office of Works were made on site but on one occasion twelve stools, two trestles, two joined tables and four forms were transported from store in London to Woking.[96] This was an exception as generally cheap furniture was more economical to make new than to transport.

There was also a variety of items made from metal, ranging from silver gilt down to pewter. Perhaps most conspicuous were the clocks. In January 1532 'the glasinge of iii frames for clockis' was undertaken at Hampton Court.[97] There, in the

327. Gilt metal clock, mainly early sixteenth century. Probably formerly owned by Henry VIII, as the weights are engraved with his and Anne Boleyn's initials and mottoes. It is typical of the high-quality decorative clocks and decorative metalwork found in the royal interiors.

328. Cast of bronze candlesticks originally intended for Henry VIII's tomb but now in Ghent.

329. A pair of cast-iron firedogs from Knole House, Kent. The tops of the dogs bear the arms of Henry VIII, the initials HR (Henricus Rex) and the falcon of Anne Boleyn. They were almost certainly formerly royal property which passed to Sir Thomas Boleyn, Anne's brother, who had them at Hever Castle, Kent.

In the King's and Queen's lodgings the most common form of candle-holder was the wall-sconce, although lanterns are occasionally mentioned. Cavendish describes the wall-sconces at Hampton Court in 1527 '. . . the plates that hung on the walls to give lights in the chamber were of silver and gilt, with lights burning in them . . .'.[100] Two years later at Hampton Court the smith made eight tinned brackets to hold wainscot bowls or plates for candles; six of them were sent to Greenwich for the 'king's chamber' the other two remained at Hampton Court.[101] These were relatively humble pieces, grander were the seventeen candlesticks of 'metalle guilte to be fastned to a walle' found at Whitehall in 1547.[102] Sconces were either hung, like the Whitehall ones, from ropes of gold with golden tassels,[103] or spiked into the wall; in a gallery at

privy chamber a clock stood on a carved pillar with a green fringed top.[98] Most often, however, they stood on wall-mounted brackets as in the background of Holbein's More family group (fig. 298). A single clock survives from Henry's collection and is now in the Royal Library, Windsor (fig. 327).[99]

Before man overcame darkness more efficiently with gas and electric light, the hours of daylight governed his existence more than almost anything else. The Court tended to go to bed earlier in winter as the days were shorter. Candles were the principal source of light for the upper courtiers and they were highly expensive. Just as rations of food were specified in the household lists, so were candles. Indeed for the staff of the Lord Steward's department candles were a luxury and rush-lights had to suffice.

244

Hampton Court there was a copper candlestick 'sett in the waynscotte'.[104] In addition to wall-sconces, candles were mounted on a standish or candlestand. Some of the freestanding candlesticks and candelabra were highly elaborate, one at Whitehall having '2 branches with vices guilte and painted the foote beinge foure square. In the toppe thof an antique boy with thinge wyndynge rounde aboute his legge'. On a larger scale there were in the same building two great standing candlesticks built on timber pillars.[105] These may have been similar to the great candelabra built for Henry VIII's tomb, but never used. These (fig. 328) are now the only surviving examples of large-scale light fixtures from Henry VIII's reign.

Epilogue

THE DEATH OF HENRY VIII was truly the end of an era. None of his children, as they succeeded in turn, could rival his energy in building, nor indeed, did they have the opportunity to, for the dead King's residences rapidly became a liability. The history of royal building in England between 1547 and 1660 is largely one of the struggle to maintain the existing Henrician buildings whilst modernising their interiors. Neither the later Tudors, nor the early Stuarts succeeded in building residences to rival Henry VIII's Hampton Court, Whitehall or Greenwich; they barely managed to maintain the houses already standing.

The reasons for the general maintenance of the residential status quo after Henry's death are not only to be found in the fact that he had left the Crown exceptionally well provided for numerically; nor can they be fully attributed to lack of finance or lack of imagination — Charles I would willingly have completed his plans for a new Whitehall. A more important factor was that the royal houses as mechanisms for government and Court life continued to fit the requirements of subsequent monarchs; little change occurred in the structure of the Court. Of course the protectorship of Edward I and the marital status of Elizabeth I had organisational consequences, just as did the fact that James I and Charles I were married with children, but the plan of the early Tudor house could serve both. Certainly, James I formally shifted the architectural and organisational emphasis of the household from the Privy Chamber to the Bedchamber, but this change had largely taken place in the last years of Henry's reign — it caused no revolution in royal planning.

Just as there was no functional need to rebuild Henry's houses, neither was there a stylistic need, at least during the sixteenth century. After the Reformation many of the artistic currents that flowed so freely in Henry's reign dried up. Architectural decoration turned in on itself; indeed it is possible to suggest that the Henrician royal houses themselves became source-books for Elizabethan designers and architects. After 1600 however, the Henrician houses were becoming old fashioned and the alterations and modifications enumerated in the Works accounts become more fundamental than before.

Thus, despite the Commonwealth and Charles II's architectural ambitions, in 1688 William and Mary found that their principal residences, Whitehall, Hampton Court and St James's were essentially Tudor buildings. Even more significantly, when Sir Christopher Wren set about rebuilding these and others of the King's houses he recreated in them the essential elements of planning developed in the reign of Henry VIII. The King's apartments at Hampton Court built for William III reflect exactly the layout of rooms in the Tudor wing that they replaced. Particularly there, but also at Whitehall, Wren used Henry VIII's infrastructure — at Hampton Court his culverts, water-supply system and kitchens continued to serve the Courts of William III and the first two Georges.

So, while the death of Henry VIII marked the end of an era in one sense, in another it was the start of one: a long period in royal domestic building during which that 'phoenix for fine masonery', Henry VIII, dominated, from his grave, generations of royal builders and architects.

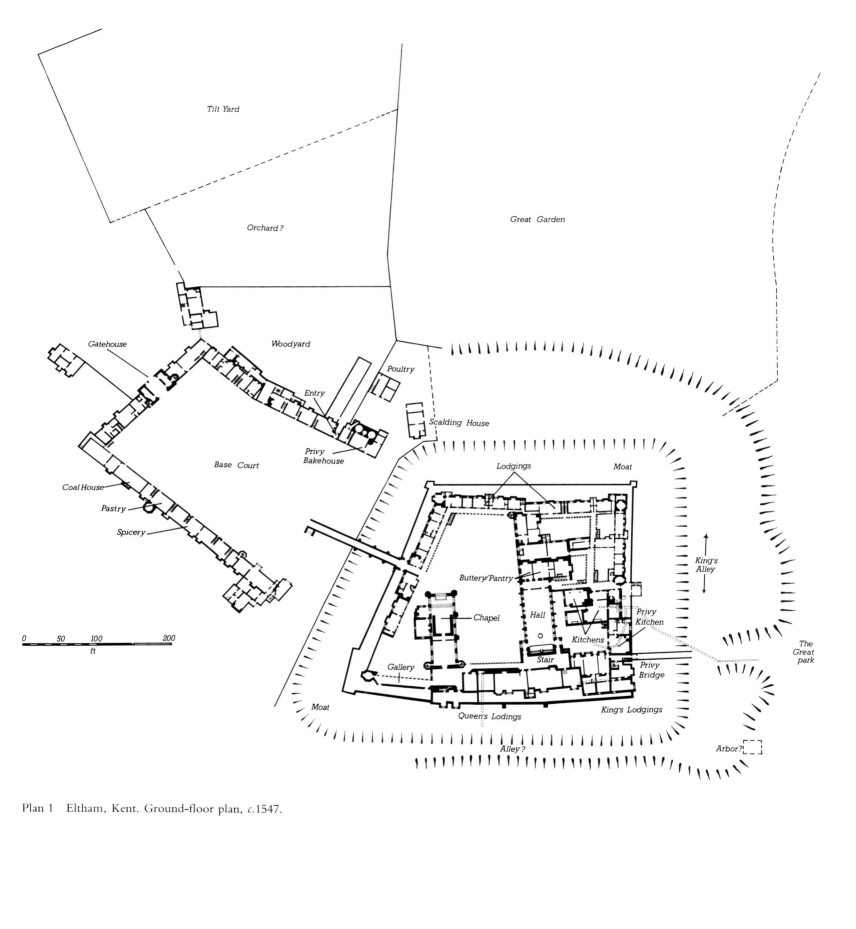

Tilt Yard

Orchard?

Great Garden

Gatehouse

Woodyard

Poultry

Entry

Scalding House

Privy
Bakehouse

Base Court

Coal House

Pastry

Spicery

Lodgings

Moat

Buttery/Pantry

Chapel

Hall

Privy
Kitchen

Kitchens

King's
Alley

Stair

Gallery

Privy
Bridge

The
Great
park

Moat

Queen's Lodings

King's Lodgings

Alley?

Arbor?

0   50   100   200
           ft

Plan 1   Eltham, Kent. Ground-floor plan, c.1547.

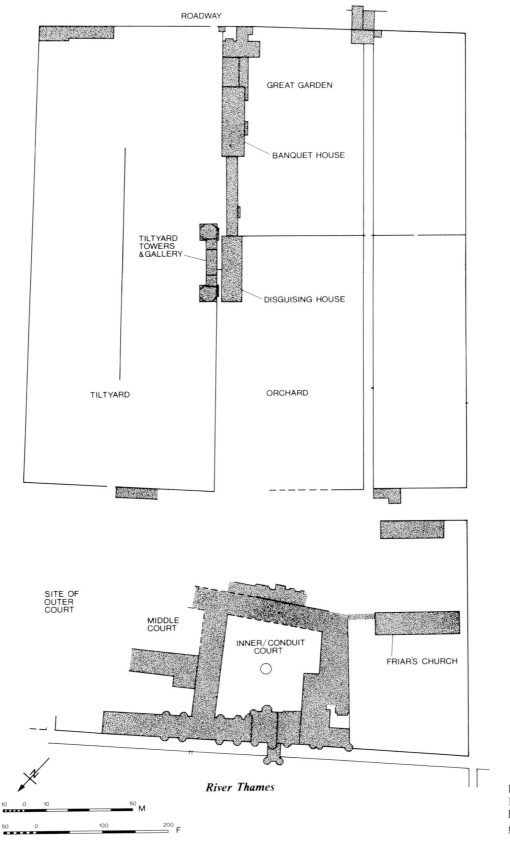

ROADWAY

GREAT GARDEN

BANQUET HOUSE

TILTYARD
TOWERS
& GALLERY

DISGUISING HOUSE

TILTYARD

ORCHARD

SITE OF
OUTER
COURT

MIDDLE
COURT

INNER/CONDUIT
COURT

FRIAR'S CHURCH

River Thames

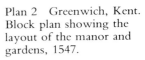

Plan 2 Greenwich, Kent.
Block plan showing the
layout of the manor and
gardens, 1547.

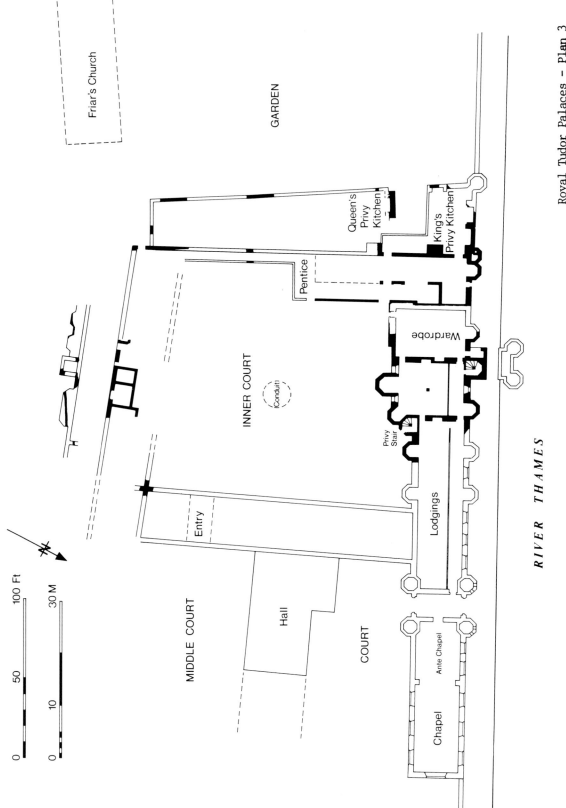

Friar's Church

GARDEN

Queen's
Privy Kitchen

King's
Privy Kitchen

Pentice

Wardrobe

INNER COURT

(Conduit)

Privy
Stair

MIDDLE COURT

Hall

COURT

Entry

Lodgings

Ante Chapel

Chapel

RIVER THAMES

0   50   100 Ft

0   10   30 M

Royal Tudor Palaces – Plan 3

Plan 3   Greenwich, Kent. Ground-floor plan, c.1547.

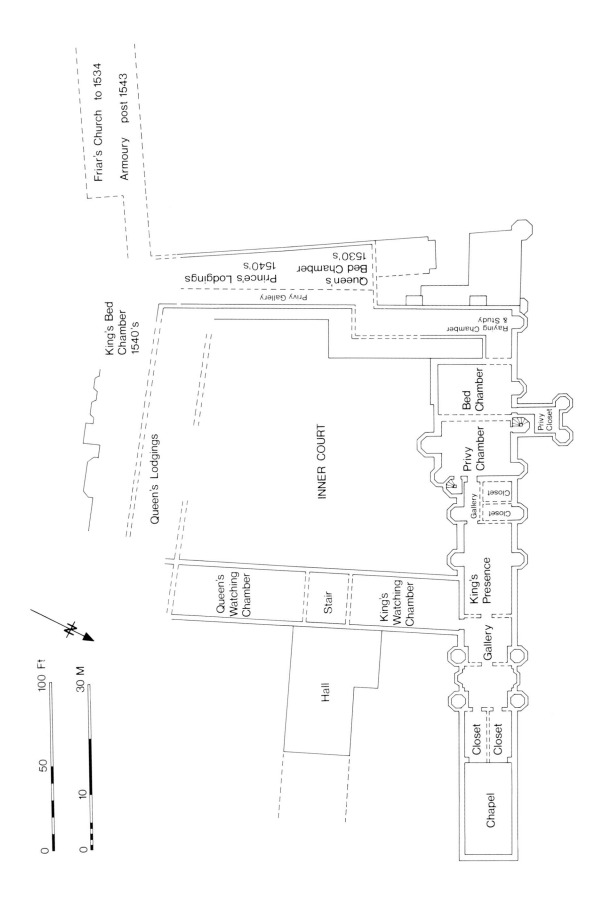

Plan 4   Greenwich, Kent. First-floor plan, c.1547.

Friar's Church to 1534
Armoury post 1543

Queen's Bed Chamber 1530's

Prince's Lodgings 1540's

Privy Gallery

Raying Chamber & Study

King's Bed Chamber 1540's

Queen's Lodgings

INNER COURT

Bed Chamber

Privy Chamber

Privy Closet

Gallery
Closet
Closet

Queen's Watching Chamber

Stair

King's Watching Chamber

King's Presence

Hall

Gallery

Chapel

Closet
Closet

100 Ft
50
0

30 M
10
0

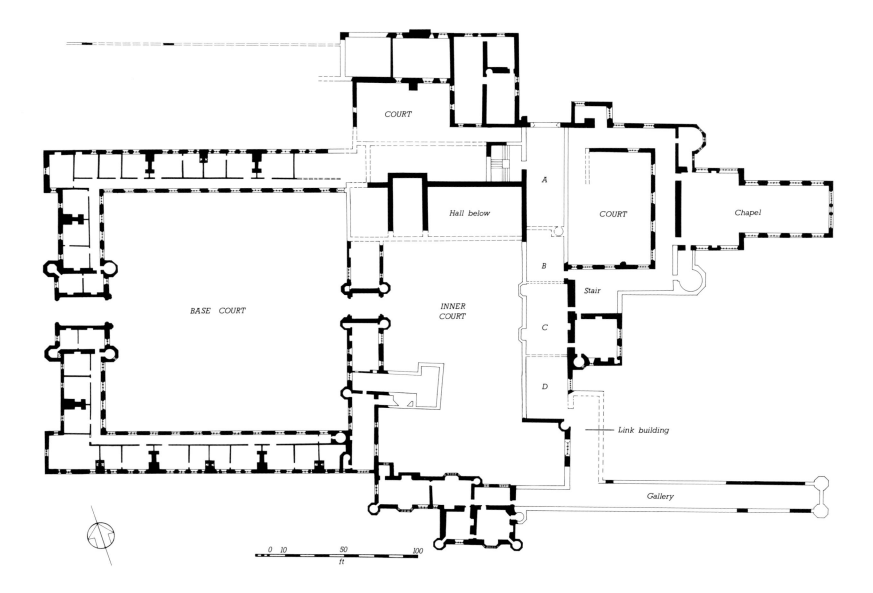

Plan 5 Hampton Court, Surrey. First-floor plan, 1529. A: outer chamber; B: ?presence chamber; C: ?privy chamber; D: ?bed chamber.

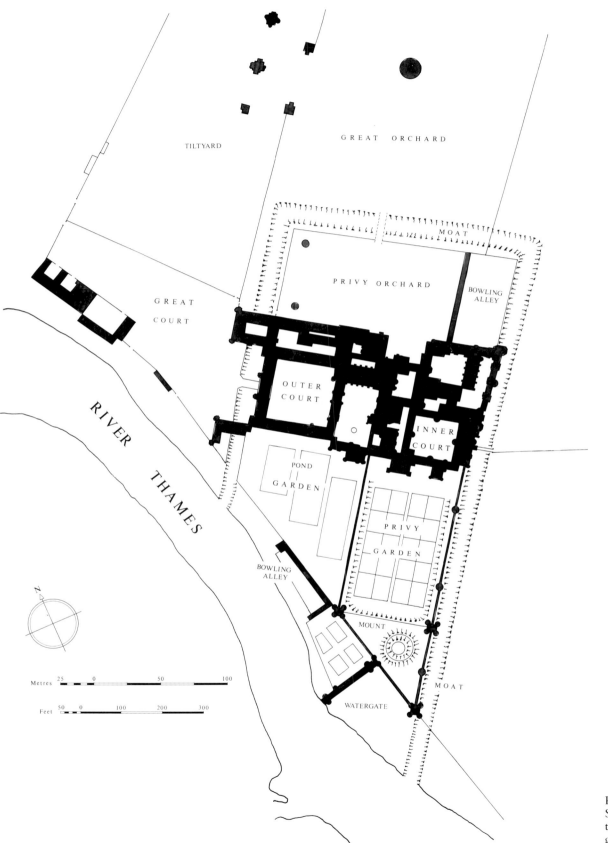

TILTYARD

GREAT ORCHARD

MOAT

GREAT
COURT

PRIVY ORCHARD

BOWLING
ALLEY

OUTER
COURT

INNER
COURT

RIVER THAMES

POND
GARDEN

PRIVY

GARDEN

BOWLING
ALLEY

MOUNT

N

Metres 25 0 50 100

Feet 50 0 100 200 300

WATERGATE

MOAT

Plan 6 Hampton Court,
Surrey. Block plan showing
the layout of the manor and
gardens, 1547.

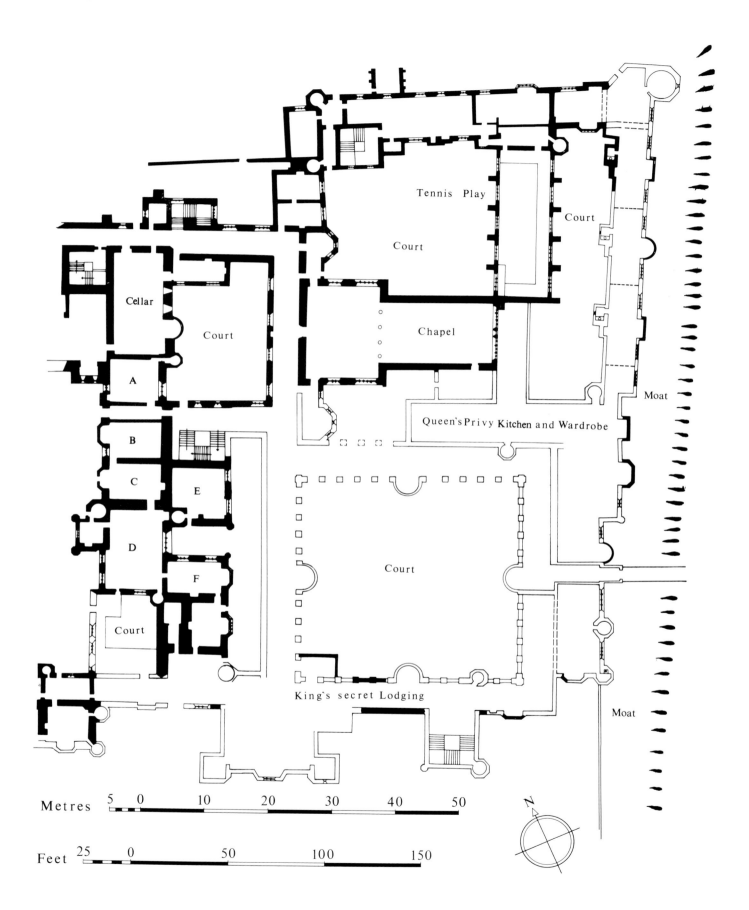

Tennis Play

Court

Court

Cellar

Court

Chapel

A

Queen's Privy Kitchen and Wardrobe

B

C

E

D

Court

F

Court

Court

King's secret Lodging

Moat

Moat

Metres 5 0 10 20 30 40 50

Feet 25 0 50 100 150

N

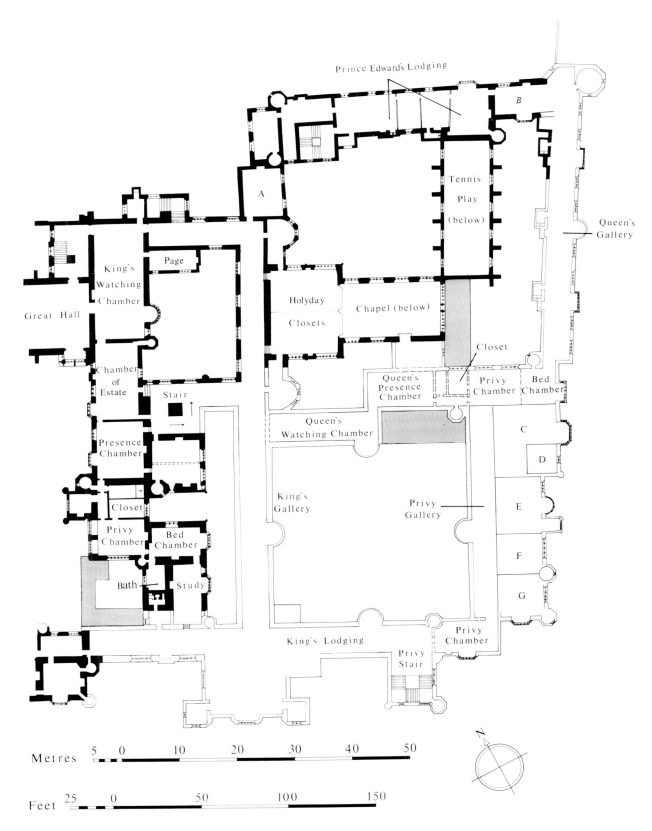

Prince Edward's Lodging

B

A

Tennis
Play
(below)

Queen's
Gallery

King's
Watching
Chamber

Page

Holyday
Closets

Chapel (below)

Great Hall

Closet

Chamber
of
Estate

Stair

Queen's
Presence
Chamber

Privy
Chamber

Bed
Chamber

Presence
Chamber

Queen's
Watching Chamber

C

D

Closet

King's
Gallery

Privy
Gallery

E

Privy
Chamber

Bed
Chamber

F

Bath

Study

G

King's Lodging

Privy
Chamber

Privy
Stair

Metres

5 0 10 20 30 40 50

Feet

25 0 50 100 150

N

Plan 7 (facing page)
Hampton Court, Surrey.
Ground-floor plan, 1547.
A, B, C, D: 1520–26,
Wolsey's reception rooms;
1526–36, Princess Mary's
lodgings; 1536–9, A, a
lodging for courtiers, B and
C, the Queen's wardrobe of
the beds, D, the King's
wardrobe of the robes;
1539–47, courtier lodgings
(A, probably Anthony
Denny, B and C, probably
Thomas Heneage); E:
king's privy kitchen; F:
1529–c.1536, office of the
chamber.

Plan 8 Hampton Court,
Surrey. First-floor plan,
1547. A: council chamber,
1529; B: council chamber,
1540; C: Queen's bed
chamber; D: tower on east
front; E: privy chamber;
F: withdrawing chamber;
G: King's bed chamber.

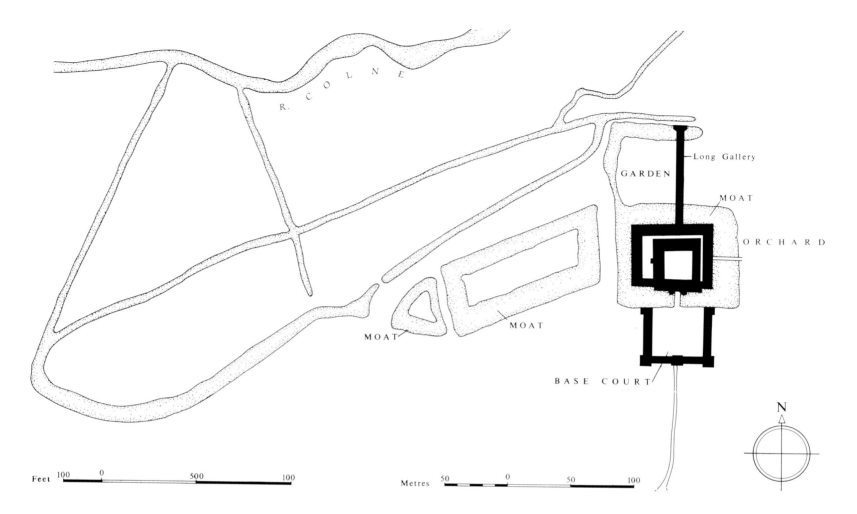

R. COLNE

Long Gallery

GARDEN

MOAT

ORCHARD

MOAT

MOAT

BASE COURT

N

Feet 100   0   500   100

Metres 50   0   50   100

Plan 9   The More, Hertfordshire. Block plan showing the layout of the manor and gardens, 1547.

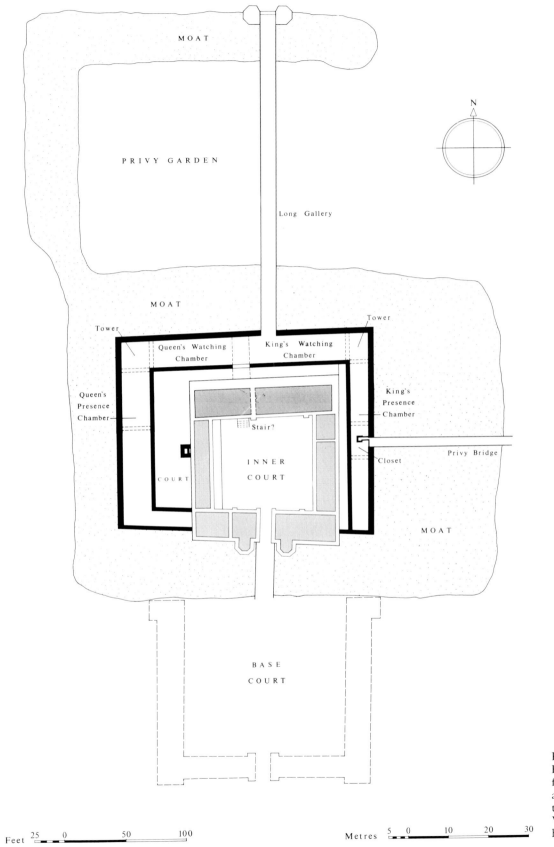

MOAT

PRIVY GARDEN

N

Long Gallery

MOAT

Tower

Tower

Queen's Watching
Chamber

King's Watching
Chamber

Queen's
Presence
Chamber

King's
Presence
Chamber

Stair?

Privy Bridge

Closet

INNER
COURT

COURT

MOAT

BASE
COURT

Feet   25   0   50   100

Metres   5   0   10   20   30

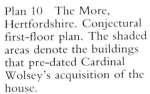

Plan 10   The More,
Hertfordshire. Conjectural
first-floor plan. The shaded
areas denote the buildings
that pre-dated Cardinal
Wolsey's acquisition of the
house.

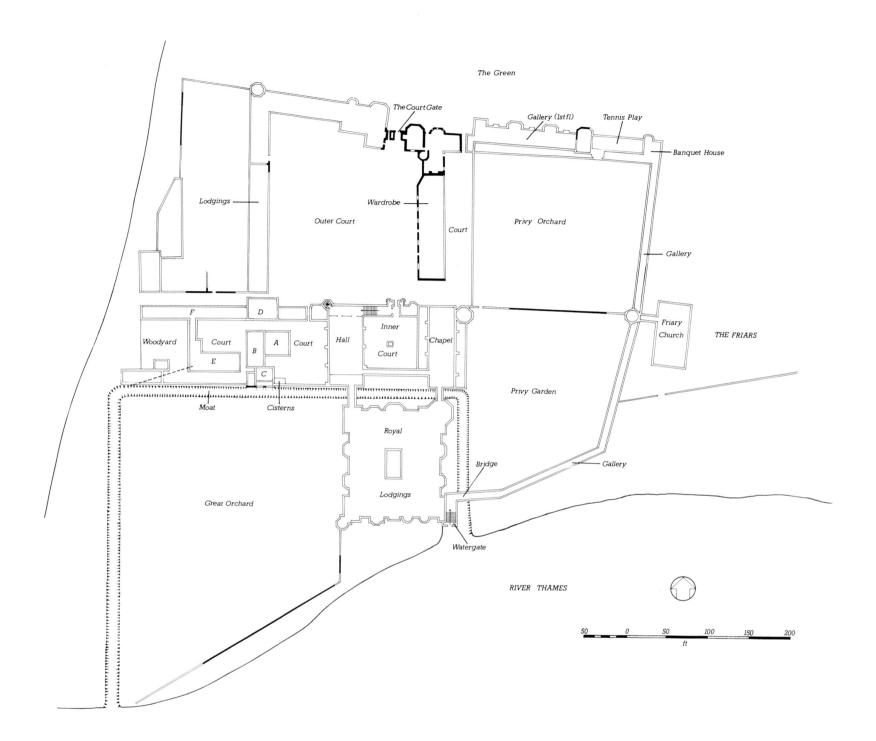

The Green

The Court Gate

Gallery (1st fl)

Tennis Play

Banquet House

Lodgings

Wardrobe

Outer Court

Court

Privy Orchard

Gallery

F

D

Woodyard

Court

A

Court

Hall

Inner

Court

Chapel

Friary
Church

THE FRIARS

B

E

C

Privy Garden

Moat

Cisterns

Royal

Lodgings

Bridge

Gallery

Great Orchard

Watergate

RIVER THAMES

50   0   50   100   150   200
ft

Plan 11   Richmond, Surrey. Layout of the manor and gardens. A: great kitchen; B: larders; C: watergate; D: tower; E: pastry-room; F: poultry-room.

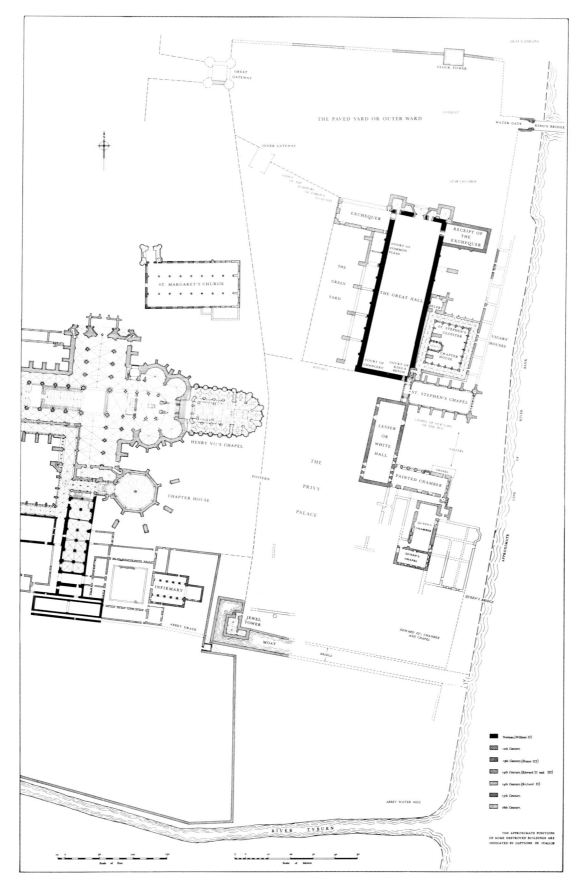

THE PAVED YARD OR OUTER WARD

GREAT GATEWAY

CLOCK TOWER

DEAN'S LODGING

WATER GATE   KING'S BRIDGE

CONDUIT

INNER GATEWAY

STAR CHAMBER

EXCHEQUER

RECEIPT OF THE EXCHEQUER

ST MARGARET'S CHURCH

COURT OF COMMON PLEAS

THE GREEN YARD

THE GREAT HALL

ST STEPHEN'S CLOISTER

CHAPTER HOUSE

VICARS' HOUSES

KITCHEN

COURT OF CHANCERY   COURT OF KING'S BENCH

ST STEPHEN'S CHAPEL

HENRY VII'S CHAPEL

CHAPEL OF OUR LADY OF THE PEW

LESSER OR WHITE HALL

GALLERY

POSTERN

THE

PRIVY

PALACE

CHAPTER HOUSE

PAINTED CHAMBER

CHAPEL

QUEEN'S CHAMBER

QUEEN'S CHAPEL

INFIRMARY

JEWEL TOWER

EDWARD III'S CHAMBER AND CHAPEL

ABBEY DRAIN

MOAT

BRIDGE

QUEEN'S BRIDGE

ABBEY WATER MILL

RIVER TYBURN

Scale of Feet

Scale of Metres

THE APPROXIMATE POSITIONS OF SOME DESTROYED BUILDINGS ARE INDICATED BY CAPTIONS IN ITALICS

Norman (William II)
12th Century.
13th Century (Henry III)
14th Century (Edward II and III)
14th Century (Richard II)
15th Century.
16th Century.

Plan 12   Westminster Palace. General historical plan.

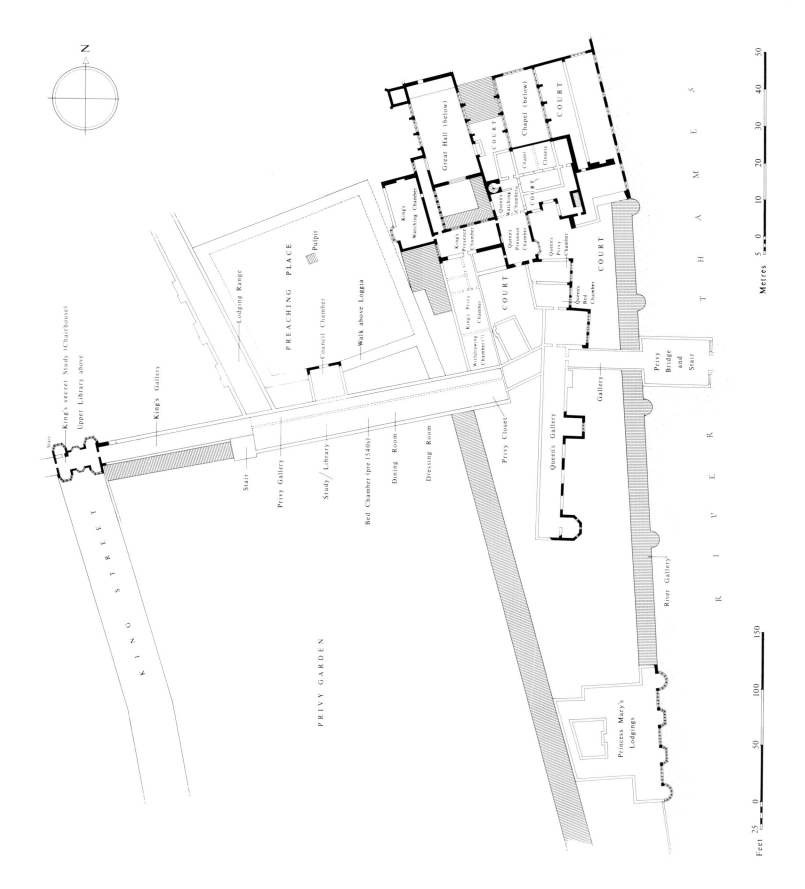

N

KING STREET

King's secret Study (Chairhouse)
Upper Library above

Stair

King's Gallery

Lodging Range

PREACHING PLACE

Pulpit

Council Chamber

Walk above Loggia

PRIVY GARDEN

Stair

Privy Gallery

Study / Library

Bed Chamber (pre 1540s)

Dining Room

Dressing Room

Withdrawing
Chamber(?)

King's
Watching Chamber

Great Hall (below)

King's
Presence
Chamber

King's Privy n
Chamber

COURT

COURT

COURT

Queen's
Watching
Chamber

Queen's
Presence
Chamber

Queen's
Privy
Chamber

Chapel

Chapel (below)

Closets

COURT

Queen's
Bed
Chamber

COURT

Privy Closet

Queen's Gallery

Gallery

Privy
Bridge
and
Stair

River Gallery

Princess Mary's
Lodgings

T H A M E S

R I V E R

Feet   25   0   50   100   150

Metres   5   0   10   20   30   40   50

Plan 13   Whitehall Palace. First-floor plan, c.1547.

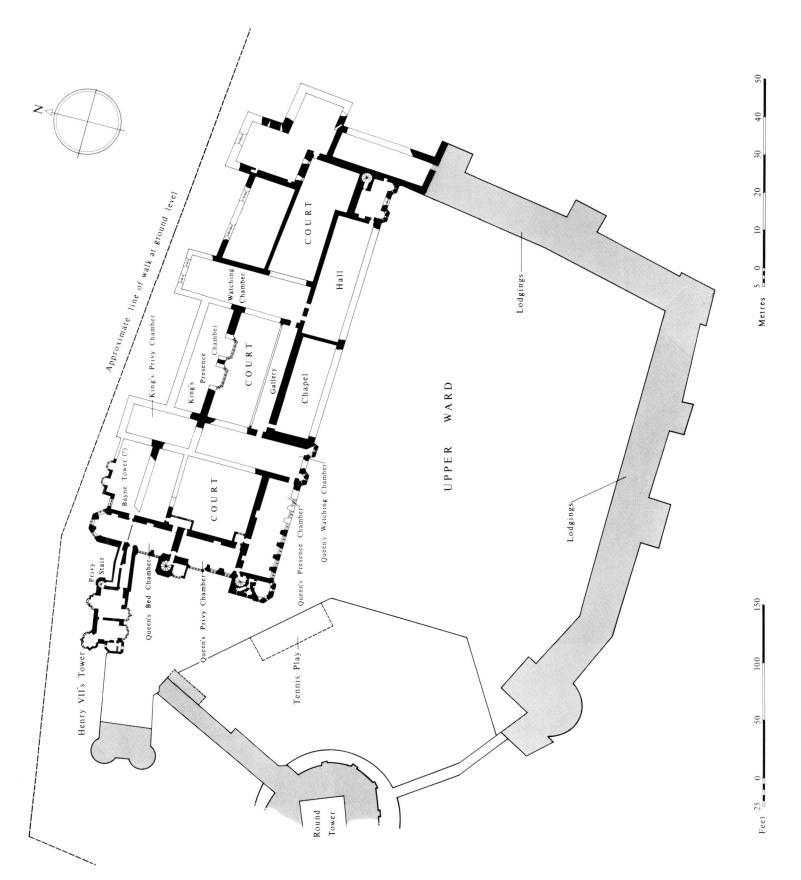

N

Approximate line of walk at ground level

King's Privy Chamber

King's Presence Chamber

Watching Chamber

COURT

Hall

COURT

Gallery

Chapel

UPPER WARD

Lodgings

Lodgings

Bayne Tower (?)

COURT

Queen's Presence Chamber

Queen's Watching Chamber

Privy Stair

Queen's Bed Chamber

Queen's Privy Chamber

Henry VII's Tower

Tennis Play

Round Tower

Feet 25 0 50 100 150

Metres 5 0 10 20 30 40 50

Plan 14 Windsor Castle, Berkshire. First-floor plan, c.1547.

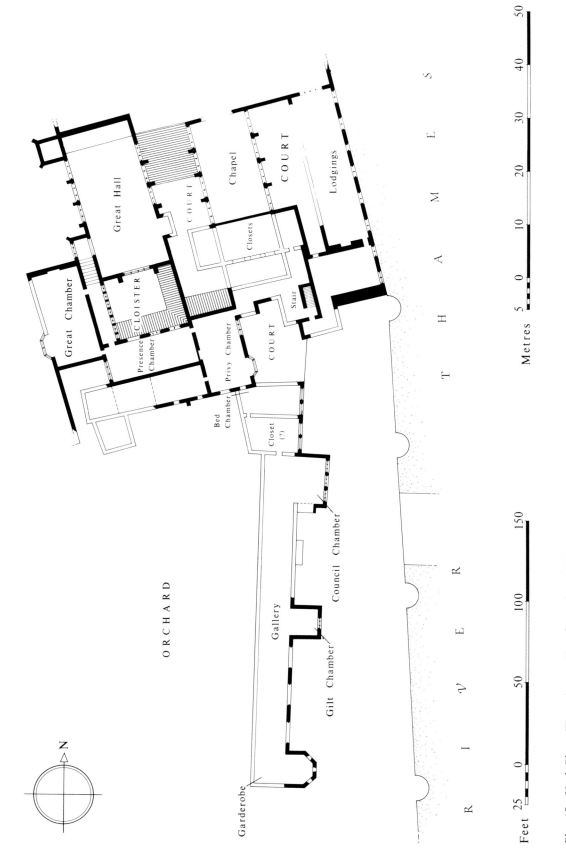

ORCHARD

N

Great Chamber

Great Hall

Presence Chamber

CLOISTER

COURT

Privy Chamber

Closets

Chapel

COURT

Bed Chamber

Stair

Lodgings

Closet (?)

COURT

T H A M E S

Gallery

Council Chamber

Gilt Chamber

Garderobe

R I V E R

Feet 25   0   50   100   150

Metres 5   0   10   20   30   40   50

Plan 15 York Place, Westminster. First-floor plan, 1529.

Notes

Abbreviations

Acts of the Privy Council	*Acts of the Privy Council*, ed. J. R. Dasent et al., n.s., 46 vols (London, 1890–1964)
AJ	*Archaeological Journal*
Arch. Cant.	*Archaeologia Cantiana*
BL	British Museum or British Library
Bod. Lib.	Bodleian Library, Oxford.
Cal. SP. Milan	*Calendar of State Papers and Manuscripts Existing in the Archives and Collections of Milan*, ed. A. B. Hinds (London, 1912)
Cal. SP. Dom.	*Calendar of State Papers Domestic*
Cal. SP. Span.	*Calendar of Letters, Documents and State Papers Relating to Negotiations between England and Spain preserved in the Archives at Simancas and Elsewhere*, ed. G. A. Bergenroth, P. de Goyangos, G. Mattingly and R. Tyler (London, 1862–1965)
Cal. SP. Ven.	*Calendar of State Papers and Manuscripts Relating to English Affairs Existing in the Archives and Collections of Venice and other Libraries of North Italy*, ed. R. L. Brown, G. Cavendish-Bentinck, H. F. Brown and A. B. Hinds, 38 vols (London, 1864–1940)
Cavendish	*The Life and Death of Cardinal Wolsey by George Cavendish*, ed. R. S. Sylvester (Early English Text Society, CCXLIII, 1959)
Chronicle of Calais	J. G. Nicols, ed., 'The Chronicle of Calais', Camden Society, o.s. xxxv (1846)
CPR	*Calendar of Patent Rolls*
EETS	Early English Text Society
EHR	*English Historical Review*
'English Royal Palaces'	S. J. Thurley, 'English Royal Palaces, 1450–1550', unpub. Ph.D. thesis (London, 1991)
Hall	*The Lives of the Kings: The Triumphant Reign of Henry VIII, by Edward Hall*, ed. C. Whibley, 2 vols (London, 1904)
Henry VIII and Hampton Court	S. J. Thurley, 'Henry VIII and the Building of Hampton Court: A Reconstruction of the Tudor Palace', *Architectural History*, 31 (1988), pp. 1–51.
Henry VIII's Kitchens	Simon Thurley, 'The Sixteenth-century Kitchens at Hampton Court', *Journal of the British Archaeological Association*, CXLIII (1990), pp. 1–28
HJ	*Historical Journal*
HO	*A Collection Ordinances and regulations for the Government of the Royal Household* (Society of Antiquaries, 1790)
JBAA	*Journal of the British Archaeological Association*
HKW	H. Colvin, gen. ed., *The History of the King's Works*, vols I–IV (1962–83)
LAMAS	*London and Middlesex Archaeological Society*
L&P	*Letters and Papers Foreign and Domestic of the Reign of Henry VIII*, catalogued, J. S. Brewer, 2nd ed. revised and enlarged, R. H. Brodie, 21 vols (London, 1861–3)
LTR	*London Topographical Record*
NUL	Nottingham University Library
Post-Med. Arch.	*Post-medieval Archaeology*
PRO	Public Record Office
RCHM	Royal Commission on Historical Monuments
RIBA	Royal Institute of British Architects
SAC	*Surrey Archaeological Collections*
Statutes of the Realm	*Statutes of the Realm*, 11 vols (1810–28)
VCH	*Victoria County History*
WAM	Westminster Abbey Muniments

NOTES TO CHAPTER 1

1. C. Given-Wilson, *The Royal Household and the King's Affinity; Service, Politics and Finance in England 1300–1413* (London, 1986), pp. 2–5, 18; *HKW*, I, p. 42.
2. Given-Wilson (1986), p. 15.
3. *HKW*, I, pp. 491–550.
4. *HKW*, I, p. 109.
5. Four new lodges were built in the New Forest in 1358–61 (*HKW*, II, p. 984). Satellite houses around Windsor were acquired — Foliejohn, Hampstead Marshall and Wynchemere — and also East Worldham in Hampshire (*HKW*, I, p. 244).
6. C. Drage, 'Nottingham Castle', *Transactions of the Thoroton Society*, XCIII (1989), pp. 38–41.
7. P. W. Curnow, 'The Wakefield Tower, Tower of London', *Ancient Monuments and their Interpretation: Essays presented to A. J. Taylor*, M. R. Apted, R. Gilyard-Beer and A. D. Saunders, eds (London, 1977), pp. 155–89; *HKW*, II, pp. 710–14.
8. The evidence for the discussion of Henry's work at Westminster can be found in *HKW*, I, pp. 494–504; H. M. Colvin, ed., *Building Accounts of King Henry III* (Oxford, 1971); P. Binski, *The Painted Chamber at Westminster* (Society of Antiquaries of London, 1986); E. W. Brayley and J. Britton, *The History of the Ancient Palace and Late Houses of Parliament at Westminster* (London, 1836), pp. 21–76.
9. S. Thurley and D. Honour, *Royal Domestic Accommodation at the Tower of London in the Thirteenth Century* (forthcoming).
10. *HKW*, I, pp. 504–5.
11. *HKW*, II, pp. 1013–16; *HKW*, II, pp. 1007–9.
12. The sources on which the following are based are: W. H. St John Hope, *Windsor Castle: An Architectural History* (London, 1913), I, pp. 187–98; II, pp. 567–70; *HKW*, II, pp. 870–83.
13. St John Hope (1913), pp. 187–90.
14. Ibid., pp. 365, 553, 556.
15. *HKW*, I, p. 245; II, pp. 997–8.
16. *HKW*, II, pp. 994–1000.
17. This interpretation of the development of Richmond differs substantially from that given in *HKW*, II, pp. 994–1003. 'English Royal Palaces', pp. 74–84, goes a long way towards this but has now been superseded by the work of Mr John Cloake who kindly let me read the draft of his chapter on the Lancastrian palace from his forthcoming book on Richmond. 'English Royal Palaces' understimates the extent of the works of Henry VI who clearly completed the main donjon (*CPR* (1429–36), p. 2; PRO E364/70 rot H; PRO E101/479/7; PRO E101/496/8; PRO E101/503/12; PRO E101/503//15). Therefore Henry VII found a completed fifteenth-century donjon and not as suggested the unfinished remains of one.
18. J. R. Kenyon, 'The gunloops at Raglan Castle, Gwent', J. R. Kenyon and R. Avent, eds, *Castles in Wales and the Marches* (Cardiff, 1987), pp. 161–72; A. Emery, 'The Development of Raglan Castle and Keeps in Medieval England', *AJ*, 132 (1975), pp. 151–86; A. J. Taylor, *Raglan Castle, Gwent*, 14th imp. (HMSO Cardiff, 1979).
19. *HKW*, II, pp. 684–5.

NOTES TO CHAPTER 2

1. J. Fortescue, *The Governance of England*, C. Plummer, ed. (Oxford, 1885), p. 125.
2. G. Kipling, *The Triumph of Honour* (Leiden, 1977), p. 163; idem, 'Henry VII and the Origins of Tudor Patronage', *Patronage in the Renaissance*, G. F. Lytle and S. Orgel, eds (Princeton, 1981), pp. 119, 113.
3. *The Ethics of Aristotle*, J. K. Thompson, trans., rev. edn. (Harmondsworth, 1988), pp. 150–51.
4. Ibid., p. 150.
5. Ibid., p. 151.
6. J. Skelton, *Magnificence*; P. Neuss, ed. (Manchester, 1980), pp. 24–6.
7. J. Skelton, 'Magnificence', P. Happe, ed., *Four Morality Plays* (Harmondsworth, 1987), p. 225.
8. M. Letts, ed., 'The Travels of Leo of Rozmital', *Hakluyt Society*, 2nd ser., CVIII (1957), p. 45.
9. A. H. Thomas and I. D. Thornley, *The Great Chronicle of London* (London, 1938), p. 215. On this subject see also B. Wolffe, *Henry VI* (London, 1981), pp. 10–13, 95–6.
10. Fortescue (1885), pp. 352–3.
11. See also A. D. Fraser Jenkins, 'Cosimo de' Medici's Patronage of Architecture and the Theory of Magnificence', *Journal of the Warburg and Courtauld Institutes*, 33 (1970), pp. 162–70.
12. *Cavendish*, p. 72.
13. *Hall*, p. 26.
14. Ibid., pp. 190–91.
15. Ibid., pp. 192–3.
16. *L&P*, IV (ii), no. 3185.
17. J. S. Brewer, *The Reign of Henry VIII*, 2 vols (London, 1884), II, p. 219.
18. O. Cartellieri, *The Court of Burgundy* (London, 1929); chap. 1 gives a brief history of the rise and fall of the dukes of Burgundy.
19. R. Vaughan, *Charles the Bold* (London, 1973), p. 193.
20. idem, *Valois Burgundy* (London, 1975), p. 184; Cartellieri (1929), pp. 62–3.
21. R. Vaughan (1975), p. 176; idem, *Philip the Bold* (London, 1962), pp. 195–6.
22. For these artistic productions see R. Vaughan, *Philip the Good* (London, 1962), pp. 188–207; idem, *John the Fearless* (London, 1966), pp. 228–36; idem (1973), pp. 169–81; Cartellieri (1929), pp. 207–17; R. Vaughan (1975), pp. 164–76; J. Huizinga, *The Waning of the Middle Ages* (Harmondsworth, 1972), pp. 232–52; F. Deuchler, *Die Burgunderbeute* (Berne, 1963), *passim*.
23. Cartellieri (1929), p. 54.
24. Vaughan, *Philip the Good*, pp. 161–2; A. B. Ferguson, *The Indian Summer of English Chivalry* (Cambridge, 1960), pp. 18–19; Cartellieri (1929), pp. 77–9; J. Huizinga, 'The Political and Military Significance of Chivalric Ideas in the Middle Ages', *Men and Ideas, essays by J. Huizinga*, J. S. Holmes and H. Van Marle, eds (London, 1960), pp. 196–206.
25. Cartellieri (1929), p. 57; Vaughan, *Philip the Good*, pp. 161–2.
26. Vaughan, *Philip the Bold*, pp. 193–5; Cartellieri (1929), p. 164–70; Vaughan (1975), pp. 163–6.
27. Vaughan, *Philip the Good*, p. 137.
28. Cartellieri (1929), chap. 2.
29. Vaughan, *Philip the Good*, p. 136.
30. D. Thompson, *Renaissance Paris* (Berkeley, CA, 1984), p. 30.
31. Vaughan (1975), p. 190.
32. Vaughan, *Philip the Good*, pp. 135–6.
33. M. Letts, *Bruges and its Past* (London, 1926),

pp. 35–8; Vaughan, *Philip the Good*, p. 136.
34. Letts (1926), p. 37.
35. S. Schneebarlg-Perelman, *Les Chasses de Maximilian: Les Enigmas d'un chef d'oeuvre de la tapisser* (Brussels, 1982).
36. P. Santenoy, 'Le Palais des ducs de Bourgogne sur le Codenberg à Bruxelles', *Les Arts et les artistes à la cour de Bruxelles* (Brussels, 1934), pp. 15–38, 123.
37. J. Hollestelle, *De Steenbakkerij in de Nederlanden* (Brussels, 1961), pp. 270–77; B. Marrey and Marie-Jean Dumont, *La Brique à Paris* (Paris, 1991), pp. 18–21.
38. Frans Doperé and William Ubregts, *De donjon in Vlaanderen, architectuur en wooncultuur* (Leuven, 1991) [English summary, pp. 101–2].
39. J. L. Boulton, *The Medieval English Economy* (London, 1980), pp. 287–320. On the transmission of ideas see also Ferguson (1960), pp. 17–21.
40. Vaughan (1973), p. 42.
41. C. Ross, *Edward IV* (London, 1983), p. 95.
42. S. Bentley, ed., 'Tournament between Lord Scales and the Bastard of Burgundy, AD 1467', *Excerpta Historica* (London, 1833), pp. 171–222; S. Anglo, 'Anglo-Burgundian Feats of Arms at Smithfield, June 1467', *Guildhall Miscellany*, II, no. 7 (1965).
43. Vaughan (1973), p. 48.
44. S. Bentley, 'Marriage of the Princess Margaret, Sister of Edward IV, AD 1468', *Excerpta Historica* (1833), pp. 223–39; Cartellieri (1929), pp. 159–61; C. Weightman, *Margaret of York* (Gloucester, 1989), pp. 30–60.
45. N. Davis, ed., *The Paston Letters and Papers*, 2 vols (Oxford, 1971–5) I, pp. 538–9.
46. Vaughan (1973), p. 71.
47. *Britain in Bruges* (exh. cat, Bruges, Stadhuis, 1966), pp. 25–7.
48. Ross (1983), pp. 153–4; idem, *Richard III* (London, 1981), pp. 19–20; C. A. J. Armstrong, *England, France and Burgundy in the Fifteenth Century* (London, 1983), pp. 410–11; W. H. St John Hope, *Windsor Castle: An Architectural History*. (London, 1913), II, pp. 427–9.
49. Ross (1983), p. 220; Armstrong (1983), pp. 414–5.
50. S. McKendrick, 'Edward IV: An English Royal Collector of Netherlandish Tapestry', *Burlington Magazine* (Aug. 1987), pp. 521–4.
51. M. Kekewich, 'Edward IV, William Caxton and Literary Patronage in Yorkist England', *Modern Language Review*, LXVI (1971), p. 482. For a selection of illustrations see E. Hallam, ed., *The Chronicles of the Wars of The Roses* (London, 1988), pp. 230–72.
52. S. Anglo, *Spectacle, Pageantry and Early Tudor Policy* (Oxford, 1969), pp. 98–9.
53. A full discussion of this document is in A. R. Myers, *The Household of Edward IV* (Manchester, 1959), pp. 1–49.
54. *HO*, pp. 19–20.
55. J. Rous, *Historia Regum Angliae*, T. Hearne, ed. (Oxford, 1745), p. 211.
56. J. Skelton 'On the Life and Death of the Noble Prince, King Edward IV', P. Henderson, ed., *The Complete Poems of John Skelton* (London, 1948), p. 2.
57. L. Toulmin-Smith, ed., *Leland's Itinerary*, 5 vols (London, 1964), I, p. 5; *HKW*, II, p. 650; *Northants* (RCHM, 1982) I, p. 45; *Northants* (*VCH*, 1906) II, p. 573.
58. Toulmin-Smith (1964), I, pp. 95–6.
59. This interpretation differs slightly from that in C. Drage, 'Nottingham Castle', *Transactions of the*

Thoroton Society, XCIII (1989), pp. 54–60.

60. 'English Royal Palaces', pp. 34–5, Drage (1989) p. 59.

61. *HKW*, I, pp. 534–7; ibid., II, pp. 912, 915.

62. St. John Hope (1913), pp. 238–9.

63. Ibid., p. 240.

64. W. Darrell, *The History of Dover Castle* (London, 1786), pp. 37, 26, 36.

65. *HKW*, I, pp. 536–7.

66. See references listed in *HKW*, II, p. 936, n. 7. Also PRO E101/496/21 and E101/497/1 ff. 1–3. Literature on the hall is listed in *HKW*, II, p. 930, n. 3; p. 936, n. 4. For the archaeology see H. Woods, 'Excavations at Eltham Palace 1975–9', *LAMAS*, 33 (1982), pp. 214–66.

67. For Edward's visits to Eltham see R. Brook, *The Story of Eltham Palace* (London, 1960), pp. 30–32.

68. *HKW*, II, p. 931.

69. Woods (1982), pp. 220–26.

70. *HKW*, II, p. 936.

71. 'English Royal Palaces', pp. 40–41.

72. Woods (1982), pp. 218–26.

73. *Henry VIII's Kitchens*, p. 5.

74. M. Wood, *The English Medieval House* (London, 1981), pp. 99–121.

75. D. Austin, 'Barnard Castle, Co. Durham: First Interim Report', *JBAA*, CXXXII (1979), pp. 50–72; 'Second Interim Report', ibid., CXXXIII (1980); 'Barnard Castle, Co. Durham', *Château Gaillard*, ix–x (1982), pp. 293–300.

76. P. Hayes and L. Butler, *Sandal Castle Excavations 1964–1973* (Wakefield Historical Publications, 1983); P. Horrox and P. W. Hammond, *British Library Harleian Manuscript 433*, 4 vols (Upminster, 1979–83), I, p. xxviii.

77. T. Hearne, *Joannis Rossi Antiquarii Warwicensis Historia Regum Angliae* (Oxford, 1745), p. 215.

78. Toulmin Smith (1964), p. 40; *Warwickshire*, (*VCH*, 1969), p. 454; P. Curnow, *Warwick Castle* (1971), MS with Society of Antiquaries, London; F. W. Dobson, 'Nottingham Castle, Recent Explorations and Some Historical Notes', *Transactions of the Thoroton Society*, XIII (1909), pp. 143–59; RIBA Smythson Collection I/21; *Architectural History*, V (1962), p. 85.

79. P. Tudor-Craig was the first to ascribe the Spy Tower and lodgings to Richard III in idem, *Richard III* (exh. cat., London, National Portrait Gallery, 1973), p. 71.

80. P. A. Faulkner, 'Sudeley Castle', *AJ*, 122 (1965), pp. 189–90. But see the doubts cast on this in A. Emery, 'Ralph, Lord Cromwell's Manor at Wingfield Castle . . .', *AJ*, 142 (1985), pp. 334–5; Emery suggests that the state rooms were Richard's but the donjon was earlier.

81. D. Verey, *Gloucestershire and the Forest of Dean, The Buildings of England* (Harmondsworth, 1979), pp. 438–9; M. Thompson, *The Decline of the Castle* (Cambridge, 1988), p. 86. A building account is in Horrox and Hammond (1979–83), II, p. 227.

NOTES TO CHAPTER 3

1. R. A. Griffiths and R. S. Thomas, *The Making of the Tudor Dynasty* (London, 1985), pp. 47–8, 58–60.

2. ibid., pp. 69–73.

3. Michael Jones, Gwyn I. Meirion-Jones, Frédéric Guibal and Jon R. Pilcher, 'The Seigneurial Domestic Buildings of Brittany: A Provisional Assessment', *Antiquaries Journal*, LXIX (1989), pp. 73–99; M. Jones, 'The Defence of Medieval Brittany', *AJ*, 138 (1981), p. 190; A. Mussat, 'Le Château de Vitre et l'architecture des châteaux bretons du XIVe au XVI siècle', *Bulletin Monumental*, 133 (1975), pp. 156–64; Michael Jones and Gwyn I. Meirion-Jones, *Wonderful Châteaux in Brittany* (Rennes, 1991).

4. Griffiths and Thomas (1985), pp. 75–131; A. V. Antonovics, 'Henry VII, King of England by the Grace of Charles VIII of France', *Kings and Nobles in the Later Middle Ages: A Tribute to Charles Ross* R. A. Griffiths and J. Sherborne, eds (Gloucester, 1986), pp. 169–84; S. B. Chrimes, *Henry VII* (London, 1987), pp. 29–39 and app. B.B.

5. C. L. Salch, *Dictionnaire des châteaux et des fortifications du moyen age en France* (Strasbourg, 1979), pp. 443–4; Jones (1981), p. 190; Mussat (1975), p. 154.

6. Compare with Warwick Castle (fig. 30).

7. Salch (1979), pp. 833–4; Mussat (1975), p. 155.

8. L. Hautecoeur, *Histoire du Louvre* (Paris, 1928), pp. 7–11; M. M. Maurice Berry and Michel Fleury, eds, *L'Enceinte et le Louvre de Philippe Auguste* (Paris, 1990), *passim*; M. Whiteley, 'La Grande Vis; Its Development in France from the Mid-fourteenth to the Mid-fifteenth Centuries', A. Chastel and J. Guillaume, eds, *L'Escalier dans l'architecture de la Renaissance* (Tours, 1985), pp. 15–19.

9. W. Anderson, *Castles of Europe* (London, 1970), pp. 192–3; R. Allen Brown, *English Castles* (London, 1954), p. 152; M. W. Thompson, *The Decline of the Castle* (Cambridge, 1987), pp. 23–30; Jones, et al. (1989), pp. 82, 87–90.

10. Chrimes (1987), p. 119.

11. What appears here is a condensed version of that in 'English Royal Palaces', pp. 74–84. There, as here, full acknowledgement to the work of Mr John Cloake is given.

12. A. H. Thomas and I. D. Thornley, eds, *The Great Chronicle of London* (London, 1938), p. 286.

13. Ibid., p. 295; PRO E101/415/3 f. 56v.

14. *HKW*, III, p. 195; PRO E36/214 ff. 39, 46v, 54, 152v; BL Add. MS. 59899 f. 68.

15. G, Kipling, ed., *The Receyt of the Ladie Kateryne*, EETS, (1990), pp. 71–3.

16. *SAC*, V (1871), p. 78.

17. NUL MS. Ne.02 f. 216v; *SAC*, V (1871), p. 78.

18. *SAC*, V (1871), p. 78; NUL, MS. Ne.02 f. 216v.

19. Kipling (1990), p. 73.

20. Whiteley (1984), pp. 15–20.

21. Kipling (1990), p. 73.

22. R. Coope, 'The Long Gallery: Its Origins, Development, Use and Decoration', *Architectural History*, 29 (1986), pp. 42–51; the gallery at the Church of St Cross, Winchester, should be added to the list of examples cited on pp. 44–5.

23. *HKW*, II, p. 725.

24. The first reference is in July 1501: S. Bentley, *Excerpta Historica* (London, 1833), p. 125. Further payments that year were in October and November. The accounts continue in BL Add. MS. 59899 f. 4v and PRO E36/214 f. 21.

25. PRO. E101/474/13 printed in J. Bayley, *The History and Antiquities of the Tower of London* (London, 1921), p. xxvi.

26. 'English Royal Palaces', pp. 68–71.

27. A full account of the construction of Greenwich can be found most conveniently in S. Thurley, 'Greenwich Palace', *Henry VIII, a European Court in England*, D. Starkey, ed. (exh. cat. Greenwich, Royal Maritime Museum, 1991), pp. 20–25; 'English Royal Palaces', pp. 85–90, 138–44, 229–37.

28. Bentley, (1833), p. 116; BL Add. MS. 59899 ff. 4v, 24, 63; BL Add. MS. 59899 ff. 62v, 63, 68, 79.

29. W. Douglas Simpson, 'The Building Accounts of Tattershall Castle 1434–1472', *Lincoln Record Society*, 55 (1960); M. W. Thompson, 'Tattershall Castle', *AJ*, 131 (1974), pp. 317–21; idem, *Tattershall Castle* (National Trust, 1977); W. Douglas Simpson, 'Buckden Palace', *JBAA*, 3rd ser., II (1937), pp. 121–30; *Essex* (RCHM, 1921) II, pp. 69–72; H. D. Barnes and W. Douglas Simpson, 'The Building Accounts of Caister Castle, 1432–1435', *Norfolk Archaeology*, 30 (1952), pp. 178–88.

30. R. Allen Brown, *English Castles* (London, 1976), pp. 39–41; Thompson (1987), pp. 28–9.

31. Frans Doperé and William Ubregts, *De donjon in Vlanderen, architecture en wooncultuur* (Leuven, 1991), pp. 101–2.

32. BL Add. MS. 59899 f. 24.

33. C. L. Kingsford, *A Survey of London by John Stow* (Oxford, 1908), I, pp. 66–7.

34. 'English Royal Palaces', pp. 91–2; P. Marsden, 'Baynards Castle', *Medieval Archaeology*, XVII (1973), pp. 162–3; J. H. MacMichael, 'Baynards Castle and Excavations on its Site', *JBAA*, XLVI (1890), pp. 173–84.

35. M. Girouard, *Life in the English Country House, a Social and Architectural History* (London, 1978), pp. 14–80; D. Starkey, 'The Age of the Household: Politics, Society and The Arts c. 1350–c. 1550', *The Later Middle Ages*, S. Medcalf, ed. (London, 1981), pp. 225–305. See also D. A. L. Morgan, 'The House of Policy: The Political Role of the Late Plantagenet Household, 1422–1485', *The English Court from the Wars of the Roses to the Civil War*, D. Starkey, ed. (London, 1987), pp. 25–70.

36. D. Starkey, 'Representation by Intimacy. A Study in the Symbolism of Monarchy and Court Office in Early Modern England', *Symbols and Sentiments. Cross-cultural Studies in Symbolism*, I. Lewis, ed. (London, 1977), pp. 188–224; Philippe Aries and Georges Duby, eds, *A History of Private Life II: Revelations of the Medieval World* (Harvard, 1988), pp. 397–423.

37. D. Starkey, 'Introduction: Court History in Perspective', Starkey (1987), p. 3.

NOTES TO CHAPTER 4

1. F. J. Furnival, *Description of England*, ed. W. Harrison (London, 1877), pp. 267–8, 270.

2. Kings from the time of Aethelwold had been closely involved in their own building projects (*HKW*, I, p. 13). Of the medieval kings Henry III and Edward III were particularly closely involved and provide the only real comparison with Henry VIII (*HKW*, I, pp. 94, 162–3). In the fifteenth century Henry VI had participated in the designs for Eton and King's (L. F. Salzman, *Building in England*, Oxford, 1967, p. 5, app. B). Henry VII had interfered with the design of the hall roof at Woodstock (*HKW*, IV, p. 350) and specified items for the design of his tomb (A. Higgins, 'On the Work of Florentine Sculptors in England . . .', *AJ*, 51 (1894), p. 138).

3. William Thomas, *The Pilgrim: A Dialogue on the Life and Actions of King Henrie the Eighth*, ed. J. A.

Froude (London, 1861), p. 79.

4. PRO SP1/71 f. 20, (*L&P*, v, no. 1298); *Hall*, i, p. 319; idem, ii, p. 23; *Chronicle of Calais*, p. 86; L. Baldwin-Smith, *Henry VIII: The Mask of Royalty* (London, 1971), p. 218; *HKW*, iv, pp. 375–77; PRO SP1/95 f. 63–63*v* (*L&P*, xix (ii), no. 592); PRO SP1/216 f. 75–75*v* (*L&P*, xxi (i), no. 507); *Chronicle of Calais*, p. 126; *Hall*, ii, p. 313; *HKW*, iv, pp. 748–9.

5. The closet at Greenwich contained 'divers plattes in a case of yellow clothe' and a 'case of tin with a platt'. In the closet next to his bedchamber there were 'two patterns for bridges' and more importantly 'one payer of sissors twoo paire of compas twoo drawing irons and a penne of steele', BL Harl. MS. 1419a ff. 58, 57*v*. In the secret wardrobe at Hampton Court there were 'cases of instruments' and 'xii platts and carts of sondry forts', BL Harl. MS. 1419 ff. 252–4. In the upper library at Whitehall there were 'mappes' PRO E315/160 f. 106.

6. BL Add. MS. 10109 f. 197*v*. Platts were often, but not always, 'drawn at the kings commandement', at Hampton Court for instance in 1536: PRO E36/243 p. 600.

7. *Cal. SP. Ven.*, iii, no. 664; *L&P*, v, no. 1187.

8. *Cal. SP. Span.* (1531–3), pp. 566–7 (*L&P*, v, no. 1633); PRO E36/239 p. 86; NUL MS. Ne03 f. 14*v*.

9. S. Anglo, *Spectacle, Pageantry and Early Tudor Policy* (Oxford, 1969), p. 219; *Henry VIII and Hampton Court*, p. 24.

10. An example at Hampton Court is in PRO E36/237 p. 367.

11. PRO E351/3322; PRO E36/251 p. 174.

12. An example is at Whitehall in the 1540s, Bod. Lib. MS. Eng. Hist. b192/1 f. 32*v*.

13. ibid., f. 75. At Whitehall there seems to have been a fairly major collapse in the 1540s when a surgeon in Charing Cross was paid for 'curing and healyng of sondrye artificers and labourers whiche were hurte in the said workis', Bod. Lib. Vet. E 1b.6.

14. For details of these see *HKW*, iv, pp. 147–8, 344, 282–3, 74–5; *HKW*, iii, pp. 261–2.

15. The account given here is a summary of that in 'English Royal Palaces', pp. 104–21.

16. M. B. Honeybourne, 'The Fleet and its Neighbourhood in Early and Medieval Times', *LTR* xix (1947), pp. 13–87; *L&P*, i (i), no. 357 (43); BL Cott. MS. Claudius E VI f. 52.

17. S. Thurley, 'The Domestic Building Works of Cardinal Wolsey', *Cardinal Wolsey: Church, State and Art*, eds S. Gunn and P. Lindley (Cambridge, 1990) p. 83.

18. PRO E36/236, p. 92; PRO E36/236 pp. 108, 166*v*.

19. A. F. Pollard, *Wolsey* (London, 1929), pp. 306–8, 307n.; *HKW*, iii, p. 189; Salzman (1967), app. A, pp. 411–12; PRO E36/236 f. 71; E. G. O'Donoghue, *Bridewell Hospital* (London, 1923), p. 41; PRO E101/517/23; PRO E36/216 p. 124*v*; PRO SP1/29 p. 129 (*L&P*, iii (ii), no. 3678); PRO SP1/26 f. 237*v*.

20. 'English Royal Palaces', pp. 104–19.

21. Bod. Lib. Rawl. MS. D 777 ff. 38*v*, 40, 48*v*; 'Biographical Memoir of Henry Fitzroy, Duke of Richmond and Somerset', *Camden Miscellany*, iii (1855), p. lxxx.

22. Thurley (1990), pp. 87–91; S. Thurley, et al., *Hampton Court 1100–1530*, English Heritage Archaeological Monograph (forthcoming).

23. See the 1782 survey of the castle in BM Stowe.

24. See the 1586 survey in PRO LR2/115 f. 34, 40*v*.

25. See the inventory PRO Prob 2/199; Maurice Howard kindly provided me with a transcript of this.

26. Bod. Lib. Rawl. MS. D 777 f. 40.

27. Thurley (1990), pp. 93–4.

28. For a fuller version of this section see 'English Royal Palaces', pp. 122–5.

29. See fig. 61 and *HKW*, iv, p. 174, n. 6. See also in National Monuments Record under New Hall.

30. *CPR* (1485–1494), p. 367.

31. PRO E36/215 f. 212*v*, 214; PRO E36/215 f. 215*v*.

32. PRO E36/235 p. 738.

33. H. Ellis, ed., *Original Letters*, 3rd. ser., 4 vols (London, 1846) i, p. 186.

34. *HKW*, iii, pp. 213–4.

35. He was paid for 'his counsell in devisynge the seide tombe' and for supervising the workmen who included Torrigiano and Meynnart Wewick: R. Forsyth Scott, 'On the Contracts for the Tomb of the Lady Margaret Beaufort', *Archaeologia*, lxvi (1914–15), pp. 370–72.

36. PRO E36/216 f. 132. We also learn of the hall, parlour and closet in a furnishing account (PRO E101/622/31) and in an Elizabethan survey 'the great chamber and the halpace at eyther ende lyeth upon shores' (PRO SP12/4 no. 57).

37. A fuller account of this section can be found in 'English Royal Palaces', pp. 126–31.

38. PRO E101/497/1.

39. PRO E101/497/1 p. 4.

40. *Cal. SP. Ven.*, iii, no. 219.

41. Bod. Lib. Rawl. MS. D 776 f. 98*v*.

42. PRO E101/497/1 p. 1 (item 4).

43. PRO E101/497/1 p. 2 (items 7 and 8).

44. Ibid.

45. The gallery from the king's lodgings (presumably the same as that from the chapel) was extended to enable it to reach the chapel (PRO E101/497/1 p. 2, item 8) and it is referred to as leading to the old bedchamber, i.e. the bedchamber was at the north end of the chapel gallery.

46. *L&P*, iv (iii), no. 5750 (p. 2559).

47. *Chronicle of Calais*, p. 82. See also S. Anglo, *Spectacle Pageantry and Early Tudor Policy* (Cambridge, 1967), pp. 142–3; PRO SP1/20 f. 77; Clement Urmandson was working for Wolsey in the late 1520s: BL MS. Cott. Titus. B.1. f. 328 (*L&P*, iv (iii), no. 6390).

48. The primary sources used below are *Hall*, i, pp. 189–93; *Chronicle of Calais*, pp. 79–83; Stephen Bamforth and Jean Dupèbe, trans. and eds 'Francisci Francorum Regis et Henrici Anglorum Colloquium', *Renaissance Studies*, 5, (1991), pp. 69–83; *Cal. SP. Ven.*, iii, nos 50, 60, 69, 83, 88, 94. Secondary accounts: 'English Royal Palaces', pp. 132–137; S. Anglo (1967), pp. 142–3; J. G. Russell, *The Field of Cloth of Gold* (London, 1969), pp. 37–47.

49. *Cal. SP. Ven.*, ii, no. 94.

50. Ibid.

51. 'On one side is the King's lodging, on the other the Queen's and between them, two very large banqueting halls', *Cal. SP. Ven.*, ii, no. 88. It was in fact a single hall divided by tapestry 'The entrance hall extending the whole length of the building . . . was disproportioned . . . [and] had been divided into two by tapestry', *Cal. SP. Ven.*, ii, no. 94.

52. *Hall*, p. 191; *Cal. SP. Ven.*, ii, no. 60, p. 41; *Rutland Papers, Camden Society*, o.s. xxi (1842), pp. 39–40.

53. The only link with Wolsey found so far is that the

chapel was remodelled in 1519 (*L&P*, ii (iii), no. 483) and prominent amongst the decorations were Wolsey's cardinal's arms (Bod. Lib. Rawl. MS. D 777 f. 172*v*).

54. PRO E36/215 ff. 16*v*, 24*v*, 30, 39*v*, 65, 83, 97*v*, 199*v*, 260.

55. PRO E36/215 f. 230.

56. PRO E36/216 ff. 11*v*, 14*v*, 17, 19*v*.

57. *Hall*, i, p. 84–6.

58. PRO E36/215 ff. 112, 267.

59. PRO E36/216 f. 34; *L&P*, iii, no. 483.

60. P. Dixon, *Excavations at Greenwich Palace 1970–71* (Greenwich and Lewisham Archaeological Society, 1972), pp. 16–17.

61. These facts are taken from *HKW*, iv, under the relevant headings.

62. *Henry VIII and Hampton Court*, pp. 13–16 and especially p. 28.

63. *Cal. SP. Span.*, iv (i), pp. 303–4.

64. *Cal. SP. Span.*, iv (ii), p. 154.

65. H. J. M. Green and S. J. Thurley, 'Excavations on the West Side of Whitehall, 1960–2, Part I: From the Building of the Tudor Palace to the Construction of the Modern Offices of State', *LAMAS* (1990), pp. 90–91.

66. E. W. Ives, *Anne Boleyn* (Oxford, 1986), pp. 226–8.

67. Anglo (1967), pp. 13, 49, 282.

68. E. W. Ives (1986), pp. 219–9.

69. The next section is based on 'English Royal Palaces', pp. 167–90, 269–77; *Henry VIII and Hampton Court*; *Henry VIII's Kitchens*; Thurley (1990), pp. 76–102; idem, 'Hampton Court 1100–1530', op. cit.; H. J. M. Green and S. Thurley (1990), pp. 59–130; S. Thurley, et al., 'Excavations on the East Side of Whitehall Palace 1938–1978' (forthcoming).

70. Thurley (1990).

71. PRO OBS1/1419.

72. *Henry VIII and Hampton Court*, pp. 13–16.

73. F. Lesuer, *Le Château de Blois* (Paris, 1970), pp. 119–24; J. Guillaume, 'Comprendre Chambord', *Dossier technique des monuments historiques*, 2 (1983); M. Chatenet, 'Une Demeure royale au milieu du XVIe siècle: La Distribution des espaces au château de Saint Germain-en-Laye', *Revue de L'Art*, 81 (1988), p. 25; idem, *Le Château de Madrid au Bois de Boulogne* (Paris, 1987), pp. 99–105; A. Blunt, *Art and Architecture in France 1500–1700* (Harmondsworth, 1982), p. 51.

74. *HKW*, ii, p. 912, for example; *HKW*, iv, p. 14.

75. *HKW* notes 'the relatively slight importance assumed by the state staircase in the planning of English Palaces' (*HKW*, iv, p. 14). But, as is shown, below the state stair or *grande vis* was a central feature in the plans of all the King's late houses.

76. *Statutes of the Realm*, 28 Henry VIII, c. 12.

77. Gervase Rosser and Simon Thurley, 'Whitehall Palace and King Street, Westminster: The Urban Cost of Princely Magnificence', *LTR*, xxvi (1990), pp. 57–77.

78. S. Thurley, 'Greenwich Palace', *Henry VIII: A European Court in England*, ed. D. S. Starkey, (exh. cat., Greenwich, National Maritime Museum, 1989), pp. 20–25; 'English Royal Palaces', pp. 229–37.

79. 'English Royal Palaces', fig. 123.

80. PRO OBS1/1419.

81. G. H. Cook, ed., *Letters to Cromwell and Others on the Suppression of the Monasteries* (London, 1965), p. 145.

82. Ibid. pp. 145–6.

83. Ibid. p. 199.

84. Ibid. p. 201.
85. Ibid. p. 202.
86. PRO OBS1/1419.
87. PRO E101/459/22. Another monastic house heavily used by Henry VIII but not acquired was Waltham Abbey. It had been visited by Henry VII at least once and Henry VIII at least nineteen times. Why it was not appropriated is unclear, perhaps it was felt that the house of Enfield was close enough. Possibly as it was the last abbey to be dissolved the King's money and enthusiasm had run out while his attention had turned to coastal defences.
88. Cook (1965), p. 242.
89. Henry also used the archiepiscopal palaces of Charing and Otford. In both 1520 and 1522 he travelled to Dover via Otford, Charing, Canterbury and Rochester (*Hall*, I, pp. 187, 245, for example). The King acquired these episcopal manors from Cranmer in addition to the monastic houses; Otford in 1537 and Charing in 1545 (*HKW*, IV, pp. 63, 217).
90. *Cavendish*, p. 45.
91. *Rutland Papers*, Camden Society, o.s. XXI (1842), pp. 81–3; *Chronicle of Calais*, p. 169; 'Wriothesley's Chronicle', I, Camden Society, n.s. XI (1875) pp. 109–10.
92. *L&P*, III (ii), p. 1541; *Hall*, I, p. 181.
93. See pp. 115–18.
94. *HKW*, IV, pp. 123–4.
95. *HKW*, IV, pp. 375–7.
96. *HKW*, IV, pp. 70, 355.
97. PRO E351/3199.
98. 'English Royal Palaces', pp. 246–7.
99. 'English Royal Palaces', pp. 247–57.
100. *Henry VIII and Hampton Court*, pp. 16–21.
101. E.g. Bod. Lib. Rawl. MS. D 784 ff. 28, 30; Bod. Lib. Rawl. MS. D 784 f. 163; Bod. Lib. Rawl. MS. D 783 f. 203.
102. BL MS. Lansdowne Roll 14.
103. *HKW*, IV, pp. 6–7.
104. The comprehensive picture can be found in S. Thurley, et al., 'Excavations on the East Side of Whitehall Palace 1938–1969' (forthcoming).
105. Ibid.
106. *HKW*, IV, p. 180.
107. *Acts of the Privy Council* (1547–50), p. 191.
108. 'Raysyng the blokys in the parke hygher that the kyngs grace may nott only gett upon hys horse easlye but lyght downe upon the same', Bod. Lib. Rawl. MS. 781 f. 34; Bod. Lib. Rawl. MS. D 781 f. 197v; PRO E315/160 f. 133v. The White-hall bed was enlarged in 1543 (PRO E315/160 f. 29v) and the Hampton Court one in 1536 (PRO E36/237 f. 599).
109. Visits were made in 1511, 1518, 1520, 1523, 1529, 1531, 1532, 1534, 1539 and 1543 (PRO OBS1/1419).
110. This was the case in 1518, 1520, 1529 (twice), 1532, 1534 (twice), 1539 (three times) and 1543 (twice) (PRO OBS1/1419).
111. PRO E351/414 printed in J. Dent, *The Quest for Nonsuch* (London, 1962), pp. 281–3.
112. See pp. 73–4.
113. *HO*, p. 160.
114. West Sussex Record Office, PHA 1630, p. 687.
115. An inventory of Whitehall Palace taken in April 1543 has a series of marginal notes to the effect that certain furnishings were taken from Whitehall to Oatlands and Nonsuch in July 1545. These included four cloths of estate, three bedsteads and a quantity of tapestry (PRO E315/160). A further reference to the use of tents can be found in a book of payments made by Nicholas Bristowe in the Loseley Manuscripts (Guildford Muniment Room Loseley MSS 2). Barges were used to transport 'tentes and joyned howses' from London to Hampton Court and Oatlands, thence to Chobham and back to London. Henry visited Chobham on 22–3 August 1546. The tents were probably to accommodate the Court there, another lesser house.
116. A. Cook, 'Oatlands Palace, an Interim Report', *SAC*, lxvi (1969), pp. 1–9; *HKW*, IV, pp. 205–19; 'English Royal Palaces', pp. 298–300.
117. PRO LR2/297.
118. PRO E36/237 p. 925.

NOTES TO CHAPTER 5

1. *Cavendish*, p. 92; PRO SP1/48 p. 181 (*L&P*, IV (ii), no. 4367).
2. PRO SP1/21 f. 42 (*L&P*, III (i), no. 957).
3. PRO SP1/180 f. 73 (*L&P*, XVIII, no. 902).
4. *Hall*, I, p. 221; 1526: PRO SP1/39 p. 75–7 (*L&P*, IV (ii) no. 2407 (2)); 1528: PRO SP1/35 f. 76 and PRO SP1/235 f. 266 (*L&P*, Add. I, no. 589); 1530: BL Lansdowne MS. 1 f. 210 (*L&P*, IV (iii), no. 5965); 1535: PRO SP1/93 p. 237 (*L&P*, VIII, no. 989); 1537: PRO SP1/116 p. 38–9 (*L&P*, XII (ii), no. 430); 1541: BL Add. MS. 9835 f. 2 (*L&P*, XVI, no. 677); and 1541: Historic Manuscripts Commission, 3rd Report (1872), p. 194. An undated list (probably from the 1530s) is in BL Add. MS. 9835 ff. 2–8.
5. *Hall*, I, p. 165.
6. PRO SP1/39 f. 75 (*L&P*, IV (ii), no. 2407).
7. H. Ellis, ed., *Original Letters*, 3rd. ser., 4 vols (London, 1846), I, p. 346.
8. S. Bentley, *Excerpta Historica* (London, 1833), p. 94; PRO SP1/195 f. 178 (*L&P*, IXX, no. 688).
9. *HO*, p. 43.
10. On the political aspects of the progress see: S. Anglo, *Spectacle, Pageantry and Early Tudor Policy*, (Cambridge, 1967); N. Samman, 'The Tudor Court During the Ascendency of Cardinal Wolsey', unpub. Ph.D. thesis (Bangor, 1988).
11. L. M. Cantor and J. Hatherly, 'The Medieval Parks of England', *Geography*, 64 (1979), pp. 78–9; O. Rackham, 'The King's Deer', *Nonsuch in Context*, ed. M. Biddle (Sutton Libraries, forthcoming).
12. W. Lambarde, *Perambulation of Kent*, ed. R. Church (Bath, 1970), p. 473.
13. S. B. Chrimes, *Henry VII* (London, 1987), p. 306.
14. See his chamber accounts: PRO E36/214 ff. 136v, 138.
15. *HO*, pp. 158–9.
16. Clearly an excuse but also a real pursuit; *Cavendish*, p. 97.
17. In 1545 raised to an honour (*L&P*, XX (ii), no. 850 (24)) and protected by strict game laws (*L&P*, XX (ii), no. 1129).
18. A. G. W. Murray and Eustace F. Bosanquet, eds, 'Excerpts from the Manuscript of William Dunche', *The Genealogist*, n.s., XXX (1914), pp. 153–4.
19. Rackham (forthcoming).
20. *HKW*, IV, p. 40.
21. 33 Henry VIII, c.37, *Statutes of the Realm*, III, (1817), p. 876; G. S. Thompson, 'Ampthill: Honour, Manor, Park, 1542–1800', *JBAA*, 13 (1950), p. 14.
22. *Cavendish*, p. 69
23. Possibly a reversal of roles, as Edward IV seems to have used Greenwich on hunting trips, see the quotation above.
24. W. Lambarde, *Perambulation of Kent* (London, 1826), p. 473.
25. A. R. Myres, ed., *The Household of Edward IV* (Manchester, 1959), pp. 89, 21; *HO*, pp. 160–61; T. Percy, ed., *The Northumberland Household Book* (London, 1827), pp. 39, 366; K. Mertes, *The English Noble Household, 1250–1600* (Oxford, 1988), p. 15.
26. *Cal. SP. Span.*, IV (i), no. 411, p. 691; *L&P*, XVI, no. 1457; *L&P*, XVI, no. 59; *L&P*, V, no. 308, p. 144; Samman (1988), pp. 56, 29.
27. Rackham (forthcoming); R. J. Knecht, *Francis I* (Cambridge, 1988), pp. 85–6; see also Cavendish's description of a French royal hunt *Cavendish*, pp. 92–3.
28. On this point see also J. S. Brewer, *The Reign of Henry VIII* (London, 1884), II, p. 159.
29. *L&P*, XVI, no. 941.
30. Samman (1988), pp. 51–3.
31. See PRO SP1/195 ff. 167–183v (*L&P*, IXX, no. 688) for example; Samman (1988), p. 61.
32. PRO SP1/17 p. 4 (*L&P*, II (ii), no. 4326 (2)); see also *L&P*, III (ii), no. 3375; for the itinerary of the Duke of Richmond in 1525 see *L&P*, IV (i), no. 1540.
33. *L&P*, III, no. 3375.
34. *L&P*, IV, no. 1577 (12) and (13); PRO SP1/28 pp. 235–40 (*L&P*, III (iii), no, 3375). See also D. Loades, *Mary Tudor* (Oxford, 1989), pp. 28–30, 45, 116–17.
35. BL Add. MS. 9835 f. 23v.
36. G. Kipling, ed., *The Receyt of the Ladie Kateryne*, (EETS, 1990), pp. 68–9; See also *HO*, p. 57.
37. *HO*, p. 198.
38. PRO E36/215 f. 16v.
39. PRO E36/215 f. 199v. These are shown on a plan of 1693, PRO MB 329, and on another of 1728, RIBA Drawings Collection, D 8/3.
40. PRO E36/245 p. 129; *HKW*, IV, p. 142.
41. NUL MS. Ne.02 ff. 141v, 118v.
42. Bod. Lib. Rawl. MS. D 781 f. 1.
43. Bod. Lib. Rawl. MS. D 777 f. 163; Bod. Lib. MS. Film 308 f. 52.
44. Myres (1959), p. 40; A. Woodworth, 'Purveyance for the Royal Household in the Reign of Queen Elizabeth', *American Philosophical Society*, n.s., XXXV, (i) (1945), pp. 3–89; A. Haynes, 'Supplying the Elizabethan Court', *History Today* (Nov. 1978), pp. 729–37.
45. *HO*, p. 65.
46. BL Add. MS. 21116 f. 13v.
47. *HKW*, I, p. 57.
48. BL Add. MS. 10109 f. 187.
49. Bod. Lib. Rawl. MS. D 781 f. 127.
50. Bod. Lib. MS. Eng. Hist. b 192/1 f. 26; Bod. Lib. Rawl. MS. D 781 f. 96v.
51. Bod. Lib MS. Eng. Hist. b. 192/1 f. 3.
52. *L&P*, V, p. 314.
53. PRO OBS1/1419.
54. Bod. Lib. Rawl. MS. D 775 ff. 26–53v.
55. BL Cott. Titus B.1 f. 323v (*L&P*, III (ii), no. 2130).
56. *Cal. SP. Ven.* (1558–80), no. 71.
57. Ellis (1846), II, p. 19.
58. The statistics below are taken from Henry VIII's itinerary in PRO OBS 1/1419.
59. This takes into account the fact that the King made ninety visits to houses that he later acquired.
60. Samman (1988), Table B shows the following figures for the first half of the reign (% of nights

outside royal houses) 1510 and 1511 — 19%; 1515 — 7%; 1519 — 15%; 1521 — 4%; 1522 — 27%; 1525 — 21%; 1526 — 31%; 1529 — 10%.

61. W. Harrison, *Description of England*, ed. F. J. Furnival (London, 1877), p. 270.
62. PRO PROB 2/199.
63. *Henry VIII and Hampton Court*, pp. 1–2.
64. *HO*, p. 160.
65. Early in the reign, before the fire which devastated Westminster Palace, Henry, like his father before him, spent considerable time at Westminster. But after its destruction and before the construction of Bridewell in 1515–22 Henry was forced to use Lambeth Palace, the house of the archbishops of Canterbury. Between 1510 and 1520 Henry paid at least ten visits there staying for over fifty days. In 1514 the Court stayed between 28 January and 3 March (PRO OBS 1/1419). See also D. Gardiner, *The Story of Lambeth Palace* (London, 1930), pp. 74–7. The pattern changed in the 1520s with the building of Bridewell and Newhall. The King spent much time at these two houses before 1530 and they both served to reduce the time the itinerant Court spent out of royal buildings.
66. *HO*, p. 160.
67. *HO*, p. 40.
68. Bod. Lib. MS. Eng. Hist. b.192/1 f. 14*v*.
69. *HO*, p. 41.
70. *HO*, f. 155.
71. *L&P*, xvi, no. 380 (f. 47).
72. *Cavendish*, p. 71.
73. In Henry VIII's inventory taken on his death the contents of the removing Wardrobe are listed (BL Harl. MS. 1419 ff. 394–8).
74. PRO SP1/126 p. 207 (*L&P*, xii (iii), no. 1147).
75. Bod. Lib. Rawl. MS. D 775 f. 31*v*.
76. PRO. E36/239 p. 417; E36/237 p. 529.
77. PRO. E351/3206.
78. BL Harl. MS. 1419.
79. PRO. E36/215 f. 251*v*. In addition, Richard III kept his Privy Wardrobe at the Tower (BL Harl. MS. 433 f. 337).
80. Bod. Lib. Rawl. MS. D 775 f. 55.
81. Bod. Lib. Rawl. MS. D 781 f. 25b.
82. BL Add. MS. 10109 f. 60*v*.; Bod. Lib. Rawl. MS. D 777 f. 194*v*.
83. BL Add. MS 21116 f. 8.
84. Ibid., f. 15.
85. BL Harl. MS. 1419.
86. *L&P*, v, no. 784.
87. Murray and Bosanquet (1914), p. 96; *HO*, pp. 85, 235, 215–16.
88. *The Parish of St Margaret Westminster*, ii, *Survey of London*, xiii, (1930), pp. 38–9.
89. *HO*, p. 164; D. Loades, *Mary Tudor* (Oxford, 1989), p. 348.
90. Princess Mary used the Queen's barge in 1523, PRO SP1/28 pp. 235–40 (*L&P*, iii, no. 3375); (*L&P*, xix, no. 688).
91. *Hall*, i, p. 246.
92. PRO SP46/1 ff. 120–120*v*.
93. Ibid.
94. PRO SP3/9 f. 6 (*L&P*, xiv (i), no. 967); S. Bentley, *Excerpta Historica* (London, 1833), p. 97.
95. Bod. Lib. MS. Eng. Hist. b192/1 ff. 43, 47, 47*v*.
96. W. Lambarde, *A Perambulation of Kent* (London, 1826), p. 473.
97. Bod. Lib. Rawl. MS. D 776 f. 181.
98. Ibid., f. 185.
99. Ibid., p. 193; see also Longleat, Wilts, MS. Misc. xxx f. 17.
100. *Henry VIII and Hampton Court*, p. 17.

101. *L&P*, ii (ii), no. 2896.
102. *Hall*, ii, p. 277.
103. *The Chronicle of Calais*, p. 93.
104. B. Hellyer and H. Hellyer, *The Astronomical Clock, Hampton Court Palace* (London, 1973).
105. C. L. Kingsford, 'Historical Notes on Medieval London Houses', *LTR*, (1916), pp. 59–63. This was also the case during the reign of Henry VII who granted the house to Elizabeth of York (BL Add. MS 59899 f. 26*v*).
106. *L&P*, i (i), g. 94 (35).
107. *Hall*, i, p. 179.
108. PRO SP1/83 f. 174 (*L&P*, vii, no. 552); *L&P*, xiii (ii), p. 174; *L&P*, v, g. 1139 (32); PRO E36/241 pp. 597, 580; *L&P*, x, no. 243 (24).
109. *L&P*, xii (ii), no. 975; *L&P*, xv, nos 899, 901; *L&P*, xvi, g. 503 (25), p. 241; *L&P*, xix (i), g. 141 (65), p. 83; no. 1036, p. 644.
110. *Henry VIII and Hampton Court*, pp. 13, 28, 41.
111. PRO SP1/21 pp. 45–8 (*L&P*, iii (i), no. 970); *L&P*, iii (ii) no. 2585; PRO SP1/28 pp. 235–40 (*L&P*, iii (ii), no. 3375); *Cal. SP. Ven.*, iii, p. 287; PRO SP1/79 f. 121 (*L&P*, vi, no. 1186); Loades (1989), pp. 36–75.
112. *L&P*, vi, no. 1296. For Mary's revenge see: *CPR* (1548–9), p. 21. See also *Cal. SP. Dom.* (1547–80), p. 5.; Loades (1989), p. xi.
113. Bod. Lib. Rawl. MS. D 776 f. 229; NUL MS. Ne.01 f. 301; *L&P*, x, no. 1137; Loades (1989), pp. 99–107. BL Cott. MS. Vesp. cxiv, ff. 104–5.
114. Bod. Lib. Rawl. MS. D 780 f. 19.
115. BL Add. MS. 10109 ff. 192, 117, 211, 201. Her rooms at Otford are mentioned in the 1547 survey printed in C. Hesketh, 'The Manor House and Great Park of the Archbishops of Canterbury at Otford', *Arch. Cant.*, 31 (1915), p. 17; PRO E101/504/2 f. 76*v*.
116. Bod. Lib. MS. Eng. Hist. b192/1 f. 49.
117. Many references, e.g.: PRO E36/239 p. 564, E36/244 p. 274; Bod. Lib. Rawl. MS. D 780 f. 23*v*.
118. J. G. Nichols, *Literary Remains of King Edward the Sixth* (Roxburghe Club, 1857) pp. xxiv–xxxvii.
119. *Henry VIII and Hampton Court*, pp. 30–31.
120. It should be noted that there is no mention of lodgings for Edward in the accounts of the 1540s relating to Whitehall. This can be explained by the fact that he had his own house at St James's.
121. BL Add. MS 10109 f. 177; *L&P*, xxi (ii) no. 571; Bod. Lib. Rawl. MS. D 781 f. 188; *L&P*, xxi, nos 50, 1206; O. Millar, *The Tudor, Stuart and Early Georgian Pictures in the Collection of Her Majesty the Queen* (London, 1963), pp. 64–5.
122. BL Harl. MS. 1419B f. 383.
123. *Cal. SP. Span.*, xi, p. 214.
124. Parts of the palace were still called the 'prince's lodging' in 1588–9 (PRO E351/3225).
125. *HKW*, iv, p. 246; R. Strong, *Henry Prince of Wales and England's Lost Renaissance* (London, 1986), pp. 64–35, 210–12.
126. 22 Hen. VIII c.17, *Statutes of the Realm*, iii, pp. 338–44; 27 Hen. VIII c.51; ibid. iii p. 621.
127. BL Add. MS. 6113 f. 62; PRO SP1/35 ff. 209–18; *Northants*, ii, (*VCH*, 1906) p. 552; *St-Martin-in-the-Fields*, ii, *Survey of London*, xviii, p. 86; C. L. Kingsford, 'Historical Notes on Medieval London Houses', *LTR*, x (1916), p. 62; 'Wriothesley's Chronicle', i, *Camden Society*, n.s., xi (1875), p. 53.
128. Bod. Lib. Rawl. MS. D 781 ff. 188, 191, 203, 193.
129. *L&P*, xix (i), no. 1036, p. 644; B. White, *Mary Tudor* (London, 1935), p. 116; *VCH Middlesex*, (1911) ii, pp. 394–5; *L&P*, xix (ii), nos 726, 794;

F. Madden, *The Privy Purse Expenses of the Princess Mary* (London, 1831), pp. 134–6.
130. *HKW*, i, pp. 97–8, 244.
131. For example, Robert Manning, Keeper of Hampton Court was involved with the maintenance of Oatlands and Hampton Court (PRO E36/244 p. 274; E36/235 p. 391). At Woking the Keeper, Anthony Browne, likewise appears in the accounts (Bod. Lib. Rawl. MS. D 776 f. 182*v*).
132. BL Add. MS. 21116 f. 13*v*.
133. R. Horrox and P. W. Hammond, *BM. Harl. MS. 433* (Upminster, 1982), iii, p. 253.
134. There is a list of keepers at Whitehall Palace in 1541 and the keepers of the privy garden, great garden, pheasants, palace gate, fish ponds and park gate are listed. These men were, of course, relatively humble (Bod. Lib. MS. Eng. Hist. b. 192/1 f. 3).
135. 'English Royal Palaces', pp. 457–9; M. Howard, *The Early Tudor Country House* (London, 1987), pp. 29–30.
136. PRO E36/252 p. 414.
137. H. J. M. Green and S. J. Thurley, 'Excavations on the West Side of Whitehall, 1960–61', *LAMAS* (1990), p. 78.
138. PRO E36/237 p. 522.
139. Bod. Lib. Rawl. MS. D 777 f. 216.
140. NUL MS. Ne.02 ff. 312–16; PRO E36/235 p. 343.
141. *HO*, p. 60.
142. BL Add. MS. 10109 f. 119.
143. PRO E36/235, p. 77.
144. PRO E36/239 p. 28.
145. BL Add. MS. 10109 f. 96; *L&P*, xiii (ii), p. 528; *L&P*, v, p. 759.
146. Bod. Lib. MS. Film 308 f. 87.
147. L. B. Smith, *A Tudor Tragedy* (London, 1961), p. 183.
148. PRO E101/504/2 f. 62.
149. Bod. Lib. MS. Eng. Hist. b.192/1.
150. Engraved in A. Pugin, *Examples of Gothic Architecture* (London, 1850), i, p. 25; C. Blair, 'The Most Superb of all Royal Locks', *Apollo* (1966), pp. 493–4.
151. Bod. Lib. Rawl. MS. D 776 f. 29*v*; D 780 f. 11*v*.
152. NUL MS. Ne.03 f. 127.

NOTES TO CHAPTER 6

1. J. R. Hale, *Renaissance Europe* (London, 1971), pp. 58–9.
2. *Hall*, i, pp. 59–77, 83–95, 113–18; M. Cruickshank, *Henry VIII and the Invasion of France* (London, 1990), pp. 1–40.
3. A list of 'those who went to war with the king' can be found in PRO SP1/2 f. 111, (*L&P*, i (i) no. 1176); *Hall*, pp. 92, 117; J. J. Scarisbrick, *Henry VIII* (Harmondsworth, 1971), pp. 59–60; Cruickshank (1990), pp. 126–8.
4. P. Vergil, 'Anglica Historica', ed. D. Hay, *Camden Society*, o.s. xxix (1844), p. 6.
5. They are listed in *L&P*, i (i) no. 2227.
6. *Hall*, i, p. 175.
7. See a full discussion of this in D. Starkey, 'Intimacy and Innovation: The Rise of the Privy Chamber, 1485–1547', *The English Court*, D. Starkey, ed. (London, 1987), pp. 84–6; idem, *The Reign of Henry VIII* (London, 1985), pp. 13, 76–7; J. S. Brewer, *The Reign of Henry VIII*, 2 vols (London, 1884), ii, pp. 433–4.
8. C. H. Clough, 'Relations between England and

the Court of Urbino 1474–1508', *Studies in the Renaissance*, XIV (1967), pp. 202–18; R. Jones and N. Penny, *Raphael* (New Haven and London, 1983), pp. 6–8, n. 29.

9. *Hall*, I, p. 40.

10. S. Anglo, *Spectacle, Pageantry, and Early Tudor Policy* (Oxford, 1969), pp. 98–113.

11. Ibid., p. 113, attributes the change in type of tournament to 'a simple change in fashion'. Here, I hope a more convincing reason for the change is offered.

12. *Cal. SP. Milan*, I, no. 669; *L&P*, I (ii) no. 2391.

13. R. Strong, *Splendour at Court, Renaissance Spectacle and Illusion* (London, 1973), pp. 37–76.

14. The first mention of the word 'antique' that I have found so far is in January 1516 (*L&P*, II (ii) p. 1495).

15. J. Schulz, 'Pinturicchio and the Revival of the Antique', *Journal of the Warburg and Courtauld Institutes* (1962), pp. 46–9; A. Schmarsow, 'Das Aufkommen der Grottesken in der Dekoration der Renaissance', *Jahrbuch der Königlich-preussischen Kunstsammlungen*, 2 (1881), pp. 131–43.

16. Schulz (1962), p. 48 and n. 40.

17. See Jones and Penny (1983), pp. 190–97 for an introduction and references.

18. An additional useful introduction is P. Ward-Jackson, *Mainstreams and Tributaries in European Ornament from 1500 to 1750* (Victoria and Albert Museum, 1969), pp. 2–15, 44.

19. Janet S. Byrne, *Renaissance Ornament Prints and Drawings* (exh. cat., New York, Metropolitan Museum of Art, 1981), p. 50.

20. Ibid., pp. 72–5; W. Rieder, 'French Sixteenth-century *Boiserie* and Furniture', *Apollo*, CVI/189 (1977), pp. 350–51.

21. For the whole of this subject in France see W. Prinz and R. G. Kecks, *Das französische Schloss der Renaissance* (Berlin, 1985), pp. 297–330.

22. Elizabeth Armstrong, 'English Purchases of Printed Books from the Continent, 1465–1526', *EHR* (1979), pp. 268–90.

23. A. F. Johnson, *The First Century of Printing at Basle* (London, 1926), pp. 18–19; J. Rowlands, *Holbein, The Paintings of Hans Holbein the Younger* (Oxford, 1985), pp. 18–19, 60.

24. I Richard III, *Statutes of the Realm*, II, p. 489; BL Add. MS. 59899, f. 79v.

25. H. Vogtherr, *Ein frembds und wunderbars Kunst-buechlin allen Molern Bildschnitzern Goldschmiden Steinmetzen Schreinern Platnern Waffen un Messerschmiden hochnutzlich zu gebrauchen der gleich vor nie keins gesehen oder inn den Truk kommen ist* (Strasburg, 1538).

26. BL Harl. MS. 1419A f. 157.

27. Ibid. f. 56v.

28. BL Add. MS. 34809; H. M. Nixon, *Five Centuries of English Bookbinding* (London, 1978), p. 32. I am grateful to Dr James Carley for his comments.

29. *L&P*, XVI, no. 941.

30. A transcription of the will is in E. Auerbach, 'Vincent Volpe: King's Painter', *Burlington Magazine*, XCII (1950), p. 226.

31. BL Cott. MS. Calig. D. vii f. 218 (*Chronicle of Calais*, pp. 84–5).

32. A. Young, *Tudor and Jacobean Tournaments* (London, 1987), p. 46; R. J. Mitchell, *John Tiptoft* (London, 1938); O. Pächt and J. J. Alexander, *Illuminated Manuscripts in the Bodleian Library, Oxford, Italian School* (Oxford, 1970), p. 62.

33. T. Campbell, 'Of Silk and Gold', *Country Life*, CLXXXV, no. 41, pp. 92–5; S. Anglo (1992), pp. 32–3; W. G. Thompson, *A History of Tapestry*

from the Earliest Times until the Present Day (3rd edition, London, 1973), pp. 119–124, 152–60.

34. A. C. Fox Davis, *A Complete Guide to Heraldry* (London, 1950), pp. 452–76; H. Stanford London, *Royal Beasts* (The Heraldry Society, 1956), pp. 3–6; A. Payne, 'Medieval Heraldry', *The Age of Chivalry*, (exh. cat., London, Royal Academy of Arts, 1987), pp. 55–9; J. Cherry, 'Heraldry as Decoration in the Thirteenth Century', M. Ormrod ed., *England in the Thirteenth Century*, Proceedings of the 1989 Harlarton Symposium (Stamford, 1991), pp. 123–34.

35. A. R. Wagner, *Heralds and Heraldry in the Middle Ages* (Oxford, 1939), pp. 9–10.

36. 33 Henry VIII cap. 14, *Statutes of the Realm*, III, p. 850; also, Anglo (1992), pp. 28–39.

37. J. G. Nichols, 'Notices of the contemporaries and successors of Holbein', *Archaeologia*, XXXIX, p. 24.

38. BL Cott. MS. Calig. D. vii, f. 202 (*Chronicle of Calais*, p. 89).

39. College of Arms MS. Vincent 152, ff. 93–108; L. Campbell and F. Steer, *A Catalogue of the Manuscripts in the College of Arms Collections* (College of Arms, London, 1988), p. 389; H. Stanford London (1956), p. 6; see also A. R. Wagner, *The Records and Collections of the College of Arms*, (Burke's Peerage Ltd, 1962), p. 26.

40. T. Woodcock and J. M. Robinson, *The Oxford Guide to Heraldry* (Oxford, 1990), pp. 172–9. *HKW*, III, pp. 192–3, 210–18. A. Young (1987), pp. 11–42.

41. This element was re-carved in the 1960s but an original royal coat of arms one survives at Beaulieu (fig. 136).

42. PRO E36/244 p. 287; H. Stanford London, *The Queen's Beasts* (London, 1953).

43. *Hall*, I, p. 156.

44. A. Pettegree, 'The Foreign Population of London in 1549', *Proceedings of the Huguenot Society of London*, XXIV (1984), pp. 141–6; M. Carlin, 'The Urban Development of Southwark, c. 1200–1550' (unpub. Ph.D. thesis, University of Toronto, 1983), pp. 510–39; G. Rosser, *Medieval Westminster* (Oxford, 1989), pp. 182–96; D. R. Ransome, 'Artisan Dynasties in London and Westminster in the Sixteenth Century', *Guildhall Miscellany*, II (1964), pp. 236–47.

45. P. M. Ryan, 'Fifteenth-century Continental Brickmasons', *Medieval Archaeology*, 30 (1986), pp. 112–13.

46. PRO E36/243 p. 418, E36/241 p. 345; PRO E36/241 p. 282.

47. W. Page, ed., 'Letters of Denization and Acts of Naturalisation for Aliens in England 1509–1603', *Huguenot Society*, VIII (1893). See also T. Wyatt, 'Aliens in England before the Huguenots', *Proceedings of the Huguenot Society of London*, I (1953) XIX.

48. See also Benno M. Forman, 'Continental Furniture Craftsmen in London 1511–1625', *Furniture History* (1971), pp. 94–109

49. Ransome (1964), *passim*.

50. Bod. Lib. Rawl. MS. D. 781 f. 40v; PRO E101/504/2 f. 57v; NUL MS Ne02 f. 139v–40; BL Add. MS 10109 f. 80v.

51. PRO SP1/23 p. 38 (*L&P*, III (ii), no. 1530).

52. 14 and 15 Henry VIII c.2. *Statutes of the Realm*, III, p. 208.

53. D. R. Ransome, 'The Struggle of the Glaziers' Company with the Foreign Glaziers, 1500–1550', pp. 12–20 (in a journal whose title I failed to record); J. A. Knowles, 'Disputes Between English

and Foreign Glass-Painters in the Sixteenth Century', *Antiquaries Journal*, V (1925), pp. 148–57.

54. E. Auerbach, *Tudor Artists* (London, 1954), pp. 15–16; PRO E36/239 p. 94–5; E36/241 p. 379; E36/241 p. 493.

55. *Chronicle of Calais*, pp. 84–5.

56. PRO SP1/20 f. 79–80; *Chronicle of Calais*, pp. 84–5; S. T. Bindoff, 'Clement Armstrong and his Treatises of the Common Weal', *EHR*, 14 (1944–5), pp. 69–71.

57. Auerbach (1954), p. 16. Nichols (1862) p. 25.

58. BL Harl. MS. 442 f. 159 (*L&P*, XVI (i) no. 1); BL Harl. MS. 6989 f. 88 (*L&P*, XVI (i) no. 9).

59. A. Higgins, 'On the Work of Florentine Sculptors in England in the Early Part of the Sixteenth Century; with Special Reference to the Tombs of Cardinal Wolsey and King Henry VIII', *AJ*, 51 (1894), pp. 164, 192–4, 207–16; P. Lindley, 'Playing Checkmate with Royal Majesty? Wolsey's Patronage of Italian Renaissance Sculpture', *Cardinal Wolsey, Church, State and Art*, S. Gunn and P. Lindley, eds (Cambridge, 1990), pp. 279–81.

60. Auerbach (1954), 'Vincent Volpe', pp. 222–7.

61. Auerbach (1954), pp. 55–7; Nichols (1862), pp. 32–7.

62. PRO LC 2/2 f. 63

63. Auerbach (1954), p. 57; *HKM*, III, pp. 44–5.

64. BL Royal MS 14. B IV. A.

65. M. Biddle, 'Nicholas Bellin of Modena, An Italian Artificer at the Courts of Francis I and Henry VIII', *Jnl. Brit. Arch. Assn.*, XXIX (1966), p. 115; Nichols (1862), pp. 37–8.

66. *State Papers*, I, p. 484.

67. BL Add Charter 1262.

68. Page (1893), pp. 108, 176, 215.

69. *L&P*, XIX (ii) no. 216. No case for his involvement in Nonsuch is made here but it should be noted that Biddle's argument on p. 121 of Biddle (1966) takes no account of the fact that he has a better documented connection with Mantua than Bellin.

70. For the plausible evidence of Modena's involvement at Mantua see Biddle (1966). See also R. Pouncey, 'Girolamo da Treviso in the service of Henry VIII'. *Burlington Mangazine*, XCV (1953), pp. 208–11; id., 'Aggiunte a Girolamo da Treviso', *Arte Antica e Moderna* (1961), pp. 209–10; 'Girolamo da Treviso', *The Genius of Venice* (exh. cat., London, Royal Academy of Arts, 1983), p. 172.

71. K. W. Forster and R. J. Tuttle, 'The Palazzo del Tè', *Journal of the Society of Architectural Historians*, XXX, 4 (1971), pp. 267–93; Gianna Suitner and Chiara Tellini Perina, *Palazzo Tè in Mantua* (Milan, 1990), pp. 77–81.

72. The definitive discussion of this is in *HKW*, III, pp. 25–45.

73. For example: PRO E36/237, p. 519; E36/241, p. 225; E36/243, p. 600.

74. PRO E36/251, p. 106; E36/252, p. 416.

75. PRO E36/245, p. 353.

76. *L&P*, XIV (i), no. 398; *L&P*, XV, p. 166.

NOTES TO CHAPTER 7

1. F. Heal, *Hospitality in England* (Oxford, 1990), pp. 40–43.

2. Quotation taken from M. Girouard, *Life in the English Country House* (London, 1978), p. 30.

3. *HO*, pp. 110–11.
4. S. Thurley, 'The Domestic Building Works of Cardinal Wolsey', *Cardinal Wolsey: Church, State and Art*, S. Gunn and P. Lindley, eds (Cambridge, 1991), pp. 91–3.
5. 'English Royal Palaces', pp. 212–13.
6. For the details of this, see 'English Royal Palaces', pp. 273–80.
7. J. Shelby, *John Rogers: Tudor Military Engineer* (Oxford, 1967), pp. 34–46, but see my re-interpretation which differs in some important respects, 'English Royal Palaces', pp. 308–11.
8. For Dartford see 'English Royal Palaces', pp. 247–55; for Canterbury, pp. 256–9; for St James's, pp. 214–28; for Oatlands, pp. 298–300.
9. Bod. Lib. Rawl. MS. D 784 ff. 22v, 24, 210.
10. *Henry VIII and Hampton Court*, pp. 10–12.
11. R. Hennell, *The History of the King's Body Guard and the Yeomen of the Guard* (London, 1904), p. 60.
12. *HO*, pp. 146–7; A. G. W. Murray and Eustace F. Bosanquet, 'Excerpts from the Manuscript of William Dunche' *The Genealogist*, n.s. xxx (1914), p. 22.
13. PRO E36/215 f. 16v, for example.
14. G. Kipling, ed., *The Receyt of the Ladie Kateryne* (EETS, 1990), p. 10; Stephen Bamforth and Jean Dupèbe, trans. and eds, 'Francisci Francorum Regis et Henrici Anglorum Colloquium', *Renaissance Studies*, v (1991), p. 7; G. W. Groos, *The Diary of Baron Waldstein* (London, 1981), pp. 73–4; see also W. B. Rye, *England as Seen by Foreigners* (London, 1865), pp. 104–5.
15. *HO*, p. 151.
16. PRO. E36/235 p. 77.
17. BL Add. MS. 6113.
18. BL Add. MS. 6113 f. 113.
19. *HO*, pp. 152, 109.
20. *HO*, p. 153.
21. *HO*, p. 38.
22. *HO*, p. 153.
23. *HO*, p. 151–2.
24. J. Stevens, *Music and Poetry in the Early Tudor Court* (Cambridge, 1978), pp. 301–3.
25. *Hall*, pp. 174–6.
26. E. K. Chambers, *The Elizabethan Stage*, 4 vols (Oxford, 1923), i, pp. 21–3.
27. *L&P*, iii, no. 197; Bod. Lib. Rawl. MS. D 781 f. 22v.
28. For both of these uses see, for example, *Henry VIII and Hampton Court*, pp. 16, 37.
29. BL Add. MS. 21116, f. 8v.
30. *HO*, pp. 111–17.
31. *Cal. SP. Span.* (1531–3), p. 617 (*L&P*, vi, no. 212); see also *L&P*, iv (i), no. 2215.
32. For another see College of Arms MS M 8 f. 65v.
33. PRO E36/243 p. 488; PRO E36/242, p. 48; *HO*, p. 153.
34. For example *L&P*, iii (i), no. 896.
35. *Cal. SP. Ven.*, ii, no. 918.
36. J. S. Brewer, *The Reign of Henry VIII* (London, 1884) ii, p. 106. This was the same behaviour as adopted by Wolsey. When the King's officers arrived at Cawood to arrest him they found his household officers dining in the great hall, Wolsey ate apart in 'an upper chamber', ibid. ii, p. 437.
37. Rye (1865), p. 107.
38. *HO*, p. 153.
39. *Cal. SP. Ven.*, ii, no. 918 (p. 398); *Cal. SP. Ven.*, ii, no. 105.
40. For dozens of examples see the three books of ceremonials BL Add. MS. 6113, Harl. MS. 6074 and Add. MS. 21116. Also: PRO SP1/128 f. 30

(*L&P*, xiii (i), no. 24); Brewer (1884), i, pp. 9, 416, ii, pp. 149, 151, 372–3; 'Wriothesley Chronicle', *Camden Society* (1987), pp. 44, 60; *Hall*, ii, pp. 20, 167; *L&P*, iii, no. 896; *L&P*, xiii (i), no. 24.
41. *L&P*, xiv (ii), no. 783.
42. It was probably also a sound-barrier between the two areas, allowing the privy chamber to be quiet if the presence chamber was filled with courtiers.
43. *HO*, p. 156.
44. *HO*, p. 51. Note the temporary arrangement of this. The clerk erected a travers to separate the King and the priest, the gallery and closet plan created a permanent room for the services.
45. PRO E36/243 p. 487.
46. *Cal. SP. Ven.*, ii, no. 1287.
47. For example *L&P*, v, p. 309.
48. PRO E36/216 f. 106v.
49. PRO E36/216 f. 69v.
50. Bod. Lib. Rawl. D 781 f. 50v.
51. At Greenwich 'the clerestoury over the altar in the said closett' (Bod. Lib. Rawl. MS. D 775 f. 50). See 'English Royal Palaces', app. i, for the evidence for the closet at Hampton Court.
52. J. Bayley, *History and Antiquities of The Tower of London* (London, 1921), p. xxxii.
53. PRO E36/239 p. 36.
54. J. Bayley (1921), p. xxxiii.
55. NUL MS. Ne02 f. 23.
56. BL Harl. MS. 1419A f. 251 is the list for Hampton Court.
57. PRO SP1/35 ff. 209, 224.
58. PRO SP1/16 f. 225 (*L&P*, ii (ii), no. 4072).
59. PRO SP1/195 f. 173.
60. *L&P*, x, no. 699 (pp. 289–91); *L&P*, iii, no. 689.
61. 'Narrative of the visit of the Duke of Najera to England in the year 1543–4 written by his secretary Pedro de Gante', *Archaeologia*, xxiii (1831), p. 351.
62. Murray and Bosanquet (1914), p. 97.
63. *HO*, pp. 154–7.
64. 'English Royal Palaces', pp. 452–56.
65. 'Rutland Papers', *Camden Society*, o.s. xxi (1842), pp. 82–3.
66. PRO E36/216 f. 88; PRO SC12/9/28.
67. Bod. Lib. Rawl. MS. D 776. f. 9v; Bod. Lib. Rawl. MS. D 777 f. 105v.
68. PRO E36/238 p. 523; PRO E36/242 p. 51; E36/238 p. 524.
69. PRO SC12/3/13 (mention of a lease on the back cover); PRO SC6/ Hen VIII/ 2103; A. G. Rosser and S. J. Thurley 'The Urban Cost of Princely Magnificence: Henry VIII and the Destruction of Medieval King Street', *LTR* (1990), pp. 57–77; WAM 36711.
70. This information has been kindly provided by Mr John Cloake, from an appendix to his book on Richmond Palace.
71. *Cavendish*, p. 123; *Hall*, ii, p. 56; Thurley (1990), p. 91.
72. *L&P*, xii (ii), app. 44; *L&P*, xiii (i), no. 855; *L&P*, xiv (i), no. 574; ibid., xiv (ii), no. 782; *Cavendish*, p. 233.
73. State Papers, i, p. xiii n.
74. *L&P*, iv, no. 1792; NUL MS. Ne.01 f. 43.
75. Bod. Lib. Rawl. MS. D 777 f. 189.
76. *HO*, pp. 167–208; *L&P*, iii (i), no. 704. *Archaeologia*, xxi (1827), p. 180.
77. *Cavendish*, p. 93; *Cal. SP. Span.* (1529–30), pp. 215, 235, 253, 257; A. F. Pollard, *Wolsey* (London, 1929), pp. 237–9.
78. 'English Royal Palaces', pp. 452–6.
79. *L&P*, xx, no. 982. For another example see *L&P*,

iv (ii), no. 4009.
80. *Cavendish*, p. 48.
81. But *Cavendish*, p. 128, shows that even men like Wolsey would have lodgings in a lesser house assigned by a harbinger.
82. BL Cott. MS. Vesp. cxiv ff. 104–5; transcribed in *Henry VIII and Hampton Court*, pp. 44–5.
83. 'Rutland Papers', *Camden Society* (1842), pp. 82–3.
84. Ibid., pp. 86–93.
85. PRO E101/517/23 item 5.
86. 'Rutland Papers' (1842), p. 76; *L&P*, xiv, no. 781.
87. PRO E36/215 f. 265.
88. PRO E36/214 f. 130v.
89. PRO E36/215 f. 72; *L&P*, xvi, no. 380 (f. 139).
90. For this see D. Loades, *The Tudor Court* (London, 1986), pp. 167–8.
91. *L&P*, v, no. 614; E. G. O'Donoghue, *Bridewell Hospital: Palace, Prison, Schools* (London, 1923); Bod. Lib. Rawl. MS. D 777 f. 38; PRO SP1/87 f. 30 (*L&P*, vii, no. 1428); PRO SP3/18 f. 21 (*L&P*, xiii, no. 1162).
92. *L&P*, viii, no. 1018.
93. O'Donoghue (1923), p. 96.
94. Bod. Lib. Rawl. MS. D 777 f. 35.
95. *L&P*, viii, no. 402 (*Cal. SP. Span.*, v (ii), no. 214).

NOTES TO CHAPTER 8

1. PRO. E36/239 p. 38.
2. *Henry VIII and Hampton Court*, p. 3.
3. PRO E36/251 pp. 7, 28.
4. Discussion of these issues, in the paragraph below, requires a consideration of several important and differing viewpoints: D. R. Starkey, 'The King's Privy Chamber, 1485–1547', University of Cambridge Ph.D. thesis (1973); idem, 'Intimacy and Innovation: The Rise of the Privy Chamber 1485–1547', *The English Court*, D. Starkey, ed. (London, 1987) pp. 71–118; P. Gwyn, *The King's Cardinal* (London, 1990), pp. 555–65; Greg Walker, 'The Expulsion of the Minions of 1519 Reconsidered', *HJ*, 32 (1989) pp. 1–16.
5. D. Starkey, 'Court and Government', *Revolution Reassessed*, D. R. Starkey and C. Coleman, eds (Oxford, 1986), pp. 39–40; Starkey (1973), p. 121.
6. *HO*, p. 154.
7. *HO*, pp. 155–6, cap. 59–60 indicates that the King rose from his bedroom and entered the privy chamber next door to dress and shave.
8. G. W. Bernard, 'The Rise of Sir William Compton, Early Tudor Courtier', *EHR*, 96, (1981), pp. 757, 772–5.
9. D. Starkey (1973), p. 182; G. R. Elton, 'Tudor Government: The Points of Contact. III: The Court', *Transactions of the Royal Historical Society*, 5th ser. 26 (1976), p. 214.
10. A full archaeological reconstruction of the range is in S. Thurley, et al., 'Excavations on the East Side of Whitehall Palace 1938–1978' (forthcoming).
11. PRO E315/160; BL Harl. MS. 1419A ff. 63–206.
12. PRO E315/160 f. 105v.
13. PRO E315/160 f. 123.
14. 'Wriothesley's Chronicle', i, *Camden Society*, n.s., xi (1875), p. 45.
15. PRO E315/160 f. 105v; BL Harl. MS. 1419A f. 176v.
16. An introduction to this famous historical battleground can be found in: D. Starkey, 'Court, Council and Nobility in Tudor England', *Princes,*

Patronage and the Nobility, R. G. Asch and A. M. Birke, eds (Oxford, 1991), pp. 175–203; G. R. Elton, *The Tudor Revolution in Government* (Cambridge, 1953), pp. 60–5, 316–69; John Guy, 'The Privy Council: Revolution or Evolution?', *Revolution Reassessed* C. Coleman and D. Starkey, eds (Oxford, 1986), pp. 59–86; G. R. Elton, 'Tudor Government', *HJ*, 31 (1988), pp. 431–4; David Starkey, 'Tudor Government: The Facts?', *HJ*, 31 (1988), pp. 923–31.

17. In 1533 we learn that glass was mended in 'iii wyndowes in the cownsell chamber within the same [great] gallery on the northe syde', J. Bayley, *History and Antiquities of the Tower of London* (London, 1921), p. xxxii. The structure which housed the chamber can be seen on the Haiward and Gascoigne map and was situated on top of the gate in the medieval wall.

18. Thurley, et al. (forthcoming).

19. 'Bordyng off too wyndowys in a chamber in the greatt gallarii callyd the Counsell chamber' (Bod. Lib. Rawl. MS. D 777 f. 38*v*). This structure can be seen on the 'Agas' view (fig. 55) and part of it was excavated in 1978; D. Gadd and T. Dyson, 'Excavations at 9–11 Bridewell Place and 1–3 Tudor Street', *Post-Med. Arch.*, 15 (1981), fig. 5.

20. *Henry VIII and Hampton Court*, p. 8.

21. Henry VII's council chamber at the tower was in the upper story of the King's Tower, J. Bayley (1921), pp. xxiv, xxvi, xxx, xxxi.

22. Thurley, et al. (forthcoming).

23. *HO*, p. 171.

24. A full discussion of the lodgings at Hampton Court is in *Henry VIII and Hampton Court*, pp. 32–4, 42–4.

25. *HO*, p. 157; *Cal. SP. Span.*, VI (ii), no. 74, p. 168.

26. Brian Tuke to Wolsey 23 June 1528, BL Cott. MS. Titus B.1. f. 306 (*L&P*, IV (ii), no. 4409).

27. BL Add. MS. 6113 f. 89; *L&P*, XIX, no. 459; 'Narrative of the Visit of the Duke of Najera to England in the year 1543–4 Written by his Secretary Pedro de Gante', *Archaeologia*, XXIII (1831), p. 351; Bod. Lib. Rawl. MS. D 781 f. 22*v*.

28. NUL MS. Ne01 f. 301*v*.

29. *HO*, p. 360.

30. N. Cuddy, 'The Revival of Entourage: The Bedchamber of James I, 1603–1625', *The English Court: From the Wars of the Roses to the Civil War*, D. Starkey, ed. (London, 1987) pp. 174–95.

31. This idea is discussed in the last chapter of Starkey (1973).

32. BL Harl. MS. 1419 f. 118*v*; Thurley, et al. (forthcoming).

33. PRO E315/160 f. 133*v*.

34. PRO E315/160 f. 105*v*; Bod. Lib. MS. Eng. Hist. b192/1 f. 2.

35. BL Harl. MS. 1419A ff. 91, 111–13.

36. *Henry VIII and Hampton Court*, pp. 3–6, 42; S. Thurley, 'Greenwich Palace', *Henry VIII: a European Court in England*, D. Starkey, ed. (exh. cat. Greenwich, National Maritime Museum, 1990), pp. 23–4.

37. *L&P*, III, no. 835.

38. G. Kipling, ed., *The Receyt of the Ladie Kateryne* (EETS, 1990), pp. 46–7; J. J. Scarisbrick, *Henry VIII* (Harmondsworth, 1968), pp. 250–51.

39. *Cal. SP. Span.* (1527–9), no. 600; *Cal. SP. Span.*, IV (i), no. 224 (p. 351).

40. BL Add. MS. 21116 f. 27.

41. G. W. Barnard, 'The Rise of Sir William Compton, Early Tudor Courtier', *EHR*, 96 (1981), p. 757.

42. *HO*, p. 125.

43. Bod. Lib. Rawl. MS. D 775, f. 82*v*; *L&P*, VI, nos 948, 1004.

44. PRO E36/244 pp. 413, 415.

45. The More, Bod. Lib. MS. Film 308 f. 85.

46. *L&P*, XXI (ii), nos 675, 684; *Cal. SP. Span.*, IX, pp. 6–7.

47. *Henry VIII and Hampton Court*, pp. 4–5.

48. An inventory of a cabinet survives in BL MS. Edgerton 2679; BL Harl. MS. 1419A ff. 54*v*, 56*v*, 59.

49. D. Starkey (1986), pp. 43–4; Bod. Lib. Rawl. MS. D 775 f. 71*v*; PRO E315/160 f. 267.

50. J. H. Nicolas, *The Privy Purse Expenses of Elizabeth of York: The Wardrobe Accounts of Edward the Fourth* (London, 1830), pp. 125–6.

51. G. Kipling, *The Triumph of Honour* (Leiden, 1977), pp. 31–40; M. McKisack, *Medieval History in the Tudor Age* (Oxford, 1971), pp. 1–5; James P. Carley, 'John Layland and the Foundations of the Royal Library: The Westminster Inventory of 1542', *Bulletin of the Society for Renaissance Studies*, VII (1989), pp. 13–22.

52. For example, PRO E36/239 p. 34. *Henry VIII and Hampton Court*, pp. 7–8.

53. Bod. Lib. Rawl MS. D 775 f. 66; BL Add. MS. 10109 f. 95*v*.

54. BL Cott. MS. Otho CX, f. 225*v* (*L&P*, X, no. 798).

55. *Historical Manuscripts Commission, Bath*, II (1907), p. 10.

NOTES TO CHAPTER 9

1. C. Given-Wilson, *The Royal Household and the King's Affinity; Service Politics and Finance in England 1300–1413* (New Haven and London, 1986), pp. 11–13.

2. *HO*, pp. 208–40; P. Gwyn, *The King's Cardinal: The Rise and Fall of Thomas Wolsey* (London, 1990), pp. 366–8, 563–4; D. Loades, *The Tudor Court* (London, 1986), pp. 59–72 (parts of this should be treated with caution).

3. *HO*, pp. 211–2.

4. *HKW*, I, p. 503, II, p. 912; T. B. James and A. M. Robinson, 'Clarendon Palace, the History and Archaeology of a Medieval Palace and Hunting Lodge near Salisbury, Wilts', *Society of Antiquaries of London*, XLV (1988), pp. 82–5.

5. M. Howard, *The Early Tudor Country House* (London, 1987), figs, 44, 50, 52.

6. For an earlier episcopal example see *Henry VIII's Kitchens*, p. 5.

7. A. R. Myres, *The Household of Edward IV* (Manchester, 1959), pp. 3–49; C. Ross, *Edward IV* (London, 1974), p. 260; Kate Mertes, 'The Liber Niger of Edward IV: A New Version', *Bulletin Of the Institute of Historical Research*, 54 (1981), pp. 33–9.

8. M. Letts, ed., 'The Travels of Leo of Rozmital', *Hakluyt Society*, 2nd ser., cviii, (1957), pp. 46–7.

9. All these and more are printed in F. J. Furnivall, ed., 'Early English Meals and Manners', EETS, o.s., 32 (1868).

10. *HO*, pp. 110–16; F. J. Furnivall and John Rusell, 'Book of Nurture', 'The Book of Courtesy', EETS, o.s., 32 (1868), pp. 115–239. For some of the many other sources see M. Girouard, *Life in the English Country House* (London, 1978), pp. 319–20, and Kate Mertes, *The English Noble Household 1250–1600* (London, 1988), pp. 194–215.

11. *HO*, pp. 162–92.

12. A different and fuller account of the Hampton

Court kitchens is in *Henry VIII's Kitchens*, pp. 1–28; S. J. Thurley, *The Tudor Kitchens at Hampton Court Palace*, souvenir guidebook (Hampton Court Palace, 1990).

13. NUL MS. Ne03 f. 40; *Henry VIII's Kitchens*, p. 22.

14. For example Whitehall (plan 13), Bridewell (fig. 54) and Richmond (plan 11).

15. PRO E36/241, p. 360. An account for the green baize also survives, PRO E36/237 p. 597.

16. *L&P*, XXI, no. 1212.

17. *Henry VIII's Kitchens*, pp. 16–18.

18. N. Pevsner and J. Harris, *Lincolnshire, The Buildings of England* (Harmondsworth, 1973), pp. 243–4.

19. For example, PRO E36/242 p. 24; BL Royal MS 14B IVA, IVB; BL Lansdowne Roll 14; *L&P*, X, no. 266, g.33.

20. BL Cott. MS Claudius, E. vi f. 137.

21. J. Bayley, *The History and Antiquities of the Tower of London* (London, 1821), p. xxii.

22. Bod. Lib. Rawl. MS. D 777 f. 182.

23. H. A. Napier, *Historical Notices of the Parishes of Swyncome and Ewelme* (Oxford, 1858), pp. 198–207.

24. Christopher K. Currie, 'Fishponds as Garden Features, *c.* 1550–1750' *Garden History*, 18 (1990), pp. 22–46.

25. PRO E36/236 pp. 54*v*, 56.

26. For example, PRO E36/243 p. 83; PRO E36/239 p. 340; BL Add. MS. 59899 f. 79; NUL MS. Ne01 f. 55; PRO E36/214 f. 152*v*; PRO E36/252 p. 509.

27. Bod. Lib. Rawl. MS. D 784 f. 29.

28. Ibid f. 29; Bod. Lib. Rawl. MS. D 784 f. 190*v*.

29. Bod. Lib. Rawl. MS. D 776 f. 119.

30. This does not invalidate my point about the location of the kitchen in relation to the hall, for we have no idea where the Lancastrian hall was.

31. Bod. Lib. Rawl. MS. D. 776. f. 23*v*; MS. D 781 f. 10; Longleat House, Wilts, MS. Misc. xxx f. 9.

32. Bod, Lib. Rawl. MS. D 781 f. 189; BL Add. MS. 101019 f. 69.

33. NUL MS. Ne01 f. 29*v*; *Henry VIII's Kitchens*, p. 20; *HO*, pp. 233–4.

34. BL Add. MS. 101019 f. 69; NUL MS. Ne02 f. 134*v*.

35. *Cal. SP. Span.*, XIII, p. 31.

36. See A. Woodworth, 'Purveyance for the Royal Household in the reign of Elizabeth I', *Transactions of the American Philosophical Society*, n.s. XXXV/(1), p. 62.

37. BL Edgerton MS. 2358; PRO E36/216 f. 24.

38. *HO*, p. 158.

39. *L&P*, VIII, no. 440: D. Loades, *Mary Tudor* (Oxford, 1989), pp. 80–81.

40. J. G. Nichols, *Literary Remains of King Edward VI* (Roxburghe Club, 1857), pp. xxviii–xxx.

41. Bod. Lib. Rawl. MS. D 783 f. 23*v*; PRO E101/497/1 p. 2 (item 6); Bod. Lib. MS. film 308 f. 219; Bod. Lib. Rawl. MS. D 777 f. 39*v*.

42. *HKW*, IV, p. 141.

43. BL Add. MS. 10109 f. 60; NUL MS. Ne02 f. 134*v*.

44. Bod. Lib. Rawl. MS. D 784 f. 7*v*; NUL MS Ne03 f. 57.

45. Above pp. 122, 138; *Cal. SP. Span.*, IX, pp. 6–7.

NOTES TO CHAPTER 10

1. *HKW*, I, p. 75.

2. Glyn Coppack, *Abbeys and Priories* (London,

1990), pp. 81–99; *HKW*, I, pp. 549–50.

3. M. A. Lower, 'Notes Respecting Halnaker, Boxgrove, etc. from a Survey temp. Queen Elizabeth I', *Sussex Archaeological Collections*, 9 (1859), p. 223; *L&P*, v, p. 751; Longleat House, Wilts, MS. Misc. xxx, f. 23.

4. BL Royal MS. 14B IVA.

5. At a later date the supply to the house was augmented by a conduit from Hyde Park (PRO Works 4/8).

6. PRO E315/414.

7. J. Dent, *The Quest for Nonsuch* (London, 1962), pp. 50–51.

8. For a survey see PRO Works 14/257.

9. BL Add. MS. 10109 f. 181; E. Ford, *A History of Enfield in the County of Middlesex* (Enfield, 1873), p. 78, pl. opp. p. 84; F. R. J. Pateman, et al., 'St Thomas à Beckets Well, Otford', *Arch. Cant.*, LXX (1956), pp. 172–6; PRO Works 14/2618.

10. PRO E36/215 ff. 261*v*, 276*v*.

11. PRO E36/216 f. 83; *L&P*, III, no. 483; PRO E101/504/2 f. 36–36*v*; PRO Works 16/132; J. M. Stone 'Greenwich: Its Underground Passages, Caverns, etc.', *Transactions of the Greenwich Antiquarian Society* (1913), pp. 262–8; PRO MP 253.

12. S. Bentley, *Excerpta Historica* (London, 1831), p. 121; C. Williams, *Thomas Platter's Travels in England in 1599* (London, 1937), pp. 220–21; NUL MS. Ne.01 f. 343*v*; NUL MS. Ne01 ff. 337–343*v*. See also *HKW*, II, fig. 72, p. 1011.

13. *HKW*, pp. 315–7.

14. PRO E36/243 p. 380, E36/237 p. 124, E36/241 p. 241, E36/244 p. 136, E36/241 p. 544, E36/237 p. 124.

15. PRO E351/3199.

16. PRO Works 5/145 f. 251.

17. Although the upper chamber was damaged by the fall of a tree caused by bomb blast in the war (PRO Works 14/1937).

18. J. W. Lindus Forge, 'Coombe Hill Conduit Houses and the Water Supply of Hampton Court Palace', *Surrey Archaeological Collections*, LVI (1959), pp. 3–14. Forge's attribution to Wolsey is exploded here.

19. NUL MS. Ne01 f. 337.

20. PRO Works 19/15/14.

21. PRO E36/239 p. 120.

22. C. L. Kingsford, *The Early History of Piccadilly, Leicester Square, Soho and their Neighbourhood* (Cambridge, 1925), pp. 15–17.

23. Bod. Lib. Rawl. MS. D 781 f. 31.

24. *HKW*, I, p. 550; II, pp. 926, 934, 998.

25. PRO E36/214 p. 142.

26. F. J. Furnivall, ed., 'Manners and Meals in Olden Times', EETS, 32 (1868), pp. 66–7, 179.

27. BL Add. MS. 6113 ff. 106*v*–7.

28. *Henry VIII and Hampton Court*, pp. 5–6.

29. BL Add. MS. 10109 ff. 83–4; Bod. Lib. Rawl. MS. D 776 ff. 72*v*, 75; BL Harl. MS. 1419 f. 362*v*.

30. *Hall*, I, p. 255.

31. Léon de Laborde, ed., *Les Comptes des bâtiments du roi, 1528–1571* (Paris, 1877), I, p. 108. They survived until the reconstruction of 1697.

32. Williams (1937), p. 221.

33. PRO E315/160 f. 48*v*.

34. BL Harl. MS. 1419 f. 362*v*.

35. BL Harl. MS. 1419 f. 61–61*v*.

36. PRO E36/243 p. 604.

37. *L&P*, XIII(ii), no. 585.

38. A. Boorde, 'A Compendyous Regyment or a Dyetary of Helth', EETS, o.s. 10 (1870).

39. Hampton Court Heath Archive.

40. *HO*, pp. 148–9.

41. Boorde (1870), p. 239.

42. Bod. Lib. MS. Film 308 f. 148*v*; *L&P*, v, p. 751.

43. Bod. Lib. Rawl. MS. D 776 f. 229*v*.

44. Bod. Lib. MS. Film 308 f. 247.

45. *L&P*, x, no. 674.

46. Boorde (1870), pp. 236–7.

47. P. L. Hughes and J. F. Larkin, eds, *Tudor Royal Proclamations*, 3 vols (1964–9), I, p. 405.

48. Bod. Lib. Rawl. MS. D 777 f. 203*v*.

49. Ibid., f. 160; *L&P*, v, p. 322; PRO E36/215 f. 251*v*.

50. E. L. Sabine, 'Latrines and Cesspools of Medieval London', *Speculum* (1934), pp. 303–21; G. Coppack, (1990), pp. 97–8.

51. *Henry VIII and Hampton Court*, pp. 26–7.

52. H. Woods, 'Excavations at Eltham Palace, 1975–9', *LAMAS*, 33 (1982), p. 234.

53. PRO E315/160 f. 52*v*; Bod. Lib. MS. Film 308, f. 39–39*v*; Bod. Lib. Rawl. MS. D 780 f. 238*v*.

54. BL Add. MS. 21116, f. 15.

55. Furnivall (1868), p. 179.

56. PRO SP 1/47 ff. 56–7 (*L&P*, IV (ii), no. 4005); PRO SP 1/153 f. 117 (*L&P*, XIV (ii), no. 153).

57. Bod. Lib. Rawl. MS. D 780 f. 191; BL Harl. MS. 1419 f. 62*v*; NUL MS. Ne02 f. 205.

NOTES TO CHAPTER 11

1. G. Kipling, ed., 'The Receyt of the Ladie Kateryne', *EETS* (1990), pp. 73–4.

2. Quoted in M. L. Bruce, *The Making of Henry VIII* (London, 1977), p. 89.

3. S. Anglo, *The Great Tournament Roll of Westminster* (Oxford, 1968), app. v.

4. For a discussion of the individual complexes see the following: for Whitehall, H. J. M. Green and S. J. Thurley, 'Excavations on the West side of Whitehall 1960–62', *LAMAS* (1990), pp. 59–130; for Hampton Court; *Henry VIII and Hampton Court*, pp. 12–13, 29, figs 1–2; for Greenwich see 'English Royal Palaces', pp. 138–43, 443.

5. T. Elyot, *The Boke Named the Governor*, ed., H. H. S. Croft, 2 vols (London, 1880), I, pp. 169–171.

6. A. Boorde, 'A Compendyous Regyment or a Dyetary of Helth', 1542', *EETS*, e.s. x (1870), p. 248.

7. Elyot (1880), pp. 290–4.

8. A. R. Myers, ed., *The Household of Edward IV: The Black Book and Ordinance of 1478* (Manchester, 1959), p. 129.

9. See above pp. 138–41.

10. BL Harl. MS. 69 f. 5b (*L&P*, I, no. 467).

11. 12 Richard II c.6; II Henry IV c.4, *Statutes of the Realm*, II (London, 1816), pp. 57, 163.

12. *Statutes of the Realm*, III (London, 1817), pp. 58–62, 665, 837–41.

13. J. Marshall, *The Annals of Tennis* (London, 1878), p. 63.

14. A. Young, *Tudor and Jacobean Tournaments* (London, 1987); S. Anglo, *The Great Tournament Roll of Westminster* (Oxford, 1978).

15. Young (1987), p. 15. See also Viscount Dillon's diagram in 'Tilting in Tudor Times', *AJ*, 55 (1898), fig. 2.

16. S. Bentley, *Excerpta Historica* (London, 1833), pp. 203–4; Viscount Dillon and W. H. St John Hope, eds, *The Beauchamp Pageant* (London, 1914), ff. 15–16.

17. *HKW*, IV, p. 287. Another example of a tem-

porary tiltyard set up by Henry VII is that at Sheen in 1492 (Bentley, 1833, p. 89).

18. PRO E36/215 f. 4*v*.

19. See above, also PRO E36/215 f. 221, 230.

20. Anglo (1978), app. v.

21. Green and Thurley (1990), pp. 75–6.

22. PRO E36/245 p. 25.

23. PRO E36/239 p. 553.

24. *Henry VIII and Hampton Court*, p. 39.

25. H. S. Scott, ed., 'The Journal of Sir Roger Wilbraham', *Camden Society Miscellany*, x (1902), p. 59.

26. *Chronicle of Calais*, p. 86.

27. S. Anglo, 'The Hampton Court Painting of the Field of Cloth of Gold Considered as an Historical Document', *Antiquaries Journal*, 46 (1966), pp. 300–303; on p. 303 there is a diagram showing the arrangement as indicated by all the reports.

28. Bod. Lib. MS. Film 308 f. 8*v*.

29. Bod. Lib. MS. Film 308. f. 36.

30. NUL MS. Ne.02 f. 35*v*.

31. See also NUL MS. Ne.01 ff. 24, 34, 37*v*; MS. Ne.02 f. 119*v*.

32. NUL MS. Ne.01 f. 28.

33. NUL MS. Ne.01 f. 13.

34. Anglo (1978), pp. 19–20.

35. On this see A. B. Ferguson, *The Indian Summer of English Chivalry* (Cambridge, 1960), pp. 3–32, especially p. 23.

36. B. Castiglione, *The Book of the Courtier*, trans. G. Bull (Harmondsworth, 1976), p. 63.

37. A. Scaino, *Trattato del Giuoco Della Palla di Messer 1553*, ed. W. W. Kershaw (London, 1951), p. 11.

38. Scaino (1951), p. 161.

39. For the mode of play see both Marshall (1878) and A. de Luze, *La Magnifique histoire du jeu de paume*, trans, and ed. R. Hamilton (repr. London, 1979), and for sixteenth-century rules Scaino (1951).

40. De Luze (1979), pp. 14–15, 171.

41. William Shakespeare, *Henry V*, Act 1, Scene 1.

42. R. Vaughan, *Valois Burgundy* (London, 1975), pp. 186, 177; de Luze (1979), p. 25; J. J. Jusserand, *Les Sportes et jeux d'exercise dans l'ancienne France* (Paris, 1901), p. 252.

43. A. H. Thomas, *The Great Chronicle of London* (London, 1937), p. 207.

44. The accounts of 1494 are only known from a partial transcription by Craven Ord printed in S. Bentley, *Excerpta Historica* (London, 1831); the references to tennis are on pp. 98, 101 and 102.

45. *HKW*, III, p. 258.

46. De Luze (1979), p. 15; S. Anglo, 'The Court Festivals of Henry VII', *Bulletin of the John Rylands Library*, 43 (1960–61), pp. 12–45.

47. Bod. Lib. Rawl. MS. D 776 f. 120*v*.

48. BL Cott. MS. Vesp. CXII. f. 285*v*.

49. PRO E101/517/23 no. 34.

50. *Hall*, I, p. 28; *Cal. SP. Ven.*, II, no. 1287.

51. *Hall*, I, p. 225; later leases on the site of Blackfriars and Bridewell mention the sites of two tennis-plays. Folger Shakespeare Library, Washington, DC, MS L.b.39; 393, f. 1.

52. Green and Thurley (1990), pp. 92–8; *L&P*, VI, no. 578 (25); *Henry VIII and Hampton Court*, p. 12.

53. Bod. Lib. Rawl. MS. D 776 ff. 76, 88; D 775 f. 51*v*; D 777 ff. 162*v*, 191*v*; NUL MS. Ne.02 f. 134; Bod. Lib. Rawl. MS. D 781 f. 13*v*; PRO E351/3232, E351/3217; Bod. Lib. Rawl. MS. D 780 f. 7.

54. De Luze (1979), p. 276; *L&P*, v, pp. 305, 312;

L&P, XVIII (ii), no. 529 (24); *Henry VIII and Hampton Court*, pp. 12–13; NUL MS. Ne02 f. 39; N. H. Nicolas, *The Privy Purse Expenses of Henry VIII* (London, 1827), p. 283; Marshall (1878), p. 8; J. Schofield, ed., 'The London Surveys of Ralph Treswell', *LTR*, 135 (1987), fig. 25.

55. Bod. Lib. Rawl. MS. D. 775 f. 51*v*; PRO E36/237 f. 172; work at Hampton Court has exposed areas of original wall plaster which is covered in several layers of black sooty paint.

56. BL Harl. MS. 1419A f. 59*v*; BL Harl. MS. 2284 f. 31; *Cal. SP. Ven.*, IV, no. 105 (p. 61). 'English Royal Palaces', pp. 433–4.

57. Boorde (1870), p. 239; Elyot (1880), I, pp. 294–6.

58. PRO E36/241 pp. 8, 589, 632; E36/245 p. 190; E36/239 p. 630.

59. Bod. Lib. Rawl. MS. D 780 ff. 190*v*, 191.

60. Bod. Lib. Rawl. MS. D 780 ff. 162–162*v*.

61. Ibid. f. 174.

62. PRO E36/241 p. 632; Bod. Lib. Rawl. MS. D 775 f. 57.

63. PRO E36/244 p. 229.

64. Bod. Lib. Rawl. MS. D 780 f. 40.

65. Nicolas (1827), pp. 20, 209, 210, 211, 212, 216, 229, 278.

66. G[ame] Cock, ed., *Cockfighting and Game-Fowl — From the Notebooks of Herbert Atkinson* (London, 1938), p. 73. In 1509 Dr John Colet ordered that scholars at St Paul's School were not to indulge in cockfighting (G. R. Scott, *The History of Cock-fighting*, London, n.d., p. 98); R[ichard] H[oulett], *The Royal Pastime of Cock-fighting or the Art of Breeding, Feeding, Fighting and Curing Cocks of the Game* (London, 1709).

67. Green and Thurley (1990), pp. 87–90.

68. Bod. Lib. Rawl. MS. D. 775, ff. 55, 61, 65*v*, 66.

69. 'A place in the galarye over the bowlyng allaye ffor the quene to syte in to see the cocke ffeyhttyng', Bod. Lib. Rawl. MS. D. 775 f. 56*v*.

70. R. Graziani, 'Sir Thomas Wyatt at a Cockfight, 1539', *Review of English Studies*, n.s., 27 (1976), p. 301.

71. Bod. Lib. Rawl. MS. D. 775 f. 55; Bod. Lib. Rawl. MS. D. 776 f. 43; Nicolas (1827), p. 206.

72. Pace to Wolsey, *L&P*, III (i), no. 950.

73. *Cal. SP. Span.*, VI (ii), no. 84 (p. 185); *L&P*, XVIII (ii), no. 41; *L&P*, XXI (ii), no. 46.

74. *L&P*, XVI, no. 1089.

75. Bod. Lib. MS. Film 308 f. 41; Rawl. D 775 f. 1; Rawl. MS. D. 777 f. 111; *L&P*, XIV (ii), no. 781 (p. 316).

76. *Cal. SP. Span.*, V (ii), p. 21; Bod. Lib. Rawl. MS. D 781 f. 36; MS. Film 308 f. 86*v*.

77. NUL MS. Ne02 ff. 148, 156, 162, 178, 191*v*; *L&P*, XIV (ii), no. 152; Bod. Lib. Rawl. MS. D. 781 f. 106; NUL MS. Ne02 f. 256.

78. PRO E36/215 f. 54; E36/215 f. 143.

79. *L&P*, XVII, no. 1153.

80. *L&P*, XVI, no. 311.

81. *L&P*, XVIII, (ii), no. 240.

82. *Hall*, II, p. 38.

83. *L&P*, IX, no. 525.

84. Bod. Lib. Rawl. MS. D 781 f. 117, 120*v*; Bod. Lib. Rawl. MS. D 780 f. 198.

85. Bod. Lib. Rawl. MS. D 775 ff. 32*v*, 50*v*; MS. D 776 ff.2, 2*v*, 3, 8, 32*v*.

86. Christine Weightman, *Margaret of York, Duchess of Burgundy, 1446–1503* (Gloucester, 1989), p. 139.

87. BL Add. MS. 59899 f. 67.

88. *L&P*, I, no. 2391, (p. 1058).

89. *L&P*, I, no. 4284; BL Add. MS. 10109 f. 88*v*.

90. Bod. Lib. Rawl. MS. D 781 f. 106; BL Add. MS. 10109 f. 141*v*.

91. NUL MS. Ne02 f. 136*v*.

92. Bod. Lib. Rawl. MS. D 776 f. 9*v*.

93. Bod. Lib. Rawl. MS. D 776 f. 224; Rawl. MS. D 780 f. 155*v*.

94. Bod. Lib. Rawl. MS. D 781 f. 22; NUL MS. Ne01 f. 15*v*.

NOTES TO CHAPTER 12

1. C. Given-Wilson, *The Royal Household and the King's Affinity* (New Haven and London, 1986), p. 67.

2. W. Ullmann, ed., 'Liber Regie Capelle: a manuscript in the Biblioteca Publica, Evora, *Henry Bradshaw Society*, 92 (1961).

3. A. R. Myres, *The Household of Edward IV* (Manchester, 1959), p. 35.

4. Ibid., p. 50.

5. Ibid., p. 51.

6. *HKW*, I, pp. 124, 247, 965, 1012. For non-royal parallels see, J. M. Lewis, 'The Chapel at Raglan and its Paving Tiles', *Castles in Wales and the Marches, Essays in Honour of D. Cathcart King*, J. R. Kenyon and R. Avent, eds (Cardiff, 1987), pp. 144–6.

7. *City of Cambridge*, (RCHM, 1959) I, pp. lxxviii-lxxx; *City of Oxford*, (RCHM, 1939) p. xxi.

8. R. Bowers, 'The Cultivation and Promotion of Music in the Household and Orbit of Thomas Wolsey', *Cardinal Wolsey: Church, State and Art*, S. Gunn and P. G. Lindley, eds (Cambridge, 1991), p. 180.

9. Ibid. p. 191.

10. *HO*, p. 161.

11. S. Thurley, 'Greenwich Palace', *Henry VIII: A European Court in England*, (exh. cat., Greenwich, National Maritime Museum, 1990), pp. 22–3.

12. H. Colvin, *Unbuilt Oxford*, (New Haven and London, 1983), pp. 2–4 and especially fig. 4; *City of Oxford* (RCHM, 1939), pp. 15–19, 69–76.

13. J. Newman, 'Cardinal Wolsey's Collegiate Foundations', Gunn and Lindley (1991), p. 112.

14. R. Bowers (1991), pp. 181–3.

15. PRO E36/216 f. 116*v*; *Cal. SP. Ven.*, II, no. 918; *L&P*, VII, no. 1507. Also *L&P*, XXI(i), no. 1227.

16. See above pp. 127–8. *L&P*, XIV (ii), no. 163; *L&P*, V, no. 564; *L&P*, III, no. 689.

17. BL Add. MS. 21116 ff. 11*v*, 17–17*v*.

18. *L&P*, XVIII (i), no. 873.

19. 'English Royal Palaces', pp. 138–43.

20. PRO E36/239 p. 512.

21. M. Dowling, 'Anne Boleyn and Reform', *Journal of Ecclesiastical History*, 35 (1984), pp. 35, 38–41; J. J. Scarisbrick, *Henry VIII* (London, 1968), pp. 538–57, 616–9; A. G. Dickens, *The English Reformation*, rev. edn. (London, 1981), pp. 254–6.

22. *The Parish of St Margaret Westminster*, II, *Survey of London*, XIII (1930), p. 88.

23. PRO. E101/474/19 (*Survey of London*, XIII, p. 88).

24. *HKW*, I, pp. 265–6.

25. *HKW*, IV, pp. 195–6.

26. *L&P*, V, no. 941; *L&P*, VI, no. 1111; Bod. Lib. Rawl. MS. D 775 f. 95.

27. G. Kipling, ed., *The Receyt of the lady Kateryne*, EETS (1991), p. 73.

28. Stephen Bamforth and Jean Dupèbe, eds and trans., 'Jacobus Sylvius, Francisci Francorum Regis et Henrici Anglorum Colloquium', *Renaissance Studies*, V (1991), pp. 73–5.

29. PRO E101/497/1 f. 3.

30. Bod. Lib. vet E 1b7; PRO E36/236 f. 53*v*; PRO E36/244 p. 75.

31. It should be noted that this reference comes from 1588/9 (PRO E351/3225).

32. H. Wayment, 'Twenty-four Vidimuses for Cardinal Wolsey', *Master Drawings*, XXIII/4, pp. 503–16.

33. PRO E36/244 f. 96.

34. H. Wayment, 'Stained Glass in Henry VIII's Palaces', *Henry VIII: A European Court In England*, D. Starkey, ed. (exh. cat., Greenwich, National Maritime Museum, 1990), pp. 28–31.

35. PRO E36/215 f. 178.

36. PRO E36/241 p. 410.

37. Bowers (1991), p. 184.

38. BL Add. MS. 59899 f. 23; PRO E36/215 f. 54.

39. PRO E36/215 f. 6*v*.

40. PRO E36/215 ff. 168, 263; PRO E36/216 f. 71; PRO E36/215 f. 186*v*.

41. PRO E36/216 f. 7*v*.

42. Bod. Lib. Rawl. MS. D 777 f. 45*v*; PRO E36/239 p. 619.

43. BL. Harl. MS. 599 ff. 116*v*, 119.

44. PRO E36/243 p. 687; E36/239 pp. 619, 634.

45. I. Smullen, 'Organ Blowing', *Country Life* (April 14, 1988); Longleat House, Wilts, MS. Misc. XXIX f. 11; NUL MS. Ne.01 f. 39; Bod. Lib. Rawl. MS. D 777 f. 162*v*; Bod. Lib. Film 308 f. 18; Bod. Lib. Rawl. MS. D 780 f. 6.

46. PRO E36/215 f. 212*v*; *Cal. SP. Ven.*, II, no. 555.

47. PRO E36/245 f. 140; *L&P*, XII, no. 911.

48. *L&P*, XII, no. 1060.

49. *Cal. SP. Ven.*, II, nos 624, 918.

50. For a contemporary list of venues see BL Harl. MS. 6074 f. 3. Greenwich was the location on twenty-four years.

51. Bod. Lib. Rawl. MS. D 781 f. 23; Rawl. MS. D 780 f. 40.

52. NUL MS. Ne02 f. 135.

53. PRO E36/236 f. 53*v*.

NOTES TO CHAPTER 13

1. *Chronicle of Calais*, pp. 54–7.

2. For example Bod. Lib. MS. film 308 f. 225*v*.

3. T. Borenius 'The Cycle of Images in the Palaces and Castles of Henry III', *Journal of the Warburg and Courtauld Institutes*, VI (1943), pp. 40–50.

4. PRO E351/3322.

5. Bod. Lib. Rawl. MS. D 780 ff. 33, 91.

6. PRO E36/239 p. 36.

7. C. Lloyd and S. Thurley, *Henry VIII Images of a Tudor King* (Oxford, 1990), pp. 44–5.

8. P. Binski, *The Painted Chamber at Westminster* (Society of Antiquaries, 1986), pp. 33–45.

9. G. Kipling, ed., 'The Receyt of the Lady Kateryne', EETS, 296 (1990), p. 72.

10. PRO E36/252 p. 468, PRO E351/3203, E351/3215, E351/3221.

11. J. Sherwood and N. Pevsner, *Oxfordshire, The Buildings of England*, (Harmondsworth, 1975), p. 496.

12. E. Croft-Murray, *Decorative Painting in England 1537–1837* (London, 1962), p. 18; D. Starkey, 'Ightam Mote: Politics and Architecture in Early Tudor England', *Archaeologia*, CVII (1982), pp. 157–8.

13. PRO E36/252 p. 631.

14. BL Harl. MS. 1419 f. 246.

15. PRO E36/237 p. 452; E36/239 p. 28; *L&P*, III, no. 1093.

16. BL. Harl. MS. 1419 f. 245.

17. Ibid., f. 56*v*.
18. See, for example, BL Harl. MS. 1419 ff. 246–50, 136–136*v*.
19. A. S. Cavallo, *Textiles. Isabella Stewart Gardner Museum* (Boston, MA, 1986), pp. 166–7; N. A. Reath, 'Velvets of the Renaissance, from Europe and Asia Minor', *Burlington Magazine*, 50 (1927), pp. 298–304. I am grateful to Mr Tom Campbell for these references.
20. *Cal. SP. Span.* (1531–3), no. 880 (*L&P*, v, no. 696).
21. BL Harl. MS. 1419 f. 206.
22. S. Bamforth and J. Dupèbe, trans. and eds, 'Francisci Francorum Regis et Henrici Anglorum Colloquium', *Renaissance Studies*, 5 (1991), p. 71.
23. For these portraits see J. Rowlands, *Holbein: the Paintings of Hans Holbein the Younger* (Oxford, 1985). A portrait of Sir Nicholas Carew belonging to the Duke of Buccleuch has similar damask hangings in the background.
24. For help on this subject I an indebted to Mr Tom Campbell who is currently completing a Ph.D. at London University on the tapestry collection of Henry VIII.
25. T. Campbell, 'Of Silk and Gold', *Country Life*, vol. CLXXXV, no. 41, pp. 92–5. This is a convenient summary of Mr Campbell's unpublished researches.
26. *Cavendish*, p. 72.
27. NUL MS. Ne02 f. 210.
28. Ibid. Another example, at Langley, is on f. 214.
29. *L&P*, IV, no. 1792.
30. W. G. Thompson, *A History of Tapestry* (London, 1930), pp. 239–63.
31. Bod. Lib. Rawl. MS. D 777 f. 194*v*.
32. Surviving windows at Hampton Court show this. See also, for example, Bod. Lib. Rawl. MS. D 775 f. 50; Bod. Lib. Rawl. MS. D. 775 ff. 50*v*–51.
33. Bod. Lib. Rawl. MS. D 775, f. 52.
34. Bod. Lib. Rawl. MS. D 775 ff. 26, 26*v*, 32.
35. NUL MS. Ne02 f. 145*v*.
36. BL Harl. MS. 1419 f. 239.
37. PRO E36/252 p. 631.
38. PRO E101/497/1.
39. *Thomas Cranmer*, by Gerlach Flicke (London, National Portrait Gallery, no. 535).
40. Bod. Lib. Rawl. MS. D 776 ff. 236, 238–238*v*.

41. Bod. Lib. Rawl. MS. D 776 ff. 211.
42. J. Rowlands, *The Age of Durer and Holbein: German Drawings 1400–1500*, (exh. cat., London, British Museum, 1988), pp. 247–8; J. Bayley, *The History and Antiquities of the Tower of London* (London, 1921), p. xxxi; PRO E36/253 pp. 577, 589, BL MS. Royal 14b IVA.
43. PRO E36/241 p. 631.
44. NUL Ne.01 f. 204*v*; C. Gilbert, J. Lomax and A. Wells-Cole, *Country House Floors 1660–1850* (exh. cat., Leeds, Temple Newsam House, 1987), p. 27.
45. *L&P*, II, p. 1493.
46. *L&P*, XIV(ii), no. 435, g. 19; Gilbert, Lomax and Wells-Cole (1987), pp. 96–7.
47. D. King and D. Silvester, *The Eastern Carpet in the Western World* (exh. cat., London, 1983), pp. 18–19; D. King, 'The Inventories of the Carpets of King Henry VIII', *Hali*, 5 (1983), pp. 287–96.
48. P. Mellbye-Hansen, *The Danish Coronation Carpets* (Copenhagen, 1987), pp. 16–17.
49. T. B. James and A. M. Robinson, *Clarendon Place*, Society of Antiquaries at London (1988), pp. 226–9.
50. Kipling (1990), p. 72.
51. Ibid., p. 73.
52. Bod. Lib. Rawl. MS. D 780 f. 25*v*.
53. BL Add. MS. 21116.
54. *L&P*, v, p. 312.
55. P. Binski (1986), pp. 13–14.
56. P. Eames, *Medieval Furniture* (Furniture History Society, 1977), pp. 85–7.
57. *HO*, pp. 121–2.
58. V. Chinnery, *Oak Furniture: The British Tradition* (Woodbridge, 1990) pp. 319–45.
59. PRO E101/425/14.
60. *Cal. SP. Span.*, VII, no. 99; *L&P*, XIX (i), no. 529.
61. Bod. Lib. MS. b.192/1 ff. 60–61.
62. BL Harl. MS. 1419 ff. 232*v*, 233.
63. *Henry VIII and Hampton Court*, pp. 32–8; 'English Royal Palaces', p. 236.
64. NUL MS. Ne01 ff. 27, 28*v*.
65. PRO E36/252 pp. 581, 633, 641.
66. *L&P*, IV, no. 1792.
67. NUL MS. Ne02 f. 274.
68. Kipling (1990), p. 66.
69. *HO*, p. 115.

70. Kipling (1990), pp. 36–7.
71. *Chronicle of Calais*, p. 55.
72. BL Add. MS. 21116 f. 8*v*, 11*v*.
73. NUL MS. Ne.02 f. 130*v*.
74. BL Harl. MS. 1419a ff. 54, 244.
75. Bod. Lib. MS. Eng. Hist. b.192/1 f. 6*v*.
76. NUL MS. Ne.01 f. 33*v*.
77. BL Harl. MS. 1419a f. 56.
78. For a full discussion see Eames (1977), pp. 55–72; V. Chinnery, *Oak Furniture: The British Tradition* (Woodbridge, 1990), pp. 319–45; P. Glanville, *Silver in Tudor and Early Stuart England* (Victoria and Albert Museum, 1990), pp. 36–40.
79. *Chronicle of Calais*, p. 55. In 1547 a buffet at Hampton Court was covered in painted leather, BL Harl. MS. 1419 f. 249.
80. BL Harl. MS. 1419 f. 87.
81. D. Starkey, ed., *Henry VIII: A European Court in England*, (exh. cat., Greenwich, National Maritime Museum, 1991), pp. 126–35.
82. Kipling (1990), p. 66.
83. Ibid., p. 76.
84. Ibid., p. 58.
85. Glanville (1990), p. 204.
86. Chinnery (1990), p. 341; Eames (1977), pls 60–61.
87. Bod. Lib. Rawl. MS. D 781 f. 15.
88. PRO E36/241 f. 278.
89. Many examples, but see PRO E36/241 f. 424.
90. Bod. Lib. Rawl. MS. D. 777 f. 181*v*.
91. WAM 12257 f. 45.
92. For example Bod. Lib. Rawl. MS. D 775 f. 64.
93. NUL MS. Ne.01 f. 242.
94. A whole account survives from 1547 detailing much work (PRO E101/424/11).
95. PRO E36/241 p. 443.
96. BL Add. MS. 10109 f. 200.
97. PRO E36/252 p. 582.
98. BL Harl. MS. 1419 f. 244.
99. C. Jagger, *Royal Clocks* (London, 1983), pp. 232–9.
100. *Cavendish*, p. 73.
101. BL Harl. MS. 1419 p. 124.
102. PRO E36/239 f. 91.
103. BL Harl. MS. 1419 f. 137.
104. Ibid., f. 245.
105. Ibid., f. 137.
106. Ibid., f. 106, also f. 135*v*.

Illustrations

278

(Crown copyright. Historic Royal Palaces. Photograph: Cliff Birtchnell.)

287. Henry VIII's Psalter, *Henry VIII Reading in his Bedchamber*, 1540. (By permission of the British Library (Royal MS 2A XVI f.3).)

288. Hans Holbein the Younger, *Solomon and the Queen of Sheba*, c.1535. (The Royal Collection © 1993 Her Majesty The Queen.)

289. Henry VIII enthroned, as depicted in the 1563 edition of Foxe's *Acts and Monuments.*

290. Hans Holbein the Younger, *Mary Wotton, Lady Guildford*, 1527. (The Saint Louis Art Museum. Purchase (1:1943).)

291. Loseley Park, Guildford. Painted decoration, possibly from a royal house. (From Loseley Park. Photograph: Cliff Birtchnell.)

292. Italian furnishing fabric, 1475–1525. (Isabella Stewart Gardner Museum, Boston (T27w62).)

293. Hans Holbein the Younger, *Jean de Dinteville and Georges de Selve, ('The Ambassadors')*, 1533. (Reproduced by courtesy of the Trustees, the National Gallery, London.)

294. German school, *Queen Elizabeth Receiving Dutch Emissaries*, c.1585. (Staatliche Kunstsammlungen, Kassel.)

295. Hans Holbein the Younger, *William Wareham, Archbishop of Canterbury*, 1527. (Service Photographique de la Réunion des Musées Nationaux, Paris.)

296. Hans Holbein the Younger, *Sir Thomas More*, 1527. (Copyright The Frick Collection, New York.)

297. Hans Holbein the Younger, *Thomas Cromwell*, 1542–3. (Copyright The Frick Collection, New York.)

298. Hans Holbein the Younger, *The Family of Sir Thomas More*. (Öffentliche Kunstsammlung, Kupferstichkabinett Basel (1662.31).)

299. Hans Holbein the Younger, *Henry VIII and the Barber-surgeons*, 1540. (The Worshipful Company of Barbers.)

300. *The Triumph of Bacchus* from the Brussels series *The Triumph of the Gods*, early 1540s. (The Royal Collection © 1993 Her Majesty The Queen.)

301. Stained-glass roundel bearing the Tudor royal arms, c.1540. (By courtesy of the Board of Trustees of the Victoria and Albert Museum (C.452–1919).)

302. Hans Holbein the Younger, *Sir Henry Guildford*, 1527. (The Royal Collection © 1993 Her Majesty The Queen.)

303. A chimney-piece, from Henry VII's tower at Windsor Castle (1500–engraved before its destruction. (The Royal Collection © 1993 Her Majesty The Queen.)

304. St James's fireplace, drawing. (By permission of the British Library (Add. MS 36370 f.120).)

305. St James's fireplace, photo. (The Royal Collection © 1993 Her Majesty The Queen.)

306. Three engravings recording the visit of Marie de' Medici to the English Court in 1638. (Reproduced by courtesy of the Trustees of the British Museum (Mm3-19, Mm3-20, Mm3-21).)

307. Hampton Court, Surrey. Fireplace built by Cardinal Wolsey and installed in the presence chamber of Catherine of Aragon's lodging. (Crown copyright. Historic Royal Palaces. Photograph: Cliff Birtchnell.)

308. Design for a fireplace, attributed to Hans Holbein the Younger, c.1540. (Reproduced by courtesy of the Trustees of the British Museum (1854-7-8-1).)

309. Sixteenth-century rush matting from Hampton Court, Surrey. (Crown copyright. Historic Royal Palaces. Photograph: Simon Thurley.)

310. Westminster Palace. Wooden patera from the ceiling of the painted chamber. (By courtesy of the Trustees of Sir John Soane's Museum.)

311. *Henry VIII*, attributed to Hans Eworth, c.1545. (The Board of Trustees of the National Museums and Galleries on Merseyside (The Walker Art Gallery, Liverpool).)

312. Windsor Castle, Berkshire. Ceiling from Henry VII's tower (1500–2). (The Scottish Record Office (RHP 13775).)

313. Hampton Court, Surrey. Leather-mâché roundels from the ceiling of the watching chamber, 1536. (Crown copyright. Historic Royal Palaces. Photograph: Cliff Birtchnell.)

314. Hampton Court, Surrey. Diagrams of the chapel ceiling, from the Office of Works, 1920. (The Public Record Office, London.)

315. Hampton Court, Surrey. The chapel ceiling. (Crown copyright. Historic Royal Palaces.)

316. Joined tester bedstead, English oak, 1500–21. (Courtesy of Victor Chinnery and Huntington Antiques.)

317. Hanging cradle, c.1500. (The Museum of London.)

318. Painted oak bedhead, 1539. (Glasgow Museums: The Burrell Collection.)

319. Edward IV enthroned, from a mid-fifteenth-century Flemish manuscript. (MS Royal 15 E IV f.14 British Library, London/Bridgeman Art Library, London.)

320. The Winchester Chair, reputedly used at the marriage Queen Mary I. (The Dean and Chapter of Winchester. Photograph: John Crook.)

321. The Great Seal of Henry VII and the third Great Seal of Henry VIII (1542). (Public Record Office, London.)

322. The Great Bible, detail of frontispiece, 1541. (The Royal Collection © 1993 Her Majesty The Queen.)

323. Part of a seating plan for Anne Boleyn's coronation. (By permission of the British Library (MS Harley 41 f.12r).)

324. *Henry VIII Enthroned*, from a Plea Roll, Trinity term 1517. (The Public Record Office, London (KB27/1130).)

325. Antonio Mor, *Mary I*, 1554. (Isabella Stewart Gardner Museum, Boston.)

326. *The Field of Cloth of Gold* (detail) by an unknown artist, c.1545. (The Royal Collection © 1993 Her Majesty The Queen.)

327. Gilt metal clock, mainly early sixteenth century. (The Royal Collection © 1993 Her Majesty The Queen.)

328. Cast of bronze candlestand originally intended for Henry VIII's tomb; now in Ghent. (By courtesy of the Board of Trustees of the Victoria and Albert Museum (1865–47).)

329. A pair of cast-iron firedogs from Knole House, Kent. (National Trust Photographic Library/Sackville Collection.)

Index